EGO TRIP'S BIG BOOK OF RACISM!

ego trip's™

BIG BOOK OF RACISM!

SACHA JENKINS, ELLIOTT WILSON, CHAIRMAN JEFFERSON MAO, GABRIEL ALVAREZ & BRENT ROLLINS

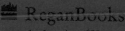
ReganBooks

An Imprint of HarperCollinsPublishers

HarperCollins books may be purchased for educational, business, or sales promotional use. For information please write: Special Markets Department, HarperCollins Publishers Inc., 10 East 53rd Street, New York, NY 10022.

FIRST EDITION
Designed by the Brent Rollins Design Machine at ego trip, NYC
Assistance by Jen Tadaki, Julie Gueraseva, Nicolas Miraglia

Photos:
AP/Wide World Photos: pgs. 11, 36, 53, 63, 236
Nicole Campon: pg. 117
Aaron Counts: pgs. 264-265
Ben Higa: pg. 49
Chairman Jefferson Mao: pgs. 49, 234-235
Nicolas Miraglia: pgs. 20, 272
Photofest: pgs. 75, 132, 148-149, 176-177, 245
Brent Rollins: pgs. 77, 288-289
Ross Schwartzman: pgs. 20, 59, 160, 166-167, 201-207, 214, 247, 257-259
Strenphoto: pgs. 104-105
© Peter Turnley/CORBIS: pgs. 28, 33, 75
Oliver Wang: pgs. 219, 262-263

Illustrations:
Devin Flynn: pgs. 181-183
Nathan Fox: pg. 101
Ebon Heath @ (((stereotype))): pgs. 184-185
Todd James: pgs. 2-3, 108, 212-213, 242-243, 246-247, 264-265, 272-275, 278-281, 284-287

Photo on pg. 72 courtesy of Ricky Powell
Illustration on pg. 209 courtesy of the Japanese American National Museum, Los Angeles, CA
T-shirt on pg. 217 courtesy of Ronnie Lin
License on pg. 255 courtesy of Rodney King

Printed on acid-free paper

Library of Congress Cataloging-in-Publication Data

Ego trip's big book of racism / Sacha Jenkins . . . [et al.] — 1st ed.
p. cm.
ISBN 0-06-098896-7 (alk. paper)
1. United States—Race relations—Humor. I. Title: Big book of racism. II. Jenkins, Sacha.

PN6231 .R25 E37 2002
305.8'002'07—dc21 2002067967

04 05 06 ❖/QW 10 9 8 7 6 5 4 3 2

Due to our strong personal convictions, we wish to stress that this book in no way endorses a belief in racism. We just hate everybody.

TABLE OF CONTENTS.

ANOTHER FORWARD FOREWORD FROM TED BAWNO.

Humans are computers programmed by God, flawed by a major bug—the racism bug. And there's no virus protection program strong enough to stop the hate.

I am not a racist. I am a human being. With feelings—mixed ones. For those who don't know, I am Theodore Aloysius Bawno. But you can call me "Ted." ("Teddy Ted," to all you marmalade ladies.) It's been *threeeeeee looooonnnnng yeeeeeaaaars* since I've come down off of my high horse and addressed you wild cowboys and -girls. Been busy. I'm here in the Philippines—actually, the Philip(Morris)pines—growing tobacco for the revolution. But more on that later.

Time for a refill. Some of you may have tasted my juice—a little elixir from back in the day known as Tab. Yeah, that calorie-scarce brew was ahead of its day. (I *still* say Diet Coke was ten years too late. And fuck Lee Iacocca. Delorean's coke, on the other hand, was always there when I called *and* always on time . . . just joshin', John, we all know you were innocent.) You see, time is money. And time is on my side. Yes it is. I may be an old geezer, but I'm not that much older than pasty Black Sabbath bassman Willie-O "Geezer" Butler—one of the forefathers of heavy titanium music.

Speaking of butlers, it was my own houseboy, Guillermo Watson, a Black Mexican (or "Blaxican" as he refers to himself, though I prefer "wetblack") from Watts, California, who begged me for years to publish the be-all-end-all book of Black American musical factoids and keloids. Elementary, *homes*, if you deduced that that pithy tome turned out to be *ego trip's Book of Rap Lists*—hip hop's answer to the telephone book, you pity-party patsies. My good friend Chris Rock has called it, and I quote, "The best book I ever read—and I can't read!" *Newsweek*? They just loved it. *Rolling Stone*—Jann and his boys? Ditto. (I was really counting on a little love from *Sister 2 Sister*, but, oh well. Black chicks still dig me.)

It makes me proud to know that the legacy of my print media empire still rules like Henry the 8-Ball—a psychic drug dealer I knew from my old Hackensack, New Jersey, days. Sure, I could keep cranking out rap books from here to Grand Cayman or Kingdom Come, whichever cums first. But, to quote another great Black man, B.B. King, that thrill is gone. Books about race music are cool. But books about . . . racism? *Fuego, amigo!*

ego trip's Big Book of Racism! is that fire. Read it, stand next to it, but don't get burned (and definitely don't burn it, all you numb nutses). This ain't no game, muh'fuckas; *BBOR!* will stomp a mudhole in this country's rump, chump. If you want a makeover, go see Jenny Jones. If you want an academia nut's view of racism, then visit www.cryfreedom.com/stiritup, or catch reruns of *Tony Brown's Journal* on the Nashville Network. But if you want to be touched by an angel and ain't afraid to laugh at your bad self, cry at your ignorance, and push your own wig back in amazement, then have I got the perfect-bound bonanza for you!

Once again, it was *my* idea, but I'm willing to give my house nizzle, Guillermo, and my staff of coloreds at *ego trip*, some credit. Yes, *BBOR!* is about race. It is about these mixed feelings we all have. But what a mixed blessing it is. The best of both worlds, even.

Discrimination is bad. It took me fifty years, and several of my own landmark court cases, to learn this painful truth. (FYI, my most inexcusable crime: the time I got busted for keeping "colored only" water coolers at the office way back in nineteen hundred and eighty-six.)

I know 9/11 ain't no joke. These are coptic times. Still, does anybody remember laughter? Humor is good, okay? And anything I do is gonna send good vibrations across the nation and have the best of intentions. The Bawno™ name will always—and I mean *always*, people— produce the quality you and your redblooded (or redboned) American, bison-burger-swilling clan can count on. The *ego trip* iron flag still waves "hello" to all you readers and ride-or-die-ers.

That's why I'm going wild on the Philippines behind the bush with my trophy comrade-in-camouflage, E! television's busty Brooke Burke, training gorillas (and Guillermo) to be guerillas. (Jeez, the body and blood of Christ is all over this stinkin' place. Lord, help us. Now. I implore You.) Once again, I'm prepared, never scared, and hard to kill. Whatchu think all the guns is for? When the ship goes down, I'm *really* gonna be ready this time. It's a long way to the top if you wanna partake in the takeover. Bawno and Judy Regan, we runnin' this book shit. Together.

Excelsior!

Theodore Aloysius Bawno

August 20, 2002
Manila, Philippines

P.S.: I swallowed a bug.

In the beginning, *everything* was black.

Not Black as in "African-American," but black as in "New York City 1977 power-outage" black. So even if there *were* people around, no one knew it 'cause they couldn't see each other. That means everybody would've had dark skin, even if they didn't. And that's how it was. So there. *Nyah-nyah.*

And then one day, God only knows why—BOOM!—somebody turned the lights back on for the very first time. Suddenly, there was all this "stuff" floating around looking to get together and mingle like it was happy hour at Plato's Retreat: gases formed into liquids, liquids shaped into solids, and solids fused into impenetrable, Gibraltar-like holiday fruit-cake. And when the rest of the dust finally settled, somehow mankind jumped up on the scene and in effect said, "I'm here. Let's party." And so they did. People clustered into different corners and caroused amongst themselves. Some brought their finest booze. Others brought bean dip. Another hooked up some positively dynamite lasagna. It was an affair to remember. But then somebody just had to go and spoil the fun by asking aloud:

. . . THE CHINESE

There are regional variations in the legends of the Goddess Nu Gua (also referred to as *Ku Gua, Nu Kua* and *Nu Wa*!!—got you all in check), but they all agree that *she* created humankind. And humankind was colored yellow, dear fellows. You see, after the Earth was formed Nu Gua decided to make people because the planet was vacant and she was lonely. Taking yellow clay, she shaped and brought to life many folks. However, this was taxing work (even for a supreme deity) so Nu Gua ingeniously took a rope, dragged it through the mud, and shook it. The labor-reducing move resulted in several blobs of mud drops that were used to create new but lesser races of folks. (And thus, the unfortunate tradition of inferior, hastily assembled, "made in China" products came to be.) The ones already molded from yellow clay became the aristocracy; those from the mud became the lower classes.

. . . THE FLATHEAD / SALISH INDIANS

This particular tribe explains the arrival of the red and white man vis-à-vis the tale of Old Man Coyote (representing "The Good") and his adversary Mountain Sheep (representing "The Baa-aa-aad"). Long ago, Old Man Coyote often cried that he was lonely to the Father of the world, Old-Man-in-the-Sky. Tired of his howlin', Old-Man-in-the-Sky instructed Old Man Coyote to collect red soil in a satchel and return it to him so that he might create people to be his buddies.

And so he went traveling for quite a long time until he found a mountain abundant with red earth and filled the satchel. Travel-weary, Old Man Coyote then fell asleep. He was later found by Mountain Sheep, who decided to play a joke on him and filled the lower half of the sack with white soil before running away to hide. (Oh, Mountain Sheep, you rascal, you.)

Old Man Coyote awakened during the night and returned his sack to Old-Man-in-the-Sky. So in darkness Old-Man-in-the-Sky took the clay, and unable to see that they were two different colors,

made two sets of men and women, and placed them back in the pouch. When Old Man Coyote took them out in the morning, he was astonished to see that the two pairs were colored different. Realizing this must have been the result of Mountain Sheep's trickery, he separated the people. He deposited the white ones on land near a big salt hole and kept the red ones with him to keep him company. (The white ones wound up so salty, they eventually ran rampant and gold-[bum]rushed the red ones' real estate.)

. . . THE HOPI INDIANS

All of humanity, the Hopi legend goes, originated underground. (Keep it real, keep it gutta!) Man first emerged from a single hole in the earth and was greeted by a mockingbird. With more authority than a grade school hall monitor, this little aviary wonder bestowed the tribes (as well as all other races) with their identities, telling each who emerged to the surface, "You shall be Navajo, and speak that language," "You shall be Hopi, and speak Hopi," and so on and so forth.

. . . THE JEWS / CHRISTIANS

The Genesis passages of the Old Testament tell the story of Noah's three sons—Ham, Shem, and Japheth—who are the ancestors of the entire world's population. As it turns out, Ham sees (and possibly molests) his father after the old man has passed out drunk (and naked). (What was up with that? Heathen.) This act brings a curse upon him and his descendents. It has been said that Ham represents Blacks (the cursed), Shem represents the Jews (the blessed Semites), and Japheth represents Caucasians.

Later on, the greatest story ever told gets even iller when a buncha folks choose to rebel against God by building the Tower of Babel, a structure so tall, it was a veritable stairway to heaven. (Word to Robert Plant. Amen.) This so pissed off the Big Man Upstairs that he scrambled the singular common language of man into many languages so that these delinquents could not communicate with each other and work against Him. People consequently separated along common language lines and in time dispersed across the globe. (Just for kicks, try to imagine God's stance on bilingual education. It makes the noggin spin.)

. . . THE MORMONS

No tales of a "big bang" in the heart of darkness here, buddy-boy. But *The Book of Mormons* is still capable of droppin' bombs—like the part about how the Nephites (righteous true believers) are characterized as "white and exceedingly fair and delightsome," while the Lamanites (nonbelievers who committed sin) became cursed with dark skin. The *BOM* never explicitly states which racial group the Lamanites belong to, but it's generally agreed that they represent the American Indians. (Check the description found in Alma 3:5, which states that their heads were "shorn," they were "naked, save it were skin which was girded about their loins" and they carried plenty of "bows" and "arrows." Sound like honest to goodness Injuns to us.)

Others interpret the text's references to Lamanite "blackness" to literally mean persons of African-American descent. Few, however, have ever doubted that the Nephites were Caucasian. So let's recap: Nephites = white and good. Lamanites = American Indian or Black and bad. (But they forgot Samsonite—a variety of colors and styles; sturdy and reasonably priced.)

. . . THE NATION OF ISLAM

According to founder W.D. Fard (a/k/a Fard Muhammad), the universe began seventy-six *trillion** years ago. The theory (called the Truth) is that from darkness came the atom, from the atom came the earth, and from the earth came the Original Man (the Creator), who assumed the name Allah and cre-

ated others in his own image—dark skin, "good" hair, and fine features, sorta like Billy Dee Williams circa *Mahogany*. These Black Asiatic people first inhabited East Asia, then began dispersing across the world over the course of several millennia.

Some migrated to Africa, where their hair became nappier, their noses broader. Others traveled to India, where they acquired red skin. (But due to their religious dissent, these same people would eventually be banished from Asia and sent packing far across the Bering Strait, straight to what we now know as the Americas.) The last people—the whites—were created via scientific experiments conducted by the evil genius Dr. Yacub, who sought to destroy his own Black people. Grafted from the (designer) genes of the Original Man, white people are a race of genetically inferior, treacherous and deceitful "devils" who can't dance and presumably all talk (in "nerd voice") like this.

. . .THE SCIENTIFIC EGGHEAD EVOLUTIONISTS

Dishonorable Dr. Yacub notwithstanding, the scientific community generally agrees on the evolutionary origins of humans. However, it is with the arrival of Homo Erectus (nearly two million years ago) where views differ regarding actual racial development. One theory, the "Multiregional Model," is that dispersed Homo Erectus communities across the globe concurrently developed their specific racial characteristics apart and unbeknownst to each other.

The "Replacement Model" theory maintains that around 200,000 years ago Homo Erectus evolved into the more advanced Homo Sapiens in Africa, who then spread across the globe, creating many communities where they would develop unique racial traits. This suggests that the various races are more recent developments and, therefore, all of humanity is even more closely related, whether you like it or not, brohannon.

Then again, there are continuing

studies that simultaneously refute and support both these arguments. Well, that's just freakin' great. We can see it now, a T-shirt that reads: I SENT MY CHILD TO THE FINEST SCIENTIFIC INSTITUTION MONEY COULD BUY AND ALL HE CAME UP WITH IS NON-CONCLUSIVE EVIDENCE.

. . . THE SHILLUK PEOPLE OF AFRICA

Blame (or thank) the existence of different races on Jouk, the big dawg being who wandered about the globe fashioning each racial / ethnic group from soil found in their respective homelands. So when Jouk discovered white sand that's where he created white dudes 'n' dudettes. From the mud of Egypt's Nile River he created brown guys 'n' gals. And where he found black earth—the Shilluk's land, for example—he molded him some ebony mens 'n' womens. (Sure, we're being silly, but that's because they're all Jouks! Ha ha!)

. . . THE WORLD CHURCH OF THE CREATOR

This group prefers to endorse questionable "facts" to support their argument of white racial superiority. In particular, TWCC cites a professedly "objective" yet subjectively titled book, *March of the Titans—A History of the White Race* (Ostara Publications, 1999). In a nutshell, these nutcases contend that the diverse characteristics of humanity were predetermined due to inherent genetic makeup. In other words, they were born to roll like the master race.** Why? They don't really say. But they do provide blatantly biased evidence placing the precursors to modern-day Caucasians at the center of every "advanced" civilization without acknowledging or explaining the development of other racial types. (Making it an absolute must-read for fans of science fiction.)

*Not to be confused with gazillion.

**Not to be confused with Masta Ace, a master emcee in his own right.

DISGRACISM.

CHAPTER 1

YOUR PERSONAL WORST: A RACISM QUIZ.

Pop quiz, anyone? Be it math, HIStory, ebonics—everybody loves a pop quiz. But as the great rapper Guru once sang, "The SAT is not geared for the lower class / So why waste time even trying to pass?" It's been test-proven— tests don't always play fair. Bigotry is a popular pastime. And it still is. Now for the first time ever comes an opportunity to level the cultural playing field once and for all, and ponder the intriguing question: What do you get when you put Joe Clark, Mr. Hand (R.I.P.), and Jaime Escalante in a room together? (Answer: Three *esés* the hard way—even harder than Chinese 'rithmetic.)

1. **Are you a racist?**
A. Yes.
B. Probably.
C. Definitely.
D. All of the above.

2. **You ain't Black.**
   When you see a Black person, you:
A. Feel guilty.
B. Smile . . . nervously.
C. Say, "Slap me some skin, on the Black hand side, baby-baby."
D. Run.

3. **You a honky. When you see a person of another ethnicity, you:**
A. Get crazy horny. (You one horny honky.)
B. Expect to lose your job. Soon.
C. Inform him, in an extremely polite tone, that deliveries are at the back entrance only, *José.*
D. Run.

4. **Finish this sentence: "The Blacker the berry . . .**
A. . . . the sweeter the Jews."
B. . . . the more rotten that shit is. Throw it away."
C. . . . the darker the daddy."
D. . . . the better the chance it's Wesley Snipes at an after-hours wine-tasting with his ganjah-smoking mellow, Woody Harrelson. (Light anotha.)"

5. **You can always tell a Latin family by:**
A. Counting the chickens.
B. The decibel levels.

C. Trying this simple trick: Yell, "*Migra!*" and if they run, they His*panic.*
D. The red furniture.

6. **The development of science has allowed a great many advantages in our daily lives. These improvements are moving at an accelerated rate. However, as far as you know, Orientals talk "funny" because:**
A. Godzilla got them hella shook.
B. Their tongues are slanted, too. (Ay ya! *That's* racist.)
C. Too much MSG. (Mangled Speech Gene.)
D. They hate your ignorant ass and are doing it to fuck with you (better known as "ancient Chinese secret").

7. **The phrase "Peace in the Middle East" is poignant because:**
A. They sure do kill a lot of muthafuckas out there.
B. It rhymes.
C. "Blessed in the Midwest" don't sound right.
D. It will never happen.

8. **A Caucasian male leaves for work at 7:00 on Monday morning. He lives on the west side of town, about ten miles away from his destination. He arrives at his office at 8:00 A.M. On the other side of town, a person of color also leaves home at 7:00 A.M. He or she arrives:**
A. Late.
B. After a quick stop at the boodah spot, right on THC-CP Time.
C. Wednesday.
D. At the unemployment line.

9. **A cracker is:**
A. A delicious, flaky, baked, sometimes-buttery, waferesque morsel.
B. One of them Rice Crispies niggaz.
C. Not to be confused with the monster from *Clash of the Titans*.
D. You, you dumb-ass cracker.

10. **Which breed of dog would not be uncommon cuisine on a southeast Asian menu?**
A. Terrier. Excellent with a white chablis. Sublime!
B. German shepherd. Great with a hearty pilsner or stout. *Das Boot!*
C. Collie. Lassie is splendid with a mango *lassi*. Beyotch, watch yourself!
D. Bullmastiff. Divine with a cherry-lime rickey or a breezy mint julep. Fo-sheezy!

11. **"BMW" stands for:**
A. Black Man's Wish.
B. Better Move, Whitey.
C. Bitch Made Whiteboy.
D. Bought My Wife, too.

12. **Who would you vote off the island first?**
A. Clint Black. (He's white.)
B. Barry White. (He's Black.)
C. Rita Moreno. (She's Boricua.)
D. Tattoo.

13. **The 1950s ushered in the era of the Cold War, a decades-long standoff between the United States and the Soviet Union. In the early 1990s, that conflict ended because:**
A. Russia agreed to take back Yakoff Smirnov.
B. The moose and squirrel games of Boris and Natasha got crazy. Real crazy.
C. George H. Dubya Sr. hated Iraqis more than Slavs.
D. The U.S. loves Soviet poontang. *Better than Eskimo Pie!*

14. **Saddam Hussein looks like:**
A. He's so damn insane. (Get it? Good.)
B. The President of the Swarthy Gentlemen's Club . . . for Men.
C. He's quick to get in that ass.
D. A really hammered Mexican with a *muy gigante* tortilla chip on his shoulder.

15. **Before September 11, 2001, you thought Osama bin Laden was:**
A. Sir Alec Guinness' character in *Star Wars*.
B. The $6.95 lunch special at your local Curry Hut.
C. The scientific term in Arabic for lopsided desert-donkey testicles.
D. Just another towelhead.

16. **Who is most dangerous?**
A. Afrika Bambaataa.
B. China Chow.
C. Kathy Ireland.
D. Alex English. (Hint: He's Black, and he's a very dangerous scorer.)

17. **RAHOWA stands for:**
A. Racial Holy War.
B. What TV talk-show host Rolanda might say to her sister if she caught her in bed with her hubby.
C. Real Arabs Have Oil Wells Aplenty.
D. What an excited Asian *Happy Days* fan says upon meeting Ron Howard for the first time.

18. **Who picks up the white trash?**
A. Welfare.
B. Ricki Lake's limousine service.
C. Vicodin.
D. Black thugz.
E. Lizzie Grubman.

19. **At which of the following places are Hispano holy rollers most likely to sight visions of Jesus and Mary:**
A. A Jesus and Mary Chain album cover.
B. The local bodega, because Jesus (pronounced *hay-zoos*) and Maria run it.
C. In the cotton candy at Shea Stadium.
D. At the border.

20. **From where does the Chinese Dragon Lady learn her powers of seduction?**
A. Vietnamese Hooker Academy.
B. Japanese Geisha Finishing School.
C. www.manilamail-orderbrides.com.
D. Some Korean slut.

21. **Since they were actually separated at birth, the only real difference between African-Americans and Italian-Americans is:**
A. The suits. The Crips wear FUBU. The wops wear Armani. (But the burgers are Ronald's.)
B. The sauce. BBQ drives Blacks bananas. Marinara makes the *paisans* go Buttafucco for Coco Puffs.
C. The sex. The monkeys can swing all-nighters. The goombahs go for the gold medallion.
D. The slammer. C'mon, y'all saw *The Green Mile* and *Goodfellas*.

22. **Dr. Angelo Saxon, PhD, a wealthy Caucasian male (of course), walks into his well-mannered boudoir one fine Wednesday evening. To his dismay, he encounters his blondish nymphet wife, Mandy, in their king-sized Ethan Allen waterbed with . . .**
A. Ferdinand, their uninhibited, untamable, and undocumented landscape artiste, who's feeding her chalupas and beating her Chihuahua senseless. ¡Amor es Perros!
B. Carmine, their in-house Haitian culinary sensation, taste-testing her French dip with his rotund rolling pin in hand. *Oui*, he'll rock you, Amadeus!
C. Lateisha, the saucy and sassy Filipina nanny, ankles-to-panties, spanking that fanny. Word to Manny (the chauffeur).
D. Manny, who's been hitting off Lateisha—*and* Angelo—on the low. (He's bisexual, you know.)

23. **On some Jimmy Stewart shit, a despondent Dr. Saxon races his silver Jaguar XJE to Old Miller's Bridge, the local suicide jump-off. Before taking the Nestea plunge, and leaving no doubt in anyone's mind that he's softer than wet Charmin, he yells . . .**
A. "Wetbacks!"

B. "Blackmale!"
C. "Nia Peeples!"
D. "Whitewater!"

24. **Are tan lines racist?**
A. Yes, because they perpetuate Carnal Sander's fried chicken theory: The white meat's the best (and it's finger-lickin' good).
B. No, just rednecks.
C. Maybe. George Hamilton ain't worked steadily in years.
D. *¡Suntanama!*

25. **Why do African-Americans love to dance?**
A. Cuz they freaks.
B. They're slaves to the rhythm. (Ta-dow! That's *really* racist.)
C. They want to practice what they will eventually do on your grave, honky.
D. The devil made them do it.

26. **Complete the following lyric: "In a white room, with black curtains . . .**
A. . . . at the (police) station."
B. . . . at the arraignment."
C. . . . at the movies with Roger Ebert and his Black wife."
D. . . . at the racetrack." (FYI: Black Curtains, a 2-to-1 favorite.)

27. **It's the annual Puerto Rican Day parade. Boricuas from all across this great nation will descend upon the Manzana Grande to commemorate:**
A. ass.
B. Ass.
C. ASS!
D. AZZ! Boo-yow!

28. **Which of the following is not controlled by the Jews?**
A. Hebrew National.
B. Beanie Sigel.
C. Judo. (Not to be confused with "jew dough." They got that on lock.)
D. Palestine.

29. **Can't we all just get along?**
A. No.
B. Absolutely not.
C. I don't think so.
D. No espeka Englis.

30. **Ignorance is:**
A. Bliss.
B. A cancer.
C. Everywhere.
D. *ego trip's Big Book of Racism!*

ADD IT UP: If you answered A for any question, you are a racist. If you answered B for any question, you are a bigot. If you answered C for any question, you are flamingly biased. If you answered D for any question, you wantonly discriminate against races/ethnicities other than your own. If you answered E for any question, guess what? You're absolutely right!

"hymies." "hymies." "hymies." "hymies."

"rag heads." "rag heads." "rag heads." "rag heads."

"nigger." "nigger." "nigger." "nigger."

"little brown ones." "little brown ones." "little brown ones."

"white niggers." "white niggers." "white niggers."

"wetbacks." "wetbacks." "wetbacks." "wetbacks."

"gook." "gook." "gook." "gook." "gook."

AMERIKKKAN BABBLE ON: A SELECTIVE GUIDE TO POLITICKIN' OFF PEOPLE OF COLOR AND OTHER CAMPAIGNFUL FIGURES OF SPEECH.

GIVE ME LIBERTY OR GIVE ME DEATH.
★ PATRICK HENRY, 1775

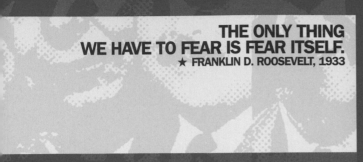

THE ONLY THING
WE HAVE TO FEAR IS FEAR ITSELF.
★ FRANKLIN D. ROOSEVELT, 1933

ASK NOT WHAT YOUR COUNTRY
CAN DO FOR YOU—ASK WHAT YOU CAN
DO FOR YOUR COUNTRY.
★ JOHN F. KENNEDY, 1961

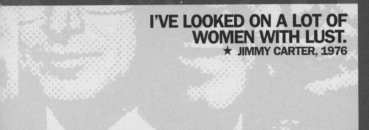

I'VE LOOKED ON A LOT OF
WOMEN WITH LUST.
★ JIMMY CARTER, 1976

These are but a few of the great examples of political yakety yak that have galvanized this great land of fruited plains, fingerwaves of grain, and purple hills (and pills) majesty. Still, for every inspired word emphatically exhorted by our political leaders, there are those that are eyebrow (and ire) raisers—statements that have been mumbled, fumbled, and grumbled under their breath, away from the microphone, or assumed to be off-the-record. (A suggestion to all political aspirants: Practice saying, "Is this thing on?") Here's an example—just a little sample—of some of the more notorious slips-of-the-tongue that have earned the regret of their originators and have left significant portions of our multicultural melting pot red, white, and bruised.

GOVERNOR SPIRO T. AGNEW (R-MARYLAND)

Relatively unknown when selected as Richard Nixon's running mate in the 1968 presidential election, the Greek-American Agnew more than made up for his obscurity on the campaign trail, where he made reference to Polish-Americans as "Polacks." Not long after his Pole prodding, the Spiromaniac noticed slumbering, Asian *Baltimore Sun* journalist Gene Oishi as the two rode on an airplane. The future veep jokingly quipped, "What's the matter with the fat Jap?"

The breaking news of the gyro-induced gaffe led to more Agnew media scrutiny, which was pivotal to Spiro's later downward political spiral. In 1973, he pleaded no contest to accepting bribes and corporate kickbacks during his gubernatorial reign, leading to a three-year probation, a $10,000 fine, and his resignation from the vice presidency. (Wonder what would've happened if he had called the guy a "napping nip"?)

REVEREND JESSE JACKSON

Never mind his crusade for civil rights alongside Dr. Martin Luther King Jr., his leadership of economic self-help organization Operation Push, his role as world conflict healer, or even his thrilling, Public Enemy–sampled declaration at 1972's Wattstax concert in Los Angeles ("Brothers and sisters! I don't know what this world is coming to!"). Jackson's "Hymietown" slight against the Jewish community in January of 1984 is the funky stuff legends are made of.

Speaking *negro a negro* to *Washington Post* reporter Milton Coleman during his bid for the U.S. presidency, J.J.'s jokey allusion to New York City as a Hebrew hub and Jews as "hymies" was thought to be off-the-record. However, Coleman allowed the remark to be appropriated by a fellow *Post* reporter for an article chronicling Jackson's already-stressed relationship with the Jewish-American community.

Eddie Murphy lampooned the controversy on *Saturday Night Live* by portraying Jackson as the Teddy Pendergrass–like lead singer of an R&B troupe pleading "Don't let me down, Hymietown." But for Jackson there wasn't a damn thing funny, as he found himself in the middle of a media feeding frenzy—all the while denying making the statements. Compounding his woes was the vocal support of Nation of Islam leader Minister Louis Farrakhan—who the American media almost unanimously vilified as anti-

Semitic—and physical protection by the Nation's security personnel, the Fruit of Islam. By late February, Jesse admitted to making the remarks and looked to prominent Jewish leaders for reconciliation.

VICE PRESIDENT GEORGE H. W. BUSH (R)

Speaking to his potna, President Ronald Reagan, George H. W. Bush, pointed out his son Jeb's biracial, Mexican-American rugrats as they deplaned in New Orleans for the 1988 GOP convention. He was, however, unaware that PA system microphones were on, recording and broadcasting his clumsy term of endearment for all the world to hear: "That's Jebby's kids.* The little *brown* ones." They were, in fact, the *only* three tykes coming off the aircraft. (It's not like they had to be picked out of a lineup of rambunctious munchkins.) Though granddaddy Bush's comment pissed off Latino Democrats, he was elected president anyways, lending credence to the theory that you can offend "brown" folks in this country without it amounting to a hill of beans.

SENATOR ERNEST FRITZ HOLLINGS (D-SOUTH CAROLINA)

In addition to acting against the civil rights–era zeitgeist by flying the Confederate flag over the state capitol (where it remains today), this former South Carolina governor also derisively mocked Jesse Jackson's Rainbow Coalition as the "Blackbow Coalition," branded California Senator Alan Cranston's Latino supporters "wetbacks" during the race for the 1984 Democratic presidential nomination, and called former Ohio Senator Howard Metzenbaum "the senator from B'nai B'rith." But for all his exploits, the Fritz Cracker has more often than not escaped the scrutiny that has befallen others.

In fact, in his fifty-plus years in the political arena, Fritz has only really caught heat once—for characterizing African delegates attending a 1993 international trade meeting in Switzerland as cannibals. "Everybody likes to go to Geneva. I used to do it for the Law of the Sea conferences and you'd find these potentates from down in Africa, you know, rather than eating each other, they'd just come up and get a good square meal in Geneva."

Hollings' unappetizing attempt at humor finally incurred some long overdue outcry. Hey, Verne. Now playing in Africa: *Ernest Goes to Hell.*

SENATOR CONRAD BURNS (R-MONTANA)

By contrast, the Treasure State senator (no relation to Conrads Bain, Janis, or Muhammad) has found himself in hot water more times than Jacuzzi-bound *Blind Date* couples. Running for office in 1994, it seemed that Burns was more interested in winning the title of "Mr. Insensitivity" than winning a senate seat. First, the evil Mr. Burns (sans Smithers) broke out the n-word in an anecdote to a newspaper editorial board. Then, during a televised debate that same year, he offended the Native Americans of his own state by referring to their tribes using the dicey "those people" pejorative.

In a March 1999 speech to the Montana Equipment Dealers Association, Burns got carried away while commenting on the U.S. dependency on foreign supplies such as oil

*Not to be confused with Jerry's Kids.

and called Arabs "ragheads." He later explained his inappropriate remark by saying, "I was wound up and getting it going." Spoken like a true con(rad) man.

CONGRESSIONAL REPRESENTATIVE BARBARA BLEWSTER (R-ARIZONA)

The ultraconservative state rep must love the taste of toenail polish, 'cause she's probably put her foot in her mouth more times than any other elected freshman. Back in May 1999, the *Arizona Republic* recounted the many examples of Punky Blewster's hot air: The time she told Jewish legislator Barbara Leff that she didn't look Jewish because she didn't have a "big hook nose." Then there's the comment she made to Black Democrat Leah Landrum that "slavery wasn't that bad." Or even that life has been "just fine" for Blacks since the Emancipation Proclamation.

At least she was "progressive" enough to add that Blacks are more intelligent than Native Americans, who are "not smart enough to do what they need to do to get ahead," and that "even African-Americans are more advanced than Native Americans." (Flattery will get you everywhere, toots.)

Some unfairly criticize her because she's a Mormon, yet her displays of ignorance may lead one to believe she's simply a *moron*. In response to her critics, Blewster claimed that she was misquoted, saying, "I respect and admire very much the progress that Black Americans have made." Misquote this: *You've* come a long way, Babs.

SENATOR JOHN MCCAIN (R-ARIZONA)

Candidates say the darndest things—sometimes repeatedly. And "gook" is not the word to play, particularly if you're a Vietnam vet running for the presidential candidacy. From his turbocharged tour bus, the aptly christened *Straight Talk Express*, 2000 chief exec hopeful McCain didn't just give it to ya straight, he gave it to ya raw—as in opening up old wounds.

When questioned early in his White House bid about his casual use of the g-word, McCain—never one to Ho Chi mince words—admitted that he often used the epithet in reference to his torturous captors, the Viet Cong. While he maintained that the term didn't reflect his enmity toward Vietnamese people in general, he nonetheless continued to use the slur when given the opportunity to discuss his history as a POW. McCain's persistent usage of "gook" insulted not only Vietnamese-Americans but many Asian-Americans across the country, leading a coalition of national Asian organizations to condemn the Arizona senator's insensitivity. And he lost, too. Sorry, Charlie. We mean, Johnny.

LIEUTENANT GOVERNOR CRUZ BUSTAMENTE (D-CALIFORNIA)

If you're gonna make a burger, make it a Whopper®. And if you're gonna make a blunder, make it during Black History Month 2001 and upset *everybody*. Sorta like Cali's highest-ranking Latino politico did while addressing a crowd of 400 at the Coalition of Black Trade Unionists annual awards and scholarship fundraiser. Running down a list of leaders and labor organizations—many of which had the term "Negro" attached to them, and hence not inappropriate given their historical context—keynote speaker Bustamente at one point blew up the spot by mistakenly substituting "nigger" for "Negro." Bussa Bus busted the wrong move, and got cold busted as an estimated 100 angry attendees walked out. Predictably, he was left with a (black) stain on his political career.

SENATOR ROBERT C. BYRD (D-WEST VIRGINIA)
You might wonder how in this day and age an ex-Klansman could hold elected office. Byrd's clandestine past bit him in the ass in 1999 when a fifty-four-year-old letter he'd written to segregationist Mississippi Senator Theodore Bilbo (rhymes with "dildo") emerged with the following card-carrying sentiments: "Rather I should die a thousand times . . . than to see this beloved land of ours become degraded by race mongrels, a throwback to the blackest specimen from the wilds." YiKKKes!

The eighty-four-year-old, seven-term Senator Bobby Byrd (man, you know *he* ain't got soul) owned up to his egregious remarks soon after their discovery, and condemned his own ignorance. He expressed his shame, and attributed his words to "a dangerous tunnel vision [that] leads young people today to join gangs or hate groups." (Or the U.S. Senate.)

But the light at the end of Bobby's tunnel still looks dim. Byrdman dropped another foul load during a March 5, 2001, *Fox News Sunday* interview when he presented his (presumably enlightened) view on the subject of racial tolerance: "You can't go to heaven if you hate anybody . . . There are white niggers. I've seen a lot of white niggers in my time—I'm going to use that word." Incredibly enough, this convoluted "white niggers" spiel was something that his dear mama told him as a child to warn him *against* racial prejudice. (Not that it mattered either way. Senator Byrd voted against the 1964 Civil Rights Bill.) Ay yo, "white" Rob—as brother Black Rob would say—that's like, "Whoa!"

JOHN COOKSEY (R-LOUISIANA)
The attacks on the World Trade Center and the Pentagon shook America to its deepest core. It shattered lives, antagonized nerves, and, as evidenced by the kooky speech of Representative John Cooksey, rattled loose some darn tootin', good ol' fashioned racism, the savory kind your color-of-hospital-bedsheets grandpaw ate for dinner every Tuesday 'n' Thursday night (and sometimes Sunday if he was lucky).

At a press hearing one week following the terrorist strikes, Cooksey boiled over when he told the media that the FBI should be on the lookout for suspects with "a diaper on his head and a fan belt wrapped around the diaper."

On the one hand, tips on extracurricular uses for fan belts and other useful trailer-trash gems are one of the great fringe benefits of having Southern-bred politcos in office. Still, there's a time and place for everything. Save crass racist descriptions like the one above for country club time, Johnny Boy. (Or re-election time.)

Critics showed no Luvs to the anti-Arabic snaps cooked up by Cooksey. Not only was the statement outrageous, it also advocated racial profiling—which is illegal. Finally, he hemmed and hawed, "[If I] offended Arab-Americans, I regret my choice of words." That's right, shit-for-brains, "towelheads" always sounds better than "diaperheads." Duh!

HATE TO THE CHIEF: M-1 OF DEAD PREZ'S FAVORITE DEAD PRESIDENTS . . . *

1.
2.
3.
4.
5.

*"None of them. I'm happy that they're dead. I'm glad that LBJ is gone because he created COINTELPRO and [the] Vietnam [war]. I'm glad he's outta here. The U.S. government is an enemy to our people."

. . . AND HIS HONORARY BLACK PRESIDENTS.

"These are people who are honorary heroes of our community. And fuck Lincoln!"

1. TUPAC SHAKUR
He exemplified everything that young Black people feel.

2. MALCOLM X
The greatest emcee that ever lived.

3. FRED HAMPTON SR. (OF CHICAGO'S BRANCH OF THE BLACK PANTHER PARTY)
Because of his ability to analyze the world and show us a way out of our problems. *He* was our Black President in 1969.

4. DR. KHALID MUHAMMAD (OF THE NEW BLACK PANTHER PARTY)
Because of his effort to bring Black power to the forefront for young Black people. Uhuru.

Biasboard® TOP 40 — AMERICA'S HOTTEST ETHNIC TARGETS™

FROM APRIL 1, 2002

THIS YEAR	YRS ON CHART	PEAK POSITION	ETHNIC GROUP — CURRENT HIT AND PREVIOUS HITS.
1	2	1	• • • • HOT SHOT DEBUT • • • • **AFGHANS** "911 IS NOT A JOKE" PREVIOUS HITS: N/A
2	23	1	**IRAQIS** "AXIS: BOLD AS EVIL PART I" PREVIOUS HITS: "I'm Kuwaiting for the Man," "Wooly Bullies," "Hussein in the Membrane"
3	23	1	**IRANIANS** "AXIS: BOLD AS EVIL PART II" PREVIOUS HITS: "1979," "Khomeniac"
4	29	3	**ARABS** "DUDE LOOKS LIKE AN AFGHAN" PREVIOUS HITS: "Grease Is the Word," "Arabcadabra"
5	55	2	**PALESTINIANS** "SUICIDE BOMBER SOLUTION" PREVIOUS HIT: "The Great Pretender (Arafat)"
6	23	21	**PAKISTANIS** • • • GREATEST GAINER • • • "DUDE LOOKS LIKE AN ARAB" PREVIOUS HITS: "Dancing in the Street (and Burning Our Flag)," "(Taxi) 'Stan"
7	95	5	**EAST INDIANS** "YOU REMIND ME (OF AN AFGHAN)" PREVIOUS HITS: "Passin' Me By," "Mr. Cabdriver"
8	226+	1	**AFRICAN-AMERICANS** • • • PACESETTER • • • "GET BACK (TO AFRICA WHERE YOU STILL BELONG)" PREVIOUS HITS: "Shock the Monkey," "I Want It All (Reparations)," "Chain Gang"
9	226+	1	**NATIVE AMERICANS** "RED, RED WHINE" (TOMAHAWK FUNK MIX) PREVIOUS HITS: "Don't You Forget About Me," "This Land Is My Land"
10	52	1	**KOREANS** "AXIS: BOLD AS EVIL PART III" PREVIOUS HIT: "Theme from M*A*S*H"
11	152	1	**CHINESE** "I BELIEVE I CAN'T FLY (OVER YOUR AIRSPACE)" PREVIOUS HITS: "Red, Red Whine" (East Side Mix), "Coolies in Cali"
12	35	38	**ISRAELIS** "STOP BEING GREEDY" PREVIOUS HIT: "You Can't Always Get What You Want (Palestine)"
13	152	2	**JEWISH-AMERICANS** "C.R.E.A.M." PREVIOUS HITS: "Tighten Up," "Money (That's What They Want)"
14	157	2	**MEXICANS** "WORKING DAY AND NIGHT (FOR LESS THAN MINIMUM WAGE)" PREVIOUS HITS: "Roaches," "Jaime's Got a Gun," "Borderline"
15	61	1	**JAPANESE** "DIDN'T YOU ALMOST OWN IT ALL" PREVIOUS HITS: "Don't Stop 'til You Get Enough (of Our Industry)," "You Dropped a Bomb on Me"
16	170+	4	**WHITE TRASH** "1ST OF THA MONTH" PREVIOUS HITS: "Money for Nothing," "Get a Job"
17	20	11	**DOMINICANS** "CRIME AFTER CRIME" PREVIOUS HIT: "Feel Like Makin' Crack"
18	41	12	**COLOMBIANS** "COCAINE" PREVIOUS HIT: "White Lines"
19	52	7	**PUERTO RICANS** "PROTECT YA VIEQUES" PREVIOUS HITS: "Cuts Like a Knife," "Jailhouse Rock," "Burning Down the (Blair) House"
20	39	2	**VIETNAMESE** "ALWAYS SOMETHING THERE TO REMIND ME" PREVIOUS HITS: "Bang a Viet Cong (Get It On)," "Welcome to the Jungle"
21	27	22	**CAMBODIANS** "SO WAT CHA SAYIN'?" PREVIOUS HITS: "Boat People (Got No Reason to Live)"
22	4	28	**INDONESIANS** "CREEPIN' ON AH COME UP" PREVIOUS HIT: "Yo! Bum Rush the Embassy"
23	226	3	**FRENCH** "WHERE DID OUR LOVE GO?" PREVIOUS HIT: "Mean Mr. French Mustard"
24	132	10	**ITALIANS (CATHOLICS)** "DON'T STAND SO CLOSE TO MY SON, THE ALTAR BOY" PREVIOUS HITS: "Happiness Is a Warm Gun and My Mother's Cannoli," "Back Stabbers"
25	152	2	**IRISH (CATHOLICS)** "PAPA DON'T PREACH . . . AND DON'T TOUCH MY CHILD" PREVIOUS HITS: "Street Fighting Man," "Mashed Potato Time"
26	61	1	**GERMANS** "EVERY BREATH YOU TAKE (WE'LL BE WATCHING YOU SAUERKRAUTS)" PREVIOUS HITS: "Another Brick in the Wall," "Blitzkrieg Bop"
27	57	1	**RUSSIANS** "STEADY MOBBIN'" PREVIOUS HITS: "Cold as Ice," "Evil Ways," "Union of the Snakes," "Sledgehammer (& Sickle)"
28	130+	3	**POLACKS** "FOOLISH" PREVIOUS HIT: "Cold Gettin' Dumb"
29	30	3	**HAITIANS** "EBONY AND HIV" PREVIOUS HITS: "Voodoo Chile," "Who Can It Be Now (Running Your Country)?"
30	41	1	**CUBANS** "THE BOY IS MINE (ELÍAN GONZALEZ)" PREVIOUS HITS: "Refugee," "I Shot the Sheriff (But I Couldn't Kill Castro)"
30	20	27	**NIGERIANS** "HEROIN" PREVIOUS HIT: "Down on the Corner (Selling Fake Rolexes)"
32	100+	4	**FILIPINOS** "SHINY HAPPY PEOPLE" PREVIOUS HITS: "Suspicious Minds," "(Cheap) Work to Do"
33	30+	28	**JAMAICANS** "DON'T LET THE GREEN GRASS FOOL YOU" PREVIOUS HIT: "Slip Sliding Away on a Bobsled"
34	23	22	**NICARAGUANS** "STANDING ON THE VERGE OF GETTING ALONG" PREVIOUS HITS: "Contra-versy," "Save the Last Sandinista for Me"
35	17	32	**AFRIKANERS** "DIAMONDS AND PEARLS" PREVIOUS HIT: "It's My Party and I'll Cry Zionism If I Want To"
36	226+	2	**MULATTOS/HALF-BREEDS** "DARK SIDE OF THE OCTOROON" PREVIOUS HIT: "Dazed and Confused"
37	100+	34	**GREEKS** "HIT IT FROM THE BACK" PREVIOUS HIT: "Superfreak"
38	9	21	**CANADIANS** "LOSING OUR RELIGION (BASEBALL—FUCK THE BLUE JAYS)" PREVIOUS HIT: N/A
39	104	1	**SPANISH** "BULL OF CONFUSION" PREVIOUS HIT: "Life in the Facist Lane"
40	226+	1	**BRITISH** "THE KIDS ARE ALL RIGHT FOR NOW" PREVIOUS HITS: "Help!" (WWII Mix), "Breaking Up Is Hard to Do" (1776 Mix)

ILLEGAL ALIENS
WHITE U.S. POLITICIANS NEVER COMPLAIN ABOUT.

ARROGANT AFRIKANERS
AUSSIE ARSEHOLES
NITWIT-ISH BRITISH
CANADIANS
NOT-SO-GREAT DANES
FANCY LADS FROM FINLAND
HOES FROM HOLLAND
ICELANDIC IGNORAMI*
SWISS MISSES

*Who give you the cold shoulder.

BILL ADLER CHOOSES THE TOP 10 INTERNATIONAL JEWISH CONSPIRACIES OF ALL TIME.

1. CHRISTIANITY Number One Son was a Hebe. 2. CAPITALISM Blame it on the Rothschilds. 3. COMMUNISM It started with Marx, brother. 4. ANTI-COMMUNISM Norman Podhortez and his fellow travelers. 5. PSYCHOANALYSIS Herr Professor Freud at your service. 6. SHOW BUSINESS An MGM Production. 7. JAZZ A nefarious plot of Blacks and Jews intended (according to the Nazis) "to uproot the racial instinct of the people and tear down blood barriers." 8. THE HOLOCAUST It never really happened. The Jews made it all up to guilt the world into giving them Israel. 9. THE ATTACK ON THE WORLD TRADE CENTER You think it was bin Laden? Impossible. "No Arab could have done this," a prominent Egyptian columnist explained. *"Arabs are always late!"* So, whodunit? Those wily Israelis, whose secret service, the Mossad, hijacked the planes to provoke a U.S. revenge attack against the Arab world. 10. BARBRA STREISAND We're truly, deeply sorry.

Bill Adler, coauthor of Jew on the Brain *(1992) and former director of publicity at Rush Artist Management (1984–1990), is still slightly too young to be an Elder of Zion. (And he has never made any money from the music industry.)*

THREE KINGS RUNNIN' THANGS. JEFF, STEVE-O AND DAVEY G. DON'T HAVE TO DREAM ABOUT GETTIN' PAID.

DIFF'RENT HOAX FOR DIFF'RENT FOLKS: 10 RACIAL RUMORS WORTH TALKING ABOUT.

1. **BLACK LUNG DISEASE**
   The packaging of Marlboro cigarettes warned that you'd not only get cancer from smoking 'em (if you got 'em), but a healthy dose of hate as well. During the mid-'80s, paranoid watchdogs claimed that when the box was turned sideways, the brand of smokes' distinctive red chevron resembled a "K" that repeated itself three times—on the front, back, and one side—indicating Klan ownership or sympathy. Close scrutiny of the Philip Morris crest also revealed that the negative space between the horses' legs looked like little hooded Grand Dragons holding the slogan "Veni, vidi, vici" ("I came, I saw, I got carcinoma").

2. **COAT CHECK**
   Mid-'80s, LL Cool J–endorsed clothing label TROOP was not only the original FUBU (Friggin' Ugly, Butt Ugly!), but it was also rumored to be owned by—guess who?—the Klan! By the end of the decade, hip hoppers everywhere believed that the once-popular name brand was an acronym for Total Reign Over Oppressed Peoples (prompting MC Shan to exhort "Puma's the brand 'cause the Klan makes TROOP" on his classic rap composition "I Pioneered This"). The company, however, was actually owned by the KJJ—a Korean and two Jews.

3. **NOT-SO-THIN LIZZY CAUSES A TIZZY**
   A 1992 tale had it that designer Liz Claiborne was kicked off *Oprah* when she declared that she didn't design for Black women because their hips were too big. This, despite the fact that she never appeared on the show. Meanwhile, the clothing line still faces boycotts ten years later. And Oprah's bigger than ever.

4. **WICKED LIQUID**
   Hearsay circa 1991 had it that Tropical Fantasy, the discount-priced, ghettocentric, fructose-laden concoction from the great borough of Brooklyn, made The Black Man sterile. (Hence, TBM's continued preference for that cool, refreshing, and sperm-count-friendly drink, malt liquor.) You'd think any excuse to throw away those Trojans would be embraced. ("C'mon, baby, I'm shootin' blanks.") However, the scuttlebutt was unfounded, leaving only one thing certain: Niggaz in the 'hood still be havin' too many seeds. Slow down, baby.

5. **"MADE FROM THE BEST STUFF ON EARTH—BLACK SWEAT"**
   The early '90s packaging of the successful Snapple ice tea (which goes great with an all-white-meat bucket o' Church's Fried Chicken) satisfied those with a thirst for racial rumors. Conspiracists misconstrued the label's large, illustrated ship to be a slave vessel, with minute depictions of chained Africans and Klansmen(?!) in the background. The image was actually of the Boston Tea Party. Fueling the brewhaha was the presence of a small, conspicuous "K"

off to the side. The chugaluggin' goyim among us thought it pointed to a Klan connection. And that ain't kosher.

6. **THAT (RACIST) THING**
According to a Caucasoid caller to the *Howard Stern Show* in 1996, Lauryn Hill—fresh off the multiplatinum success of the Fugees—had made statements on MTV to the effect of, "I'd rather have my children starve than have white people buy my music." No evidence ever surfaced to confirm that she'd said anything of the sort. She may be miseducated, but she ain't misbehavin'. (Unless you count that Rohan shit.)

7. **COAT CHECK, PART 2**
Evidently, the paranoia grapevine loves them some Oprah. In 1996, all-American sportswear owner Tommy Hilfiger was targeted when he supposedly remarked on Ms. Winfrey's TV talkathon, "If I knew that Blacks and Asians were going to wear my clothes, I would never have designed them." Uncle Tommy never actually said it. Go ahead, ask Kidada Jones's Blackbird side. (No disrespect, Q.)

8. **TRIPLE THREAT**
A 1997-ish rumor swore that the name of Omaha, Nebraska, ska-rock group 311 was really an encrypted reference to—who else?—the Ku Klux Klan. (The eleventh letter of the alphabet is K, so 3 X K = KKK.) The lightweight rockers' name actually originates from the L.A. police code for indecent exposure. Or was it noise pollution?

9. **UNEQUAL RIGHTS**
A 1999 hoax, discharged by the misinformation superhighway, claimed that people of color could be identified if an even number appeared as their social security number's fifth digit. Thus, your nonwhiteness was advertised to prospective employers, lenders, and loan sharks. Not true: You better work—bitch.

10. **YOU'VE GOT HATE MAIL**
Circa 2000, a mass-forwarded e-mail told recipients to type the following sentence into Word for Windows: "I'd like all niggers to die." You were then instructed to highlight the sentence and choose the thesaurus. The program returned a responded suggestion of "I'll drink to that." All this leads one to believe that the pale (and pale yellow) programmers at Microsoft were not only unscrupulous, but big-time bigots as well. Compu-geeks chalked it up to a bad programming glitch. ("I'll drink to that" showed up as the response to any sentence that began with "I'd like . . .") Of course, the bigger question is what in tarnation would compel anyone to type in that phrase in the first place. That's not very PC—ha ha ha!

(By the way, that other rumor, that Bill Gates is the devil, is true.)

CONSPIRACISM: FINDING THE HIDDEN HATE IN ORDINARY, EVERYDAY THINGS.

Here's the deal, bucko. Only the most alert race-savvy spectators regularly read between the lines. Not many realize that there are ugly messages prevalent in even the most seemingly benign products. Keeping this in mind, we the *et* watchers provide this much-needed public service alert. You might call us paranoid androids, but PLEASE do not disregard our warnings.

ADVANCE WHITE TOOTHPASTE
A/k/a mean Gleem, knawmean?

BIG BROWN BAG
¡Ay! Why does the help always have to be brown? Because it represents cheap Latin labor that carries that weight—a long time.

IVORY SOAP
The great white wash.

CHEESE NIPS
Little yellow squares—the *otaku* of the snack world.

HOOD MILK
New England's heifer secretion isn't available in chocolate flavor. No wonder Black athletes hate playing in Boston.

SPIC AND SPAN
Cleans and disinfects sans stress from INS.

WITE OUT
Invented by Monkee Mike Nesmith's momma. Any Black Monkees' fans out there?

MAJOR ACCENT HIGHLIGHTER MARKER
The yellow ones of this brand are most common—coincidence?

AND WHAT ABOUT...?

BILLIARDS
There's something fishy about a game that starts with a single white ball violently busting up a peacefully united congregation of coloreds. The contest culminates in hateful ecstasy once the eight ball (the black ball) is successfully knocked down a hole like a (tar) Baby Jessica. Oh, and everything also ends automatically if the white ball unintentionally falls down the same hellish hole. In other words, if whitey ain't playin', there's no goddamned game!

BOWLING
The ultimate sporting manifestation of great white guilt. Think about it: A hulking, rolling ebony behemoth of a ball steamrolls passive, pear-shaped white pins again and again . . . and again. If the ball doesn't accomplish its mission, it's back to the gutter (a/k/a da streetz, a/k/a da ghetto). It ought to be the Black man's favorite sport—except for the fact that the white man got three fingers all up in his shiznit! A Black man can't do nuthin' by hisself!

BROWN EGGS
Hard as they might try to be down, there ain't no sunny side to being these little brown ones. Inside, they're just as good as the white ones. But you'd never know because you never buy them, you racist. Fuck you.

BROWNIES
Like Mexicans, Jamaicans, and Hawaiians, they're *chronic*ally associated with carrying marijuana. Either that, or they're rolling with nuts (as in weirdos).

DOMINOES
They're otherwise pure black squares tainted by little white spots that dictate where they go, where they meet, and who they connect with. They ain't playin' Sun City, and we ain't playin' dominoes! Never again.

INSTANT RAMEN NOODLES
They're a tight-knit group that won't separate unless subjected to harsh elements or chemical abuse (a/k/a "Oriental Flavor").

#2 PENCILS
Skinny, yellow, and always second-class citizens. And they're good at tests.

PHONOGRAPH RECORDS
They're black, twelve inches (or at least no less than seven inches), and they get the white girls shaking their rumps. No wonder there was a massive conspiracy to erase the bass. Genocide is a muh'fucka.

RICE (THE WHITE KIND)
It sticks together. And it's thrown at weddings . . . with extra force at interracial nuptials.

SAUERKRAUT
The name itself is outlandish Auslander slander. This German condiment gets the dils.

WATERMELON SEEDS
Natural selection in its most discriminatory form. You can digest the white ones, but not the black ones. That's no Fruitopia. No way. Nuh-uh.

COONSKIN CAPS

WHITE GUYS CALLING NONWHITES "BRO"

 THE FRITO BANDITO

THE PAPER BAG TEST

LAWN JOCKEYS

WHITE SLAVERY RINGS

"GHETTO BLASTERS"

THE SAMBO'S RESTAURANT CHAIN

WHAT EVER HAPPENED TO...?

COINTELPRO

JEWFROS

POLACK JOKES

CALLING MARTIAL ARTS FILMS "CHOP SOCKY" FLICKS

THE BROW

WHITE FLIGHT

RACIALLY CLEVER ADVERTISING CAMPAIGNS

LAMBADA, THE FORBIDDEN DANCE

MALCOLM X HATS

"RACE-TRAITORS"

RAMBO FLICKS

PEOPLE ASSUMING THAT ALL BLACK

 KHOMEINI SUCKS

"FUCK IRAN" BUTTONS

THE YOUNG LORDS

DON RICKLES

LITTLE ITALY

AFRICA MEDALLIONS

JENNIFER GREY'S NOSE

SLOWPOKE RODRIGUEZ

CALLING HEROIN "THE WHITE LADY"

"RACE MUSIC"

THE BLACK ROCK COALITION

"KISS ME, I'M IRISH"

BLACK VENTRILOQUISTS

ADONNA'S LATIN PHASE

RACIST JOKE BOOKS

ERETS

BASEBALL PLAYERS NAMED "WHITEY"

PINKOS

THE 3RD BASS WORLD UNITY TOUR

EÑOR NAUGLES

PRINCE SPAGHETTI DAY

ASIAN SERVANT BOYS

WESTERNS

ITH PAGERS ARE DRUG DEALERS

USING "COTTON PICKIN'" AS AN ADJECTIVE

MAMA CELESTE

WANG CHUNG

POLITICAL BLACK ATHLETES

THE INTELLIVISION MAN
WILL TAKE US TO THE PROMISED LAND:
SELECTED RACIAL MILESTONES AND GLITCHES
IN VIDEO GAME HISTORY. BY GABE SORIA

Back in 1972, no fuss was ever made over the fact that there were no Black people in *Pong*, the revolutionary video game that took the nation by the joystick. That's because there were no people at all in *Pong*—no Nubians, no white people, no Asians, no nothing, except some busy-ass blips. And it was beautiful. The prehuman era of video games was an electronic Eden, a polygonal paradise, a nerd nirvana. It was an abstract wonderland where politics rarely entered the picture.

Enter the Intellivision Man, the de facto mascot of the Mattel Electronics gaming system (and one of my racial heroes). This little pixilated fella, the cruder-than-crude digital equivalent to a cave painting, was so iconic and so blank he was nobody and everybody at the same time. A two-bit everyman, he was a blank slate for video game players of all ethnicities on which to imprint their personalities.

But as the industry developed and the graphics improved, more attention was given to detail. Things like skin tone now existed in computer programming. Sadly, it would be the graphic exposure of too much skin and blatant racism that would figure prominently in video games' fall from innocence.

The X-rated *Custer's Revenge*, created by a company called Mystique for the Atari 2600 in 1982, caused an uproar for the digitalized degradation of its sick premise. You *are* General George Armstrong Custer. Avoiding the arrows of unseen braves raining down on your pale treacherous ass, you run across the screen (without much difficulty) wearing only a dusty cavalry hat, a boogery 'kerchief 'round your red neck, some horse-shit-stained boots, and armed with a powerful erection. An *erection!* Your prize? A busty, butt-naked American Indian lass tied to a pole waiting for you to "score" as a fanfare of "Charge" is played. The instructional manual downplayed the rape by stating: "Watch how the maiden smiles and kicks up her heels and Custer 'flips his lid.' " (It also recommended: "If the kids catch you and should ask, tell them Custer and the maiden are just dancing.")

No fooling; this game actually existed. Heavily protested, *Custer's Revenge* deservedly lost much of its distribution. Looking back, about the only thing Mystique got right was that ol' George sure was a nasty son of a bitch.

From the get-go, sports titles were popular. Released in 1983 to capitalize on the growing fever surrounding the next year's Olympic Games in Los Angeles, *Track & Field* by Konami featured one basic character, a short-short-wearing, mustache-sporting male athlete who came in many variations, one decidedly Negroid. Notable for the fact that the characters' running and jumping skills were based solely on their player's capacity for repetitive button pushing and timing and not inherently on their skin color, which explains why white men actually won the 100-yard dash in this game.

Pac-Man wouldn't go straight to the ghetto until the '90s (unless you count the cop Sean Penn played in the 1988 movie *Colors*). That's when Mandingo Entertainment hit the world with an adaptation of the Robin Harris animated feature *Bebe's Kids* for the Super Nintendo and the hip hop-inspired street basketball game *Rap Jam Vol. 1*. The *Vol. 1* thing turned out to be incredibly optimistic, as Mandingo's noble efforts to cut out the white and Japanese middlemen in the making of substandard vid-game fare went largely unnoticed by the gaming public. The company disappeared, unmourned, a short time later. (Incidentally, why a company making Black-themed video games would name itself Mandingo and not produce a game based on the 1975 flick of the same name—a miscegenation-'n'-boxing classic—defies all logic known to man.)

In 1996, the aptly titled *Shellshock*, an episodic tank combat simulation for the Sega Saturn and Sony PlayStation, dropped a bomb on the lily-white playing field. Yes, indeed, you commanded an entirely Black cast that amounted to the A-Team if it were made up entirely of Mr. Ts, mercenaries who roamed the land defending the defenseless and trading quasi-jive talk. Would have made an excellent film starring Richard Roundtree, Sidney Poitier, and Richard Pryor.

Not many people were laughing when copies of *Diehard Gamefan* (Volume 3, Issue 9) hit the newsstands. The worst nightmare of magazine production is having an obvious mistake printed in the final product. Normally, publications utilize "dummy" text (usually innocuous Latin phrases or a nonsense jumble of words) in early layouts while they wait for the writer to turn in the actual arti-

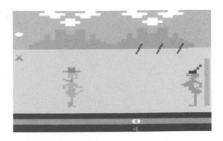

cle. So having dummy text printed would be embarrassing. But when you're a video game magazine that relies heavily on product that originates from the Land of the Rising Sun and your dummy text includes the phrase "little Jap bastards" as seen in *Diehard Gamefan*'s preview for *College Football USA '96*, well, embarrassing isn't quite the word for it. Oddly enough, these guys love Japanese people. Really!

In terms of technology, video games will only get better now that we're in the twenty-first century. (Just ask those little Jap bastards.) But racial representation still has a long way to go. Boxing video games, much like the football and basketball titles, is where you will find most of the Black characters. Old school joints like Activision's Atari 2600 *Boxing* used the classic dichotomy of Black fighter versus white fighter, a trend that would evolve to feature more ethnic types such as Nintendo's multicultural coin-op *Punch-Out!!*, which featured an Italian boxer named, get this, Pizza Pasta. (No one really grumbled about it, though.)

Perhaps the most debated character to jump in the ring is Afro Thunder, the utterly buffoonish "star" of *Ready 2 Rumble*, which also includes Mexican, Hawaiian, Arabic, Thai, and other non-Anglo brawlers. Thunder, an obvious descendent of Kid Quick from *Punch-Out!!*, is absolutely ridiculous. He has an Afro that would qualify him for membership in the Sylvers, he prances around like Little Richard on an overdose of James Brown pills, and his trash-talkin' street patter is *waaay* beat. Interestingly enough, he was designed by a Filipino artist and physically modeled after a real person. The thing is, in light of the always flamboyant and controversial behavior of professional boxers, Afro Thunder might just come off as being a little less over the top and more of a role model than his live counterparts, as scary as that sounds.

Computerized Latinos, on the other hand, haven't made much noise at all. Those few characters that do make it can sometimes cause a panic, as seen by Activision's 1999 *Toy Story 2* video game, based on the Disney cartoon.

Under fire was the bad guy that kids had to kill in order to advance to the next level, a bushy-mustached, sombrero-on-the-*cabeza*, bullet-bandolier-across-the-chest *bandido* chubster. Now if that isn't a Mexican stereotype, then there's no such thing as Corinthian leather. (All right, so Mr. Rourke pulled a fast one on you gringos. Obviously, you're all still rather angry.)

As it stands, almost all the main video game characters continue to be made of Caucasoid computer chips. Non-Cauckies are usually relegated to secondary (subservient) roles or cast as villains. Asian characters are almost always some type of ninjas. Arabs will probably continue to be portrayed as terrorists for decades to come. Blacks are usually nonthinking muscleheads. And even when whites are becoming the minorities, like in the sports category, you can often find that one honky who at crucial times can throw impossible 100-plus-yard TDs or incredibly swish full-court three-pointers at the buzzer.

Arguments about racial misrepresentations in the video game world are endless. (Xatrix Entertainment is cleverly carving out a racial niche with titles like Redneck Rampage and Kingpin, a battle-for-the-'hood shoot-'em-up.) With hundreds of thousands of games available, the ones mentioned here are but a drop in the two-bit bucket. So, yes, right now there might be some Samboesque Black folks shuckin' it up in video games made and released only in Japan, a place that controls a large part of the industry but where there isn't that much racial diversity. (And let's not forget that stateside plenty of KKK-endorsed video games for your PC are popping up everywhere on the Internet as technology advances.) All of which points us back to the Intellivision Man, that pan-ethnic guru who seemed to have been saying all along, "Everything might be all right, if y'all just chill the hell out."

Writer/musician/cerveza expert Gabe Soria is a former editor at Videogames *magazine. He's half-Black and half-Mexican and immensely enjoys the fact that he has a large selection of stereotypes to choose from.*

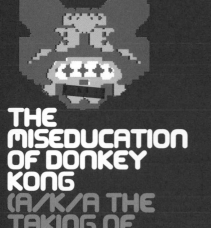

THE MISEDUCATION OF DONKEY KONG
(A/K/A THE TAKING OF PAULINE 1, 2, 3).

Game. It's what real players need to have to survive. Ask the original DK(NY) hustla, Donkey Kong (representing the Big Apple, baby pops). It was within the evil streets of NYC's concrete jungle that this misunderstood ape man's saga became world infamous. Here is his back story. A fitness instructor who possessed all the right moves in the barbell room, good ol' Kong could slap the medicine ball like a mentholated Puerto Rican on a graffiti-festooned handball court. He exuded power. But while physically imposing—many would even say *intimidating*—on first sight, he was, in fact, a soft-spoken simian when one got to know him. He was a credit to his race. The ape race. The Black race. At least that's how a lot of *you* see it.

But Donkey Kong's seemingly halcyon world would soon forever change. One day after a calf-muscle massage therapy session with one of his supreme clientele regulars, "Tuna" (better known to gridiron fanatics as Coach Bill Parcells), Kong received a call from the white man who signed his checks at the gym, Mike DeFazio. Kong had dutifully served his overseer for the past four years (and never once stole nuthin'), so big boss Mike trusted his monkey ass.

"Say, Kong," said Mike, "I need ya to do me a solid. Remember my *paisan* . . . uh, my dear friend Mario? He's in construction. He installed the smoke detectors and sprinklers here in the gym. Anyways, he wants his main squeeze to get the smoke outta *her* lungs, and get in shape. I told him you were just the fella to siphon out that jelly."

Kong, of course, obediently agreed, and penciled in a session for early in the A.M.—at da breaka dawn. (He had the keys to the place, you know. *That's*

trust.) It was while chomping on his third toasted corn muffin of the morning that he was interrupted by a knock on the door by a vision of loveliness. Now usually, Kong never paid the additional two dollars for white meat. He was strictly for his S.I.S.T.A.S.—Sexy, Intelligent, Sisters, Tanned Always, Sho' 'nuff. That is until Pauline, a tobacco-chewing, mahogany sweatsuit-wearing blonde with an overbite and a mild case of dandruff, stepped inside his arena. She was the closest thing to Helen Hunt Kong's hazel eyes had ever witnessed. Instantly, he was mad about her.

But while Kong was clearly smitten, he honored his professional code of fitness excellence: Thou shalt not feel up customers on the clock, or that's your ass! Two hours later after a near perfect workout, Pauline had worked up quite a sweat. She was fienin' like Jodeci for one of her trusty cancer sticks. Kong knew it was wrong. But being the nice chimp he was, he just couldn't say no—especially since Pauline had legs like Jessica Lange's.

"I'm sorry, but the only place you can get your puff on is on the roof," he explained, remembering the sensitivity of her boo Mario's state-of-the-art smoke detector/sprinkler system.

"Come with me," she insisted. "It's windy up there and I'm scared of heights."

While up on the roof, Kong and Pauline didn't realize that a perturbed Mario had stopped by to pick her up. The naturally hotheaded Italiano was late for his jobby job, and Mario cursed up a blue streak as he searched for Pauline's whereabouts. Being a stickler for all things fire-

code–related, he noticed the emergency stairwell door ajar. He knew something was up . . . the stairs. Plus the unmistakable odor of Capris had infected his olfactory nerves, and that *really* got on his nerves.

"What the hell is going on up here?" Mario yelled as he burst onto the roof. The sight of his sugar cube fraternizing with this . . . this . . . *Black* was too close for comfort. "I'm gonna freakin' murdalize both of yas!" he shrieked, as he grasped his preferred tool of war—an enormous mallet—and started swinging like Thor. It was hammer time.

Petrified, Pauline yelped the only words that popped into her pretty little head: *"Help! Help!"*

Faced with this senseless, crazed attacker, Kong's brain reacted and reverted to survival-of-the-fittest instincts: *I know what to do,* he thought, seizing one of boss DeFazio's rooftop barrels full of groovy grape—you know, the good stuff: homemade moonshine, wop-style, 1981.

"No Rocky-wannabe is gonna make a monkey outta me!" Kong growled as he began hurling barrels at a crazy rate.

EPILOGUE

Like many events in American history, Donkey Kong's plight has been twisted into a whirlwind of lies and deceit. This ape ain't no dumbbell with an incurable case of jungle fever. No, friends, he was simply at the wrong place at the wrong time—with the wrong white woman. And while millions will undoubtedly continue to view him as a super villain against vanillin civilians, we know the truth. And now you do, too. Ape recognize game. Game recognize ape. Thanks, Nintendo!

Riot

THE BEST OF TWENTIETH-CENTURY CIVIL UNREST.

On!

NOT OKAY IN OK
TULSA, OKLAHOMA—MAY 31–JUNE 1, 1921

On the night of May 31, a crowd of whites gathers at the Tulsa courthouse to witness the lynching of a Black shoe-shine man who, according to a fabricated story in the local newspaper, had attempted to rape a white woman. A Black crowd gathers to protect the innocent man from the bloodthirsty mob. However, after a skirmish between the opposing groups leaves a white man shot dead, Black Tulsa is subjected to an unprecedented bloodbath. Over the next twelve hours, the once-prosperous African-American business district of Greenwood (a/k/a the "Black Wall Street") is torched by white rioters by land and from the air with explosives dropped from small airplanes. More than 1,400 Black homes and businesses—among them churches, restaurants, grocery stores, movie theaters, libraries, schools, law offices, a hospital, a bank, a post office, several private planes, and a bus system—are destroyed. The city's official death toll of mostly Black victims is initially calculated at thirty, but the Red Cross' count inflates the figure to 300. Years later, the discovery of mass graves raises the estimate of those dead to possibly thousands more.

BEAST IN THE EAST
LOS ANGELES, CALIFORNIA—JUNE 3–7, 1943

Eleven white sailors on shore leave claim to have been attacked by a group of Mexican-American youths adorned in zoot suits—a style of dress stereotyped as *pachuco* hoodlum gear. Seeking payback later that evening, more than 200 sailors take a fleet of taxicabs to the center of Los Angeles' Mexican-American barrio, East L.A., and begin indiscriminately attacking anyone rocking a zoot suit. For the next four nights, American servicemen—sailors and soldiers—continue their battle on the community. All the while, cops turn a blind eye and act as passive accomplices to the violence. The June 21 issue of *Time* magazine later reports that, "The police practice was to accompany the caravans of soldiers and sailors in police cars, watch the beatings, and jail the victims." At midnight on the night of June 7, military authorities finally stop the rioting by declaring the city off-limits to their personnel. Though hundreds of *pachucos*—many not even wear-

DESTROY AND REBUILD (BUT MOSTLY DESTROY): AN L.A. STREET SOLDIER SALUTES THE '92 REBELLION.

ing zoot suits—are arrested, no sailors or soldiers are prosecuted for their lawlessness. The servicemen are, in fact, widely heralded by the local press. A June 7 *Los Angeles Times* headline reads: ZOOT SUITERS LEARN LESSON IN FIGHTS WITH SERVICEMEN.

DETROIT RACE CITY, PART 1
DETROIT, MICHIGAN—JUNE 20–21, 1943
Detroit is the most important industrial center in the country during World War II. But the huge influx of Blacks from down south filling the city's factory jobs gradually transforms the city, nicknamed the "Arsenal of Democracy," into an overcrowded metropolis that residents cynically redub the "Arsehole of Democracy." On the night of June 20, at an amusement park called Belle Isle, multiple incidents of fighting between Black and white teenagers erupt. Two false rumors—that whites have thrown a Black woman and her baby off the Belle Isle Bridge and that a Black man has raped and murdered a white woman on the bridge—circulate throughout the rest of Detroit. In response, Black mobs loot and destroy white-owned businesses while whites attack streetcars carrying Black passengers, and gather outside the Black-patronized Roxy Theater to assault moviegoers. It isn't until the next night, when whites invade the destitute Black ghetto (ironically named Paradise Valley), that U.S. Army troops are finally called in to shut down the city. In the end, the death toll totals nine whites and twenty-five Blacks—seventeen of them killed by white policemen. Nearly 700 people are injured in the melee and the damage is assessed at $2 million.

WATTS UP
WATTS, CALIFORNIA—AUGUST 11–16, 1965
Coming just a year after passage of the Civil Rights Act of 1964, the Watts riots show the world that all is still not good in the 'hood. A twenty-one-year-old Black man, Marquette Frye, is stopped and arrested by white police officers during the evening on a drunken-and-disorderly driving charge near his home in the South Central L.A. neighborhood of Watts. Frye's brother and mother plead with the offi-

cers to release Marquette, but the cops refuse and, after a scuffle, arrest them as well. A growing crowd of onlookers spit on the officers and pelt them with rocks and bottles. The disgruntled mob begins setting small fires, before the whole shebang escalates into one of U.S. history's most notorious outbursts of urban rage. For six days, African-Americans and Latinos loot and firebomb large sections of inner-city Los Angeles—targeting white-owned (largely Jewish-owned) businesses—and coin the catchphrase "Burn, baby, burn" a decade before the Trammps cut "Disco Inferno." Snipers shoot at firemen attempting to extinguish the blazes, the result of the L.A. Fire Department's prejudicial hiring practices and ill treatment of Black firemen. The National Guard eventually regains control and institutes a curfew zone covering 46.5 square miles. Thirty-four people die, 4,000 are arrested, and damage estimates reach $40 million.

DETROIT RACE CITY, PART 2
DETROIT, MICHIGAN—JULY 23–25, 1967
The "long hot summer" of 1967 sees the ruckus brought to several major cities—among them New York, Washington, Chicago, and Newark, where riots leave twenty-six dead and 1,500 injured. Once again, though, the Motor City takes the title of strife-life capital. After police execute an early-morning raid on the United Community and Civic League, an illegal bar/gambling spot in a Black neighborhood, a crowd gathers in protest after rumors spread of police brutality. In a short time, the protests turn to looting and burning of white-owned stores. Mindful of the city's history of police overreaction to minor incidents, authorities elect not to send extra officers to the scene and even impose a local news blackout in the hopes of keeping a lid on the situation. Both tactics backfire as rioters rage unchecked. They begin burning down Black businesses and homes as well as white ones, spreading the affected area to fourteen square miles. When the smoke clears, forty-three are dead, 7,000 arrested,

1,300 buildings destroyed, and 2,700 businesses looted with property damage totaling $22 million.

RAY OF BLIGHT:
KING ASSASSINATION RIOTS
NUMEROUS CITIES—APRIL 4–11, 1968
After Martin Luther King Jr. is assassinated in Memphis, Tennessee, rioting erupts in more than 120 cities across the map. In Chicago, Mayor Richard J. Daley orders police to "shoot to kill" riot participants. In Washington, D.C., President Lyndon B. Johnson deploys the 82nd Airborne Division to control the chaos. Meanwhile, rioters in downtown Trenton loot a sporting goods store and drive golf balls down city streets like ticked-off Tiger Woodses at dodging police officers as the city burns. Nationwide forty-six die; with 2,600 injured. Ironically, in normally tense Boston, there is relative peace as James Brown's concert at Boston Garden is broadcast live on local television on the night of the assassination, keeping folks indoors and entertained.

GET OFF THE BUS
BOSTON, MASSACHUSETTS, 1974–1976
On June 21, 1974, Federal Judge W. Arthur Garrity orders that Boston public schools achieve racial balance via the forced busing of students from designated Black neighborhoods to schools in designated white neighborhoods and vice versa. The decision escalates simmering tensions between the two areas most visibly affected by the plan—the Black ghetto of Roxbury and its white Irish-Catholic counterpart, South Boston—and immediately makes Garrity the most hated man in Boston. For the next three years, police-escorted buses of Black students enter white areas amid hurled bricks, bottles, and epithets, earning the Hub the dubious nickname "the Little Rock of the North." Despite the in-school presence of metal detectors, police officers patrolling hallways and cafeterias, and even snipers assigned to nearby rooftops, racial fighting breaks out daily. The ferocity of antibusing demonstrations is captured in a Pulitzer Prize–winning photograph by Stanley Forman taken outside

Boston City Hall in which a Black attorney is seen being jabbed by a white man using an American flag pole.

MIAMI SOUND CLASH
MIAMI, FLORIDA—MAY 17–20, 1980
Twelve years before the Rodney King verdict, Miami endures the murder trial of thirty-three-year-old Black insurance executive Arthur McDuffie. In December 1979, McDuffie is arrested after a high-speed chase and dies after being repeatedly struck by white policemen brandishing heavy flashlights. Police initially attempt to cover up the murder by claiming the chase ended in McDuffie's accidental death when his motorcycle crashed. The trial, which takes place before an all-white jury after a change of venue, ends with the acquittal of four white officers. Subsequent rioting in Miami's Liberty City ghetto claims eighteen lives and causes $100 million in damage. Miami, rife with resentment amongst African-Americans due to economic opportunities lost to incoming Cuban, Nicaraguan, and Haitian immigrants, will suffer through several more race-fueled disturbances in the '80s.

THE CROWN HEIGHTS AFFAIR
CROWN HEIGHTS, BROOKLYN, NEW YORK—AUGUST 19–23, 1991
A seven-year-old Black child, Gavin Cato, is struck and killed when a car in the motorcade of the rabbi Menachem Schneerson spins out of control onto the sidewalk. Angry Black residents of the largely West Indian community begin beating the car's driver, Yosef Lifsh, before he is taken to the hospital by a privately run Jewish Hatzolah ambulance. The news that Lifsh will not be arrested by police spreads through the area. Later that evening, an angry mob chases down twenty-nine-year-old Australian rabbinical scholar Yankel Rosenbaum and stabs him to death in retaliation. Four days and three nights of turmoil engulfs the neighborhood. Jewish residents are beaten, cars are overturned and set on fire, and stores are looted and firebombed as Crown Heights' Black majority releases its long-standing frustration with the neighborhood's eco-nomically and politically empowered Orthodox Jewish minority. Hundreds of police officers in riot gear eventually restore order, but Black New York City mayor David Dinkins is heavily criticized by Jews for the New York Police Department's slow response to the chaos. In concert performances thereafter, even A Tribe Called Quest's Phife Dawg alters his lyrics to "Can I Kick It?" from "Mr. Dinkins would you please be my mayor?" to "Mr. Dinkins was a shitty fuckin' mayor."

ROYAL (BLACK 'N') BLUE
LOS ANGELES, CALIFORNIA —APRIL 29–MAY 1, 1992
You love to hear the story again and again: Black motorist Rodney King is stopped by white police officers in the early morning hours of March 3, 1991, after his 1988 Hyundai sedan is allegedly clocked at 110 miles per hour. King is ordered out of his car, told to lie on his stomach, and is repeatedly kicked, struck with nightsticks, and shocked with a Taser gun by police as a resident in a nearby apartment complex records the violence with his video camera. The world is outraged upon viewing the eighty-one-second videotape. But not as outraged as L.A.'s inner-city dwellas on April 29, 1992, when a jury of ten whites, an Hispanic, and a Filipino finds all four cops charged for excessive force not guilty. Rioting, looting, and arson erupt across Los Angeles, with its epicenter at the intersection of Florence and Normandie Avenues. White motorists are pulled from their cars and assaulted, including truck driver Reginald Denny, whose beatdown is broadcast live from a TV news helicopter.

But the racial acrimony isn't limited to Black versus white. Black-Korean relations are also strained in the wake of the Latasha Harlins murder trial (in which a local Korean store owner who'd fatally shot a Black teen for shoplifting in March 1991 was sentenced only to probation), and many Korean-owned businesses are pillaged in the chaos. The rioters themselves are of diverse ethnic affiliations. Of the nearly 17,000 arrested almost 37 per-cent are Latino, 30 percent Black, 7 percent white, and 26 percent "unknown." The final tally: fifty-two dead, nearly 3,000 injured, and a billion dollars in property damage.

DISHONORABLE MENTION:
YAK ATTACK
GERALDO, NEW YORK, NEW YORK —NOVEMBER 3, 1988
During the taping of a Geraldo Rivera talk show on the subject of Nazi skinheads, a brawl breaks out between two guests—John Metzger, leader of the White Aryan Resistance Youth, and Black activist Roy Innis of the Congress for Racial Equality. Amidst the bedlam of fisticuffs and audience members storming the stage, a chair strikes Geraldo in the face, breaking his nose. Tuff break, homes. (Then again, G-man is a Puerto Rican Jew with a somewhat Semitic schnozz—so no one really notices the "snap.")

BLACK BY POPULAR DEMAND:
TOP 10 THINGS BLACK PEOPLE "TOOK" FROM WHITEY.

10. Stage diving **9.** Ecstasy abuse **8.** Crappy romantic comedies **7.** All-terrain vehicles **6.** Excessive tattooing **5.** Fixation on brand name designer apparel **4.** Every ghetto, every city **3.** Straightening hair/dying hair blond **2.** The n-word **1.** Hatred for Blacks

TOP 10 REASONS LATINS STEAL.

10. Skyrocketing Similac prices **9.** Never learned how to say "borrow" **8.** A latent indigenous trait that makes them want to take shit back **7.** Too much rap (though a lot of them learn English from it, it's a bad influence) **6.** The more ignorant and thugged out you are, the more it drives the *jainas loca* **5.** Ask Ruben Rivera **4.** You heard them before, they don't need no stinkin' badges **3.** You do crazy *caca* when you're drunk **2.** They get so horny, they can't keep their hands to themselves **1.** That European blood

10 BLACKS THAT BLACKS SHOULD BE ASHAMED OF... AND THE REAL REASONS WHY.

1. **MARION BARRY**
Because that *kufi* you used to rock looked just plain goofy. Someone should've called the fashion police.

2. **JOHNNIE COCHRAN**
How any self-respecting attorney could defend troubled *Diff'rent Strokes* star Todd Bridges and look himself in the mirror every morning is beyond us.

3. **MINISTER LOUIS FARRAKHAN**
Abandoned a budding calypso singing career before it really even had a chance to take off. Such unfulfilled promise. Tsk, tsk.

4. **JESSE JACKSON**
Been rappin' since the '70s and *still* ain't got no record contract? What a disgrace to the race.

5. **R. KELLY**
Any Black man who would record a duet with Celine Dion should get his head checked.

6. **DON KING**
In a 1988 *Playboy* interview, he claimed not to use chemicals in his hair. Liar, liar, pants on fire!

7. **SPIKE LEE**
Girl 6 is still unavailable on DVD. Spike, brother, we believed in you.

8. **AL SHARPTON**
Why would anyone stop touring with James Brown just to get into politics? Disgraceful.

9. **O.J. SIMPSON**
Because *Naked Gun 33 1/3* wasn't as slammin' as the first two. Juice, how do you sleep at night?

10. **MIKE TYSON**
We still haven't forgiven you for guesting on a song by overhyped hip hop flash-in-the-pan Canibus. How can you live with yourself?

LOVE 4 ALLAH Y'ALL: 10 REASONS BLACK PEOPLE LOVE GOD SO GODDANG MUCH.

10. Hope floats.
9. Can't box wit' 'im. (Arms too short.)
8. Jesus was broke, too. (Hallelujah!)
7. It's hell on earth. Heaven must be better.
6. Reverend Creflo Dollar. (Ka-ching!)
5. Church's Fried Chicken. (Can we get an "amen"—and a side of biscuits?)
4. Because He's easy like Sunday morning.
3. More Gospel musicals for e'ry-body.
2. Used to kissing a honky's ass. (Don't realize He's Black.)
1. Because Black is beautiful. And God don't like ugly.

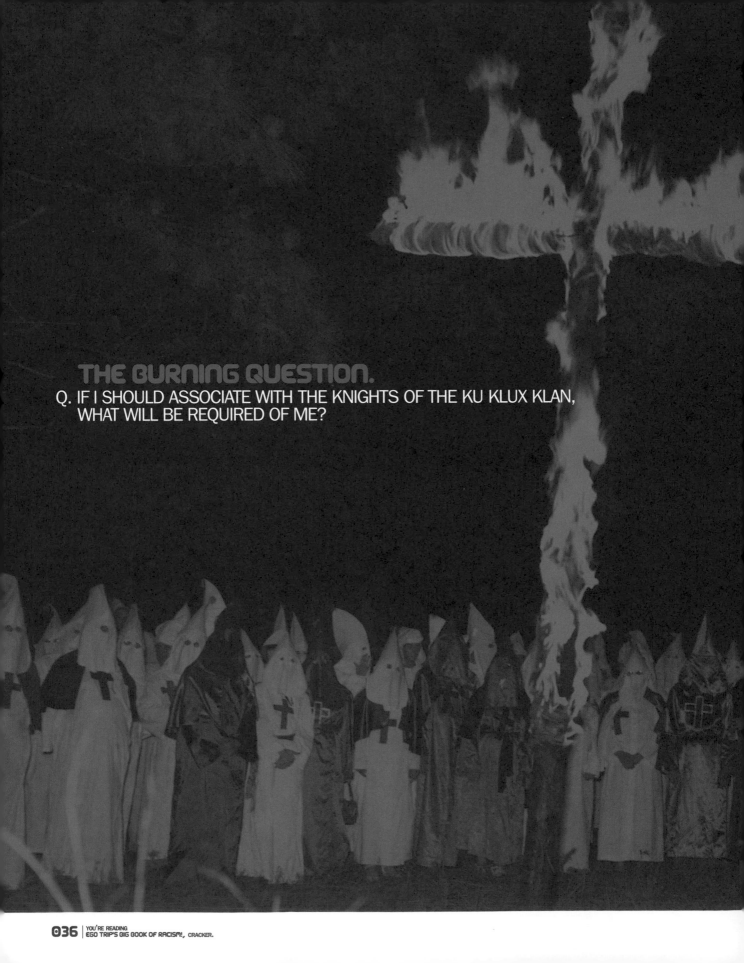

THE BURNING QUESTION.

Q. IF I SHOULD ASSOCIATE WITH THE KNIGHTS OF THE KU KLUX KLAN, WHAT WILL BE REQUIRED OF ME?

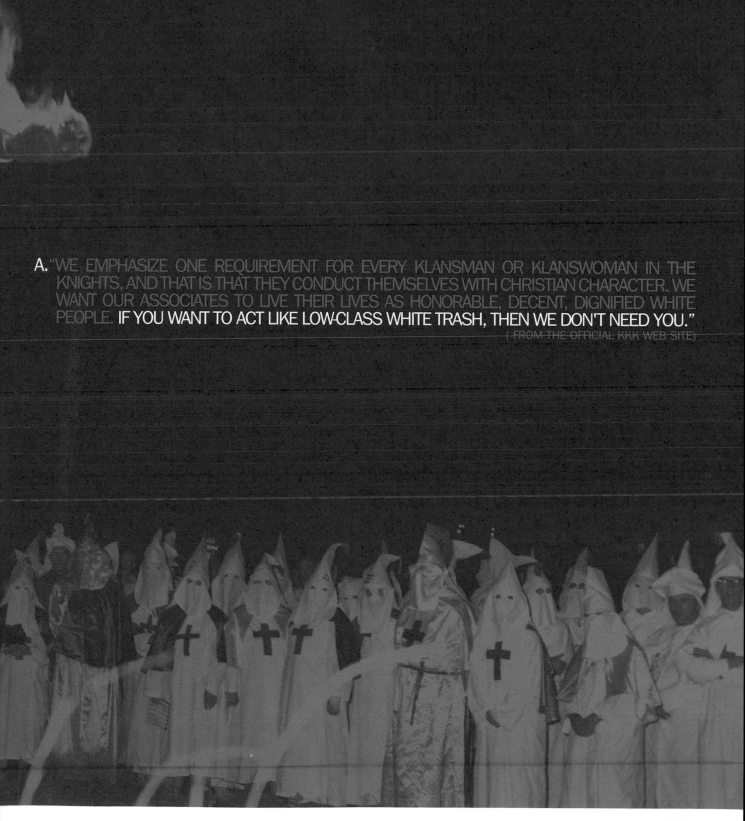

A. "WE EMPHASIZE ONE REQUIREMENT FOR EVERY KLANSMAN OR KLANSWOMAN IN THE KNIGHTS, AND THAT IS THAT THEY CONDUCT THEMSELVES WITH CHRISTIAN CHARACTER. WE WANT OUR ASSOCIATES TO LIVE THEIR LIVES AS HONORABLE, DECENT, DIGNIFIED WHITE PEOPLE. **IF YOU WANT TO ACT LIKE LOW-CLASS WHITE TRASH, THEN WE DON'T NEED YOU.**"

(FROM THE OFFICIAL KKK WEB SITE)

ACT NOW. GRAND DRAGONS ARE STANDING BY...
ACTUAL THINGS YOU WILL RECEIVE IN A PLAIN (PROBABLY WHITE) ENVELOPE AFTER JOINING THE KNIGHTS OF THE KU KLUX KLAN BY PAYING A $35 MEMBERSHIP FEE.

1. "Free" orientation video.
2. "Beautiful certificate" verifying your association in the Klan. Suitable for framing. Or framing others.
3. Membership "passport" card.
4. Welcome letter from National Director Thomas Robb.
5. Information on how you can come up in the white supremacy game.
6. Pledge book.

BUT, WAIT. THERE'S MORE! YOU'LL ALSO GET . . .

7. The *White Patriot* monthly.
8. Bimonthly activity report as well as *Robb's Victory Report*.
9. Invitation to the National Klan Congress in Harrison, Arkansas.

AND MOST IMPORTANTLY . . .

10. "A rewarding experience as you work toward a better understanding of Klan philosophy, our struggle, and [the] return of White Christian Revival in America. We can't do it overnight, but each person who dedicates himself or herself to our cause and remains persistent in their beliefs and goals brings our nation one step closer to a rebirth of Christian self-government. We will help you make that step."

SO, ARYAN, WHAT ARE YOU WAITING FOR?
VISA OR MASTERCARD ACCEPTED. AND THEY DON'T TAKE AMERICAN EXPRESS.

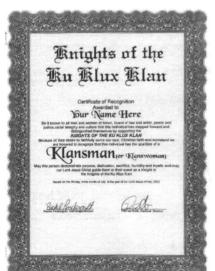

Knights of the Ku Klux Klan

Certificate of Recognition
Awarded to

Your Name Here

Be it known to all men and women of honor, lovers of law and order, peace and justice, racial integrity and culture that this individual has stepped forward and distinguished themselves by supporting the
KNIGHTS OF THE KU KLUX KLAN
Because of their desire to faithfully serve our race, Christian faith and homeland we are honored to recognize that this individual has the qualities of a

Klansman (or Klanswoman)

May this person demonstrate purpose, dedication, sacrifice, humility and loyalty and may our Lord Jesus Christ guide them in their quest as a Knight in the Knights of the Ku Klux Kan

Issued on the 4th day, in the month of July, in the year of our Lord Jesus Christ, 2003

KATCH AS KATCH KAN:
6 KATCHY KKK T-SHIRT SLOGANS.

1. "The Original Boyz N The Hood."
2. "They may take your flag. . . . But I'll be damned if they take mine!" (Klansman standing in front of Confederate flag.)
3. "Klan Kids Kare."
   (Also in smaller type: "Stand up for your people," "Love your heritage," "White and proud," and "Love Jesus.")
4. "It's LOVE not HATE."
5. "You wear your X and I'll wear MINE!"
   (Klansman standing in front of Confederate flag.)
6. "Property of KKK (-XXL-) Athletic Dept."

WHERE'S FRANKLIN? UNCOVERING PEANUTS' "MISSING" COLORED PANELS.*

If you came of age at any point in the latter half of the twentieth century, Sundays meant certain things: Tarzan flicks (with commercials for *der Kommisar* Johnny Weismuller's swimming pools), a hearty meal of Swanson's delectable Salisbury steak washed down with a cup o' Ovaltine plus a Campbell's bean-soup enema (day of purging, you know), liver snacks for Fido, and a rousing game of pickle, pocket pool, or pinochle, *pendejo*. And Peanuts.

The late, great Charles M. Schulz's paean to childhood was a perfect slice of Americana (Ameri-con-ya) right down to

* 'Toon in: This is a parody, people. Anybody who thinks otherwise must be nuts.

the racism. Franklin, the sole recurring soul brother of any color in Big Snoop Dogg's backyard (although half-Mexican/half-Swedish *beisbol* phenom José Peterson once made a brief appearance), had to eat table scraps after table dances, and suffer all kinds of other indignities, none of which you saw in the funny papers—till now.

PISTACHIOS: THE LOST HONEY ROASTED PEANUTS.

Franklin wasn't the only honey-roasted Peanut conspicuously absent from Schulz's illustrated Aryan playland. The following is a list of other minor(ity) characters who for some reason or another never caught on and found themselves exiled from the 'Nuthouse. Exactly why is anyone's guess.

CHUEY SUAREZ
Shirtless and shiftless, Chuey was perpetually scared shitless that Lucy Van Pelt would call the INS on his ass and pelt him with stale Dolly Madison cupcakes. We can only guess that she did.

LIL' HONDA
Maybe the reason no one ever saw Peanuts' lone Asian character is because, like all confused, repressed members of the model minority, she was too busy studying for early entry to MIT—at age eight.

MO(HAMMAD)
Lil' Mo was a proposed Middle Eastern character more pungent than Pig Pen (hummus—comin' atcha). Linus, nonetheless, coveted his headwear. A whole Allaht.

PELTIER
Something of a guru to Peppermint Patty, Peltier was also something of an instigator. The other kids' parents didn't like him (or his kind)—and not just because he secretly espoused the virtues of 'shrooms.

"JEW BOY"
Hasidic and highly antisocial, "Jew Boy" was a mystery. No one was quite sure what this kid's deal was. (Rumors of inbreeding ran amok throughout the neighborhood.) Oh, and his family was on welfare.

UNCLE REBUS.

Everyone loves a rebus puzzle—a chance to tickle that brain muscle (coochie-coochie-coo!)

1. WATCH THIS DIRTY LAUNDRY.

Chi+  +

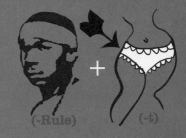

(-Rule) (-t)

M+  a   +er

(-C)

2. NO JOAQUIN IN L.A.

4. ENEMY MINE.

  M+ BEST

(-d)

5. IT'S RED ALL OVER.

(-ckel) (-p)

They're fun, and Fun never discriminates. Until now. Behold the racially rambunctious rebus.

 +

  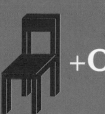 

3. YOU REMIND ME OF MY JEEP.

W+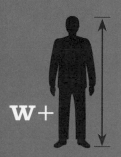

6. YOU'LL CATCH HIM REDHANDED.

 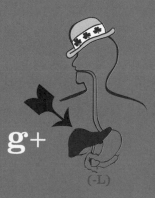

7. TAKING OUT THE GARBAGE PALE KIDS.

8. VEXED TEX-MEX HEX.

(-d)

9. WRONG DIVISION.

10. ¿QUE HORROR ES?

ANSWER KEY:

[1] "Chinese, Japanese, dirty knees, look at these." [2] Make a run for the border. [3] "I'm part Cherokee." [4] "Some of my best friends are Black." [5] "A fight, a fight, a nigger and a white." [6] Indian giver. [7] "Fuck you, white trash!" [8] "Remember the Alamo." [9] Separate but equal. [10] "It's Giuliani time."

Baseball. Apple Pie. Racism. Except for maybe the occasional CIA-sponsored third world puppet regime, you really can't get more American than that. Bigotry, hatred, and ignorance built this country and keep it rolling. Ford tough. Dodge different. Why do you think the rest of the world is not-so-secretly jealous of us? They wish they could perfect what we got. But we've got it on lock. And to prove it we'll "take you there," like the Staple Singers used to croon. So c'mon, everybody, let's all get down: hop aboard the *ego trip* Winnebago as we randomly shamble along onto some of our favorite and not-so-favorite sites across this land of ours. Cold little places in our even colder hearts we like to call . . .

RACE LAND U*S*A*

Bigotry! Violence! Xenophobia! Wish You Were Here!

TURN

ALASKA

NOT-SO-FUN FACT: The Alaska Native Claims Settlement Act of 1971 removed the sovereign status of Indian nations in Alaska. As a result, approximately forty-four million acres of oil and timber-rich territories previously belonging to Native Americans were turned into U.S. assets. (Presto!)

1 4th Ave. Between C & D Sts.
⬧ Anchorage

When in downtown Anchorage, why not cruise along this particular block and retrace the path of the three white teens who went on a paintball gun drive-by spree in January 2001. Their targets were Eskimos, some of them apparently drunk. The ignorant trio proclaimed, "We're going to nail some Eskimos—also known as 'muktuks,'" as they captured the whole nasty episode on video. Schmuck-tucks.

2 Chinaman Lagoon ⬧ Pavlof Bay

This golden pond's name is like water torture.

3 Negrohead Mountain ⬧ Yukon-Koyukuk
Blackhead summit.

ARIZONA

NOT-SO-FUN FACT: Despite being observed in other states since 1986, Arizona did not approve the Martin Luther King Jr. holiday until 1992, after successful protest and boycott campaigns by a coalition of angry citizens. Hey AZ, better late than nigga.

4 Chevron Gas Station
⬧ 7956 E. University Dr., Mesa

Where Sikh-practicing East Indian immigrant Balbir Singh Sodhi was murdered by reactionary patriot Frank Silva Roque, who mistook Sodhi for an Islamic Arab shortly after 9/11.

5 Squaw Tits ⬧ Maricopa

Epithet-christened summit whose name is sure to make Native American ladies see red.

CALIFORNIA

NOT-SO-FUN FACT: California's conservative stronghold is in Orange County. How can you tell? The *Orange County Register* reports that in the early '90s the Newport Beach police was fond of using the radio code "NIN" ("Nigger In Newport") whenever officers spotted

certain types of individuals in the area (and they weren't talking about Puerto Ricans).

6 11700 Block of Foothill Blvd.
⬧ Lakeview Terrace

Location where Rodney King was beaten by police after he was stopped for speeding.

7 Broxton Ave. ⬧ Westwood Village

Once-popular upscale collegiate 'hood where Asian advertising art director Karen Toshima was killed in January 1988, caught in gun crossfire from Black gangbangers wreaking havoc outside their South Central 'hood. The incident led to a rise in racial paranoia that infected the City of Angels well into the next decade.

8 "Caution: Mexicans Crossing" Sign
⬧ Hwy. 5, San Diego

"Deer Crossing" signs aren't uncommon in select parts of California. But in Southern California, the "Crossing" signage gets *muy* ethnic. So don't be surprised if while cruising the southern part of the state you notice the international symbol for "Warning: Undocumented Immigrants Attempting to Cross Highway on Foot." *Familia*, hotstepping hurts.

9 Chico

For a town whose name means "little boy" in Spanish, Chico (not to be confused with Chino) sure has an Asian fixation. The locals will fill you in about the legend of the underground network of Chinese opium dens that lie beneath the downtown district, or the curious, not-so-great walls of lava rocks in neighboring fields that were allegedly placed there by Chinese laborers in the nineteenth century.

10 Davis High School
⬧ 315 W. 14th St., Davis

Thong Hy Huynh was stabbed to death on these grounds by two white students in 1984 after he and three other Vietnamese students were taunted with racial slurs for several weeks.

11 Empire Liquor Market Deli
⬧ 9127 S. Figueroa St., Los Angeles

Convenience store in which fifteen-year-old Black patron Latasha Harlins was shot and killed by forty-nine-year-old female Korean shopkeeper Soon Ja Du after Harlins attempted to shoplift a bottle of juice and scuffled with Du.

12 International Market
⬧ 1381 Las Tunas Dr., San Gabriel

Grocery store where within a week of 9/11, Egyptian shop-owner Adel Karas was shot and killed, apparently mistaken for a terrorist.

13 Japanese Tea Garden
⬧ Golden Gate Park, San Francisco

Curiously, this is the birthplace of the *Chinese* fortune cookie. Confucius say, "Confusion."

14 Lake Merritt Apartments
⬧ 1200 Lakeshore Ave., Oakland

Former penthouse home of Black Panther leader and light-skinded heartthrob, Huey P. Newton. Ironically, in the early '90s the building's owner (a Japanese investment company) was accused of forcing out elderly and Black tenants in its attempt to convert the units to condos.

15 Long Beach Arena
⬧ E. Ocean Blvd., Long Beach

Site of the lowpoint of the 1986 Run-D.M.C. "Raising Hell" Tour, where Black and Mexican gang members did just that, squaring off with tragic, bloody results. Rap don't live here anymore.

16 Manzanar Relocation Center
⬧ Manzanar

Japanese internment camp that played host to December 1942 riots in which two internees were killed and ten injured by gunfire from military police.

17 Pomona Fwy. ⬧ El Monte

(Slightly lighter) shades of Rodney King: Two white Riverside County sheriff deputies were videotaped here opening a can of whoop-ass on two fleeing undocumented Mexican immigrants, a man and a woman, in April 1996. A few days later, the beaten pair filed a $70 million lawsuit against the county and were offered a place to crash by mud-people-lover Marlon Brando.

18 San Francisco International Airport
⬧ San Francisco

Loudmouth TV talk show host Morton Downey Jr.'s career crash-landed when he claimed to have been ambushed here by racist skinheads in a bathroom, surfacing with his dome half-shaved and branded with a swastika. Authorities, however, found no evidence whatsoever to substantiate his story. Because he was in town on a promotional tour, it's believed it was all a bad stunt. R.I.P., Mort.

19 Santa Teresa High School
⬧ 6150 Snell Ave., San Jose

Where a white student became upset with his Black teacher when the teacher suspended his white friend. In response, the student spray painted the teacher's name with the words "Thanks nigga" beside it. Though charged with committing a hate crime, the student was found innocent by a judge, who in a March

2002 ruling, decided that the use of the "friendly" spelling of the n-word, "N-I-G-G-A" as opposed to "N-I-G-G-E-R," precluded his act from being considered racist. Thanks for nothin', cracka.

20 Vox Soundlab Studios
⬧ 15454 Cabrito Rd., Van Nuys

Now-defunct recording facility where James Brown recorded 1968's seminal soul-power anthem, "Say It Loud, I'm Black and I'm Proud," featuring a chorus sung not by Blacks, but by young Asian and white kids!

COLORADO

NOT-SO-FUN FACT: Colorado is the home state to America's first family of ultra-right conservatism—the Coors klan, whose support of apartheid South Africa back in the '80s and discriminatory hiring practices against Blacks and Latinos are well documented. We wouldn't even be surprised if they cut off raging keggers before midnight. Fuckers.

21 7-Eleven ⬧ 1645 E. 17th Ave., Aurora

Where on Thanksgiving morning 1997, twenty-six-year-old Black female Shomie Francis claimed that a group of six whites called her "nigger" and beat her after she asked them if they were skinheads. The incident occurred when Denver area racial tension was high; a West African man had been shot and killed by a white supremacist while standing at a bus stop just a few weeks earlier. However, after witnesses stated that Francis instigated the confrontation and a store surveillance video provided no evidence of criminal conduct, no charges were filed.

22 8,960 Acres of Land Rumored
to Have Been Owned by Hitler
⬧ Four Miles from Kit Carson

After drinking all that racist Adolf Coors beer, why not relieve yourself on random parcels of land that Adolf Hitler may or may not have inherited from German relatives.

23 Home of Alan Berg
⬧ 1400 Block of Adams St., Denver

Location where Jewish KOA radio talk show host Berg was gunned down on his driveway in June 1984 by five members of Bruder Schweigen ("the Silent Brotherhood"), a neo-Nazi group.

HAWAII

NOT-SO-FUN FACT: Way back in 1893, Hawaii's Queen Liliuokalani attempted to impose a new constitution claiming more authority for native Hawaiians (a/k/a "Pacific Islanders"). But the

white leaders who occupied the government office in Honolulu overthrew the monarchy. Damn those *haoles*.

24 Chinaman's Hat ⬧ Tiny Island Off of Kaneohe Bay, Hawaii

Small, conical-shaped island that resembles an Asian *chapeau*.

IDAHO

NOT-SO-FUN FACT: Under the state's strict felony hate crime statute, someone could do jail time for just saying "nigger." (It actually happened to Lonny Rae, who did a seven-day bid for letting loose the lousy language at a 2000 high school football game in Council.)

25 Former HQ of Aryan Nations ⬧ Outside of Hayden Lake

This twenty-acre plot was the stomping ground of Richard Butler's white supremacist/anti-Semitic Aryan Nations compound. Forced out after much legal wrangling, the former "church" (of the poison mind) was scheduled to become a human rights museum.

26 Chink's Peak ⬧ Near Pocatello, Bannock County

Don't be afraid to ask the locals, "How's your mama?" That was the greeting reputedly used by the old Chinese man who once lived near this peak later named in his "honor." In later years the CP was re-christened the more PC *Chinese* Peak. (Really though, how is your ma?)

27 Indian "Massacre" Memorial ⬧ Across the Street from the Post Office, Almo

This historical marker commemorates the 1861 massacre in which 295 west-bound white settlers were killed by Indians. Only problem is, as James W. Loewen's *Lies Across America* (Touchstone, 1999) details, it was all made up. (Hey, it's the thought that counts.)

MONTANA

NOT-SO-FUN FACT: The Anti-Indian Movement, which has been labeled "inherently racist" by civil rights groups and opposes tribal government positions on all issues, is alive and well in Montana thanks to organizations such as the Flathead Reservation-based All Citizens Equal (ACE).

28 Billings

City that saw a surge in bias-related activity in 1993: KKK fliers were distributed, a Jewish cemetery was vandalized, Black church members were harassed by skinheads, Native American homes were spray-painted with epithets, and a brick was tossed through the window of a young boy's home in which a Chanukah *menorah* was displayed. In response, the community joined together to fight the hate with marches and candlelight vigils, painters union members pitched in to paint over racist graffiti, the local newspaper printed up full page menorahs that were displayed in 10,000 homes and businesses as a symbol of unity, and the anti-racism catchphrase "Not In Our Town" was spawned. What more can we say? Top Billings!

29 I-90 Rest Stop ⬧ Near Gold Creek

David Solomon, a Black man, was shot and killed here in July 1999 in front of his wife and child by Douglas Zander, a white man with whom he'd had no previous contact. Upon his arrest Zander reputedly told police his girlfriend had just left him for a Black man. Solomon had been moving his family from Spokane, Washington to their new home in Arizona when they stopped to take a rest.

30 Marias Massacre ⬧ Marias River Bluffs Near Shelby

It was here in January 1870 that six companies of U.S. troops under the command of Major Eugene Baker attacked a camp of 200 defenseless Piegan Indian women, children, and elderly people while their warriors were away on a hunt. Even government officials at the time told the *Chicago Tribune* that it was "the most disgraceful butchery in the annals of our dealings with the Indian."

NEVADA

NOT-SO-FUN FACT: In 1962, an Indian Lands Claims Commission decision acknowledged that—surprise!—the U.S. government illegally took Western Shoshone Indian land (which incidentally once covered about two-thirds of the state and is today coveted for its gold mines). However, as of April 2002, $100 million in compensation had yet to be paid to the tribe while it contested the deal's fairness. In the meantime, the government tests atomic bombs on remaining Western Shoshone territories and schemes to build a nuclear waste dump on the tribe's sacred site of Yucca Mountain. Yuck.

31 KCEP ⬧ 330 W. Washington Ave., Las Vegas

Radio station that broadcast a July

2000 interview with Clark County School Superintendent Carlos Garcia by Black student interns. "Niggers come in all colors," Garcia said. "To me, a nigger is someone who doesn't respect themselves or others." The comments provoked calls for Garcia's resignation. But after offering an emotional apology the super-sorry Super kept his gig.

32 Area Three Miles West of U.S. Hwy. 95 ⬧ Near Rome Blvd., Las Vegas Valley

Daniel Shersty and Lin Newborn of the Las Vegas Unity Skins, an anti-racist skinhead group, were found shot to death here in July 1998. Shersty, who was white, and Newborn, who was Black, were lured to the desert location by two women with whom they'd made a date. When the friends arrived with the women at the secluded meeting point, they were ambushed—shot by John Butler of the Independent Nazi Skinhead group.

33 Moulin Rouge ⬧ 900 W. Bonanza Rd., Las Vegas

Shithole apartments now occupy the location of the Moulin Rouge, Sin City's first integrated hotel / casino, which in May 1955 opened its doors to Black entertainers who previously couldn't even stay in the hotels in which they performed. Despite considerable initial success, it closed within five months of its opening—some say due to collusive activity by white-owned hotel / casinos. Craps.

NEW MEXICO

NOT-SO-FUN FACT: In 1906, the federal government seized 50,000 acres of wilderness land sacred to the Taos Pueblo Indians in the Blue Lake region of the New Mexico mountains for a national park.

34 Los Alamos National Laboratory ⬧ Los Alamos

Where falsely accused U.S. "traitor," Taiwanese immigrant scientist Wen Ho Lee clocked in before getting tossed in the clink.

35 Rio Arriba County Courthouse ⬧ Tierra Amarilla

In June 1967, forty Chicano land grant activists led by Reies Tijerina seized this courthouse in an armed raid, declaring that 2,500 square miles of state land was the rightful property of their organization, Alianza Federal de Mercedes, by order of the 1848 Treaty of Guadalupe Hildago. The National Guard was brought in and Tijerina, despite eluding authorities for a few days, was eventually captured. *Adios, revolución. Hola*, slammer.

36 Vaughn High School ⬧ E. Hwy. 60, Vaughn

In February 1997, longtime teachers Nadine and Patsy Cordova were suspended for educating their students about Cesar Chavez's farmworkers movement, and using the textbook *500 Years of Chicano History*. The school superintendent, Arthur Martinez, deemed the non-Eurocentric curriculum racially intolerant and militant. By July, the Cordovas were fired for insubordination.

OREGON

NOT-SO-FUN FACT: In 1862, Oregon adopted a law that required all Blacks, Chinese, Hawaiians(!), and mixed-race folks to pay an annual tax of five dollars. If they couldn't come up with the money, the state could force them to work maintaining state roads for fifty cents a day to pay it off. Fuck road rules.

37 "Darkey Creek" ⬧ Alsea River Basin

Renamed "Southworth Creek" in June 2002 in honor of Louis A. Southworth, a slave who bought his freedom and went on to become a respected homesteader in the area.

38 Dead Indian Rd. ⬧ Ashland

Correction: the *formerly* named Dead Indian Road—which memorialized an incident that resulted in the death of a Native American—has been renamed "Dead Indian *Memorial* Road" in honor of . . . uh, Chief Whatshizname.

39 Phi Delta Theta Fraternity at Oregon State University ⬧ 120 N.W. 13th St., Corvallis

Alma Mater to not one, but *two* hate crimes against Black student Frederick Harris. The first occurred in 1996 when then-freshman Harris was given a "golden shower" by students on an unspecified dorm balcony as he walked by. Three years later, Harris was called the dreaded n-word and subjected to lit firecrackers as he walked by the Phi Delta Theta house. We really hope he finally transferred his Black ass.

40 Deep Creek Tributary ⬧ Snake River

Site of the "Snake River Massacre," where in May 1887, thirty-one Chinese gold miners were robbed, tortured, and killed by a band of seven snow-white bandits.

UTAH

NOT-SO-FUN FACT: Utah is the home state of Senator Bob Bennett, who in 2000 made the following prediction regarding George W. Bush's bid for the Republican presidential nomination:

"Unless George W. steps in front of a bus or . . . some Black woman comes forward with an illegitimate child that he fathered within the last eighteen months . . . George W. will be the nominee." Good call, Bob.

41 Blanding

Town that features a government-built uranium mill on the White Mesa Ute Indian tribe's ancestral burial ground—just one example of what environmental activists estimate is 2 million tons of radioactive uranium contaminating Indian lands nationwide.

42 Topaz Relocation Center ♦ Topaz

The Japanese-Americans from temperate northern California who composed much of the population at this camp couldn't have been too keen on Topaz's climate. The temperatures here ranged from a balmy 106 degrees in the summer to a brisk (but never nippy) thirty degrees below zero in the winter.

WASHINGTON

NOT-SO-FUN FACT: In the '90s, African-Americans occupied twenty-two percent of the state's prison cells even though they comprised only 3.1 percent of the state population. That's what we call affirmative action, Jackson.

43 Boeing ♦ Seattle

The aerospace company has had several racial run-ins. In 1998, forty-three Black workers filed a suit claiming that they were subjected to racial hostility and bias in promotions, and Boeing forked over $15 million to settle. In 1999, Boeing shelled out $4.5 million to minority and female employees when it was discovered that there were gaps in the pay they received compared to white male workers doing the same jobs. And in late 1999, Asians of all flavors (including Vietnamese, East Indians, Filipinos, and Singaporeans) accused Boeing of denying them promotions, laying them off quicker than other ethnicities and giving them smaller raises because of the stereotype that Asians are passive noncomplainers. *Boing*!!!

44 23rd Ave. and E. Union St. ♦ Seattle

This site, where police killed Black motorist Aaron Roberts, was chosen for Central Area's July 2001 "Unity on Union" Festival. Black activist Omari Tahir-Garrett, incensed by what he deemed a disrespectful choice of location for the festivities, smacked Mayor Paul Schell in the grill with a megaphone. Upon his arrest, Tahir-Garrett requested to be sent to Africa (with reparations and a window seat).

45 KXLY ♦ 500 W. Boone, Spokane

When in lovely Spokane be sure to visit radio station KXLY, where former LAPD detective Mark "der" Fuhrman hosts his weekly talk show, "All About Crime."

WYOMING

NOT-SO-FUN FACT: In 2001, Wyoming still had "Alien Land Laws" on its books that were originally intended to prevent **Asian immigrants from owning land.**

46 Heart Mountain Relocation Center ♦ Heart Mountain

Although this camp's head count eventually peaked at over 10,000 Japanese-American internees (making it the third largest community in the whole damn state), Governor Nels Smith initially resisted its construction, saying if the Japanese were brought into Wyoming that they'd be "hanging from every tree."

47 Rock Springs

In 1885, rowdy whites set this town's Chinatown afire—literally. Twenty-eight Chinese miners were killed in the "Rock Springs Massacre," the culmination of anti-Chinese sentiment stemming from the immigrants' role as cheap labor.

48 University of Wyoming / Laramie

In 1969, Black students (fourteen of 'em) on the University of Wyoming football team were kicked off the squad after protesting the Mormon Church's ban on Black priests. One of the "Black Fourteen," Mel Hamilton, went on to become Wyoming's first Black school principal in 1996. A few years later, he was fired. Joe Clark wouldn't have taken that shit.

GREETINGS FROM LAS VEGAS, NEVADA

LONG BEACH ARENA
LONG BEACH, CALIFORNIA

ILLINOIS

NOT-SO-FUN FACT: Illinois was the native state of our sixteenth president, Abraham Lincoln, the "Great Emancipator." Unfortunately, Lincoln acted more like a great racist when he supported Illinois' "Black Law," which was passed in 1853. It called to "effectually prohibit free persons of color from immigrating to and settling in [the] state." Shame, shame, not-so-honest Abe.

1 Belleville

Where a June 1998 copycat crime of Texas' James Byrd Jr. murder took place in which three whites dragged a Black teenager alongside a sports utility vehicle.

2 Former HQ of the Illinois Chapter of the Black Panther Party
◊ 2337 W. Monroe St., Chicago

On December 4, 1969, charismatic, influential Panther leader Fred Hampton—the man who brokered peace between the city's rival, multiracial street gangs—and fellow party member Mark Clark were killed here

six Orthodox Jews walking home from Sabbath services in the Rogers Park section of Chicago. In Northbrook, an Asian-American couple in a car were shot at but not hurt as they attempted to pass Smith's Taurus. Former Northwestern University basketball coach Ricky Byrdsong, an African-American, was killed by Smith while walking with his kids by his home in Skokie. Smith wounded Blacks in separate drivebys in Springfield, then wounded a Black minister in Decatur and an Asian University of Illinois student in Urbana. Finally, after being chased by police, Smith shot and killed himself while driving on Interstate 57 in Salem.

5 Skokie Village Hall
◊ 5127 Oakton St., Skokie

Site of the National Socialist (a/k/a Nazi) Party of America's attempted rally in 1978. The Nazis chose Skokie because the Chicago suburb's population was 60 percent Jewish and included Holocaust survivors. After several court injunctions filed by the town attempting to stop the march,

THE Midwest

by police in a pre-dawn raid many Panther sympathizers have equated with an execution. Years later during a civil suit filed by Hampton's and Clark's families against the city, it was revealed that Hampton's personal bodyguard, William O'Neal, was an FBI informant who provided a detailed floor plan of the apartment used in the raid.

3 Old Comiskey Park
◊ 35th St. and Shields, Chicago

Site of the July 12, 1979 Disco Demolition Night in which local rock (a/k/a white) radio DJ Steve Dahl urged fans to bring unwanted "disco" (a/k/a R&B, a/k/a "Black") albums for a mass burning in between games of a White Sox-Detroit Tigers doubleheader. Fans hurled records through the stands during the game and a not-so-quiet riot ensued in which the field was trashed, forcing the Sox to forfeit the second game.

4 Rogers Park, Chicago; Northbrook; Skokie; Springfield; Decatur; Urbana; Salem

Ill state locales of twenty-one-year-old white supremacist Benjamin Nathaniel Smith's July 4th weekend, 1999, shooting spree. Smith wounded

an Appeals Court ruling protected the Nazis' right to assemble under the First Amendment. The story became a 1981 made-for-TV movie, *Skokie*, starring Danny Kaye. (But no truth to rumors of a more lighthearted sequel co-starring Burt Reynolds and Sally Field, *Skokie and the Bandit*.)

INDIANA

NOT-SO-FUN FACT: Indiana is the home state of Michael Jackson (remember when he did "Going Back to Indiana" with Tito and them?), who used to be Black, but now defies any adequate racial description.

6 Former Gary Public Schools Memorial Auditorium
◊ 700-734 Massachusetts St., Gary

In September 1945, 500 white students walked out of classes at Froebel High School in protest of the integration of Blacks. The strike situation escalated to the point where a local diversity group eventually recruited Frank Sinatra to give a concert here at Memorial Auditorium in the name of tolerance. No word whether "That Old Black Magic" made the set list. The site is now vacant.

7 Negro Creek ◊ Elkinsville

Never been here, but judging from its name we advise that you don't get caught here without a paddle. Or maybe a gun.

8 Korean United Methodist Church ◊ 1924 E. 3rd St., Bloomington

Site of white supremacist Benjamin Nathaniel Smith's fatal July 4, 1999 shooting

of Korean Indiana University doctoral student Won-Joon Yoon.

9 Thomas Hart Benton Mural
◊ Woodburn Hall, Campus of Indiana University, Bloomington

IU might not have Bobby Knight to push around anymore, but it does have the controversial Benton mural. Created in 1933, it depicts both positive and negative images from

argued that Catt later became a pussycat on such issues and condemned racism after women had won the right to vote.

11 Des Moines

Host city to minor league ball club the Iowa Cubs' Fan Fest luncheon, at which former manager Whitey Herzog complained that major league baseball practiced reverse discrimination regarding the filling of management jobs. This despite the fact that at the time of Herzog's comments in January 2002, only six out of twenty-nine managerial jobs were filled by minorities—far short of a full count.

12 Marshalltown

Jean Seberg, the troubled blonde star of Otto Preminger's *Saint Joan* (1957) and Jean-Luc Godard's *Breathless* (1960), was born here in 1938. A vocal supporter of the Black Panther Party, Seberg was subjected to false, FBI-propagated rumors that she'd become impregnated by one of the Panthers. The strain of the FBI campaign to ruin her, along with a pregnancy that ended in miscarriage, triggered several nervous breakdowns before she eventually committed suicide in France in 1979.

KANSAS

NOT-SO-FUN FACT: The 1862 Homestead Act opened up Native American land in "Western" territories like Kansas to homesteaders, providing title deeds for 160-acre plots (at just one dollar and twenty-five cents per acre—whatta bargain) to those willing to occupy the land for at least five years. (Sorry, mud folks, only white people needed apply.)

13 Brown vs. Board of Education National Historical Site ♦ Topeka

Site of Monroe Elementary School and surrounding grounds commemorating the landmark 1954 Supreme Court school de-segregation decision.

14 Fort Scott

Small town that provided the setting for Gordon Park's 1969 semi-autobiographical coming-of-age-and-overcoming-racism cinematic effort *The Learning Tree.*

15 Nicodemus National Historical Site ♦ Nicodemus, Graham County

Area that preserves the only remaining all-Black pioneer town founded during the Reconstruction Era. Ya, mon! Feelin' irie in-a-Kansas, mon!

Indiana's history, including robed KKK members burning a cross. Black students have objected to the display of the Klan images over the years. However, in March 2002 school chancellor Sharon Brehm announced that the mural would stay because removing it would only serve to "hide the shameful aspects of Indiana's past."

IOWA

NOT-SO-FUN FACT: According to civil rights watch dog groups, Iowa is the state most frequently targeted by anti-immigration TV advertising due to its older, largely white population and the fact that it is the host to first-in-nation presidential caucuses every four years. The commercials usually portray Hispanics as criminals who take jobs away from whites and ruin cities. Stick to HBO.

10 Carrie Chapman Catt Hall at Iowa State University ♦ Ames

Former Botany Hall was re-named for the women's rights pioneer in 1995. However, many students protested the change, citing Catt's racist ideology. She reputedly once remarked that "white supremacy will be strengthened, not weakened, by woman suffrage." Those in favor of the re-naming

MICHIGAN

NOT-SO-FUN FACT: Michigan is the birthplace of the American auto industry, whose brilliant guiding figure, Henry Ford, also happened to be a racist and Nazi sympathizer who once received the Supreme Order of the German Eagle—the highest award Hitler's Third Reich could bestow upon a non-German. Maybe Volkswagen got a bad rap.

16 Corner of Michigan and Wyoming Aves. ♦ Dearborn

Site of a shortlived (only one day in October 2000) anti-immigration billboard by Project U.S.A. The ad, which was taken down for fear of offending people, featured a wee lad and the words, "Immigration is doubling U.S. population in my lifetime." It would have been a pretty ineffective message anyway, considering the large concentration of Arab immigrants who call the neighborhood home.

17 Farmer Jack's Supermarket ♦ 9023 Joseph Campau St., Hamtramck

Where bagger Karl Petzold—who suffers from Tourette's syndrome—involuntarily

Amazingly, Ebens and Nitz never saw any jail time.

20 Public Hall ♦ 3408 Hastings St., Detroit

Where a young, destitute Elijah Poole (later the Nation of Islam's Elijah Muhammad) came to hear the teachings of W.D. Fard, who was lecturing on his own interpretation of Islam. Inspired by Fard's words, Poole sought him out after the speech to speak to him. The experience gave him new resolve to carry on with his life.

MINNESOTA

NOT-SO-FUN FACT: The state's largest Native American reservation (at 800,000 acres) is named White Earth. Who said dirt don't hurt?

21 Lindbergh Terminal ♦ Minneapolis-St. Paul International Airport

Next time you're scurrying to your connecting flight here, just be glad you're not FWA (Flying While Arab). On September 21, 2001, three Arab-American men from Utah were kicked

from nineteen geographical places because it was offensive to Native Americans. However, the 139 residents of tiny Squaw Lake have basically ignored all that shit. Bitches.

24 St. Cloud State University ♦ St. Cloud

SCSU is no cool school. Charges of anti-Semitism by three professors led to the filing of an October 2001 lawsuit against the university for discriminatory practices. Complaints from Black students that they were subject to racial epithets and police harassment resulted in a March 2002 open letter from three Black professors to high school guidance counselors, warning that the school could be "hazardous to Blacks" thinking of enrolling.

25 St. Paul

With his appearance on *The Late Show with David Letterman* in February 1999, pro wrestler turned Minnesota governor Jesse Ventura joked that the city of St. Paul's winding streets were so confusing they must have been designed by drunken Irishmen. After receiving complaints about his comments, Ventura explained that he was only trying to be funny on a funny show and that he was sorry Minnesotans had apparently lost their sense of humor. He pledged to play it straight on future late night appearances. (And no, "play it straight" was not a slur against gays and lesbians.)

NEBRASKA

NOT-SO-FUN FACT: The Nebraska Department of Correctional Services Statistics / Data Inmate Population Report states that during the '90s Mexicans represented about 2.3% of the state's population, but about 10.3% of its prison inmate population.

26 2867 Ohio St. ♦ Omaha

Where in August 1970 police officer Larry Minard was killed when a suitcase rigged with explosives detonated. Police arrested fifteen-year-old Black youth Duane Peak, who after several days of questioning delivered a deposition stating that his colleagues in the Black Panther Party-affiliated National Committee to Combat Fascism, David Rice and Edward Poindexter, were involved in the explosion. Despite the fact that they were convicted based almost solely on Peak's testimony and that many believe that the case was COINTELPRO-tampered, Rice (now known as Mondo we Langa) and Poindexter remain imprisoned today.

27 3448 Pinkney St. ♦ Omaha

On May 19, 1925, Malcolm Little (later known to the world as Malcolm

X) was born in a now-demolished house at this locale.

28 Lincoln

The state's capitol is also the hometown of neo-Nazi Gerhard Lauck (a/k/a the "Farmbelt Fuehrer"), who attempted to use web addresses with names similar to those of German governmental institutions to lure unsuspecting Internet users to his anti-Semitic sites. In January 2002, the UN's World Intellectual Property Organization ruled that Lauck was shit outta luck and had no right to use the names.

NORTH DAKOTA

NOT-SO-FUN FACT: According to the Southern Poverty Law Center's Intelligence Report, as of 2001 there was just one hate group, the National Skinhead Front, in North Dakota. (But that's still one too many, aight?)

29 Fargo

Citing low rates of both crime and cases of AIDS infections, and the pale complexion of its population, the white supremacists at David Duke's official website are convinced that Fargo is paradise. (Hey, *ego trip* saw *Fargo*. Great movie, but that shit sure as hell ain't paradise.)

30 Ralph Englestad Hockey Arena at University of North Dakota ♦ Grand Forks

Controversy engulfed the October 2001 opening of this $100 million facility when the local Standing Rock Sioux Tribe and Native American governments statewide protested the "Fighting Sioux" Indian logos emblazoned throughout it (most prominently at center ice) and the statue of Sitting Bull near the entrance as offensive. Native students had attempted to stop the university from using the "Fighting Sioux" nickname, but arena benefactor Englestad, an accused Nazi sympathizer with a Hitler fixation, threatened to pull his funding for the project unless the name stayed. Guess who won?

OHIO

NOT-SO-FUN FACT: In 2001, the Buckeye State recorded 315 hate crime incidents within its borders, and was home to seven separate branches of the KKK and four separate branches of the neo-Nazi World Church of the Creator.

31 Ohio State University ♦ Columbus

Great Black author Chester Himes attended school here in 1929 when Blacks were not allowed to live in school dormitories, use the student union, or eat in local restaurants.

THE *Midwest*

---

uttered racial slurs, offending Blacks. Petzold was fired by the chain in 1996, due to fear of customer legal action.

18 Jim Crow Museum of Racist Memorabilia at Ferris State University ♦ Big Rapids

Courtesy of sociology professor David Pilgrim, the museum is home to over 4,000 racist memorabilia items. Get yo' race on!

19 Fancy Pants Tavern ♦ 13843 Woodward Ave., Highland Park

Now abandoned, this former strip club was where twenty-seven-year-old Chinese-American Vincent Chin first encountered disgruntled white Detroit autoworkers Ronald Ebens and Michael Nitz while attempting to enjoy his bachelor party in June 1982. Fueled by xenophobic rage during the height of the "Japanese automobile import" invasion, Ebens and Nitz—who'd just been laid off from his auto plant job—mistook Chin for Japanese, and the three men became embroiled in an altercation. The feuding resumed twenty minutes later at a fast-food restaurant where Ebens bashed in Chin's skull with a baseball bat, leading to injuries which would prove fatal a few days later.

off of Northwest flight 673 heading to Salt Lake City when other passengers refused to fly if they remained on board. After being interrogated, the Arab-American men were eventually re-booked on another flight home—on Delta.

22 Photo Dock 1 Hour Photo ♦ 822 Washington Ave. S.E., Stadium Village

Film developing shop where in January 2000 college co-ed Melissa Sweeney claimed she received an intentionally placed racist photo in her returned work. Sweeney, who is white, had dropped off film for development of her and her Black boyfriend. Somehow an extra flick of a white supremacist standing at a podium draped in Confederate / Klan / swastika flags got in the mix. (Whoops!) Sweeney filed an official complaint with the Minneapolis Department of Civil Rights. Photo Dock's owners (one of whom is Vietnamese) claimed that they were "practically a minority-owned business" and that the extra photo's appearance was purely an accident.

23 Squaw Lake ♦ Itasca County

In 1995, the Minnesota state legislature eliminated the word "squaw"

Himes later cited his brief collegiate stint as his first profound experience of racial prejudice, and wrote, "If one lives in a country where racism is held valid and practiced in all ways of life, eventually, no matter whether one is a racist or a victim, one comes to feel the absurdity of life." Write on.

32 **Over-the-Rhine ▶ Cincinnati**

Economically depressed (read: Black) 'hood where the deadly shooting of unarmed teenager Timothy Thomas by a policeman led to three days of civil unrest in April 2001. Fifteen Black men had been shot and killed by police since 1995.

33 **Southern Ohio Correction Facility ▶ Lucasville**

Sure, the eleven-day 1993 Easter Sunday riot that took place here, in which nine inmates and a corrections officer were killed amidst a hostage takeover, made *Oz* look like *The Osbournes*. At least there was a silver lining of racial unity to this jailhouse ruckus: members of the Aryan Brotherhood and Black Gangster Disciples joined with Muslim inmates to protest their common oppressor, the prison authority. And when police entered the occupied cell block, they found slogans on the walls like, "Black and whites together" and "Convict unity."

SOUTH DAKOTA

NOT-SO-FUN FACT: In March 2000 the South Dakota Advisory Committee to the U.S. Commission on Civil Rights concluded that the mistreatment of Indians by whites had changed little since the 1970s. Furthermore, the racial tension within the state was determined to be worse than in prototypical prejudicial hotbed cities New York and Los Angeles.

34 **Martin**

City in which 1,200 Lakota Indians converged in February 2002 to protest longtime practices of harassment, racial targeting, and racial profiling of Native American residents by the local police.

35 **Wounded Knee ▶ Pine Ridge Reservation**

Site of the last major battle between U.S. Cavalry troops and Indian tribes, the December 1890 massacre in which 300 Sioux were killed. In February 1973 the area was re-occupied by AIM (American Indian Movement) to bring attention to Native American grievances, resulting in a gunfight with the FBI in which two agents were killed.

WISCONSIN

NOT-SO-FUN FACT: Treaties that gave American Indian tribes the right to hunt, fish, and gather in the territories that were taken from them in Wisconsin were violated for more than 100 years. (That's a long time, paleface.) Aggressive (sometimes violent) protests reached their apex in the '70s and '80s when local white fishermen opposed the Chippewa tribes spearing fish in lake fronts. Federal courts eventually decided that the Indian treaties were legitimate and should be enforced.

36 **Former Oxford Apartments ▶ 924 N. 25th St., Milwaukee**

It's now a weed-filled vacant lot. But here once stood the apartment building to which crazy Caucasoid cannibal Jeffrey Dahmer lured his Black and Asian victims for some morbid hanky-panky and, ultimately, dinner.

37 **Denny's ▶ 5501 Washington Ave., Racine**

Black pancake chef Martin Ellis alleged that on six different occasions someone anonymously posted newspaper clippings of Black sports figures like O.J. Simpson, Mike Tyson, and Michael Jordan on the staff bulletin board, and wrote his name next to the photos. When Ellis complained to the general manager that he was being racially ridiculed, nothing was supposedly ever done to rectify the problem. (Truthfully, *ego trip* prefers IHOP—it's *international*, you know.)

OVER-THE-RHINE
CINCINNATI, OHIO

ALABAMA

NOT-SO-FUN FACT: The state didn't repeal its ban on mixed marriages until November 2000. (Good thing Charles Barkley wed his white wife, Maureen, well after leaving sweet home Alabammy.)

1 **16th St. Baptist Church Adjacent to the National Civil Rights Institute**
♦ **16th St. and 6th Ave., Birmingham**
Site of the infamous Sunday morning bomb blast that killed four young Black girls and wounded twenty congregation members in 1963.

2 **Birmingham Municipal Auditorium (Now Known as Boutwell Auditorium)**
♦ **1930 8th Ave. N., Birmingham**
Famed singer / pianist Nat King Cole was no merry old soul when he played here for an all-white audience in 1956. Maybe it was because before he could complete the second song of the concert, he was knocked off his stool and attacked by white segregationists enraged by the sight of Cole and his racially-mixed crew on stage.

3 **Delta Sigma Phi Fraternity House at Auburn University**
♦ **891 Lem Morrison Dr., Auburn**
Animal house where members of the all-white Delta Sigma Phi Fraternity (and also members of Beta Theta Pi) wore KKK costumes and dressed as Blackfaced lynching victims at their October 2001 Halloween parties. The frat was subsequently suspended. Yo, frats: step off and "wake up" like *School Daze*, aight?

4 **Montgomery St. ♦ Montgomery**
Ah ha, what's that fuss? Everybody move to the *front* of the bus traveling down Montgomery Street (preferably while rockin' to OutKast's "Rosa Parks"). It's the public transportation route made famous by said Sista Rosa, the grande dame of civil rights, in 1955.

5 **Tuskegee**
Hometown to the infamous Tuskegee Experiments, in which 400 African-American men that officials from the U.S. Public Health Service knew were infected with syphilis were left untreated over a forty-year period so that the effects of the disease on Blacks could be observed.

ARKANSAS

NOT-SO-FUN FACT: In the mid-'90s, the home state of America's "first Black President," William Jefferson Clinton, was also home to the largest and most active faction of the KKK, the Knights of the Ku Klux Klan, in Harrison.

6 **Jerome Relocation Center ♦ Denson**
This Japanese-American internment camp, one of two in Arkansas, was the last to open (in October 1942), first to close (in June 1944), and housed a peak population of almost 8,500. In 1942, a local civilian shot and injured two internees on work detail in the woods thinking they were attempting to escape the camp.

7 **Mobil Service Station (Now Known as Central High School Museum Visitor Center)**
♦ **14th St. and Park St., Little Rock**
Site of the former gas station where a white mob, fueled on hate, assembled to harass the Black students known as the Little Rock Nine as they prepared to desegregate Central High in 1957.

8 **Negro Bend ♦ Drew County**
They bend, but don't break.

FLORIDA

NOT-SO-FUN FACT: Black voters reported statewide prejudicial activity by police and polling personnel during the controversial 2000 presidential election. And y'all know how that turned out. Bushwacked.

9 **9000 Block of Royal Palm Blvd.**
♦ **Coral Springs**
Where in August 1992, Asian University of Miami pre-med student Luyen Phan Nguyen voiced his objection to a racial slur directed at him while attending a party at an apartment complex. Nguyen was later fatally beaten as his attackers reportedly shouted "chink," "Viet Cong," and "*sayonara*."

10 **Cape Canaveral**
Next time you watch the latest space shuttle head out into the great blue yonder, ponder the far-out folly of far-right radio preacher Rev. Carl McIntire. In 1976 C-Mack proposed a Vietnam-war-era theme park. And to prove he meant business he even populated a simulated village with forty live Vietnamese refugees—years before *Miss Saigon* opened on Broadway.

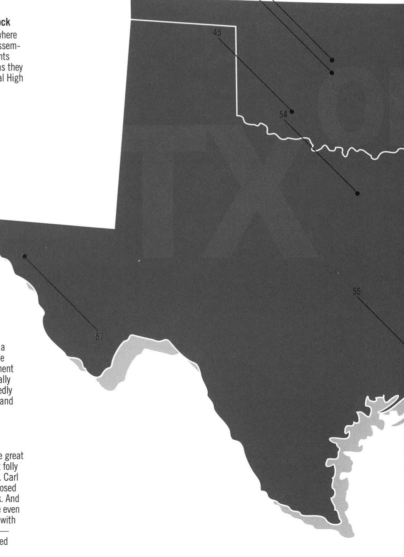

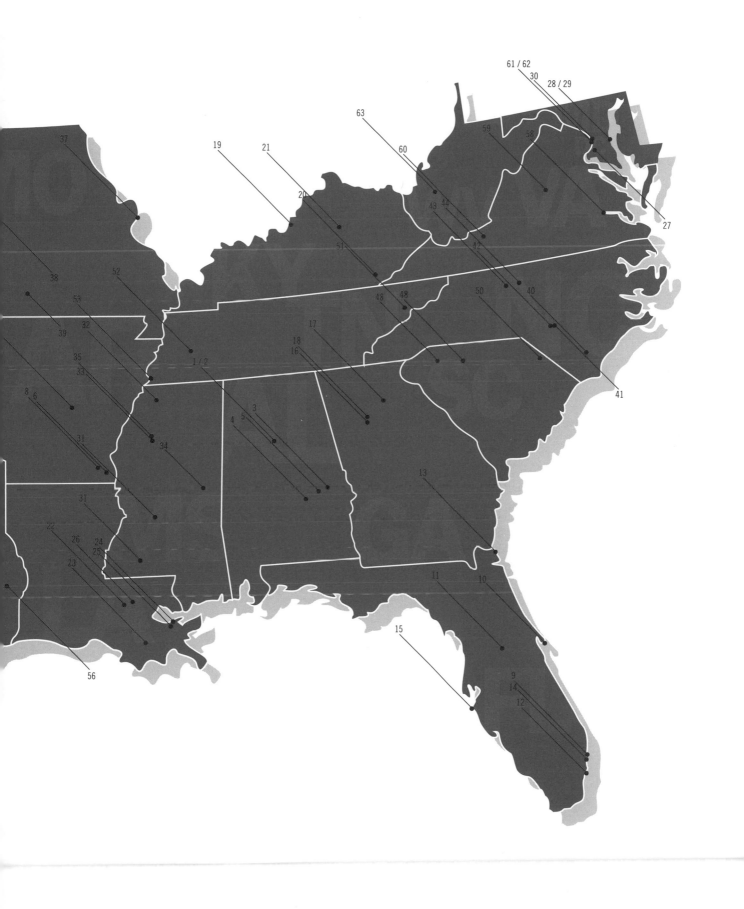

11 Denny's
♦ **State Rd. 50 Near West Oaks Mall, Ocoee**

In May 1998, a group of forty Black sixth graders and their chaperones from Baltimore on their way to Disney World stopped at this cholesterol castle to eat. You'll never guess what happened. They were ignored by the staff and left after an hour without being served. After a complaint was filed with the Office of the Civil Rights Monitor, the president of the Denny's chain apologized to the group.

12 Denny's
♦ **S. Dixie Hwy., Cutler Ridge**

In October 1999, a Black couple from Miami alleged that they were ignored for an hour while white customers were seated and served at this Denny's and filed a lawsuit against the embattled restaurant chain. Same old story, right? Wrong! Denny's responded by presenting a security video that showed the couple in the eatery for just ten minutes before exiting, and the suit was dropped

quicker than you can say, "Moons Over My Hammy."

13 Domino's Pizza
♦ **2020 Sadler Rd., Fernandina Beach, Amelia Island in Jacksonville**

G'head and order a Domino's pizza (no pork, please) while visiting the state's only remaining African-American coastal community. But while you're scarfing down that meal, pour a little liquor out for the brothas and sistas who couldn't get Domino's delivered to their doors by this pie service center in the past, and were forced to meet safety-fearing drivers at a nearby convenience store. (The red lining has since been stopped.)

14 Inverrary Country Club
♦ **3840 Inverrary Blvd., Lauderhill**

Society spot where acclaimed Black actor James Earl Jones was to receive a plaque for serving as featured speaker at Lauderhill's 2002 Martin Luther King Jr. Day ceremonies. However, city officials were shocked when they saw that the plaque they'd intended for Jones was instead inscribed, "Thank you James Earl Ray for keeping the dream alive." James Earl Ray was the man convicted of

assassinating Martin Luther King Jr. in 1968. The plaque's manufacturer called the mistake a "copy error." We call that excuse a "cop-out."

15 Jewfish Key ♦ South of Longboat Pass
"Schvartze, you never come down to visit your aunt. Oh, if your mother knew. Shame on you. *Oy vey.*"

GEORGIA

NOT-SO-FUN FACT: Amnesty International reports that out of the 3,220 Blacks lynched by mobs in the southern states of the U.S.A. between 1880 and 1930, 460 of the lynchings took place in Georgia.

16 Georgia Power Plant
♦ **South of Atlanta**

In February 2002, CBS News reported that four Black subcontractors of Georgia Power charged the utility company with widespread acts of institutional racism. Among the charges: that they'd heard racial slurs and jokes, were forced to duck falling debris, were spat on, and observed hanging nooses across the plant grounds. Two days after voicing their complaints, the subcontractors were unplugged when they were fired for tardiness.

17 Forsyth County

Largely white area in which an interracial group of civil rights supporters attempted to march in honor of Martin Luther King Jr. in January 1987, but were met by Klansmen throwing rocks and bottles and turned back. A week later over 20,000 people resumed the march for racial unity protected by state and local cops. Meanwhile, the original marchers sued the Klan for violating their rights and were awarded almost $1 million in damages, thus giving new meaning to the term *poor* white trash.

18 Martin Luther King Jr. Historic Site and Preservation District ♦ Roughly Bounded by Irwin Ave. and Courtland, Randolph and Chamberlain Sts.

Area comprised of MLK Jr.'s birth home, church, and grave site.

KENTUCKY

NOT-SO-FUN FACT: According to the American Defamation League's website, Kentucky now lays claim to the largest remaining Klan faction of today's decentralized KKK—the Imperial Klan of America (IKA) based in Powderly.

19 Kentucky Derby at Churchill Downs
♦ **700 Central Ave., Louisville**

While you're experiencing the most exciting two minutes in sports, con-

sider the fate of Blacks in world class horse racing. The first Kentucky Derby winner in 1875, Aristides, was trained and ridden by Blacks. Fifteen of the first twenty-eight Derby winners were ridden by Black jockeys, with five trained by Black trainers. Yet by the turn of the century Blacks' roles in racing had gone considerably unstable, and was largely relegated to stable help. Ain't that some horseshit?

20 Negro Knob ♦ Creekville

21 Rupp Arena at University of Kentucky
♦ **Lexington**

B-ball gym named after legendary Wildcats coach Adolph Rupp, the man responsible for bringing big time college hoops to UK. Unfortunately, Rupp was also considered by many to be a big time racist whose failure to recruit Black players resulted in the ultimate comeuppance: a loss by his all-white starting five to an all-Black starting five from Texas Western in the 1966 NCAA Championship game. (He also spearheaded the NCAA's ban on dunking. Figures.)

LOUISIANA

NOT-SO-FUN FACT (For Whites Only): If you live in the Boot State and acknowledge *any* sort of African slave ancestry, you are officially Black, thanks to a "One Drop (of Black Blood Makes You Black)" law that's been left on the books. Guess infamous Louisiana governor Huey Long was right when he reputedly remarked that the "pure white" population of Louisiana could be fed "with a nickel's worth of red beans and a dime's worth of rice."

22 "The Good Darky" Statue at Rural Life Museum
♦ **4600 Essen Ln., Baton Rouge**

A bronze statue of a subservient Black man tipping his hat. The inscription on its base states that it was erected "in Grateful Recognition of the Arduous and Faithful Service of the Good Darkies of Louisiana . . . 1927." (The "Bad Darkies" just got lynched.)

23 Raceland
An actual town. And it's not Candyland.

24 She She's
♦ **9000 Chef Menteur Hwy., New Orleans**

In N'awlins East and feelin' a bit racially randy? Then check out this Black titty-bar owned by Vietnamese proprietors. Both drinks and lap-dances are cheap. And even if you abstain from some rub-a-dub action the girls will grab your attention . . . and your little Uncle Ho.

25 Former Site of Tulane Stadium (Now the Aron Student Residences at Tulane University)
♦ **Stadium Pl., New Orleans**

The 1956 Sugar Bowl between Georgia Tech and Pittsburgh was played at the now-demolished Tulane Stadium. This despite the protests of Georgia's governor, who forbade Tech from playing because Pitt had a Black player on its squad. And that ain't sweet.

26 Walker

Town that played host to a 1976 David Duke-organized KKK rally attended by approximately 2,700 like-minded white supremacists, which made it the largest such gathering since the '60s.

MARYLAND

NOT-SO-FUN FACT: In 1664, Maryland passed the first anti-miscegenation law, prohibiting marriage between Blacks and whites.

27 1200 Block of Proxmire Dr.
♦ **Oxon Hill**

The neighborhood where Black convicted murderer "Willie" Horton invaded the home of white Clifford Barnes, beating him and then raping his fiancée, before being caught by police. Horton was out on an unguarded forty-eight-hour furlough from his correctional facility in Concord, Massachusetts. His thuggish visage was used in 1989 as racial bait by then-presidential candidate George Bush to lure voters away from opposing candidate Michael Dukakis, then governor of Massachusetts.

28 Chink's Point ♦ Annapolis
Ancient proverb: It's not polite to point

29 Denny's
♦ **2095 West St. # 1093, Annapolis**

This is the Denny's restaurant that on April Fool's Day 1993 made six uniformed Black Secret Service officers wait a whole hour for breakfast while their fifteen white co-workers gleefully clogged their arteries with delicious pork fat—on your dime, by the way. (Coincidentally, this major slight occurred the same day that Denny's promised *California*'s federal court to end discrimination towards Black customers. So who're the *real* April fools?)

30 WARW / 5912 Hubbard Dr., Rockville
You learn one thing for certain when you're driving cross country: Radio "personalities" are irritating. And some are really racist, like WARW's former morning rush hour shock jock, Doug "The Greaseman" Tracht. In

February 1999, after playing some song snippets from hip hop artist Lauryn Hill, Tracht for some reason saw fit to comment "no wonder people drag them behind trucks"—a reference to Black Texan James Byrd Jr.'s horrific, then-recent dragging death. Tracht—who reportedly also once remarked on-air about the Martin Luther King Jr. holiday, "Kill four more and we can take a whole week off"—was dismissed from the station, interestingly enough, just one day after the death sentence was handed down to one of Byrd's convicted killers.

MISSISSIPPI

NOT-SO-FUN FACT: In April 2001, Mississippi voters decided by a nearly two-to-one margin to keep its ancient-ass state flag design, which prominently incorporates the Confederate flag—a symbol many activists consider an offense to African-Americans who are descendants of slaves.

31 Alexander Center at Jackson State University ◆ Jackson

Site of May 1970 riots, which erupted in reaction to rumors that Fayette mayor Charles Evers (brother of slain civil rights activist Medgar Evers) and his wife had been killed, and subsequent confrontations between Black students and white motorists driving through campus on their way downtown. Police fired into a crowd of students assembled in front of the Alexander Center dorm, resulting in two deaths.

32 Alpha Tau Omega Fraternity ◆ University of Mississippi

ATO's 2001 Halloween party tore a page from the playbook of Delta Sigma Phi at Auburn. In a photo that wound up on the Internet, a member of the white frat was seen pointing a gun at the head of another member dressed in Blackface, kneeling and picking cotton. The chapter wound up being suspended from campus for a year. Miss-anthropes.

33 Greenwood

Greenwood is not only home to tons o' East Indian-owned motels, it also provided the setting for everyone's favorite Black / East Indian cross-cultural / racial love story, 1992's *Mississippi Masala*.

34 Mount Zion Methodist Church ◆ Longdale

Church that was attacked and burned to the ground by Klan members in June 1964. Civil rights volunteers James Chaney, Andrew Goodman, and Michael Schwerner came to investigate the incident and were murdered shortly thereafter.

35 Tallahatchie River ◆ Near Money

Black fourteen-year-old Emmett Till (a Chicagoan visiting relatives down south for the summer) was killed and his mutilated body dumped here in August 1955 after he reputedly whistled at a white woman. An all-white, all-male jury later acquitted two white men of the crime.

MISSOURI

NOT-SO-FUN FACT: "The Missouri Waltz" (a/k/a "Hush-A-Bye, Ma Baby") was adopted as Missouri's state song in 1949 despite originally featuring such racist lyrics as, "Way down in Missouri where I heard this melody / When I was a pickaninny on ma mammy's knee / The darkies were hummin' / Their banjos were strummin'." (Contrary to rumor, these lyrics were not composed by Lou Reed.)

36 Billingsly Student Center at Missouri Southern State University ◆ Joplin

Site of the school's September 2000 "Anti-Racism Day" events, for which they allotted a whopping four whole hours (8 A.M. to noon; don't oversleep!).

37 KKK's "Adopt-A-Highway" ◆ Half Mile Stretch of Interstate 55, Outside of St. Louis

Stretch of highway that the KKK won the right to sponsor in 1999 as part of the state's clean-up program in which volunteers retrieve litter along the road in return for a sign acknowledging their work. While two signs bigging-up the Klan for giving a hoot and not polluting were erected, they were quickly torn down. Eventually, however, the KKK's sponsorship was revoked for failing to continue to actually pick up the trash. Woodsy the Owl, hold ya head.

38 Municipal Auditorium ◆ Block of 13th, 14th, Wyandotte and Central Sts., Kansas City

Locale of Black super-renaissance man Paul Robeson's February 1942 concert in which he stopped his performance to protest the venue's segregation of Black and white audience members. Hundreds of white patrons walked out. Robeson was widely commended within the Black community.

39 Springfield

The town where ultra-conservative, accused racist U.S. Attorney General (and former Missouri governor and senator) John Ashcroft was raised.

NORTH CAROLINA

NOT-SO-FUN FACT: Voters have kept perpetually accused racist Republican Senator Jesse Helms in office since 1972. 'Nuff said.

40 Avis Rent-A-Car ◆ 1740 Airport Blvd., Wilmington

In May 1995, an African-American woman was denied the two minivans she had reserved for rental here. Based on this incident and several other complaints of discrimination from Black patrons at Avises throughout the Carolinas, a lawsuit was filed against the company in 1996. In a deposition, a former manager at the Wilmington franchise admitted to being instructed to make renting to Black customers more difficult. In April 1998, Avis settled with the plaintiffs for $5.4 million. We guess freedom is a road seldom traveled by the multitude . . . of Black people . . . in Avis cars.

41 Hall St. Near Campbell Ave. ◆ Fayetteville

December 1995 murder site of two Black civilians who were shot while walking down the street by three neo-Nazi skinhead soldiers from the U.S. Army's 82nd Airborne Division stationed at Fort Bragg. The soldiers were out after a night of drinking and specifically looking for Blacks to harass.

42 Osama's Place ◆ 3563 Ray Rd., Spring Lake

This Jordanian-owned café near Fort Bragg probably possesses the most unpopular name imaginable next to Hitler's (or Jar Jar Binks'). C'mon, the guy's just trying to make an honest buck. Buy a calzone or pita sam'ich, and don't forget to ask if fries go with that sheikh.

43 Wake Forest University ◆ 1834 Wake Forest Rd., Winston-Salem

Pimply, Caucasoid freshmen at Wake Forest University's fall 2000 orientation weren't guaranteed a higher education, but they were guaranteed to live out their *Higher Learning* fantasies (or fears). The school's "Blue-Eyed Orientation" subjected young Biffs and Beckys to ridicule and other forms of discrimination—all in the name of instilling empathy for those who aren't white like them—for a whole, entire *day*! Ohmigod! (Nice try, but you'll never understand the pain we feel.)

44 132 S. Elm St. ◆ Greensboro

Next time you're sittin' down snackin' on a Bojangles biscuit, think back to February 1, 1960. It was on that fateful day that four Black college students pioneered the sit-in movement at the lunch counter of this former Woolworth's to protest the custom of serving colored folk SRO. Inspired by

Having a great time in... ...Auburn, AL!

the "Greensboro Four," Black protesters commenced sit-ins at other segregated eateries state- and region-wide.

OKLAHOMA
NOT-SO-FUN FACT: In 1889, the first of five Oklahoma Land Runs categorized millions of acres of Indian lands as "unassigned" and put them up for settlement by American settlers.

45 Fort Sill
In May 1942, forty-five-year-old gardener Ichiro Shimoda of Los Angeles was shot and killed while attempting to escape the Fort Sill Temporary Enemy Alien Internment Camp despite camp guards' knowledge that he was mentally disturbed and suicidal. Shimoda's mental instability was a result of being one of the first Japanese-Americans taken from his family by the FBI after the Pearl Harbor bombing.

46 Langston
Black leaders' attempts to organize a

mass occupation of Oklahoma Land Run territories (with the intent of forming an eventual all-Black state) may never have materialized. But at least some brothas and sistas were able to form the Black township of Langston—whose hues, we might add, can't lose.

47 Mercy Hospital ◆ Oklahoma City
One day after the April 19, 1995 Murrah Federal Office Building bombing, the Oklahoma City home of pregnant Iraqi refugee Suhair Al-Mosawi was attacked by persons who believed the bombing was committed by Muslims. Al-Mosawi wound up suffering a miscarriage at this hospital.

SOUTH CAROLINA
NOT-SO-FUN FACT: Despite protests that the Confederate battle flag was a painful symbol of the slavery era, South Cakalaka didn't stop flying it from atop its state capitol until July 2000. It still ain't gone, though. The state's lawmaking bastards have merely moved it to a new, shorter pole in front of the capitol next to a monument honoring fallen Confederate soldiers.

48 Bob Jones University ◆ Greenville
Religious learning institute that finally lifted its ban on interracial dating on campus in March 2000 when university president Bob Jones III admitted to talk show host Larry King that—newsflash!—there was no actual verse in the bible that prohibited the act.

49 E. Main St. at Hwys. 49 and 215 ◆ Monarch Mill, Union County
Locale where in October 1994 white mother Susan Smith alleged she was carjacked by a Black man with her two young sons still in the backseat. For nine days she made emotional appeals to the "kidnapper" to return her kids before she finally confessed to having rolled the car herself into nearby John D. Long Lake with her sons locked inside.

50 South of the Border ◆ I-95 U.S., 301-501 Dillon
What began as a mere beer stand in 1950 has become South of the Border, the country's premiere Mexican-themed attraction, just south of the North Carolina border. Dine in the Sombrero Room Restaurant, take in the view atop Sombrero Tower, or indulge your carnal impulses in Pedro's Pleasure Dome. And all the employees, regardless of race, are called "Pedro." It's just like Tijuana, but without all those pesky, y'know, Mexicans.

TENNESSEE
NOT-SO-FUN FACT: Tennessee lays claim to the birthplace of the Ku Klux Klan, which was started in 1865 in the town of Pulaski by six former Confederate Army vets as a response to the post-Civil War Reconstruction.

51 Newport
Town that in January 2001 saw a burning cross appear on the front lawn of the home of Roland Dykes, its first Black mayor. The hate crime was the culmination of weeks of tension in Newport, and came just a few days before a scheduled Klan rally—the most public demonstration by the KKKooks in the region since 1978.

52 Johnson Grove Baptist Church ◆ Bells
One of the first Black houses of worship to be hit in a mid-'90s series of racially-motivated church fires that swept through the south beginning in January 1995.

53 National Civil Rights Museum ◆ 450 Mulberry St., Memphis
Formerly the Lorraine Motel, where Martin Luther King Jr. was assassinated in April 1968.

TEXAS
NOT-SO-FUN FACT: The Southern Poverty Law Center reports that Texas is the state with the most identified hate groups, fifty, as of 2001.

54 Coca Cola Bottling Co. of N. Texas ◆ Dallas
In May 2002, several employees of Coca Cola alleged that the beverage behemoth regularly had its workers repackage unsold, almost out-of-date cans and bottles of soda from stores in white neighborhoods and sell them to stores in minority neighborhoods. (At least you don't have to wait for quarter waters to go bad.)

55 Galveston Bay
Area that saw tensions rise between local white fishermen and immigrant Vietnamese fishermen in the late '70s and early '80s, resulting in several Vietnamese fishing boats being burned, and armed Texas Klansmen cruising the bay hanging a Vietnamese fisherman in effigy.

56 Jasper
The town in which forty-nine-year-old African-American James Byrd Jr. was murdered in June 1998. After being offered a ride by three white men while walking home one night, Byrd was taken to an isolated location, severely beaten, and then chained to the back of a pickup truck by his ankles and dragged for three miles.

57 Sierra Blanca
First the good news: After years of lobbying and protest, residents of this tiny, largely Mexican-immigrant border town succeeded in halting the construction of a radioactive nuclear waste dump within its borders in 1998. Now the bad news: From 1992 to 2001, Sierra Blanca was the dumping site for thousands upon thousands of tons of highly toxic New York City sewage, subjecting its citizens to rashes, allergies, blisters, asthma, and the pervading smell of shit.

VIRGINIA
NOT-SO-FUN FACT: In 2000, Governor James S. Gilmore III declared April Confederate History Month. (Guess uptighty whiteys were still pissed about having to add Martin Luther King Jr.'s surname to Virginia's Robert E. Lee / Stonewall Jackson holiday in 1984.) An outraged NAACP and other Black organizations threatened to boycott tourism in the state, and finally in March 2002, new Governor Mark R. Warner wisely shut CHM down.

58 Country Club of Virginia ◆ 6031 St. Andrews Ln., Richmond
Physician James Howard Cane became the first Black member of the more-than-eighty-year-old Country Club of Virginia in 1992. Interestingly enough, the club's rules never banned Blacks from the grounds and its three golf courses, it's just that no one ever joined. Cane told the *Washington Post* about his milestone move: "[Breaking racial barriers] wasn't the main reason for doing it. My children are very active, and I wanted a place that was family oriented. [And] the food is excellent." The best part: The brotha didn't even play golf.

59 Monticello ◆ 931 Thomas Jefferson Pkwy., Charlottesville
Home of a shrine to Tommy Jefferson, who had seven children with slave Sally Hemings, yet never granted her her freedom, even after he became president. Instead, he wrote *Notes on the State of Virginia* in which he described interracial sex as "a degradation to which none can innocently consent." When you visit the fabulous gift shop at Monticello, try not to laugh when you buy those bookmarks etched with one of Jefferson's hot-aired mottoes: "I have sworn upon the altar of God eternal hostility against every form of tyranny over the mind."

60 Virginia Polytechnic Institute ◆ Blacksburg
Where in 1997 a Black frat brother of Delta Sigma Pi received an email document called "Ebonic Loan Application" sent by a white "brother." Some of the lowlights of the mock application form: The multiple choices for "Place of Birth" included "Charity Hospital," "Free Public Hospital," "Cotton Patch," "Back Alley," or "Zoo." The "Current Residence" question requested the make, model, and license plate number of the applicant's car (and even inquired if it was financed or ripped-off). So giddy was the creator of the crass computerized "joke" that he ended his hateful message by exclaiming, "Please send this to as many people as possible! It took me forever to type!"

WASHINGTON D.C.
NOT-SO-FUN FACT: Thanks to an area movie theater that denied him admission, a young, 1950s Black calypso crooner who later came to be known as Nation of Islam leader Louis Farrakhan was inspired to write his song "Why America Is No Democracy." Ahh, the power of cinema.

61 **Blair House**
  ◆ **Pennsylvania Ave.**
  Between 15th and 17th Sts.
  Diagonal from the White House

On November 1, 1950, Puerto Rican Nationalist Party members Griselio Torresola and Oscar Collazo attacked the official government guest house in an unsuccessful attempt to assassinate U.S. president Harry S. Truman, who was staying there while the White House was being renovated. The pair's mission for PR independence resulted in the death of one police officer, while two others were wounded and Torresola caught one in the dome—ending his *vida* instantly. Collazo was sentenced to death, but Truman later knocked it down to life imprisonment. (He was freed in 1979 during the Carter administration.)

62 **Duke Zeibert's**
  ◆ **1050 Connecticut Ave.**

Swing through downtown D.C. and lament the closing of this old school red meat power-lunch emporium (reborn as Morton's in the late '90s). It was here that ex-Vegas bookie Jimmy "The Greek" Snyder dropped his infamous January 1988 bomb during lunch: that Blacks were better athletes because of slave plantation breeding techniques.

WEST VIRGINIA

NOT-SO-FUN FACT: The National Alliance, the neo-Nazi organization led by author William L. Pierce, PhD (who under the pseudonym Andrew MacDonald wrote the infamous *The Turner Diaries*, the pro-Aryan, race-war-is-comin', eve of destruction novel that reportedly juiced up Timothy McVeigh to act a fool), is headquartered somewhere in West Virginia's fucking boonies. (It's in Mills Point near Hillsboro, if you really want to know.) Ex-college professor Pierce might be getting old, but he's hip as hell. In order to attract young white sheep to his cause, he purchased Resistance Records, the largest white supremacist record company in America, in 1999.

63 **Multi-CAP Building**
  ◆ **1007 Bigley Ave., Charleston**

In 1999 pro-African culture organization All-Aid International Inc., in an effort to educate the masses on slavery, co-commissioned with the state a scale model of the Henrietta Marie, a 300-year-old slave ship that was discovered in the Florida Keys in 1972. Unfortunately, despite the million dollars spent on its construction and the model's success as a tourist draw, the state eventually declined ownership of it. The model was dismantled and the wrecked ship lay in boxes in the basement of the soon-to-be-sold Multi-CAP Building.

CONNECTICUT

NOT-SO-FUN FACT: Who says size matters? According to a November 2001 report from the Connecticut Regional Office of the Anti-Defamation League, extremist hate group activity in the state is "disproportionate" to its small area. No surprise from a state that hosted Klan cross burnings as recently as 1978.

1 **Foxwoods Resort Casino**
♦ 39 Norwich Westerly Rd., Mashantucket

Attention high-rolling pilgrims: waste your wampum at the Mashantucket Pequot Tribe's Foxwoods Resort Casino, which at 320,000 square feet is the world's largest. (Sorry, no beads accepted.) Don't forget to ask one of the "red" men about their proposed Asian theme park (featuring a replica of the Great Wall) designed to appease the "yellow" man's gambling jones.

2 **Sylvan Lake (a/k/a "Niggerhead Pond") ♦ Waterbury**

The North

3 **Wallingford**

Local union workers' 1999 attempts to force the town council to recognize Martin Luther King Jr.'s birthday as a holiday provoked hostility from residents angry at the idea of "lazy" public employees getting another day off. Despite the KKK's attempts to intimidate the union's ranks, the bill eventually passed two years later.

DELAWARE

NOT-SO-FUN FACT: Delaware was home base to the Cannon-Johnson Gang, one of the most notorious operations of the "Reverse Underground Railroad" in which free Blacks were kidnapped and sold into slavery.

4 **Delaware State University ♦ Dover**

Kathleen Carter, a white woman, became chairman of the education department of the historically Black DSU in 1995. But a few years later, Carter filed a discriminatory lawsuit against the school, alleging that she was harassed (even called a "white bitch" by one Black colleague) and denied tenure because of her race. A federal judge dismissed Carter's case based on lack of evidence.

5 **Negro Island ♦ Milton**

MAINE

NOT-SO-FUN FACT: It wasn't until 1977 that the lily-white state of Maine adopted legislation requiring the renaming of ten geographical locations whose names included a racial slur.

6 **AAA**
♦ Shaw's Plaza, 600 Center St., Auburn

Site of alleged discriminatory acts on the part of workers at Auburn's AAA branch toward Black patron Rhonda King in January 1997. King's attempts to renew her auto insurance policy were thwarted when she was repeatedly refused entry to the branch office while white patrons were allowed entry and served. AAAssholes.

7 **Cumberland Ave. Apartments**
♦ Cumberland Ave. Near Wilmot and Chestnut Sts., West Bayside, Portland

Locale of one of Maine's ugliest racial confrontations. In June 1998, seventeen-year-old Alan J. Shaw and a group of about ten other white youths attacked five Somali immigrant youths with sticks, bricks, and bottles. Shaw reportedly yelled, "I'm going to kill you, nigger," at nineteen-year-old Abdi Hassan Ali before hitting Ali in the head with a brick. Asked later by police why he attacked Ali, Shaw responded, "'Cause they're fucking niggers; enough said."

8 **Malaga Island ♦ Near Phippsburg**

A forty-one-acre island settled by free Blacks during the Civil War that forty-five Black and mixed race people and their families had peacefully called home for half a century. But by 1912 local white residents could no longer stand the thought of this colored colony. That's when all of Malaga's residents were mass evicted, their homes torched by state workers and the bones of their ancestors dug up. If the state of Maine had some real important plans for the land, they've kept it a secret for nearly a century. Locals say no one's lived there since.

MASSACHUSETTS

NOT-SO-FUN FACT: While like most states Massachusetts got its name and land from Native Americans, the 2000 Census reports that Native Americans compose just 0.2% of the commonwealth's population, less than one fourth of the nationwide percentage. Where they at?

9 **Brigham and Women's Hospital**
♦ 75 Francis St., Boston

Medical center where white male Charles Stuart was last seen leaving with his pregnant white wife, Carol, before he murdered her and later blamed the death on a fictional Black carjacker back in October 1989—a "fact" that racially-charged Beantown was all too ready-and-willing to initially accept. (When Stuart's lie was exposed, he committed suicide by jumping off the Tobin Bridge into the Mystic River.)

10 **Dana Farber Cancer Institute**
♦ 1 Jimmy Fund Way, Boston

Celebrated *New York Times Book Review* critic Anatole Broyard was a light-skinded Black man who lived his entire life passing as a white man. Ten days before Broyard's death in 1990, while he was laid up in the Dana Farber facility, Broyard's white wife, Sandy, broke the news of his actual racial identity to their kids on a patch of grass across the street from the Institute. (Wouldn't you have loved to be a fly on a blade of grass at that little family talk?)

11 **Merriam-Webster**
♦ 47 Federal St., Springfield

Publishing home to *Webster's Dictionary*, which caught flack in 1998 for listing the primary definition of "nigger" as "a Black person—usually taken to be offensive."

12 **Stretch between Savin Hill and Dorchester; 998 Dorchester Ave.**
♦ Boston

The locales where a young Mark Wahlberg assaulted various colored folk. In June 1986, Wahlberg and two companions chased some Black kids from their neighborhood, throwing rocks and yelling, "Kill the niggers!" Seeing the same Blacks the next day, the not-so-funky bunch chased them again, this time hitting two girls with rocks. Then in April 1988 at 998 Dorchester Ave., Wahlberg yelled epithets at and beat a Vietnamese man, Tanh Lam, with a stick in an attempt to steal the two cases of beer Lam was carrying. While Lam wound up losing one of his eyes in the brutal attack, Wahlberg served just forty-five days at the Deer Island House of Corrections and then went on to become a recording star, a Calvin Klein model, and a successful actor.

13 **Wellesley Post Office**
♦ 1 Grove St., Wellesley

It was in 1990 outside this post office in the affluent Boston suburb that Celtics rookie Dee Brown was sitting in his car, reading his mail with his fiancée when he was approached by several cops at gunpoint and forced to lie on the ground. Turns out a Black man had robbed an area bank the day before and Brown made the mistake of being Black while in the area, thus his detainment by police.

NEW HAMPSHIRE

NOT-SO-FUN FACT: New Hampshire, which possesses a minority population of only about 3 percent, became the last U.S. state to sign the Martin Luther King Jr. holiday into law in June of 1999. (The state had previously observed a generic "Civil Rights Day" holiday.)

14 **Concord Police Department**
♦ 35 Green St., Concord

Police station where white subway vigilante/fugitive Bernhard Goetz finally turned himself in on New Year's Eve 1984. Goetz had won widespread admiration for shooting and maiming one of four young Black muggers as he rode New York City's subway. This incident was viewed as a significant episode in NYC's escalating '80s racial tension.

15 **Pulaski Dr. Apartments**
♦ Off Rte. 108, Newmarket

It was in the parking lot outside this housing complex in July 2001 that sixty-two-year-old Laotian-American Thung Phetakoune was killed by thirty-five-year-old Caucasian Richard Labbe. Amidst a drunken anti-Asian tirade motivated by the Vietnam War deaths of two relatives, Labbe pushed Phetakoune, who fell and suffered fatal injuries when his head hit the pavement. Labbe reportedly later told police, "What's going on is that those Asians killed Americans, and you won't do anything about it, so I will." Ironically, Phetakoune had actually fought alongside American troops during the Vietnam conflict as a soldier in the Laotian army.

NEW JERSEY

NOT-SO-FUN FACT: In late 2000, New Jersey officials released 91,000 pages of documents confirming that racial profiling of Black and Latino drivers had been standard operating procedure by police in that state for the last decade.

16 **213 N. Broad St. ♦ Trenton**

Seventy-three-year-old white male William Horner was robbed and killed here at his junk shop in January 1948 allegedly by several light-skinded Black men. Bowing under public pressure to solve the case quickly, police arrested six Black suspects (most of whom did not fit the witness descriptions). All were subsequently found guilty by an all-white jury and given the death sentence. Lawyers from the Civil Rights Congress of the Communist Party took on the case, appealing the decision, and the convictions were overturned. In the re-trial, four of the defendants were

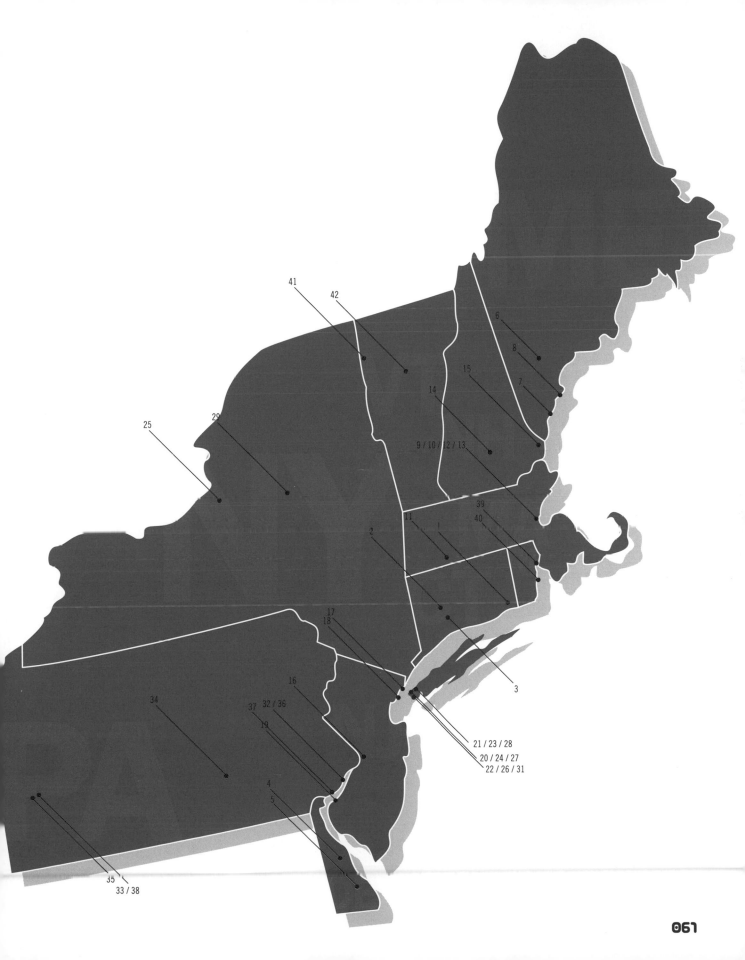

41

42

6

8

15

7

14

9 / 10 / 12 / 13

29

25

39

11

40

2

3

17

18

16

34

32 / 36

37

19

21 / 23 / 28

20 / 24 / 27

22 / 26 / 31

4

5

35

33 / 38

found not guilty, and the case of the Trenton Six attracted worldwide attention as a prime example of "Northern lynching."

17 Backyard of 19 Intervale Rd. ♦ Teaneck

Where in April 1990 Black teenager Phillip Pannell was shot in the back and killed by police despite the sixteen-year-old's attempt to raise his arms to surrender. White patrolman Gary Spath, who fired the fatal shot but was acquitted of manslaughter charges, believed that Pannell had turned to shoot at him. (A gun was found on Pannell afterwards.) The incident sparked public outcry of police racism and a tri-state media frenzy—unfortunate since Teaneck had built a reputation for racial tolerance when it voluntarily desegregated its public schools in the 1960s.

18 Ninth St. and Willow Ave. ♦ Hoboken

Where South Asian Novroze Mody, a Citibank manager, and a co-worker were walking on September 27, 1987 when they were attacked by a group of ten Latino high school students.

The North

The group reportedly shouted "Hindu! Hindu!" as they mercilessly beat Mody. He died of head injuries after a few days in a coma. The murder coincided with a wave of violence against South Asians in the Jersey City area committed by a white group calling itself the "Dotbusters"—who'd vowed in a letter to a local newspaper to "go to any extremes to get Indians to move out of Jersey City."

19 Penn's Grove High School ♦ 334 Harding Hwy., Carney's Point

It was at this school in his senior year that Bruce "I Sang For Motown" Willis participated in a white versus Black "race riot" in the cafeteria, thus leading to his expulsion. Perhaps this was, in fact, Bruno's first real encounter with twelve monkeys?

NEW YORK

NOT-SO-FUN FACT: Want racism? WE GOT RACISM. Come to the Rotten Apple and walk the streets or ride the subway for just one day. Hell, one hour. You will hear, see—even smell—something racist. We promise. And that's our *ego trip* guarantee or your money back (after we pickpocket you).

20 Bar Veloce ♦ Second Ave. and 11th St., E. Village, Manhattan

Thirty-five-year-old Black Brooklynite Steven Johnson, afflicted with AIDS and distraught by the recent death of his wife from the same illness, opened fire inside this bar, striking and harming three victims in June 2002. In the course of forty deranged minutes, he allegedly terrorized the trapped patrons by pouring kerosene on several of them and waving a barbecue lighter. After being subdued by two women and arrested by police, he told detectives, "I wanted to kill as many white people as I could."

21 Belt Pkwy. Near Cross Bay Blvd. ♦ Howard Beach, Queens

In December 1986, twenty-three-year-old Black male Michael Griffith and two Black friends stopped at the New Park Pizzeria on Cross Bay Blvd. and 157th Ave. looking for assistance when their car broke down. After getting into an altercation with some of the white locals, Griffith was struck by a car and killed on the Belt as he ran from an enraged, baseball-bat-wielding mob of white youths.

22 Borough Hall ♦ Downtown Brooklyn

Government center where in January 2002 BK Borough President Marty Markowitz caused a flap for referring to "Father of Our Country" George Washington as an "old white man" and removing G-Dub's long-displayed portrait with the intention of replacing it with one of someone who reflected "the richness of [Brooklyn's] diversity." An "old white man" his damn self, Markowitz's bold move cast aside any doubts: Brooklyn *is* the borough! Thought you knew.

23 Cross Bay Blvd. ♦ Broad Channel, Queens

A police officer and two firefighters from this virtually all-white neighborhood donned Blackface and afro wigs, tossed watermelon and fried chicken onto the crowd, hoisted a banner that read "Black to the Future, Broad Channel 2098," and re-enacted the racist dragging murder of James Byrd Jr. in Jasper, Texas at the 1998 Broad Channel Labor Day Parade. The three civil servants—who'd won the "funniest float" prize nine years straight by mocking other ethnic groups with banners reading "The Gooks of Hazzard" and "Hasidic Park"—were all fired.

24 C.U.R.E. ♦ 64 Macdougal St., Greenwich Village, Manhattan

HQ of a friendly-as-heck organization calling itself Caucasians for Reparations and Emancipation. (Good cause. Too bad it'll never happen.)

25 Denny's ♦ 2863 Eire Blvd. E., Syracuse

Where in April 1997 a group of six Asian, three Black, and one Caucasian Syracuse University students claimed that not only did they have to wait thirty minutes to be seated while other (white) patrons were given tables quickly, but they were also ejected from the premises by armed security guards. *Then* they were attacked and racially taunted by a large group of young whites who were also in the restaurant. Dang.

26 Family Red Apple Market ♦ 1823 Church Ave., Flatbush, Brooklyn

A Haitian-American woman claimed that she was assaulted by an employee at this Korean-owned grocery store in January 1990. The incident caused Black and Haitian activists to organize an ugly thirteen-month boycott of both Family Red Apple and another nearby Korean-owned grocery, Church Fruits and Vegetables. Area tension also resulted in an attack by Blacks on three Vietnamese-Americans, whom they mistook for Koreans.

27 Friars Club ♦ 57 E. 55th St., Manhattan

Site of the infamous 1993 roast in Whoopi Goldberg's honor at which her then-boyfriend Ted Danson appeared onstage in Blackface, told "nigger" and "coon" jokes (penned by Goldberg), and ate watermelon—all to the horror of a shocked audience. That's incredible.

28 Long Island Railroad Near the Merillon Ave. Station

Black nutball Colin Ferguson opened fire on a packed commuter train here, killing six citizens and wounding 19 others at approximately 5:33 p.m. on December 7, 1993. Later submitted as evidence in the bizarre, much-publicized trial that featured Ferguson acting as his own defense lawyer were notes that were found on him at the scene of the crime. They announced that Ferguson's hatred for white folks, Asians and Uncle Toms was his motive.

29 Nehasane Lake (a/k/a "Negro Lake") ♦ Herkimer County

30 Pavillion Apartment Complex ♦ 17 Carnaby Dr., Wappingers Falls

The apartment complex in this sleepy town of 5,000 is the former home of the infamous Tawana Brawley. On November 28, 1987, African-American Brawley—then only fifteen-years-old—was found in a large garbage bag, her clothing torn, smeared with feces, and graffiti-ed in charcoal with the words "nigger," "bitch," and "KKK." Brawley said that

she was abducted and sexually abused by a group of white men. However, her claims were subsequently disputed and the case became one of the significant race/justice events of the latter half of the century.

31 Northeast Corner of 69th St. and 20th Ave. ♦ Bensonhurst, Brooklyn

Corner in a primarily Italian-American 'hood where Black teen Yusef Hawkins came to look at a used car on August 23, 1989 and was instead killed by a mob of local white youths. Hawkins and his friends were mistaken for the non-white invitees rumored to be attending the birthday party of one of the gang's ex-girlfriends.

PENNSYLVANIA

NOT-SO-FUN FACT: According to online finger-pointer The Smoking Gun, Philadelphia's "Welcome to America" Independence Day 2001 brochure inadvertently acknowledged the country's racism problem. Included in the "Kids Corner" word search puzzle weren't just words like "flag" and "historic," but also far more provocative terms like "nigga," "yid," and "jap." A gaffe in the puzzle-making software? Probably. Distinctly American? *Definitely*.

32 13th and Locust Sts. ♦ Philadelphia

Intersection where white Philadelphia police officer Daniel Faulkner was killed in 1981. In a controversial trial, Black journalist/activist Mumia Abu-Jamal was convicted and sentenced to death. The fight to free Mumia has since become a major civil rights rallying cause.

33 788 Elmspring Rd., Virginia Manor; Indian Grocers at Scott Township; Ya Fei Chinese Cuisine at Robinson Town Center; C.S. Kim School of Karate at Center Township ♦ Pittsburgh Vicinity

In April 2000, thirty-four-year-old Caucasian immigration attorney Richard Baumhammer went on a racially-motivated shooting rampage in these areas. Baumhammer fatally shot his sixty-three-year-old female Jewish neighbor in the well-to-do community of Virginia Manor, shot two workers at an Indian grocery in Scott Township (killing one and leaving the other paralyzed), fatally shot the owner of the Robinson Town Center Chinese restaurant and his Vietnamese food delivery man, then killed a Black student at a martial arts school in Center Township.

34 GIANT Food Store ♦ 4211 Union Deposit Rd., Harrisburg

This supermarket chain store earned a lot of unnecessary attention in February 2002 for displaying a sign declaring, "In honor of Black History Month, we at GIANT are offering a special savings on fried chicken." (C'mon, *that's* funny.) Still, the overly PC (persnickety customers) complained and the sign was taken down. Guess that means no *chalupa* hook-up on Cinco de Mayo. *Mierda.*

35 McKees Rocks

Town whose lone police dog was accused of racial profiling in June 2002. Complaints that five-year-old German shepherd "Dolpho" displayed a penchant for attacking Black people came to a head when the canine bit a Black child bystander during a police arrest. Dolpho was taken off active duty.

36 Rocky Statue at the Spectrum
♦ Philadelphia

Maybe it's only right that Philly, a city notorious for its virulent racism, would hold onto a statue of a fictional white boxing hero (originally a prop from *Rocky II* donated as a gift to Cheesesteak Central by Sylvester Stallone) while its own real life Black heavyweight champ, Joe Frazier, remains uncelebrated. That's below the belt.

37 Swarthmore College
♦ 500 College Ave., Swarthmore

Fall 1998 at the dormitories: first-year students were asked to stand in a line according to their skin color—lightest to darkest—and talk about their feelings about being "positioned." College is like, so great.

38 Woodside Garden Apartments, 1200 Wood Ct., Burger King on Penn Ave.; McDonald's on Penn Ave.
♦ Wilkinsburg

Locales of Black male Ronald Taylor's March 2000 shooting spree targeting white victims. Taylor shot and killed a maintenance man in his apartment building on Wood St., fatally wounded another man in Burger King, and shot three other victims at McDonald's, one of them fatally. A racism-fueled suicide note he called "Personal Legit Feelings" was later found in Taylor's home.

RHODE ISLAND

NOT-SO-FUN FACT: "V-J Day" (a/k/a "Victory Over Japan Day") was celebrated in Rhode Island every August 14th from 1948 until 1995 (when it was changed to "Peace Remembrance Day") to commemorate the end of World War II. The holiday's observance coincided with periodic vandalism of Asian-owned businesses and assaults against Asian-Americans in the state.

39 Fidas Diner
♦ 270 Valley St., Providence

Black off-duty police officer Cornel

Young Jr. was shot and killed here by two fellow white officers in January 2000. The officers had mistaken Young for an armed suspect as he attempted to break up a fight.

40 Warwick City Hall
♦ 3275 Post Rd., Warwick

In September 2000, a six-foot tall Mr. Potato Head statue (which was on display as part of a statewide "Birthplace of Fun" tourism campaign) was removed from this location after local Black residents complained that the smiling, brown-skinded figure appeared sambo-ish. When asked about the "Tourist Tater's" controversial color, its designer simply said, "He's a potato. That's why he's brown."

VERMONT

NOT-SO-FUN FACT: Despite its low population of Blacks and Jews, Vermont was home to thousands of KKK supporters in the 1920s and '30s. Their **primary targets were immigrants, many** of whom were Roman Catholic.

41 University of Vermont ♦ Burlington

In a case of textbook racism, between 1894 and 1969 as part of its "Winter Carnival," the school held annual "Kake Walk" contests. These icy affairs featured white fraternity brothers in Blackface performing plantation worker minstrel dances to the delight of crowded gymnasiums full of fellow (white) students. Whatever happened to Shakespeare in the round? (Get the *Othello* outta here.)

42 Vermont Public Records Division
♦ Middlesex

Those with a eugenics jones should stop on by the VPRD and browse through the papers of scientist Henry Perkins. In the '20s and '30s, Perkins and a team of colleagues developed a plan of genetic purification in which Vermont's "degenerate" bloodlines would be eliminated in order to revive its original citizens' "old pioneer stock." No, Perkins and company weren't into clones, but they were on some ImClone (a/k/a shady) shit. Their survey resulted in the sterilization of several hundred poor, rural Vermonters, including many Abenaki Indians. Maybe you "pioneers" shoulda just gone the fuck back to Europe.

BAY RIDGE AVE. (69TH ST.) AND 20TH AVE.
BENSONHURST, BROOKLYN

Birthplace of Fun!
WARWICK, RHODE ISLAND

White folks, we the Mud Peoples of the United $nakes, in order to form a more perfect union, have decided to let the white lies die, not multiply, and let love rule. From here on out, we swear that our spears will not pierce your spheres (a/k/a your fuckin' domes). You see, we love to see you smile. We now know that when we see the whites of your eyes, that peace is the place that they're beaming from. It's a warm place. A place for us all. Together.

A R T I C L E   I
Whites, we forgive you for:

Four hundred-somethin'-somethin' years of slavery.
(Freedom-Shmeedom!)

Nasty-ass Columbus and his stank mates' disease-ridden no-love boat bringing VD to America.
(Hoody-hoo! Our genitals are on fire, but it's all good!)

Introducing Native Americans to firewater and bogarting their land for bags of worthless beads.
(You guys sure got over on *that* tom-tom club!)

Stealing California, parts of Texas, and other territories from the Mexicans.
(¡You *siesta*, you lose!)

Japanese internment camps.
(They're still a never-ending source of inspiration—for Pat Morita! *Arigato!*)

Forsaking true rock 'n' roll pioneers like Chuck Berry, Little Richard,
and Ike "Speaks wit' His Hands" Turner, and crowning Elvis the King.
(Son died on the toilet—*that's* gangsta!)

Similarly usurping blues, jazz, R&B, and hip hop for your cultural trophy case.
(At least it got you to kill that yodeling noise!)

Assassinating our leaders.
(What would we have named all those Martin Luther King Jr. Blvds. otherwise?)

Making February, the shortest month of the year, Black History Month.
(K.I.M.—keep it movin'!)

Crack.
(Inspired great son-of-a-Black filmmaker Mario Van Peebles' finest cinematic effort—*New Jack City!*)

AIDS.
(It didn't stop Magic!)

The Rodney King verdict.
(Revived that long-forgotten group activity for families of color—looting!)

Passing Proposition 187.
(Hey, this ain't no *Via Allegre*.)

The Amadou Diallo verdict.
(Confirmed our theory that wallets and the Bronx don't go hand in hand!)

The Florida electoral college.
(Just proved what we knew all along—voting don't mean shit!)

ARTICLE II
However, white folks, we do NOT forgive you for:

Casting Elizabeth Taylor as Cleopatra.
(Talk about white out!)

Howdy Doody.
(Ugly-ass puppet.)

Escargot.
(Y'all just nasty!)

The word "dude."
(It's like we totally can't stop saying it, dude!)

Calling that one show *T.J. Hooker.*
(Ha-ha, *muy* funny, *cabrones.*)

Michael Jackson.
(What y'all did to that homie's head was fucked *up!*)

The Wave.
(Sit down and watch the fuckin' game.)

Jim Carrey *and* Drew Carey.
(However, Carrie, that crazy voodoo white bitch, is down wit' us.)

Synchronized swimming.
(Bubble-blowing at its worst.)

Banning end-zone dances.
(Can't nobody hold us down.)

Starbuck's.
(Haven't you bean counters "coffee achieved" enough?)

The Gap.
(Fall into something else.)

John Travolta's comeback.
(He's only stayin' alive on L. Ron Hubbard's dime.)

Titanic.
(There's nothing romantic about drowning in some frigid-ass water
—unless, of course, you're an ice person from the Caucasus Mountains.)

Limp Bizkit and every other wack-ass crew of mic-wielding whiteys.
(You whites did okay with the blues, and damn good with rock. But to quote your own kind, we won't get fooled again.)

For never, ever putting anything by the Rolling Stones and Led Zeppelin (not even fucking *Coda,* that piece of shit)
or Pink Floyd's *Dark Side of the Moon* on sale.
(Sam Goody rocks a white hoodie.)

Tribal tattoos.
(Marks of the beast.)

Breast implants.
(Stick with Frank Perdue.)

AMENDMENT I
White folks, we thank you for:

The Beatles.
(Okay, you got us on that one.)

Nova from the originoo *Planet of the Apes.*
(Our favorite cave bitch.)

Buying out BET.
(It ain't our fault no mo'!)

CHAPTER 2

GET UR RACE ON.

THAT'S WHAT THEY ALL SAY: 25 CELEBS WHO HAVE CLAIMED OR HAVE BEEN RUMORED TO BE PART CHEROKEE INDIAN.

Kareem Abdul-Jabbar / athlete
Amil / rapper
Kim Basinger / actress
Johnny Cash / singer
Cher / entertainer
Rita Coolidge / singer
Johnny Depp / actor
Carmen Electra / actress
James Garner / actor
Brian Austin Green / actor
Jimi Hendrix / musician
James Earl Jones / actor
Tommy Lee Jones / actor
Val Kilmer / actor
Eartha Kitt / entertainer
Chuck Norris / actor
Mario Van Peebles / actor, director
Elvis Presley / singer
Della Reese / actress
Burt Reynolds / actor
Salli Richardson / actress
Pat Smear / musician
Ronnie Spector / singer
Quentin Tarantino / director
Fred Ward / actor

ARABS AMONG US: 15 WELL-KNOWN PERSONALITIES OF ARABIC DESCENT.

F. Murray Abraham / actor
1/2 Syrian, 1/2 white (Italian-American)

Paul Anka / singer
Lebanese

Yasmine Bleeth / actress
1/4 Algerian, 3/4 white (French, Russian, German)

Dick Dale / musician
1/2 Lebanese, 1/2 white (Polish)

Shannon Elizabeth / actress
1/2 Syrian-Lebanese, 1/2 white (British, French)

Salma Hayek / actress
1/2 Lebanese, 1/2 Latin (Mexican)

Casey Kasem / radio personality
Lebanese

Ralph Nader / politician, activist
Lebanese

Bobby Rahal / race car driver
1/2 Syrian, 1/2 white

Shakira / singer
1/2 Lebanese, 1/2 Latin (Colombian)

Tony Shalhoub / actor
Lebanese

John E. Sununu / politician
Palestinian

Vic Tayback / actor
Syrian-Lebanese

Danny Thomas / actor
Lebanese

Tiffany / singer
Lebanese

BONUS: NOT QUITE ARAB, BUT CLOSE ENOUGH DAMMIT...

The Hughes brothers / dynamic film-making duo
1/2 Armenian, 1/2 Black

HIPPA TO DA HAPA: ALMOST ASIAN.

Tyson Beckford / model
1/4 Chinese, 3/4 Black (Jamaican, Panamanian)

Dean Cain / actor
1/4 Japanese, 3/4 white (Welsh, French-Canadian, Irish)

Naomi Campbell / model
1/8 Chinese, 7/8 Black (Jamaican)

Phoebe Cates / actress
Mother part some kind of wonderful Asian, father white (Jewish)

Rae-Dawn Chong / actress
1/4 Chinese, 1/2 Black, 1/4 white

Ann Curry / news personality
1/2 Japanese, the rest French, Scotch-Irish, American Indian

Kirk Hammett (Metallica) / musician
1/4 Filipino, 3/4 white

Don Ho / singer
According to his Web site, "Born of Hawaiian, Chinese, Portuguese, Dutch, German parentage"

Kelis / singer
1/4 Chinese, 1/2 Black, 1/4 Latin (Puerto Rican)

Ben Kingsley* / actor
1/2 East Indian, 1/2 white (British)

Sean Lennon / musician
1/2 Japanese, 1/2 Beatle

Danica McKellar ("Winnie" from *The Wonder Years*) / actress
1/2 Korean, 1/2 white

Ming the Merciless from *Flash Gordon*** / evil ruler

Keanu Reeves / actor
1/2 Chinese-Hawaiian, 1/2 white (British)

Rob Schneider / actor
1/2 Filipino, 1/2 white (Jewish)

Mike Shinoda (Linkin Park) / singer
1/2 Japanese, 1/2 white

Jimmy Smits / actor
1/4 Dutch East Indian, 1/2 Latin (Puerto Rican), 1/4 Surinamese

Wesley Snipes*** / actor

Jennifer and Meg Tilly / actresses
1/2 Chinese, 1/2 white

Eddie and Alex Van Halen / musicians
1/2 Indonesian, 1/2 white (Dutch)

*Born Krishna Bhanji, but forced to assume an Anglo stage name so he could finally get great acting gigs only a white man gets—like playing Gandhi.

**Do you know anyone named Ming who is not part Asian?

***Included for being on the Asian dick.

30 LATINS ON THE LOW.

AZ / rapper
1/2 Dominican, 1/2 Black

Catherine Bach / actress
1/2 Mexican, 1/2 white (German)

Jean-Michel Basquiat / artist
1/2 Puerto Rican, 1/2 Black (Haitian)

David Blaine / magician
1/2 Puerto Rican, 1/2 white (Russian-Jewish)

Benjamin Bratt / actor
1/2 Peruvian (Quechua Indian),
1/2 white (British, German)

Irene Cara / entertainer
1/2 Black Puerto Rican, 1/4 Cuban,
1/4 white (French)

Mariah Carey / singer
1/4 Venezuelan, 1/2 white (Irish),
1/4 Black

Vikki Carr / actress
Mexican

Lynda Carter / actress
1/2 Mexican, 1/2 white

Chino XL / rapper
1/2 Puerto Rican, 1/2 Black

Sammy Davis Jr. / entertainer
1/2 Puerto Rican, 1/2 Black

Zack de la Rocha / singer
3/4 Chicano, 1/4 white (Irish, German)

Fabolous / rapper
1/2 Dominican, 1/2 Black

Antonio Fargas / actor
1/2 Dominican, 1/2 Black

Freddie Fender / musician
Chicano

Phil Lynott / musician
1/2 Afro Brazilian, 1/2 white (Irish)

Maxwell / singer
1/2 Puerto Rican, 1/2 Black (Haitian)

Frankie Muniz / actor
1/2 Puerto Rican, 1/2 white (Italian, Irish)

Vince Neil / musician
1/4 Mexican, 1/2 white, 1/4 Native
American

Freddie Prinze Jr. / actor
1/4 Puerto Rican, 3/4 white
(1/4 Hungarian)

Anthony Quinn / actor
1/2 Mexican, 1/2 white (Irish)

Linda Ronstadt / singer
1/2 Mexican, 1/2 white

Roxanne Shanté / rapper
1/2 Cuban, 1/2 Black

Shyne / rapper
Belizean

Jamie Lynn Sigler / actress
1/2 Cuban, 1/2 white (Jewish)

Brenda K. Starr / singer
1/2 Puerto Rican, 1/2 white

Madeline Stowe / actress
1/2 Costa Rican, 1/2 white (British)

Christie Turlington / model
1/2 Salvadorian, 1/2 white

Raquel Welch / actress
1/2 Bolivian, 1/2 white (British)

Hype Williams / director
1/2 Honduran, 1/2 Black

DISCLAIMER:
Martin Sheen / actor
white (Spanish, Irish)

SPICE GIRLS. CAMERON DIAZ VERSUS CHRISTINA AGUILERA: ¿WHO'S MORE LATIN?

C&C I.D.: FULL NAME
CAMERON: Cameron Diaz
CHRISTINA: Christina Maria Aguilera
ADVANTAGE: Christina. Although real Latinas drop the *h,* Ms. Aguilera wins with her middle moniker, Maria, the name of every other Spanish girl on the planet. (Diaz only played Mary on screen.)

AY PAPI: **LATIN PARENT**
CAMERON: Her father, Emilio, is Cuban-American.
CHRISTINA: Her father, Fausto, is Ecuadorian.
ADVANTAGE: Cameron. Word to Estevez. Even though Cami's *papi* is second generation, his name takes out the Germanesque Fausto, which sounds like the handle of an extra on *Hogan's Heroes.*

¿FEAR OF DIOS?: **RELIGIOUS DENOMINATION**
CAMERON: According to a 1996 *Rolling Stone* profile, when she was a little girl and curious about religion, her parents would drop her off at any church she chose to check out.
CHRISTINA: Catholic
ADVANTAGE: Christina. Scientific studies show 98.9 percent of all Latinos in the universe are Catholic. Really.

VIVA LA RAZA: **REPPIN' THE ROOTS**
CAMERON: "My Latin roots are very strong. All my life, because I'm blond and blue-eyed, people who aren't Hispanic can't believe that I am. And people who are Hispanic always think I'm not, because I don't look like them. Being Latin is part of who I am,

Blond, blue-eyed, and bony babes Cameron Diaz and Christina Aguilera have even more in common than what first meets the eye. Both are fast-food-loving Betties who hail from middle-class backgrounds and did stints as high school cheerleaders. Both found success in Japan early in their careers—Cameron as a pre-actress, party-hearty teen Elite model and Christina as a budding pop singer.

And they're both Latinas, *claro que si.*

See, despite their keep-it-real surnames, it's easy to forget that these two barely brown beauties have a little flavor in their genes (if not their jeans). *ego trip* investigates further and asks the *pregunta de million pesos*: ¿Quien es mas Latina? ¿Cameron o Christina?

and I bring that part to every role," she informed E! Online in 1998.

CHRISTINA: In a 2001 *Time* interview she stated: "As soon as I came to the point where we were going to release my album, the label was like, 'You know, this name, it's too difficult to pronounce.' They wanted it to be more American sounding. I said no because this is my name. It's my identity."

ADVANTAGE: Christina. Diaz is confused. As of the start of 2002, she had yet to take on a Latina role.

SHE'S BI: ¿SPEAKS SPANISH?
CAMERON: *Poco.*
CHRISTINA: *Poco*, but recorded a top-selling album en Español. (She learned songs phonetically.)
ADVANTAGE: Christina. Talk is cheap, but Aguilera is Sound(scan)ing right.

CLOSE ENCOUNTERS OF THE SAME KIND: SIGNIFICANT LATINO LOVE TRYSTS
CAMERON: Had a five-year relationship with producer Carlos de la Torre.
CHRISTINA: Dated Jorge Santos, one of her original dancers.
ADVANTAGE: Cameron. She's got five on it.

FRISKY AT FIFTEEN: TEENAGE PROMISCUITY
CAMERON: The following quote, regarding her stint as a young unsupervised model overseas, appears on countless Web sites dedicated to the down-to-earth daffodil: "Believe me, you can get into a lot of trouble being sixteen-years-old in a foreign country with no adult telling you when to come home."
CHRISTINA: In a 1999 interview with Todd

Oldham she said, "My first kiss was when I was really little 'cause I would kiss boys just for fun. My first boyfriend kiss was when I was thirteen."
ADVANTAGE: Cameron Sutra. Even without any details, we think she was wilder. Oh, yeah, baby.

FACE 2 FACE: ¿HINT OF A 'STACHE?
CAMERON: No.
CHRISTINA: No.
ADVANTAGE: Tie.

YOUR *ROPA:* ¿WEARS TIGHT, REVEALING CLOTHES?
CAMERON: *Si.* Doesn't like to brandish a bra.
CHRISTINA: *Si.* "I find that small tops that show off the belly are much sexier than a bare body. I feel I can flirt with the limits for years to come," she told MTVAsia.com in 2001.
ADVANTAGE: Cameron. There's something about perky breasts on a full-grown *señorita.*

BLUE EYES AND BLUE-LIGHT SPECIALS: DISCOUNT BRAND AFFILIATION
CAMERON: Once did an ad for L.A. Gear.
CHRISTINA: Has her own boutique at Sears.
ADVANTAGE: Christina. Although JCPenney would have been better, Sears is the brown people's Macy's.

POWDER PUFF GIRLS: MAKEUP MATTERS
CAMERON: Often appears in interviews or in public sans makeup.
CHRISTINA: *Si.* (Maybe too much. Her "Lady Marmalade" get-up led to Dee Snider lookalike jokes.)
ADVANTAGE: Christina. *Cholas* everywhere can worship her war paint.

CHICA BOOM: HOTHEADEDNESS/EMOTIONAL MISCUES
CAMERON: Previously mentioned '96 *Rolling Stone* article stated, "She swears like a longshoreman"; reportedly yelled, along with costar Leonardo "*Part 6*" DiCaprio, at rude paparazzi gathered around the set of Martin Scorcese's *Gangs of New York.*
CHRISTINA: Reportedly used F-word in front of children during taping of a Disney show and acted arrogant toward extras; was also accused of yelling at a little girl who confused her with Mandy Moore; allegedly cried when one of her hotel suites was too small.
ADVANTAGE: Christina. Yelling at kids is some Latin shit.

MI CASA, SU CASA: PENCHANT FOR DOMESTICITY
CAMERON: A 2001 *Premiere* article stated, "She can routinely be seen lugging her own peat moss across the yard of her new Hollywood Hills home, picking up her dry cleaning, or rummaging through the hinge rack at the neighborhood hardware store."
CHRISTINA: "When I moved from Pittsburgh to make my record in L.A., I lived out of a hotel. So it feels a little strange having my own place now and shopping for myself," she's confessed to *YM.*
ADVANTAGE: Our homegirl Cameron.

LA WINNER. ¿WHO GOT THE KEYS TO THE BEANERS?
Proving you ain't gotta be brown (skinded) to be down, Christina is *rubia* the right way. Free Coronas for everybody.

RICKY POWELL ON BEING A MEXICAN JEW.

I've never given it much thought—being half-Jewish and half-Mexican. I grew up with my "Jewish" mother (who isn't religious, to say the least). She ran shit but let me live.

I didn't miss having a father figure around because I liked the simplicity of our household: It was just me, my mom, and our animals (we always had dogs and cats 'cause she could never pass up a homeless one on the street). Anyway, if I did ask my mother what the deal was with our family, I don't think I really listened because I don't remember what she said.

Eventually, my grandmother told me that when I was a baby, my mother and father separated—and that he was from Mexico. I remember going to Mexico City in the summer of '68 'cause the six-ring symbol of the Olympics was all over the place. I also have vague memories of visiting some people there in a really nice house (I think they might have had loot). I don't remember really knowing who they were. But they were nice.

Aside from that, I have no connection to my Mexican roots. I grew up in Manhattan—the Village, mostly—and have lived life basically as a white guy. I never felt aware of my ethnicity despite having a good ear for soul music. As far as how I dressed, I didn't want to be considered a nerd, so I'd rock clothes that were cool at the time, such as double-knit pants (sometimes with the pant leg rolled up, which was actually considered a Puerto Rican thing), polyester shirts, and the like.

When it came to girls, I've basically dated white girls. Not because that's all I like, but you know how interracial dating can be—nearly impossible. I think most nonwhite girls are shy, hesitant, or straight-up scared to do the mixed thing. Latin girls are especially hard to hook up with. I don't know why. They've just been elusive to me. I guess I don't look swashbuckling like Zorro.

In conclusion, being a Mexican-Jew really doesn't mean a thing to me. It's trivial.

Ricky Powell—one of the world's greatest photographers—is also a magnificent philosopher. Peep his steelo at www.ricky-powell.com.

OTHER NOTABLE MEXICAN JEWS.

1. Frida Kahlo / artist
2. Raylene / porn "actress"
3. Goretex / rapper
4. The dearly departed, late-lamented Kosher Burrito on Crenshaw Boulevard, Los Angeles, California. Y'all slept!

10 REVELATIONS A BLACK MAN MUST FACE WHEN CONVERTING TO A LIFE AS A JEW.

BY HAITIAN GEORGES

1. Jewish women will fulfill their Lenny Kravitz fantasies with you.

2. Jewish parents still have a heart attack when you show up arm-in-arm with their *sheyna maidele*.

3. After attending the same temple for a year, you'll still get asked "Can I help you?" by security.

4. It's bad form to sop up the brisket gravy with *challah*.

5. It's also bad form to pour a little Manischewitz out of the Kiddush cup for the homies who ain't there for Friday night services.

6. *Yarmulkes* get no play in the 'hood.

7. When it's time to mark the beginning of the Jewish New Year at Rosh Hashanah, the rabbi doesn't appreciate your impromptu rendition of "Rumpshaker" on the shofar.

8. The Sammy Davis Jr. references don't get funnier with time.

9. Double the slavery heritage.

10. You have to get circumcised—*again!*

By the time you read this, Haitian Georges will be a full-fledged, bona fide, honest-to-Jehovah Jew. Challah!

JEW DON'T KNOW?

Lauren Bacall / actress
Beck / singer
Barbi Benton / actress
Sorrell Booke ("Boss Hogg" from *The Dukes of Hazzard*) / actor
Nell Carter / actress
Andrew Dice Clay / comedian
Ron Jeremy / porn legend
Harvey Keitel / actor
Yaphet Kotto / actor
Krusty the Clown (*The Simpsons*) / animated entertainer
Michael Landon / actor
Marilyn Monroe / actress
Natalie Portman / actress
Joey Ramone / singer
Lou Reed / singer
The Rugrats / animated characters
Rod Serling / writer
William Shatner / actor
Dinah Shore / TV personality

ALMOST EVERYTHING: 6 ETHNICALLY EVASIVE CELEBS.

PAULA ABDUL

Inhale. The ethnic origins of former Laker girl/choreographer/pop music diva (and apple of Arsenio's eye) was a curiosity in the late '80s/early '90s. During those years people speculated all kinds of things: "She's funky, so she *must* be part Black. Yet she's sassy, so she *must* be Hispanic." Her olive complexion, exotic features, and surname hinted at Middle Eastern origins, but Paula—Ms. Abdul, if ya nasty—never really gave up the goods. (No biggie, since everyone's hiding *something* in Los Angeles.) Still, ya gotta come out sooner or later, and it's since been revealed that her father is Syrian-Brazilian and her mother is Jewish–French Canadian. Exhale.

ROSARIO DAWSON

Despite a decidedly non-Hispanic surname, Dawson's screen debut as a promiscuous New York City preteen in 1995's disturbing *Kids* led many to assume that the photogenic actress is straight-up Boricua. And until the spotlight of fame shone her way in 1998 for her role as the conniving girlfriend in *He Got Game,* most folks thought that was *all* she was. But, truth be known, she's *sooo* much more. Although Dawson usually downplays her actual ethnic makeup in interviews, she does admit to being quite an ethnic cocktail. Besides Puerto Rican roots she also claims to be part Black, Cuban, Irish, and American Indian. How!

VIN DIESEL

For some time, busybodies everywhere desperately wanted to know the exact racial mix of this yoked-up action star. (It has since been reported his mom's Italian and his old man is Black.) From the looks of it, Mr. *XXX* prefers to keep things extra vague, even going so far as to write, direct, and act in a 1994 film short called *Multi-Facial* about the perils of being hard to pin down in the acting game. Still, people talk: "Is he Irish? . . . Italian? . . . German? . . . ¿¿¿*Dominicano* maybe*???*" One thing's for sure though: Dude used to be a bouncer at notorious NYC club The Tunnel back in the day. So you know he's down for whatever.

LOU DIAMOND PHILLIPS

In dog-eat-dog Tinseltown, where the "meaty" roles are few and the "minority" roles fewer, the road to success is paved with deception. And the career of racially ambiguous stud Lou Diamond Phillips is no exception. Best known for playing the pioneering rock 'n' roll Chicano Ritchie Valens in 1987's biopic *La Bamba*, Phillips's actual race-factuals were up for debate. He's admitted to being mostly Filipino, but rumors of his having American-Indian blood seemed to help cement future Latino roles such as a belligerent teenager in *Stand and Deliver* (1987). And while Hollywood and the media don't show him the kind of love they did during his *La Bamba* days, Louie's true color(s) still remains a hot Internet newsgroup discussion topic. (For the record, his moms *is* Filipino and his dad is said to be a Texan of Scottish-Irish and Native American descent.)

ROZONDA "CHILLI" THOMAS

If the racial background of this member of TLC was unknown to her legions of fans, it was through no fault of her own. Her "good" hair came from a man she never knew, and her mother barely knew—a soldier stationed in Columbus, Georgia. Apparently, pops unknowingly impregnated Chilli's Black–Native American mother and took off before Rozonda was born in 1971. But after twenty-five years of living in the dark and chasing waterfalls, Chilli's problem was solved the *new*-fashioned way: via Sally Jesse Raphael's daytime TV chat-a-thon. On an episode titled "I'm Desperate to Find My Family," Chilli was reunited at last with her father, the half Arabic, half East Indian Atlantic City casino worker Mr. Abdul Ali. Jackpot.

TIGER WOODS

What hasn't been said about the racial breakdown of America's favorite dark-skinded Happy Gilmore? Woods' reluctance to label himself as merely a "Black" pro golfer— instead of half Black, half Thai, half Chinese, a quarter American-Indian, and a quarter white—is a lot more palatable than his self-mocking catchall term, "Cablinasian." *Tigga, please.* We all know that the sunburned son-of-a-guns you swing with think of you as "Chief Chinkiniggookracker" . . . but we'll forgive ya. (By the way, your Swedish cupcake is kinda tight!)

TRANSRACIAL TWINS.

RUTHIE FROM *REAL WORLD* HAWAII AND TUPAC SHAKUR

YASSER ARAFAT AND REDD FOXX
BIZZY BONE AND KID ROCK
RICHARD GERE AND JUNICHIRO KOIZUMI (PRIME MINISTER OF JAPAN)
LIZZIE GRUBMAN AND CRAIG MACK
MASTER P AND GEOFFREY RUSH
MANUEL NORIEGA AND CREATURE FROM THE BLACK LAGOON
SCOTTIE PIPPEN AND SYLVESTER STALLONE
SNOOP DOGG AND LEE VAN CLEEF

CORNEL WEST AND GENE SHALIT

TOP 10 ITALIANS KNOWN SIMPLY BY THEIR LAST NAMES.

10. Mario (as in Super)
9. Coppola / Scorsese (tie)
8. Mussolini
7. Vinci
6. Fellini
5. Versaceda
4. Gotti
3. DeNiro / Pacino (tie)
2. Sinatra
1. Christ

TOP 10 WHITES (ACCORDING TO BLACKS).

10. Jerry Springer/Rikki Lake/Jenny Jones (a daytime TV ménage à trois tie)
9. Marshall "Eminem" Mathers
8. Sting / Phil Collins (tie)
7. Teena Marie
6. Robert DeNiro
5. Pat Riley / Phil Jackson / Marv Albert (An NBA trifecta tie)
4. Pamela Anderson
3. WJC*
2. JFK
1. Jesus

HONORABLE MENTION:
The Dutch Masters
(Let's be blunt: Rollover, White Owl)

*William Jefferson Clinton

TOP 10 BLACKS (ACCORDING TO WHITES).

10. Clarence Thomas / Ward Connerly (tie)
9. Biz Markie / Kool Keith / The Roots (tie)
8. Oprah
7. Jimi Hendrix
6. Denzel Washington
5. Michael Jordan
4. Muhammad Ali (post-Parkinson's)
3. MLK
2. Jesus
1. Uncle Tom

TOP BLACK JUNIORS (ACCORDING TO WHITES).

6. "James Evans Jr." (a/k/a "J.J." from *Good Times*)
5. Ken Griffey Jr.
4. Trevor Smith Jr. (a/k/a Busta Rhymes)
3. Sammy Davis Jr.
2. Cuba Gooding Jr.
1. Martin Luther King Jr.

BONUS: TOP WHITE JUNIOR (ACCORDING TO BLACKS).

White-owned, Black-patronized Junior's on Flatbush Avenue, Brooklyn. (The chocolate swirl cheesecake is off the Hindenburg!)

BLACKS BEHIND THE WHITES.

DONALD "CINQUE MTUME" DEFREEZE
Leader of the Symbionese Liberation Army, the otherwise white-membered revolutionary organization that kidnapped newspaper heiress Patricia "Tanya" Hearst in 1974 and "brainwashed" her into participating in a San Francisco bank robbery.

DR. DRE
Sound surgeon behind Angry Blond wit' Attitude Eminem.

FULL FORCE
Flatbush, BK, writing/producing crew behind PR princess Lisa Lisa. They first got a taste for that vanilla-scrilla as the creative force behind '80s Brit tabloid slut turned pop music slut Samantha Fox. Ten years later, they continue cranking out hits for Britney Spears, the Backstreet Boys, and 'N Stink, we mean Sync.

K.C. JONES
Cool-tempered coach of the 1986 Boston Celtics championship team that featured Caucasian stars Larry Bird, Kevin McHale, Bill Walton, and Danny Ainge, who occasionally played five whites at a time on the court.

REGINALD F. LEWIS
Late founder of food conglomerate TLC Beatrice, the first Black-owned company to boast revenues of over $1 billion.

PAUL MOONEY
Respected writer/performer that was an early comic mentor to funny girly grrrl Sandra Bernhard.

MICHAEL MOYE
Creator of white America's favorite dysfunctional family sitcom, *Married with Children*. (Cue toilet flush and laugh track.)

COLIN POWELL
Early '90s Pentagon HNIC and strategic Black brain behind U.S. award tours like Operation Desert Storm; currently heads up the Dubya administration's State Department.

MC SHAN
Once-famed Queensbridge-bred rapper who discovered great white hope of early '90s dancehall reggae, Snow.

MAURICE STARR
Puppet master behind the prototypical modern white-boy pop group, New Kids on the Block.

JERRY TIBBS
Call him Mister. Policeman/amateur photographer who discovered ever-popular '50s sexpot pin-up Betty Page on the beach at Coney Island. Tibbs' help landed Betty her first cover—for a Harlem newsprint magazine.

LESTER WILSON
Choreographer of John Travolta's dance moves in *Saturday Night Fever*. Fuck Denny Terrio.

JOHNNY WRIGHT
Manager of 'N Sync. Impressive, huh?

HONORABLE MENTION:
KEVIN CLASH—BLACK BEHIND THE ORANGE MUPPET
Soul controller behind the enormously popular Elmo. Aren't you tickled pink?

DISHONORABLE MENTION:
DON BLACK
Former Klansman who, in March 1995, put up the first hate site on the World Wide Web. P.S.: He's white.

TRIBUTE TO AN IRISHMAN.
THE JOLLY GREEN GIANT: POPULAR PEA PUSHER ON WHY IT AIN'T EASY BEING GREEN.

BY CARTER RILEY HARRIS

ALMOST SEAMUS: A PEA-WEE-SIZED MCDERMOTT, AGE SIX MONTHS.

Back in the nineteenth century, being Irish in America wasn't such a lucky thing. The countless Catholics who fled Ireland after the infamous potato famine (1845–1848) found themselves crowded into rat-infested tenements in cities like New York, Philadelphia, and Boston. Poor immigrants with bad accents, the boisterous, communal lot were disdained by the mostly Anglo-Saxon Protestants running the show. Newspaper cartoons and stage shows portrayed them as apelike, ruddy-cheeked drunks who beat each other silly with shillelaghs and got hauled off by police in paddy wagons.

Like most immigrant populations in the U.S.A., the Irish had to work their way around the stereotypes. Besides the many bridge builders, bricklayers, and factory workers, the descendants of Eire gave us some of our best actors (James Cagney, Spencer Tracy, Gene and Grace Kelly, Jackie Gleason), finest writers (F. Scott Fitzgerald, John Steinbeck, Flannery O'Connor, Eugene O'Neill), and handsomest politicians (John F. Kennedy, our only Irish Catholic President). But one of this country's greatest public figures is often inexplicably left off the list of celebrated Irish-Americans. His name is Seamus O'Shaunessey McDermott, known to most as the Jolly Green Giant.

Seamus, of course, is the most important advocate of canned and frozen vegetables in the world. It was not a future he expected growing up in South Boston's Old Colony housing projects as the youngest of four sisters and six brothers—two of whom died in infancy.

"Childhood was hard," says Seamus, now ninety-six, from his home outside Chicago.

"But there was also a lot of love and laughter."

There was also a lot of promise, at least in the case of Seamus, who maintained a B+ average and served time as an altar boy at St. Mary's Church. In the ninth grade, he was already six feet tall, 200 pounds, and fast became a high school football all-star lineman. Notre Dame scouts convinced Seamus—via a scholarship and generous under-the-table cash incentives—to reject Boston College's Eagles in favor of the Fighting Irish.

But then one fateful St. Patrick's Day, Seamus and some buddies guzzled a little too much cheap whiskey and, in keeping with tradition, went looking to punch people in the face along the parade route. Seamus fell down and got run over by, of all things, the Guinness Beer float and his left femur was shattered beyond recognition. His football days were over. One week later, Seamus' eldest brother Colin died when the crystal meth lab he had built (one of the first in the country) exploded. "Things went downhill pretty fast," he recalls. "I threw out my school books, took to the drink, and started brawling with my neighbors and the coppers, most of whom were also my neighbors."

On the road to nowhere, Seamus was sent in 1924 to stay with his mother's brother, Eddie O'Donaghue, and family in a small town called Blue Earth, Minnesota. His second week there he skipped work, polished off a case of Hamms beer, and passed out in a pea patch. "I'll never forget it," says Winston Thatcher, the owner of that pea patch and the top exec at the Minnesota Valley Canning Company. "I came home and I see this huge, primitive-looking fellow snoring peacefully among my vegetables. He just blended in so naturally. I knew right then that we had the perfect pitchman."

The next day the company signed Seamus to a contract and hired the Chicago-based Leo Burnett advertising agency to remake his image. Seamus was dressed in a leafy toga, red scarf, and pointy boots and given the name Jolly Giant. "I thought it was a little fruity at the time," he says. "But I couldn't argue with the money and they kept heat lamps on me during the colder photo shoots."

Problems arose due to Seamus' skin, which had a greenish tint owing to a condition called vertitis epidemia, an ailment that afflicts the Irish in especially wet, cold climates where there's an excess of plant life and chlorophyll. (For reasons still unclear to scientists, it only affects those with excess bone growth, namely very large or very small people—hence the myths about leprechauns.) At first pinkish makeup was used to cover over Seamus's now-eight-foot, 275-pound frame. "But it just looked ridiculous," says Thatcher. "So we came up with the idea to enhance the greenness already in his skin with dye."

The makeover paid off when housewives went crazy for canned-goods featuring the gentler, buffed-up Jolly Green Giant. Before he could thank his lucky stars, he was doing TV spots, signing autographs, and sitting courtside at Celtics games.

He became the third biggest advertising icon (after Marlboro Man and noted rival Tony the Tiger), and briefly dated Hollywood sex symbol Jane Russell (from *Gentlemen Prefer Blondes* and the eighteen-hour bra commercials). Instead of blowing his money on fancy clothes and cars, however, Seamus gave a big chunk of it to his family, church, the Green Party, and Sinn Fein (the political organization fighting for a just peace in Northern Ireland).

In the 1980s, at the height of his fame, Seamus, now in his seventies but in excellent shape thanks to rigid training and nutrition, started hanging out with Irish rockers the Pogues. He even toured briefly with the rowdy band, playing the bodhran (a traditional Irish drum). "It was a little too much fun," admits Seamus. "[Pogues' frontman] Shane MacGowan turned me on to Poteen [a form of Irish moonshine]. It tasted like the devil's piss, but I couldn't keep away from it."

His bosses at the canning company helped get Seamus into the Betty Ford Clinic (paying the tab with his royalties). While there, Seamus reacquainted himself with biblical scripture and with one special line in a William Butler Yeats poem: "Cast your eyes on other days, that we in days to come may be, still the indomitable Irishry."

His fighting spirit reawakened, he battled the bottle, but the real help came in the form of a "knockout redhead with these beautiful gams" whom he met after leaving an AA meeting.

That woman was Colleen Gallagher. "Not long after we began to date, I caught him hiding a pint of Jameson in his jacket," she says. "I told him it was me or the drink. He poured it out and got down on one knee, his bad knee, and says, 'This liquid is but a poor substitute for what I truly crave. And that is to drink from the elixir of your love for the rest of me days.' What can you say to that?" Three weeks later they exchanged Claddagh rings and said their vows. Six years after that they'd birthed two girls and three boys,

including one named Siobhan (a Gaelic name pronounced Shivawn), who became the inspiration for Sprout in later Green Giant commercials.

Seamus managed to stay straight until 1998, the year he failed to get the lead in an overseas remake of *The Incredible Hulk*. He relapsed and got caught patronizing a hooker on the southside of Chicago. (Arresting officers reportedly chanted "Ho, ho, ho!" repeatedly at the scene.) "It's nothing I'm proud of," he says, "but we all make mistakes. If we didn't, what would be the point of priests?" Forced out of the house for three months, Seamus went to confession weekly and finally sobered up. His wife found it in her heart to forgive him, "because I'm still in love with the ol' gobshite."

Late last year, Seamus retired from his pitchman gig, though his image still appears on canned and frozen foods, which means he continues to inspire children of all ages to eat their veggies, bringing about a healthier diet for millions around the globe. He is also living testament to how far a poor kid with a weird skin condition from the projects can go. Seamus O'Shaunessey McDermott has proven himself to be a brawler and a bard, a family man of strong religious and political convictions, and an ex-boozer who just might fall off the wagon at any given moment. He is, in sum, the quintessential Irish-American (give or take a few inches).

Carter Riley Harris, former executive editor of Vibe *magazine, is a screenwriter and cofounder of the Irish-American Union of Drunken Revelers.*

TOP 10 LATINS WITH *CABEZAS CALIENTES.*

1. **"TONY MONTANA"** (*SCARFACE,* 1983)
Not being able to maintain an accent throughout a three-hour film would make anybody mad. Add 300 kilos of cocaine to Al Pacino's filthy-mouthed Cuban druglord's nostrils and fuhgeddaboudit, *coño!* But America needs people like him. (One less actual spic on the silver screen . . .)

2. **AUGUSTO PINOCHET**
This Chilean dictator wasn't chillin'. Here is something you can't understand: how from 1973 to 1990 he could just kill a man or two or three. (Okay, thousands.) No wonder human-rights groups had an A.P.B. on A.P., the S.O.B.

3. **PANCHO VILLA**
Long before bin Laden, this Mexican Robin Hood pissed off his northern neighbors by invading New Mexico in 1916 and letting his gat blow. ¿The *resulto*? One intense manhunt and a sad reactionary drop in chimichanga consumption in the United States. Just so you know, gringo, the real "Panchorello" always had a mean streak—from shooting the landowner who tried to rape his sister to making it a point of not only instantly killing any backstabbers, but all their immediate male family members as well. We're not sure why he was so angry. (He didn't drink alcohol.) Some might say it was because he grew up the son of a sharecropper. Others might be of the opinion that he grew tired of watching his country overrun by *pinche gabachos*. We say it was dealing with his twenty-plus wives.

4. **FAT JOE**
He smashes champagne bottles on the *cabezas* of rappers he doesn't deem real. Former crew members end up with mysterious buck-fiftys across their grills. He's down with notorious Uptown street legend (and hot beatmaker) Showbiz. Oh, José, can't you see we don't want it with Joe?

5. **"RICKY RICARDO"** (*I LOVE LUCY,* 1951–1957)
After a long, hard day of rehearsing at the Tropicana and chasing skirts, the last thing El Rickster wanted was to arrive at his *casa* and hear about the ghetto-fabulous aspirations of his loony wifey. Fed up, he'd get red-faced and then let the rowdy redhead have it with one of them rapid-fire outbursts even other native Cubanos find hard to decipher. We suspect that Desi Arnaz had some of that fire in real life since he was the first (¿and only?) Latino to own a Hollywood studio. Better believe he was getting in some Tinseltown fucker's ass on a daily basis. (By the way, you shoulda seen Fred Mertz lose it. Whoa!)

6. **ROBERTO DURAN**
Duran-Duran is the Panamanian strong man forever known for his nickname *"Manos de Piedra"* ("Hands of Stone"), and for saying *"No mas"* ("No more") to Sugar Ray Leonard during their 1980 championship rematch. (¿*Por que?* He ain't got no patience and he hates waiting, that's why.) The boxing legend routinely punished sparring partners and came close to killing a few opponents in the ring. Known to use "foul" tactics, Roberto won world titles in four weight divisions and continued to fight until the age of fifty. In fact, he's so tough (and hotheaded) he survived a serious car wreck in 2001.

7. **"TINA"** (*DO THE RIGHT THING,* 1989)
Do the Right Thing had all the elements of a classic potboiler: the racial tension, the police brutality, the riot. Yet the scuriest thing in this Crooklyn cooker is the rage of one squeaky-voiced, ain't-never-satisfied Latina sexpot. Hotter than the thermometer on the wall (and looking good in a wet T-shirt), Rosie Perez, playing the p.o.ed Puerto Rican baby *mami*, hands in a performance that ranks up there with Ricardo Montalban's extra ticked-off extraterrestrial "Khan Noonien Singh," the first Korean–East Indian in space (*Star Trek II: The Wrath of Roarke,* 1982). But think about it. You'd be vexed, too, if the father of your child was named "Mookie."

8. **MIGUEL PIÑERO**
This Puerto Rican street poet, playwright, and occasional penitentiary resident wrote the violent prison drama *Short Eyes*, an astonishing and acclaimed literary work filled with some bad-ass mofos he no doubt partly based on real life peeps he met. And those that met Piñero all agreed, friend or foe, you never were 100 percent safe around this 110 percent thoro Boricua who lived hard till his death at the age of 41.

9. **JESUS**
Contrary to popular belief, the Christo Kid didn't always turn the other cheek. Nor did he hesitate to tell Satan where to stick it. And although he was probably best known for scoring a Top 20 hit with the feel-good chant-along "Give Peace a Chance," open your eyes (and your windows, hookah tokers) to the fact that J.High was sometimes cross before he got nailed to the cross.

10. **MONTEZUMA'S REVENGE**
Attacking quickly, without warning (just like *honquistadors*), this intestinal malady will burn your insides like Henny, gringo.

HALFTIME:
TOP 10 TRAGIC MULATTOS.

1. **MARIAH CAREY**
What does an African-American / Venezuelan father, an Irish-American mother, a great set of pipes, a million adoring fans, a jillion #1 records in a row, a domineering Italian-American ex-husband / Svengali, a trailer load of self-image issues, a propensity for "whorelike attire," a nervous break-down, a mocked and derided cinematic debut, and a failed soundtrack add up to? One poor, tortured soul with good hair. But, Mariah, you ain't a pariah. Girl, you're on fire!

2. **ROB PILATUS (MILLI VANILLI)**
Though he was blessed with green eyes, model looks, and pop star drive, Pilatus, the son of a Black American father and white German mom, lacked just one thing—talent. Correction; he *could* lip sync like a mo-fo, as was proven by the 14 million albums he and his man Fab sold as Milli Vanilli. But when word got out that the duo didn't sing a single note on any of their records (resulting in the revoca-tion of their Grammy), Pilatus suffered through public ridicule, substance abuse, an attempted suicide, failed drug rehab, being mistaken for Dennis Rodman, and ultimately, a death by overdose of alcohol and pills in 1998. As he *didn't* sing on MV's 1989 smash, "Girl I'm Gonna Miss You": "It's a tragedy for me to see the dream is over." All that, and he didn't even rank #1 on our list. Sigh.

3. **PRINCE AS "THE KID"** *(PURPLE RAIN, 1984)*
His (Black) dad beats his (white) mom. His bandmates don't understand him, or his swashbuckling pirate garb. His equally racially ambiguous girlfriend is dumb enough to jump topless into a lake in the dead of a Minnesota winter. And all he wants to do is rock. (Even more tragic: 1990's *Graffiti Bridge*.)

4. **"SARAH JANE JOHNSON"** *(IMITATION OF LIFE, 1959)*
Though Sarah Jane's official background isn't necessarily even biracial (her domestic-worker mother only indicates that her father was "almost white"), she is nonetheless the modern archetype of the tragic mulatto. Sarah Jane grows up preferring to play with white dolls, later dates white boys, and eventually leaves home to pass for white. She needs help. But little does she understand that her mom really is the help. Only after Mama Johnson passes does her sad seed return to tearfully recognize the real.

5. **HALLE BERRY**
The lovely Ms. Berry has suffered through a strike-out marriage to baseball star and Jake Steed–lookalike David Justice, a hit-and-run auto accident in which she was at the helm, an emotionally wrenching turn as her troubled role model, Dorothy Dandridge, that horrible white wig in *X-Men* (2000), and *Swordfish* (2001)—a shitty film that paid her extra loot for doing a delicious nude scene that no one saw. Her historic Best Actress Oscar triumph for 2001's *Monster's Ball* could have finally signaled the end of Halle's hell. But her second marriage, to singer Eric Benet, has not been all peachy keen, with reports surfacing that he's cheated on her. Lordy, Lordy—have mercy on Ms. Halle!

6. **BOB MARLEY**
A great orator who never knew his father, this long-locked freedom fighter and messenger of hope survived fre-quent persecution from the powers that be—including one unsuccessful assassination attempt—before eventu-ally dying before his time.

7. **JESUS**
See above.

8. **MR. SPOCK**
Half-Vulcan. Half-human. He doesn't cry. And that's sad.

9. **LISA BONET**
Fortunate to be part of *The Cosby Show*, the universe's #1-rated TV show of the '80s, the young Ms. Bonet's boneheaded hissy-fits (and no-shows) surprisingly didn't kill her career. The kooky cutie instead got her own pro-gram, *A Different World*, married fellow biracial sensation Lenny Kravitz, and birthed a beautiful baby girl. Unfortunately, she was kicked off *A Different World,* and her marriage dissolved. To add insult to (her own persist-ent self-)injury, she chose to bump uglies with Mickey "I Coulda Been a Contenda" Rourke in the devilish noir thriller, *Angel Heart* (1987). Lisa, please!

10. **VANESSA L. WILLIAMS**
The first Black Miss America was stripped of her crown after some early career softcore-porn photos of her par-taking in sapphic shenanigans appeared in *Penthouse*. Vanessa bounced back with a somewhat successful music and acting career, but faltered once more when she wound up marrying Los Angeles Lakers' cornballer Rick Fox. Truly tragic.

HONORABLE MENTION:

THE MCDLT
Composed of a burger half that stayed hot and a pro-duce portion that chilled, this short-lived Mickey D's delight was nothing short of revolutionary. But for rea-sons that have never been properly explained, the ulti-mate mulatto meal was abruptly discontinued by Ronald and company. McFuck all y'all!

BLISTEX ANYONE?
25 FAMOUS WHITE PEOPLE WITH BIG LIPS.

PAMELA ANDERSON • ANDRE THE GIANT • RICHARD ASHCROFT (THE VERVE) • KIM BASINGER • MR. BEAN • SANDRA BERNHARD • MACAULAY CULKIN • MARIO CUOMO • BEATRICE DALLE • DANIELLE FISHEL (TV'S *BOY MEETS WORLD*) • JENNIFER GARNER (TV'S *ALIAS*) • BARBARA HERSHEY (POST-OP) • ANGELINA JOLIE • DON KNOTTS • JON LOVITZ • JULIANNA MARGULIES* • MARY-KATE AND ASHLEY OLSEN • RON PERLMAN • JULIA ROBERTS • BABE RUTH** • LIV TYLER • STEVEN TYLER** • JOHN WATERS • OH YEAH . . . MICK JAGGER

*Allegedly called "Flounder Mouth" as a child by other kids.
**Were both allegedly called "Nigger Lips" as children by schoolmates. (Kids say the darndest things!)

MOTHER NATURE'S CURSE: 10 BLACK WOMEN WHO AREN'T KNOWN FOR HAVING A BIG "BACKYARD."

BRANDY
Wine is fine, liquor is quicker. But Brandy could be a little thicker.

BLU CANTRELL
Yeah, she got buck naked before she blew, but like Bill Bellamy asked, "Where's the booty?"

LAURYN HILL
No L-Boogie in her butt.

WHITNEY HOUSTON
She's built like the tip of a crack pipe. Sorry, Bobby.

KELLY (DESTINY'S CHILD)
Kelly, we don't think your jelly's ready compared to Beyoncé's bountiful, buxom (and Popeye's popcorn-chicken-enhanced) derriere.

THANDIE NEWTON
Tom Cruise's exotic *MI:2* costar's caboose is MIA.

HOLLY ROBINSON-PEETE
Why do you think Johnny Depp never caught a case of jungle fever on *21 Jump Street*?

DIANA ROSS AND HER SEED, TRACEE
Like diva, like daughter. Their minimal glutei maximi would never make *Maxim*. Maybe *Blender*.

JADA PINKETT-SMITH
You know your backing is lacking when you need a stunt ass. Just rent 1998's cinematic triumph *Woo* if you don't believe us.

SOMMORE
This Queen of Comedy even admits it her damn self: She needs s'more ass.

TOP 10 SCRUTABLE ASIANS.

1. **BRUCE LEE**
Don't get it twisted. Brucie B wasn't just out for kicks, he was determination personified—whether it came to busting race barriers in Hollywood, starring in and directing cinematic classics, passing hand (and feet) skills to Steve McQueen and Kareem Abdul-Jabbar, cutting a rug like Fred Astaire, or marrying a nice white chick.

2. **DALAI LAMA / GANDHI (TIE)**
Both brought millions to their nonviolent knees with one simple slogan: Peace is not the word to play, suckas.

3. **GODZILLA**
Yeah, this lizard king is one grumpy Gus. But you'd be, too, if your ass got woken up from a million-year slumber for no good reason.

4. **HELLO KITTY!**
Miss Japanese Thang and her adorable, small-gift / big-smile crew of characters are all about the pleasure principle.

5. **DJ Q-BERT**
This turntable superhero is just a Pinoy brotha who lets his fingers do the talking.

6. **PIZZICATO FIVE / CIBO MATTO (TIE)**
Happy music.

7. **APU NAHASAPEEMAPETILON (*THE SIMPSONS*)**
You know what's on the mind of this Kwik E Mart mogul: Slushees and the welfare of his litter of *naan*-snatchas.

8. **RODNEY YEE**
Yoga master to the stars is as *namasté* as he wants to be, baby.

9. **DINESH D'SOUZA**
No doubt, the East Indian author of *The End of Racism* is one conservative crackpot. What else would you expect from the guy who also wrote *Ronald Reagan: How an Ordinary Man Became an Extraordinary Leader?*

10. **GENERAL TSO (AND HIS WONDERFUL FRIED CHICKEN RECIPE)**
The Colonel Sanders of the Big East is strictly chicken business.

ALL-STAR ALBINOS:
A LOOK AT THE OTHER OTHER WHITE MEAT
NO ONE'S TALKING ABOUT.

THERE'S ONLY ONE SORT OF NATURAL BLONDE ON EARTH—ALBINOS.
MARILYN MONROE

Come across or merely mention albinos, and you're met with everything from tentative curiosity to outright confusion and ignorance. Nobody's smilin' when it comes to albinos. Look no further than the poetics of late rock icon Kurt Cobain to sum up the enigma that is this lost tribe: "A mulatto, an albino, a mosquito, my libido." Some of us complain about growing up not having cable. Imagine growing up not having melanin in your skin, eyes, and hair.

Yes, technically, albinism is an inherited medical condition, not a race. However, because the albino massive throughout the funky far corners of the world have been consistently shunned as outcasts to society, they essentially form a special, separate, colorless cipher whose membership crosses all traditional barriers of pigment (and even animal kingdoms).

Relegated to circus freak shows, erroneously pegged as possessors of supernatural gifts, albinos have endured a hard history for sure. Career opportunities are the ones that never knock for our *really* fair-skinded friends. However, here is a modern chronicle of some famous (and infamous) white folks even white folks don't understand. Salute.

JOHNNY AND EDGAR WINTER
These Texas-bred siblings permanently raised the bar for triple A: amazing albino achievement. The brothers Winter blazed bandstands and records with Johnny's white-hot guitar-licks and Edgar's soulful testimonies through the early '70s. But things weren't always so honky-dory. The blues brethren also sued DC Comics for once depicting them as half-human, half-worm creatures dubbed "Johnny and Edgar Autumn." Open season on albinos entered a whole new stage.

THE ZOMBIES FROM *THE OMEGA MAN* (1971)
Just what was the nonalbino white man trying to say when he created this big picture's premise? In *Omega Man*'s post-nuclear holocaust world there is a terrible plague that kills most of the earth's people. Those that don't die become player-hating albino freaks who come out at night and try to off any remaining survivors—especially if they're involved in interracial romances like stars Chuckie Heston and Rosalind Cash. To quote Rick James, that's cold. Blooded.

SALIF KEITA
Thought being Black in AmeriKKKa was rough? Try being a Black albino in Africa, where you're not only discriminated against in nearly every single facet of everyday life, but you are highly susceptible to skin cancer from the region's harsh sun rays. Albino Malian musician Keita bucked the odds and made it, albeit only upon moving to France to find acceptance and stardom. (Hey, it worked for Jerry Lewis.)

YELLOWMAN
"King" Yellowman popularized reggae dance hall chatting around the globe in the '80s, utilizing his humor, slack lyrics, arrogant swagger, and unique appearance to pull more hoes than a gang of Mexican gardeners. He even spawned at least one wannabe in colorless carbon copy Purple Man.

Yellowman was also the first Jamaican DJ to trade verses with hip hop royalty, spawning "Roots, Rap, Reggae" with Kings from Queens Run-D.M.C. back when you were still chewing on Abba Zabbas. Since the early '90s, rumors of his failing health have coincided with a sharp drop-off in public activity. But we hear he's just on the low, rub-a-dub-dubbing with honeys of all colors still a-mad-over-he.

"MOKI" THE ALBINO ASSASSIN IN *STICK* (1985)
Another dramatic setback for albino representation. Here nonalbino Anglo stuntman Dar Robinson portrays a vindictive villain out to get Burt Reynolds by any means necessary. The thrilling, climactic scene in which Moki plunges to his death from a skyscraper balcony while letting off a healthy round or twenty parallels the free-fall of portraying pigmentless people on screen in any fair way.

"POWDER" IN *POWDER* (1995)
The thrust of this film plays into the stereotype of albinos as misunderstood mystic Einsteins. After spending most of his life in a basement reading books and honing extrasensory skills, an orphaned albino teen is sent to a reform school where hick townies tease and castigate him like, as Roger Ebert described, some cross between "Cliff Robertson's Charly, the Elephant Man, Mr. Spock, E.T., and Jesus." Ebert forgot Michael Jackson. Like MJ, Powder, with his translucent skin, shy-ass personality, and penchant for fly headgear, wasn't like other guys.

KRONDON
This L.A. underground rapper is a throwback to the *hermanos* Winter—all skills, no frills. The future of the albino profile in the arts, he can be heard shining bright with Cali cohorts Self Scientific and Planet Asia on "Three Kings" or ballin' solo on singles like "James Worthee." Fellow indie microphone fiends pale in comparison.

THOUGHT THEY WAS, BUT THEY WASN'T.

Rutger Hauer
Jim Jarmusch
Nicole Kidman
DJ Ready Rock (Geto Boys)
Andy Warhol

WHITER SHADE OF PALE:
"POWDER" FEELIN' SAD AND BLUE.

CHAPTER 3

RACISM 'N' BLUES.

OLDE FOOLS FROM THE OLDE SCHOOL:
13 COLORFUL MINSTREL SONG TITLES.*

"BULL-FROG AND THE COON"—ADA JONES (EDISON, 1908) "COON TOWN CAPERS (A NEW NEGRO ODDITY)"—METROPOLITAN ORCHESTRA (BERLINER, 1897) "COONVILLE CULLID BAND"—ARTHUR COLLINS (EDISON, 1904) "COON WITH A RAZOR"—LOUIS "BEBE" VASNER (LOUISIANA PHONOGRAPH COMPANY, 1892) "DARKEY TICKLE"—VESS OSSMAN (EDISON, 1896) "EVERY RACE HAS A FLAG BUT THE COONS"—ARTHUR COLLINS (EDISON, 1900) "IF THE MAN IN THE MOON WERE A COON"—ADA

*A direct bite off of Nick Tosches' *Where Dead Voices Gather* (Little, Brown and Company, 2001)

JONES (EDISON, 1906) "LITTLE PICKANINNIES"—VESS OSSMAN (EDISON, 1899) "NIGGER IN A FIT"—VESS OSSMAN (EDISON, 1896) "NIGGER, NIGGER NEBER DIE"—ARTHUR COLLINS (EDISON, 1899) "SONGS MY MAMMY SANG FOR ME"—ADA JONES (EDISON, 1905) "THE WHISTLING COON"—GEORGE WASHINGTON JOHNSON (COLUMBIA, 1891) "WHO DAT SAY CHICKEN IN DIS CROWD?—METROPOLITAN ORCHESTRA (BERLINER, 1900)

NOTICE!

STOP

Help Save The Youth of America
DON'T BUY NEGRO RECORDS

(If you don't want to serve negroes in your place of business, then do not have negro records on your juke box or listen to negro records on the radio.)

The screaming, idiotic words, and savage music of these records are undermining the morals of our white youth in America.

Call the advertisers of the radio stations that play this type of music and complain to them!

Don't Let Your Children Buy, or Listen
To These Negro Records

For additional copies of this circular, write
CITIZENS' COUNCIL OF GREATER NEW ORLEANS, INC.
509 Delta Building   New Orleans Louisiana 70112

Permission is granted to re-print this circular

25 SOULFUL ALBUMS, SOULLESS ALBUM COVERS.

It was different back then. During the 1950s and the 1960s, Caucasians ruled, no ifs, ands, or buts about it. (Especially no butts. See Miss America for further details.)

Oh, what a happy time for George and Georgette Gringo. The aliens were coming from space, not across the border. The most colorful neighbors were the Browns (and thank goodness they didn't live up to their name). And if an Anglo ogled a bus seat taken by a Black, he asked for it. Instead of "Fuck you, you Greyhound-ridin' honky!," the response was, "Yes, sir!" Damn, it was easy. It was like music to the ears.

Ah, yes—jungle music. Universally loved (as long as whitey didn't have to look at who was playing it), hot records by Black artists sold like hot hoecakes. But some musicians were burned in the process. Take a gander at these deceptively designed LPs performed by BPs (Black Peoples) and aimed at R&B-lovin' YTs. Holla!

1. *After Hours*—Erskine Hawkins and His Orchestra (RCA, 1960)
2. *Aware of Love*—Jerry Butler (Vee-Jay, 1961)
3. *The Chantels*—The Chantels (End, 1959)
4. *Dobie Gray Sings for "In" Crowders*—Dobie Gray (Charger, 1965)
5. *Fever*—Little Willie John (King, 1956)
6. *Flamingo Favorites*—The Flamingos (End, 1960)
7. *Got a Good Thing Goin'*—Big John Patton (Blue Note, 1966)
8. *Hip Hug-Her*—Booker T. & the MG's (Stax, 1967)
9. *Hold On . . . It's Dee Clark*—Dee Clark (Vee-Jay, 1961)
10. *I Dig Chicks!*—Jonah Jones (Capitol, 1959)
11. *Land of 1000 Dances*—Chris Kenner (Atlantic, 1966)
12. *Love for Sale*—Cecil Taylor Trio and Quintet (United Artists, 1959)
13. *Miles Ahead*—Miles Davis (Columbia, 1957)
14. *Nothing Takes the Place of You*—Toussaint McCall (Now, 1967)
15. *Oh, What a Nite*—The Dells (Vee-Jay, 1959)
16. *Otis Blue / Otis Redding Sings Soul*—Otis Redding (Volt, 1965)
17. *The Paragons Meet the Jesters*—The Paragons / The Jesters (Jubilee, 1959)
18. *Please, Please, Please*—James Brown (King, 1959)
19. *Prisoner of Love*—Billy Eckstine (Regent, 1947)
20. *Sil Austin's Danny Boy*—Sil Austin (Mercury, 1959)
21. *Stay with Maurice Williams and the Zodiacs*—Maurice Williams and the Zodiacs (Herald, 1961)
22. *Swingin' Easy*—Bill Doggett and His Orchestra (King, 1959)
23. *The Tender Side of Ray Charles*—Ray Charles (Suffolk, 1978)
24. *This Old Heart of Mine*—Isley Brothers (Tamla, 1966)
25. *You Always Hurt the One You Love*—Clarence Henry (Argo, 1961)

HUNK O' BURNING CROSS: ELVIS PRESLEY, THE KING . . . OF RACISM?

BY CHRIS HOUGHTON

ELVIS WAS A HERO TO MOST / BUT HE NEVER MEANT SHIT TO ME YOU SEE / A STRAIGHT-UP RACIST THE SUCKER WAS SIMPLE AND PLAIN / MOTHERFUCK HIM AND JOHN WAYNE.
"FIGHT THE POWER"—PUBLIC ENEMY

Public Enemy may be rock 'n' roll legends themselves these days (vis-à-vis the group's induction into the annals of VH1's *Behind the Music*), but I always wondered about those lyrics—every time I heard "Fight the Power." Even when watching *Do the Right Thing* with Rosie Perez to distract me, I had to stop and think: Was Elvis Presley really a racist?

I mean, it's not like Chuck said, "Elvis was a child-marrying, mother-obsessed pervert." Or "Elvis was a straight-up pill-addicted, incontinent whale." Or even, "Elvis was stoned out of his gourd when he met President Nixon to talk about how the Beatles were . . ." You get the idea.

But was he a racist? Actually, that's a tricky question because "racist" is a slippery word. If you define "racist" as being part of a power structure designed to keep a people down, yeah, Elvis would be that. He was doing what Chuck Berry and others were doing but he was white and they weren't, so he got the mansions and they got the leftovers. But a "racist" can also be an individual, in or out of the power structure, who harbors a prejudice based on race. Was Elvis Presley one of those individuals?

OF COURSE . . . He was what he was—an uneducated white guy from the old South. According to *Elvis Aaron Presley: Revelations from the Memphis Mafia* (Alanna Nash, 1995), written by those shitkickers who hung out with Presley and changed his diapers, "He was prejudiced about Blacks, sure he was. Because of the way he grew up. His family hated Blacks, hated Jews, hated everybody. And that only came from ignorance. You have to consider the times."

ON THE OTHER HAND . . . The Mafioso makes a good point. In Memphis they would ban movies that, in the city censors' opinion, presented "too much racial mixture." Strict segregation laws prevented such mixing, and Elvis actually defied those laws on at least one occasion when he attended a fairground on a designated "colored" night. This act of defiance was appreciated by the local Black community, so you could make a case that he was pretty enlightened for his time.

NEVERTHELESS . . . One famous account has Presley saying, "The only thing a Negro can do for me is buy my records and shine my shoes"—only he didn't use the word "Negro."

THEN AGAIN . . . He probably never said it. The rumor had been circulating for a while when, in 1957, *Jet* magazine (*Jet* has been around since *then*?!) sent a reporter down to Memphis to check it out. They interviewed several Blacks who knew the young singer and decided it was probably false.

BESIDES WHICH . . . from his start at Sun Records to his death on a toilet seat, he always went out of his way to praise Black singers, which was a controversial thing to do in the '50s.

AND FURTHERMORE . . . the thing is, these Black musicians liked him right back. R&B great Ivory Joe Hunter, who'd heard the "shine my shoes" rumor and thought Elvis might be bigoted, got along great with the kid, and B.B. King, Jackie Wilson, and James Brown all admired him at least a little. They didn't lump him in with the Pat Boones of the world, they considered him someone who knew of what he sang.

YEAH, BUT . . . in the '60s Elvis would dump a woman in a second if he found out she'd ever dated a Black man. He once said he'd be damned if his daughter, Lisa Marie, would ever marry Black. This is the same Lisa Marie who was once married to Michael Jackson. He's probably safe.

So what's the verdict? Hell, you tell me. To be honest, before I got going on this story, practically the only thing I knew about Elvis Presley was that his ex-wife, Priscilla, was in the *Naked Gun* movies. I concur with Chuck—you could accurately say he didn't mean shit to me. But now, I think one of the reasons behind this guy's popularity is he's hard to pin down. He's different things to different people. To some fat housewife somewhere he's a hunk o' burnin' love, to another he's a sensitive child to be mothered. To many music critics he broke down racial barriers, to others he's a thief. Or a hero. Or a racist.

So Elvis' mind-set remains a question mark, but there is one thing my research has proven, one thing I can conclude with confidence: John Wayne was a radical right-wing S.O.B. who had the lowest opinion of Blacks imaginable. So Flavor Flav was right.

Some, but not all, of Brooklyn-based Chris Houghton's heroes do appear on stamps. Like Abbott and Costello, for instance. Those guys were really funny.

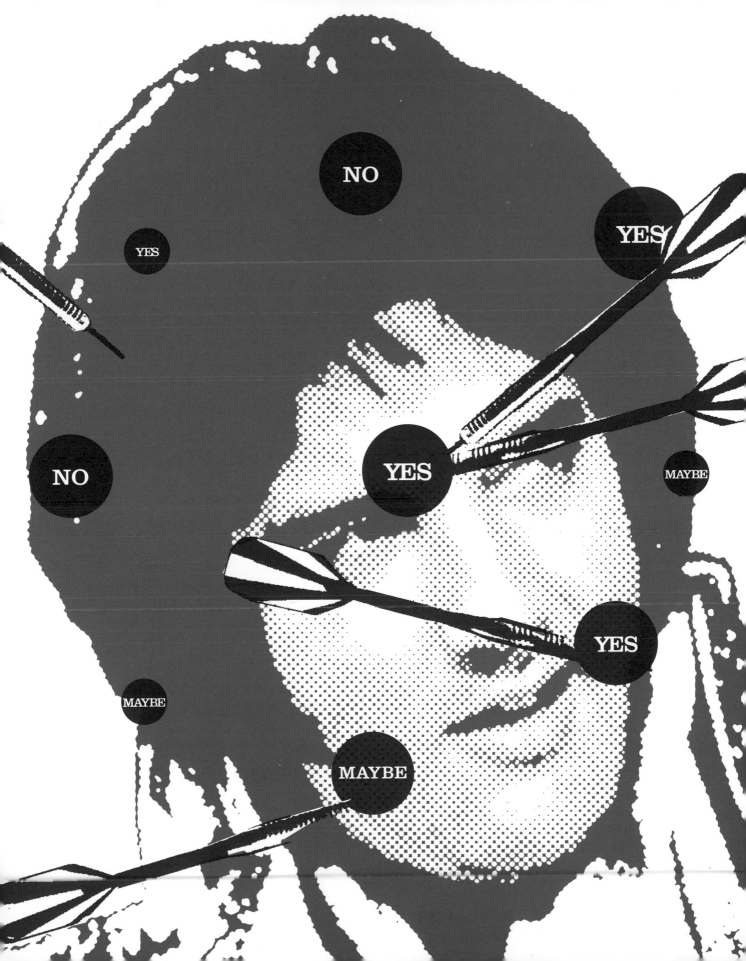

EGO TRIP'S TOP ROCK 'N' ROLL WHITE BOYS (AND GIRLS)... AND THEIR GREATEST RACIST MOMENTS.*

PHIL ANSELMO (PANTERA)

At a March 1995 show in Montreal, Anselmo angrily delivers a speech denouncing antiwhite rap acts, then goes on to equate the Black community's pleas for an end to Black-on-Black violence as, "basically saying it's okay to kill white people." He also announces, "This is our world, and tonight is a white thing."

Backstage after the show, the venue's five Black security guards are clearly upset with Anselmo, leading the singer to allegedly tell his own head of security, "Tell the niggers to stop eyeballing me." Two Black female fans of the band also visit Anselmo backstage to express their disappointment with his comments. Anselmo apologizes to them, but the fans remain unconvinced of his sincerity. One later tells the *Montreal Gazette,* "I'm not saying he's a white supremacist, but I think he isn't able to articulate himself properly and that he harbors racist views."

DAVID BOWIE

"Hitler was a terrible military strategist. But his overall objective was good. He was a tremendous morale booster." (*Playboy,* 1975)

ERIC CLAPTON

"[Y]ou know English people have a very big thing towards a spade. They really love that magic thing, the sexual thing. They all fall for that sort of thing. Everybody and his brother in England still sort of think that spades have big dicks." (*Rolling Stone,* 1968)

KURT COBAIN

"I have absolutely no respect for the English people. They make me sick. I thought I'd never say anything racist in my life, but those people are the most snooty, cocksure, anal people, and they have absolutely no regard for people's emotions. They don't think of other people as humans at all. They're the coldest people I've ever met." (*Come as You Are: The Story of Nirvana*, by Michael Azerrad. Main Street Books/Doubleday, 1993)

ELVIS COSTELLO

In March 1979 at a Columbus, Ohio, Holiday Inn, a belligerent Costello engages in an argument with members of Stephen Stills' touring entourage when he starts talking shit about America. When told by Stills' backup singer Bonnie Bramlett that his music owes a debt to American R&B, Costello responds by calling Ray Charles "a blind, ignorant nigger" and James Brown "another dumb nigger." A fight ensues in which Costello catches a bad one courtesy of Bramlett.

LIAM GALLAGHER (OASIS)

On a February 23, 1998, flight from Hong Kong to Australia on Cathay Pacific Airlines, a drunk Liam Gallagher gets into an altercation with a flight attendant over not receiving a complimentary scone. According to Oasis' tour manager, after a twenty-minute brouhaha, Gallagher eventually calms down and falls asleep. A day later, however, Gallagher is still ranting about the incident and is videotaped remarking about his Asian antagonist: "He told me to shut me mouth, and like carried on and on. And I do not like that. [He was] some panhead who wants [a] stabbing up the arse with a pickaxe." Gallagher is subsequently banned from Cathay Pacific fo' life.

IGGY POP**

"Ummm, I called a nigger a nigger in Massachusetts last week. That's pretty bold. You know what I mean? You just don't say that sort of stuff in front of 3,000 people. But he really was, I mean he was niggering. Niggering out, grabbing at my leg and microphone cord. I said 'Stop that, you damn nigger!' and that takes guts!" (*Heavy Metal Digest,* 1974)

COURTNEY LOVE

At a 1995 Hole gig at Madison Square Garden, CL makes a not-so-smooth move and attempts to get the audience to join in with her on a chant of "nigger." No one sees the need to participate. (FYI, New Yorkers prefer saying "nigga"—on their own time.)

JIM MORRISON

Three incidents involving the Lizard King's liberal use of the n-word are remembered in Jac Holzman and Gavan Daws' *Follow the Music: The Life and Times of Elektra Records in the Great*

Years of American Pop Culture (FirstMedia Books, 1998). The first involves Morrison standing drunk in the middle of Los Angeles' La Cienega Boulevard yelling at passersby, "You're all a bunch of niggers!" A second occurs at famed club the Whisky A Go-Go when, during a performance by a Black R&B act, Morrison stands on a table and yells, "Niggers! Fucking niggers can't sing! I can sing the blues better than you!"

The third also takes place at the Whisky. One night while seated with singer Eric Burdon in a booth listening to a visiting band, Morrison suddenly decides to take it to the stage. He climbs up and begins reciting poetry until the music stops and the musicians leave him alone. Then, as Burdon recalls,

[I]t turned very sour. Jim started to rap about provocation and about revolution. "You've all had your revolution and it's all over. And there'll never be another revolution, 'cause you're all niggers" . . . He went on and on about, "You're niggers," and nahnahnah, and silence fell over the club.

And then you could almost hear the hammer on this pistol from upstairs creak back. The old policeman, the private dick of the house, an old Black guy, he put his head out and drew a bead on Jim, and he said, "I'll give you niggers, you son of a bitch. Get off the fucking stage." By that time somebody called the police and they were there in seconds. [Jim] was bundled out the door, his shirt ripped off. And I think he actually broke loose from the cops on the street and slipped past them and took off bounding over the roofs of cars into the night.

NICO
"I said in Melody Maker to some interviewer that I didn't like [N]egroes. That's all. They took it so personally . . . although it's a whole different race. I mean, Bob Marley doesn't resemble a [N]egro, does he? . . . He's an archetype of Jamaican . . . but with the features like white people. I don't like the features [of Black people]. They're so much like animals . . . it's cannibals, no?" (New Wave Rock, 1979)

TED NUGENT
Nugent appears in a 1991 music video with Def Jam artist The Don for the song on which he plays guitar, "Big 12 Inch." The day of the shoot Nugent reputedly tells label head honcho Russell Simmons, "I'm a bigger nigger than you'll ever be."

Four years later in an interview with Grand Royal magazine, Nugent confirms the story.

THAT'S EXACTLY WHAT I SAID . . . I meant that I've got soul, that I don't resort to fuckin' electronic drumbeats, and I listen to James Brown and Wilson Pickett and Sam and Dave— THOSE ARE NIGGERS! THOSE ARE FUCKIN' SPIRITED, GENUINE AFRO-AMERICANS . . . BECAUSE THE BLACK GUYS WITH THIS RAP, ELECTRONIC, MAKE-BELIEVE TALENTLESS MUSIC MAKE ME WANT TO THROW UP! WHERE'S THE SOUL?

NIKKI SIXX (MÖTLEY CRÜE)
November 6, 1997. At a show in Greensboro, North Carolina, the Crüe's bassist, Nikki Sixx, sees a Black security guard harassing fans near the stage. Sixx begins directing racial slurs at the guard, then urges fans to attack the guard. A fan's videotape captures Sixx's subsequent verbal barrage. Sixx yells:

You're a big fucking Black man. You feel pretty good beating up a little girl. Fuck you! You know what, you mother-fuckers? Kick this fucking guy's ass. Kick this motherfucker's ass. There's more of you than there is of him.

How's that feel, asshole, you fucking nigger? Don't call me fucking racist, man, because then you are a fucking nigger, because nobody treats another human being like that! Suck my dick!

EDDIE VAN HALEN***
Charles R. Cross' Heavier Than Heaven: A Biography of Kurt Cobain (Hyperion, 2001) details an unfortunate encounter between the members of Nirvana and Eddie Van Halen. Backstage at Nirvana's December 1993 show at the Forum in Inglewood, California, Eddie shows up itchin' to jam with the band. Unfortunately, the famed fret-master is so sloshed that everyone blows him off, telling him

there are no extra guitars for him to play. Pointing out Black guitarist Pat Smear, Eddie says, "Well, then let me play the Mexican's guitar. What is he, is he Mexican? Is he Black?" His rant continues into what's described by an observer as "racist, homophobic banter, typical redneck [stuff]." Fed up with Van Halen's rambling, Cobain exits in disgust.

HONORABLE MENTION: OZZY OSBOURNE
"When we first played America with [Black] Sabbath, and we did Philadelphia, nobody had ever seen us or heard of us, and when I got onstage, two-thirds of the audience were Black guys. I'm thinkin', we've come to the wrong gig, man. There's this guy on the side of the stage shouting, 'Hey you, Black Sabbath.' He thought my name was Black Sabbath, this guy. Halfway through the show I said, 'What do you want, man?' He says, 'You guys ain't Black.' He fuckin' did, man. I'm going, 'What have we done?' Our first tour of America and I'm thinking, this is fuckin' weird, man. We've come to the wrong gig. Twenty-five white guys are going to get stabbed on the way out." (For the Record: Black Sabbath, edited by Dave Marsh)

---

*By the way, racist or not, all you mutha-fuckas rawk! Yeah!

**But also gets props for the insightful remark, "I don't like white American girls. They talk funny, and they tend not to have butts." (Blender, 2001)

***Actually, technically only half white boy. (Consult the Almost Asian list, page 69)

DON CORNELIUS' FAVORITE FUNKY WHITE BOYS (AND GIRLS!).

10. MOSE ALLISON

9. MICHAEL MCDONALD

8. FRANK SINATRA

7. ERIC CLAPTON
"They say he's funky. I guess because of his reputation."

6. JOE COCKER

5. STING

4. DAVID BOWIE
"He's married to a sista. He's gotta be funky."

3. BONNIE RAITT

2. MICK JAGGER

1. JAMES TAYLOR
"He's the funkiest I've ever seen . . . the funkiest nigga that ever walked."

HONORABLE MENTIONS:
Teena Marie ("Deep in her heart she's not even white"), Eminem, Elton John, and Kid Rock.

The creator and original host of television's longest-running syndicated program, Soul Train, Don Cornelius is a living legend who knows funk. Bow down and recognize, Dick (Clark).

STATION TO STATION: DON WELCOMES THE THIN WHITE DUKE TO *SOUL TRAIN*, 1976.

10 MOMENTS IN REGGAE THAT WERE NOT 100 PERCENT ONE LOVE.

BY THE DUBWISER

1978

The Clash makes beautiful music with JA dubmasters Scratch Perry and Mikey Dread, but when the UK rude boys actually go to Jamaica, they strike a sour note. Their second album, *Give 'Em Enough Rope*, opens with a pissed-off postcard from yard's, "Safe European Home": "I went to the place where every white face is an invitation to robbery / I'm sitting here in my safe European home / I don't wanna go back there again."

1980

Yellowman's "Mr. Chin" describes interracial love between an albino and a Chinese girl in less than politically correct terms: "Him have one daughter / She name Ting Ling / Me make love to her / Hear the girl start sing / Ooh long Chong long / Ooh long Chong long long."

1981

While house-sitting at Keith Richards' vacation home in Ocho Rios, Jamaica, Peter Tosh takes a liking to the place and decides to stay, ignoring Richards' telephone calls until this exchange took place, as recorded in Timothy White's book *Catch a Fire*:

Keith: "I'm coming down to the house. I need it for myself."
Peter: "If yuh come anywhere near here, I'll shoot yuh."
Keith: "You'd better make sure you know how to use that gun and make sure you get the fucking magazine the right way 'round, cos I'm gonna be there in half an hour."

1982

On a *Saturday Night Live* skit, Eddie Murphy portrays a Rastafarian musician named Tyrone Green who sings a reggae song that goes, "Kill the white people / But buy my record first," before a horrified VFW talent show audience.

1984

Scratch Perry's shaky allegiance with Island Records founder Chris Blackwell disintegrates when he tells a reporter from the *N.M.E.*:

You know, that Chris Blackwell disgusts me. He makes me want to

vomit. He invited me to the opening of the Compass Point studio in Nassau and there I saw him drink the blood of a freshly killed chicken. He thought I was into all that voodoo and obeah, and offered me some."

Perry later releases the song "Chris Blackwell Is a Vampire."

1987

Before a 1987 trial to sort out Bob Marley's estate, Danny Sims—who signed Marley to a publishing deal in 1968 and has been known to dismiss reggae as "jungle music"—explains his strategy for guiding the Rastafarian singer's career: "I discouraged Bob from doing the revolutionary stuff. I'm a commercial guy. I want to sell songs to thirteen-year-old girls, not to guys throwing spears."

1995

Two Caucasian journalists visit a three-day Niyabinghi session in a remote section of Spanish Town, on the outskirts of Kingston, Jamaica. A Niyabinghi is a gathering of Rastafarian faithful who sit around an enormous bonfire, smoke herb, and pound out a steady drumbeat while chanting down the wicked forces of Babylon. The word Niyabinghi means "death to white oppressors," although some Rastas add "Black *and* white oppressors." On this particular night, the exact meaning isn't quite clear. "That fire is for you," one agitated young Rasta tells the white visitors, thoroughly freaking them out. Several hours later, the very same Rasta climbs up on top of the roaring fire and burns himself up.

1996

Beenie Man drops science on his song "Africans," bigging-up certain downtrodden brothers in Babylon. "O. J. Simpson one thing mi did warn yuh / Say fi stick to yuh own kind / Yuh switch from yuh kind / And yuh nearly serve time / Now you bust the case / Put a smile pon your face and join the repatriation / Rodney King, look how bad dem beat him / 'Pon public television / Full time we get it straight / Dem nuh like we race / Mek we pack up and leave dis place."

1998

Sizzla unnerves the largely white crowd at Jamaica's biggest international music festival, Reggae Sumfest in Montego Bay, by proclaiming, "Fire burn all white people in Jamaica!" He also summons down fire on local newspapers, the Sumfest stage and backstage, and the queen of England.

2001

During a hotly contested final round of the World Clash between the Japanese sound Mighty Crown and the Jamaican sound Bass Odyssey, things get a bit ugly. One dubplate, Elephant Man, disses the "Chiney man from Mighty Crown with the squeeze-up eye." And Squingy from Bass Odyssey calls Mighty Crown "some likkle Japs." To which Mighty Crown replies by making fun of his rotten teeth and saying that he looks like "the perfect crackhead."

The Dubwiser is very wise. And, boy, he really can shoot a basketball, seen?

YELLOW RAP BASTARDIZATION: A BRIEF HISTORY OF RAP RECORDINGS THAT RIDICULE 'RIENTALS.

ILLUSTRATION BY NATHAN FOX

"DANA DANE WITH FAME"—DANA DANE (PROFILE, 1987)
The earliest recorded hip hop moment explicitly offensive to Asians. Recounting an intimate episode with a female companion, Dana rhymes, "Rocked it once / She said, 'Dana, please!' / I rocked it once again / She started talking Japanese / 'Choy yoi yoi yoi yoi yoi yoi / Choy yoi yoi yoi yoooiii! / Choy yoi yoi yoi ch-choy ch-choy / A-chig-a-chig-choy choy choy!' " (We're no linguists, but we're pretty sure that last part isn't really Japanese.)

"IWO JIMA"—FROZEN EXPLOSION (B-BOY, 1987)
Leave it to an obscure, guido-looking white rapper from the Midwest to take Nippon mockery to the next level. "Iwo Jima" is a mysterious Japanese cat who cold rocks the party every time he sings his whiny theme song—a tune four times more offensive than Dana Dane's faux Far Eastern improv (mainly because it's repeated in quadruplicate, aight?)

"ON THE BUGGED TIP"—BIG DADDY KANE FEATURING SCOOB LOVER (COLD CHILLIN', 1988)
Kane's sidekick Scoob dogged Asian cuisine stereotypes when he yelped, "Now now now I'ma place a order for a Scooby snack / Not at the Chinese restaurant because I don't eat cats." Not without duck sauce, anyways.

"CHINESE DELIVERY"—SHAZZY (ELEKTRA, 1990)
This thirty-five-second skit on the female rapper's debut album consists of a Chinese food deliveryman sputtering a few words in broken English over a nervous drum track. His career in rap lasted about as long as Shazzy's.

"BLACK KOREA"—ICE CUBE (PRIORITY, 1991)
O'Shea's *Death Certificate* tirade against Korean shopkeepers who mistreat their Black patrons is the stuff great hate is made of, and features morsels of inspired ignorance like, "So don't follow me up and down your market / Or your little chop suey ass will be a target / Of the nationwide boycott." Cube's Asian bashing resurfaces on two other songs from the album—the anti–jungle fever diatribe "Horny Lil' Devil" ("Go down to the corner store and beat the Jap up"), and the call for Black unity "Us" ("Too much backstabbin' / While I look out the window I see all the Japs grabbin' / Every vacant lot in my neighborhood"). Too bad no one was grabbin' all the vacant seats in the movie theater that week *Ghosts of Mars* was playing.

"I SHOT YA (REMIX)"—LL COOL J FEATURING KEITH MURRAY, PRODIGY, FAT JOE, AND FOXY BROWN (DEF JAM, 1995)
A posse extravaganza notable for Foxy's grammatically-botched, rhyme-challenged, racially-insensitive lines, "Thug niggaz give they minks to [sic] chinks / Slow down, we sip drinks, rockin' minks [sic]." A shame she didn't get her lyrics *from* Jay-Z. (And if she did, shame on a Hova.)

UNTITLED SKIT FROM *THE SCORE*—FUGEES (COLUMBIA, 1996)
This Fugees' album was a multi-zillion certified smash, so chances are you've heard the ignorant interlude in which a Chinese takeout proprietor talks like a badly dubbed character from an old school kung fu flick and whyles out on his customers for no good reason. But hopefully most of y'all just skipped it because you couldn't wait to hear "Fu-gee-la" one mo' time *again*. Ooh la la la!

"SHANGHAI"—CAM'RON (UNTERTAINMENT, 1998)
It's hell up in Harlem for some Asian gangsters running an illegal business out of a local storefront when Cam'Ron finds out. Demanding a piece of their action, Cam unleashes venomous lines like, "Blam, that's for the chink that flipped / And grabbed me like Spock on some Bruce Lee shit" over a cacophonous Far Eastern melody while a presumably Asian woman screams bloody murder in the background.

"DIDDY"—P. DIDDY AND THE BAD BOY FAMILY (BAD BOY, 2001)
Puffy's boast, "My aim is winnin' / Got Asian women that'll change my linen / After I done blazed and hit 'em," got him in hot water with Asian-American activists. We can't figure out why, since everybody knows illegal Latinos wash all the dirty laundry these days. Duh, Diddy. (Or, to quote Run-D.M.C., "Dumb Diddy Dumb Diddy Diddy Diddy Dumb Dumb.")

MOST DISHONORABLE MENTION:
In December 1995, DJ Funkmaster Flex drops an inadvertent bomb when he makes a derogatory joke about "slanty-eyed" Asians being poor drivers during his radio program on New York station Hot 97. News of Flex's comments sparks outcry from the Committee Against Anti-Asian Violence and the American Civil Liberties Union, and Flex issues a public apology.

N-WORD UP!

ROCK SONGS BY WHITES THAT EMPLOY "NIGGERS."

"ALMOST BLACK"—JAMES WHITE AND THE BLACKS (ZE, 1979) "Well, he's almost Black / Thaaat niggggaaa's white! / Well, he's got some moves / But they ain't right!"

"BLACK TRAIN"—GUN CLUB (RUBY, 1981) "Torn up on the Black Train / Torn from my southern home / Left a nigger lying dead by the river / Left the will o' the wisp to roam."

"DEVIL AND THE NIGGER"—GUN CLUB (SYMPATHY FOR THE MUSIC INDUSTRY, 1997) "The nigger and the devil / Meet down in New Orleans / He's worked so hard for so many years / Wasn't gonna get down on his knees."

"FOR THE LOVE OF IVY"—GUN CLUB (RUBY, 1981) "Well, jawbone eat and jawbone talk / Jawbone eat you with a knife and fork / I was hunting for niggers down in the dark / When suddenly I got a better thought."

"HURRICANE"—BOB DYLAN (COLUMBIA, 1976) "The judge made Rubin's witnesses drunkards from the slums / To the white folks who watched he was a revolutionary bum / And to the Black folks he was just a crazy nigger / No one doubted that he pulled the trigger."

"IRRESPONSIBLE HATE ANTHEM"—MARILYN MANSON (NOTHING / INTERSCOPE, 1996) "Everybody's someone else's nigger / I know you are, so am I / I wasn't born with enough middle fingers / I don't need to choose a side."

"LOS ANGELES"—X (SLASH, 1980) "She had to leave Los Angeles / All her toys wore out in black / And her boys had, too / She started to hate / Every nigger and Jew / Every Mexican that gave her a lot of shit / Every homosexual and the idle rich."

"NIGGER"—CLAWFINGER (METAL BLADE, 1994) "Goddamn, my man, you see I can't understand / Why you wanna say 'nigger' to your brother man / Talking Black pride then you call yourself a 'nigger' / Don't bring yourself down cuz it just don't figure."

"OLIVER'S ARMY"—ELVIS COSTELLO (COLUMBIA, 1979) "All it takes is one itchy trigger / One more widow / One less white nigger."

"ONE IN A MILLION"—GUNS N' ROSES (GEFFEN, 1988) "Police and niggers, that's right, get out of my way / Don't need to buy none of your
g o l d

"REDNECKS"—RANDY NEWMAN (REPRISE, 1974) "We're rednecks, rednecks / And we don't know our ass from a hole in the ground / We're rednecks, we're rednecks / keeping the niggers down."

chains / I today / I don't need no bracelets clamped in front of my back / Just need my ticket / till then won't you cut me some slack?"

"ROCK 'N' ROLL NIGGER"—PATTI SMITH (ARISTA, 1978) "Baby, baby is a rock-and-roll nigger / Jimi Hendrix was a nigger / Jesus Christ and Grandma, too / Jackson Pollock was a nigger / Nigger, nigger, nigger, nigger, nigger, nigger, nig-ger, nigger, nigger, nigger, nigger."

"SAINT HUCK"—NICK CAVE AND THE BAD SEEDS (MUTE/ELEKTRA, 1984) "Straight in the arms of the city goes Huck / Down the beckonin' streets of op-po-tunity / Whistling his favorite river-song . . . /And a bad-blind nigger at the piano."

"THEY AIN'T MAKIN' JEWS LIKE JESUS ANYMORE"—KINKY FRIEDMAN (ABC-DUNHILL, 1974) "He says, 'I ain't a racist but Aristotle Onassis is one Greek we don't need / And them niggers, Jews, and Sigma Nus, all they ever do is breed.'"

"WALTER WESTINGHOUSE"—THE RESIDENTS (RALPH, 1976) "He said, 'Your trust is like a crust / Too brittle and too thin' / I said, 'You're full of nigger nuts / Afrd look like Rin Tin Tin.'"

"WE'VE GOT A BIGGER PROBLEM NOW"—DEAD KENNEDYS (ALTERNATIVE TENTACLES, 1981) "Ku Klux Klan will control you / Still you think it's natural / Nigger knockin for the master race / Still you wear the happy face."

"WHO IS THE CULPRIT AND WHO IS THE VICTIM?"—SNAKEFINGER (RALPH, 1979) "Which is the model, which is the nigger and which is the chief?" and which is the rose / Which is the merchant and which is the thief / Which is the nigger and which is the chief."

WHOLE BLOODY DISCOGRAPHY—SKREWDRIVER (TRIPLE X, 1987)* Sample lyric: "Oi, oi, oi / Nigger, nigger, nigger / Oi, oi, oi."

"WHORES"—JANE'S ADDICTION (TRIPLE X, 1987)* "Way down low where the streets get bigger / I find my fun with the freaks and the niggers."

"WOMAN IS THE NIGGER OF THE WORLD"—JOHN LENNON (CAPITOL, 1975) "Woman is the nigger of the world / Yes she is . . . think about it / Woman is the nigger of the world / Think about it . . . do something about it."

HONORABLE MENTIONS:
"I AM THE WALRUS"—THE BEATLES (APPLE, 1968) John Lennon's line, "Boy, you've been a naughty girl, you let your knickers down," sounds a lot like, "Boy, you've been a naughty girl, you let your niggas down."

"WALK ON THE WILD SIDE"—LOU REED (RCA, 1972) Sweet Lou refers to his backup singers as "the colored girls," though in fact said vocalists were a triumvirate of vanilla, UK-bred heifers known as the Thunder Thighs.

*During the first Lollapalooza tour, Jane's Addiction brings out Ice-T to perform a rendition of Sly & the Family Stone's "Don't Call Me Nigger, Whitey (Don't Call Me Nigger)." Perry Farrell sings the white part, Ice-T sings the Black part. Black quartet Living Colour comes onstage afterward, and bandleader Vernon. Reid announces, "I'll never be anyone's nigger for entertainment . . ."

Darryl Jenifer

Here's the scenario: four jazz-fusion-jamming brothas—two of them actual siblings for real—from various Washington, D.C.-area Blackburbs get a whiff of ye new English phunk (à la the Sex Pistols) back in 1977. The accomplished musical youth figure, shoot, if them limeys can do this without even playing their instruments half right, then, as Brandy might say, what about us? Said baaad-ass cats soon thereafter become, well . . . *punks*; vocalist Paul "Hunting Rod" Hudson, his drummer brother Earl, guitarist Gary "Dr. Know" Miller, and bassist Darryl Jenifer flip their band's name from Mind Power to Bad Brains, and the world of hard and heavy rock 'n' roll (and, yes, mon, reggae!) is never the same.

With twenty-years'-plus worth of hardcore touring under his bass strap, Darryl Jenifer's been around the world more than Biggie, Diddy, Ma$e, and Lisa Stansfield—combined. Here, he kicks down three close encounters with that naughty "n-word" (or words of a "nigger-ish"/"nigga-ish" nature). Peep the science. It ain't nothin' nice—cuz people could have been killed (or at least punched in the face).

NIGGER-ISH / NIGGA-ISH GIBBERISH DEATH WISHES:
BAD BRAINS' DARRYL JENIFER RECALLS A TRIFECTA OF TALES FROM THE DARK SIDE.
PHOTO BY STRENPHOTO

PART 1: THE GETAWAY

We played this show down in Atlanta that I'll never forget. It was a blistering post-Brains, *Quickness*-era concert, with a whole house full of white boys kicking their own primal version of getting buck wizzy. Although that mosh shit has always been a mystery to me, it is fun to watch it all from the stage, especially when you're the cat holding the throttle.

Anyway, the show went on and, as usual, ended with one of H.R.'s perfect-10 back flips. Blooooodclot!

As I dried off backstage, I noticed a couple of skinhead characters fucking around outside our dressing room, so I gave them a Rasta-inspired "Yo!" I then heard a "yo" back at me, but this voice had a chipper, country girl's twang. I craned my head around the corner only to see three skinhead beyotches—one big, stout-looking heifer, and two sexy-ass skinhead babes who looked like they jumped straight out of a *Nazi Youth Camp Weekly* center-fold. The finest one spoke up first.

"You guys are really great. I saw y'all one time up in Carsboro," she said. Then her monsterlike friend (homegirl had short jet-black hair and rocked Spock-like sideburns, crazy tattoos, and fucked-up, big-ass boots; her fingers were all nubbed out from fighting, begging, and putting out Marlboros) said, with that typical, wild-eyed "I wanna meet the band, dude" flair, "Y'all played at my school with Fishbone!" The heifer then looked to her flyest friend and said (to me), "She [the fine one] plays the bass and can't believe she is talking to you!" Oh, word? I said to myself.

The next thing you know, Shorty started to get a bit frisky on a brother, trying with all her redneck charm to get me to take her home. We, of course, kept things conversational and friendly. Then, from out of nowhere, I felt the weight of somebody's eyes tickling my neck. I turned to discover an angry, hillbilly-looking, bald-headed motherfucker clocking me. I looked at Shorty and spoke my mind: "Yo, do you know this motherfucker?"

"Fuck him," Shorty said. "That's my boyfriend—he's an asshole boyfriend!"

So, here I am, somewhere waaay down South—and I'm like, "You better go talk to this dude . . ."

But homeboy, nonetheless, worked his way over to me and spoke his mind: "You know what? I like your band about this much," he said, leaving maybe an inch between his index finger and thumb. I swung right back with, "Word? Well, I like your bald head about this much," leaving even less air between my fingers.

By this time the tension was extremely high and I could feel that at any moment somebody was gonna get smacked. And I was waitin' for dude to hit me in the head with a coupla swift "niggers" (I could damn near feel 'em ooze out of his pores). Then Hitler's Mr. Clean came back with "I like your fucking dreads about this much."

Cut to: me physically thrusting this punk out of my face, which happened five seconds before our tour bus rounds the corner and my man Dr. Know screamed, "Yo, let's go, nigga!"

I laughed my ass off and ran across the damp Southern street and jumped on the bus. I looked out the window and saw Shorty sadly waving good-bye. I wasn't so sad. Although somebody finally did call me the n-word that night.

PART 2: DOUBLE DEUTSCH BUSTED
We were in Germany, early 1980s, at a polytechnic or some shit. The infamous Bad Brains onstage dub'n' it up with H.R. on guitar, along with Doc, Earl, our roadie Kindu on bass, and I was DJing radical yard styles when I noticed a stoutly German fellow standing right in front of me in the crowd. Mind you, this was a small college gig with no stage, so me and Hans were somewhat eye to eye, as I "bongdid-dled" on.

Boom! Hans unexpectedly lifted his sixty-ounce stein and flung every drop of his brew in my motherfuckin' face. My eyes were burning from some deep carbonation, my shirt and crown drenched down with brew.

Boom! I ran behind the amps, wiped my face off with a T-shirt, then leaped out into the crowd like a moonshine-tipsy, inbred hunter. I immediately went into a sort of a semi-crouch so my six-foot-five-inch frame wouldn't give me away. As all of this started to unfold, the band continued to jam along; they were so caught up in the tunes that they didn't see this sun get splashed.

I quickly spotted Hans—he was laughing and chatting with his comrades, so I crept up on their man and took a K9-type, twisted grip hold on his bandanna—which was conveniently tied around his neck. We then began to spin around like a helicopter ("North Carolina!"), me going, "What the fuck is your problem?" and him screaming something garbled in German (I *think* I heard "nigger" scrambled in there). I twirled his stupid ass a number of revolutions before I let him go. I then stood there in the crowd, out of breath and totally in panic mode—the whole crowd started to surround me, yelling shit in German (I'm sure they threw a coupla "niggers" in there for good measure). Right flush in front of me stood three of Hans' crew.

Boom! I saw Hans' head pop up behind one of his buddies—and at that split second someone burned the back of my arm with a fucking cigarette!

Boom! I instantly jabbed homeboy with the right cross of ages (as if I had boxing skills). This jab was so leveled that I didn't feel the center of Hans' face—but saw it and him explode in a bloody, broken white-boy nose-bridge mess. I broke back to the bus and said, "Stupid motherfuckers!"

PART 3: PAYBLACK'S A MUTHA
Nineteen hundred and eighty-nine. Paris, France. I believe Fishbone was playing, too. After the gig, we skipped back to the hotel for a little shower action. The band's chaperone, or, better yet, our French connection, told us that there was a reggae club that we should check out. So me, a couple of homies, and Soundgarden's drummer's sister, who was a very nice girl, went to the spot and walked around for a bit. Of course, there wasn't one Jamaican to be found—wall-to-wall African brothers; shiny Somalian warlord-looking motherfuckers—these gentlemen made a Black American motherfucker like myself feel white. Made Bernie Mac look light-skinded. These fellas were straight-up purple. You feel me?

Right off the bat, niggaz was peepin' me out. They saw me with this little redheaded girl; they gave me that you're-not-one-of-us look. They were pumping much Bob Marley—which is dope—but I was wanting to hear some rub-a-dub, too. At that point, I said to Shorty Redhead, "Look, let's break out and get some crepes or something." When we stepped out of the club to get a cab, I saw this six-foot-eight, Black Senegalese cat and a little shriveled-up French girl who looked like she smoked fifteen packs of Gitanes a day. The dude looked up at me as I got into the taxi and said, with the thickest, mildly feminine French accent, "Fucking cotton pickhurrre!"

He kinda threw me off. And I didn't say anything at the time because he was really big—my man had tribal scars. He was the type of motherfucker who probably had a huge spear in the trunk of his tiny Renault. He looked like a Black-ass version of Seal, if you ask me. Whatever. I didn't say it then, but I'll say it now: Fuck you, you Black bastard!!

NIGGAZ WIT' AMPLIFIERS:
EGO TRIP'S HARDEST ROCKING BLACKS OF ALL TIME.

1 IKE TURNER. JUST ASK TINA. OR NAT. **2** ROBERT JOHNSON. THE DEVIL DONE MADE HIM DO IT. **3** JIMI HENDRIX. FROM SEATTLE TO LIVERPOOL, THIS PSYCHEDELIC "MONKEY" (WHO'S GONE TO HEAVEN) SHINES. WORD TO PETER TORK. **4** BAD BRAINS. NOT BAD MEANIN' BAD, BUT BAD MEANIN' GOOD. (A GOOD CAN OF WHOOP-ASS FROM THE PIT, WHITEY. YES, RAS!) **5** (TIE) PAT SMEAR. (THE GERMS, NIRVANA, AND FOO FIGHTERS) / LITTLE RICHARD. EACH IS STRONG ENOUGH TO KEEP THE WHITE MAN IN CHECK. BUT BUILT LIKE A POWERFUL BLACK WOMAN. YOU GO, GIRLS. **6** (TIE) POLY STYRENE. (X-RAY SPEX) / TINA TURNER. THESE TWISTED SISTAS KNEW HOW TO WORK IT OUT. (ASK IKE. OR SID. OR SID'S BOO, NANCY.) **7** SLY STONE. THAT SAN FRANCISCO TREAT. **8** CHARLEY PRIDE. YOU GOTTA BE HARD BEING A BLACK MAN DOING COUNTRY MUSIC AT THE GRAND OLE OPRY. (HOWEVER, WE'RE NOT SURE IF CP EVER APPEARED ON THE GRAND OLE *OPRAH*. SHAME ON A NUH IF HE DIDN'T.) **9** FUNKADELIC. HARD DRUGS. **10** PHIL LYNOTT. (THIN LIZZIE) HE WAS BLACK IRISH (HAM HOCKS AND SHAMROCKS UP IN HERE). HE MADE "JOHNNY THE FOX" (A BREAKBEAT CLASSIC). HE SHOT HEROIN IN THE VEINS OF HIS FEET (TOO BAD THE LUCK OF THE IRISH DID HIM IN). NOW, THAT'S *REALLY* GANGSTA! **11** HALF OF SLASH. (GUNS N' ROSES) / HALF OF TOM MORELLO. (RAGE AGAINST THE MACHINE) MISCEGENATION ROCKS AND RULES, DUDE. **12** PRINCE. BLACK POWER, PURPLE PASSION. MINNESOTA PHATS. **13** MICHAEL JACKSON. BECAUSE HE WANTS TO ROCK WITH YOU. ALL NIGHT.

MESSAGE TO LENNY: YOU ONLY ROCK AS HARD AS YOU HAVE TO. WHEN WILL WE SEE YOU (ROCK) AGAIN?

FIGHT MUSIC: THE BEATLES' WHITE ALBUM VERSUS PRINCE'S BLACK ALBUM.

There's a riot goin' on in your record collection. A race riot. Whether you're the type of guy that maintains his music in a state of stylistic segregation, or a freethinking audiophile who lets Slave (a Black group, of course) cozy up next to Slayer (a band of rowdy whites and a scary Chilean) in predestined alphabetical order, know this: all those grooves aren't in sync. The ultimate stand-off in this colorful sound clash: The Beatles' *White Album* (Apple, 1968) versus Prince's *Black Album* (Paisley Park, 1987)—two opuses positioned at opposite ends of the rhythm-and-hues rainbow; the former an official white-meat classic, the latter a black market mainstay 2 real 4 Sam Goody. That's right—a fight, a fight, a fight, a Black weirdo, and four whites.

THE BEATLES	PRINCE
THAT ELUSIVE JE NE SAIS QUOI	
$34.98 at a Coconuts near you.	Try eBay, ummy-day.

ADVANTAGE: Prince. Blacks only buy bootlegs.

WORKLOAD	
Beatles (there's four of them): 30 songs (count 'em).	Prince (there's one of him—not including "Jamie Starr," "Camille," "Spooky Electric," and other sexually ambiguous alter egos in the Purple One's mirror): 8 songs.

ADVANTAGE: Prince. Those lazy limeys should have thirty-two bangers between the Fab Four of 'em. Proof again, Blacks always work (and pimp) harder.

SONG ABOUT COVETING REAL LIVE BROADS	
"Dear Prudence"	"Cindy C."
—about Mia Farrow's sister, Prudence Farrow.	—about supermodel Cindy Crawford.

ADVANTAGE: Prince. He seen more white tail than Ted Nugent, Scott Baio, and Spencer Tunick combined.

SONG ABOUT FUCKING . . . IN PUBLIC	
"Why Don't We Do It in the Road?"	"Rock Hard in a Funky Place"

ADVANTAGE: Beatles. Paul gets gangsta on that ass. Plus, whites can get away with that sweet, that nasty, that gushy stuff. Doin' it in the park? Oh, yeah. Doin' it if you're dark? Oh, no!

"Back in the U.S.S.R."
—clowns the Beach Boys, whom they made irrelevant.

"Dead on It"
—clowns rappers, who ultimately made him irrelevant.

ADVANTAGE: Beatles. Black-on-Black crime never wins.

SELF-REFERENTIAL NOD & WINK MOMENT

"Glass Onion"
—a veggie medley of past hits.

"2 Nigs United 4 West Compton"
—begins with a musical reference to "Housequake."

ADVANTAGE: Beatles. Nigs united? *Nigro, please.*

WHO YA JACKIN'?

"Ob-La-Di, Ob-La-Da"
—title ripped off from Black singer Jimmy Scott.

"Superfunkycalifragisexy"
—title ripped off from *Mary Poppins.*

ADVANTAGE: Prince. It's about time a Black man took something from a white lady other than her purse.

"BLACKEST" MOMENT

"Blackbird"
—a song that Charles Manson interpreted as a call to arms for Blacks to rise up and kill whitey.

"Bob George"
—a song in which Prince portrays some crazy motherfucker who talks shit about his manager, orders his lady around, and gets into a shoot-out when the cops show up.

ADVANTAGE: Beatles. Contrary to popular belief, whites, not niggas, are scared of revolution.

LEGACY

White Album's double-LP length symbolized that the Fab Four were losing touch with one another and going in different artistic and personal directions.

To Prince, the *Black Album* symbolized the evil, dark side of his soul. To everyone else, it symbolized Prince finally losing his mind. (He later attempted to dissuade consumers from buying it with a subliminal message in the "Alphabet Street" video—it read, "Don't buy the *Black Album.* I'm sorry.")

ADVANTAGE: Beatles. Whites have nuthin' to be sorry about. Ha-ha!

WINNER: The Beatles. Though it's close, four pasty farts take a piss on Paisley Park. Celebrate the hate.

MO' COLORFUL MATCHUPS

PRIMUS
THE BROWN ALBUM
(INTERSCOPE, 1997)
VERSUS
A LIGHTER SHADE OF BROWN
BROWN & PROUD
(PUMP, 1990)
WINNER: A LIGHTER SHADE OF BROWN.
Lightweight L.A. Chicano hip hoppers snatch the brown crown over Les Claypool and (white) company like it's *Milagro Beanfield War II.*

BLACK UHURU
RED
(MANGO, 1981)
VERSUS
REDBONE
COME AND GET YOUR REDBONE (THE BEST OF REDBONE)
(EPIC, 1975)
WINNER: BLACK UHURU.
Classic blunted Black Rasta gospel tops the provocatively named, peace-pipe partying Native American funky bunch by a natty dread.

THE SIMPSONS
THE YELLOW ALBUM
(GEFFEN, 1981)
VERSUS
YELLA
ONE MO NIGGA TA GO
(STREET LIFE, 1996)
DRAW:
Cartoon yellow white people and N.W.A.'s lost light-skinded boardsman make equally unlistenable albums, thus demonstrating that each should stick to what they do best. S'son fam: running TV comedy forever and ever. Yella: quietly fading into obscurity.

LIGHT-SKINDED VERSUS DARK-SKINDED: A (SK)IN-DEPTH DEBATE ON BLACKS IN HIP HOP.

The world is filled with pimps and hoes—and colors, too. But we're not talking the kind that you find in a Crayola box, on a peacock, or on the streets of Concrete Gangland, U.S.A. We're talking various shades of Black.

Let us tell you something about Blackness—grits and cornbread, how can you act this? Unless, by chance, you somehow missed *School Daze* (or any Spike Lee joint for that matter—Ya dig? Sho' 'nuff!), you must know that our light-skinded brothas and sistas and our dark-skinded brothas and sistas don't always see eye to eye. The great debate over which pigment gets the most props has never been fully determined. Until now.

Who better to dissect this dilemma and explore these issues than *ego trip*'s founding poppas: crazy-sexy-cool-large, "Satchmo" Jenkins and "Belafonte" Wilson? Their weapons? Great Black brains and the skin that they're in. Their playing field? The light-skinded/dark-skinded duos of the rap entertainment world.*

Let the race games begin. Blow, Satch, blow. Run, Jesse, run.

*Fuck Kris Kross.

ROUND 1: KID 'N PLAY

BELAFONTE: This is a classic group right here. Kid had a high top fade. Come on, no question.

SATCHMO: Play, he's dark-skinded. And in real life it turns out he's the player, you know what I'm sayin'? In real life he was getting more ass than Kid!

B: Kid had more talent, though. I mean look at him—Kid's fade drew the people in! Who's the marketable guy? Kid. The movies and all that Hollywood shit—you think that would've happened to two dark-skinded niggaz?

S: It's all about the darker-skinded brothas, man.

B: When Kid 'N Play fell off, where was Play? He's a failed entrepreneur. He lost his little clothing shop in Flushing, but Kid was still shining! On Grand Puba's album, *2000*, he was flippin' the hooks, singin'! And he's got shit to say. He was on *Politically Incorrect*.

S: The only reason Kid's barely getting over now is because he's light-skinded and people remember what his ass looks like and he gets into clubs for free.

B: Play is a grown-ass Black man. What kind of Black man would call himself "Play"? There's no time to play in America for the Black man! Shit is fucked up!

WINNER: BELAFONTE

ROUND 2: LORD TARIQ AND PETER GUNZ

S: You got no argument here, man. Your man looks weird!

B: He's the nicest one! He got his own deal for his own album. Tariq's deal was with Money Boss Players. Peter Gunz got his own album!

S: Lord Tariq is a God. He always shines. What is your man, some type of Puerto Rican? Is your man even Black?

B: Yeah, he's Black. Somehow. Forget that, we're all Black! The fact is that Tariq was in the underground for a long time, he didn't do shit, never got a deal—

S: Cuz he's not light-skinded!

B: Gunz comes in, energizes the whole act, sells the duo and everyone's talk-ing—Columbia signs 'em!

S: Colonel Sanders is his grandfather, that's why! Aight? They're on some Kentucky Fried Chicken shit.

B: Yo, light-skinded niggaz make things happen.

WINNER: BELAFONTE

ROUND 3: COCOA BROVAZ

 B: Steele can do the singsong style and he's a pretty-boy nigga. The bitches be lovin' them cuz of him— he's got good hair, he's shinin'!

S: Let me tell you some-thing, man. For one, my man Tek will beat his little light-skinded ass! Two, your man must be on some pretty-boy shit cuz he can't even really smoke weed. He shouldn't even be in the Cocoa Brovaz if he can't smoke weed!

B: Steele's for the bitches, man!

S: "Steele" means nothing; "Tek" is a specific item—a specific brand name!

B: You just hate him cuz he's pretty.

S: It's easier for him in this fucking coun-try! They oppressin' the dark-skinded brothers. Yo, hold your head, Tek.

WINNER: SATCHMO

ROUND 4: THE BEATNUTS

B: JuJu ain't doin' nuthin'. He don't want to go on tour. He's either at the bodega or hanging out with Haitian Mike in his Jeep.

S: Les—somebody in his family is defi-nitely white.

B: Les can flip different flows. JuJu just always tries to be hard and shit.

 S: But he is hard, man! He's dark-skinded and has had to fight his whole life!

B: He was all hard when he was singing "gimme tha ass"? Les kicked that shit for real. Les gets the ass, kid! While JuJu's singing "gimme tha ass," Les gets the ass!

S: Yeah, but see, Les tries to be on some pretty shit. Every time you see JuJu he's wearing Army fatigues, you know what I'm sayin'? He's mad fuck-ing real!

B: He's also mad cuz Les is winning!

S: Nah, I think Les' name says it all—LESS!

WINNER: SATCHMO

ROUND 5: SHOW AND A.G.

S: Come on, Show can make beats and he can rhyme.

B: Show played himself because he gave up the mic, kid. He's ain't no real emcee.

S: He gave up the mic to let A.G. finally shine. He was tired of taking out his man on the mic with his stutterin' rhymes!

B: A.G. wins cuz he wrote one of the best rhymes of all time: "Don't fuck with no devil / I'd rather marry Oprah / That's right I'm pro-Black." That shit is incredible. That's the revolution, right there!

S: That's just another light-skinded motherfucker tryin' to pretend that he's more Black. Him sayin' that is like that bitch Justin Timberlake saying, "I'm pro-Black."

B: That's if you get it twisted. The light-skinded nigga gets more dap because—

S: He's mulatto! Mulattos should stick to Lotto!

B: He had to overcome the mulatto stigma and A.G. is the man on the mic. He named himself after Andre the Giant, crushin' niggaz.

S: Show named himself after a whole industry, "Showbiz."

WINNER: SATCHMO

ROUND 6: SALT-N-PEPA

S: Come on, man, Salt looks like someone's demented cousin.

B: Salt carries the songs. She had the creative vision. When she was fuckin' with Hurby Luv Bug, she helped craft the songs. Then, when he deserted her ass, she did production and wrote rhymes and shit. She's the one who held down the group while Pepa was out there bullshittin'.

S: How's Pepa bullshittin'? She looks good. She's got a scorpion tattoo between her titties. Would someone that was light-skinded do that? No. Salt's on some light-skinded shit—"Oh, I'm better than you" bullshit.

B: Salt's holdin' it down while Pepa's tryin' to look good, gettin' her hair done every week.

S: Salt be out there sniffin' coke tryin' to hang out with Sheryl Crow an' shit. Pepa doesn't give a fuck about that white shit. She rolls with strong Black brothers. Salt's wastin' her time on some white shit.

B: Salt never sniffed coke in her life. She's goin' to heaven, kid, that's all I know.

WINNER: BELAFONTE

ROUND 7: MOBB DEEP

B: Prodigy, the new Rakim, what?! He's the dopest lyricist in the game. Havoc sounds like he's bustin' a nut with every verse.

S: That's what hip hop is, man, bustin' nuts for dark-skinded people. Your man P is from Long Island. He's not even from the Bridge. He's pretending, wanting to be down with the Bridge—sayin' that shit when he's from Long Island. He's white and he's from Long Island! That's why he's got that bullshit vocabulary, speakin' like the white man! Havoc

speaks the Black man's language! Let's not even start with Jigga-man callin' him a "ballerina."

B: Prodigy's the son of Rakim—the dopest emcee from Long Island just like Rakim.

S: Can Prodigy make beats? No. He's not better than Havoc. If Havoc can make beats and he can rhyme then—Hello!—he don't need Prodigy's light-skinded ass. Havoc solo album in '03!

B: Who says the lyrics people quote? Prodigy!

S: While your man's from Long Island, my man's "never leavin' the projects." Your man couldn't even say he's gonna stay in the projects forever cuz he's not from the projects.

B: Does Havoc still live in the Bridge? Havoc don't live in the Bridge.

S: Your man's a little mulatto from Long Island livin' in a house with white people next door.

WINNER: EVEN

ROUND 8: CAPONE-N-NOREAGA

B: Capone? Where that nigga at? What's up with that?

S: He gets locked down from time to time. He's real. He can't go around sippin' Cristal.

B: Dark niggaz is dumb.

S: Nore's from Lefrak. That's practically Rego Park.

B: Run-D.M.C., they're not from the projects. LL, he's not from the projects. P.E., they ain't from the projects and they're the greatest!

S: Your man's from the fuckin' Judd Hirsch projects. Get the fuck outta here with that Dear John bullshit!

WINNER: BELAFONTE

ROUND 9: PETE ROCK AND CL SMOOTH

S: Come on, Pete can rhyme better than CL.

B: CL's name is "Adofo." Come on. He wins.

S: Cuz he's "Adofo"? What the fuck is that?

B: He made Pete Rock's generic fuckin' horn beats work. He carried that production. Pete, that nigga fell

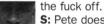

the fuck off.

S: Pete does solo albums, he's on the radio, he still produces beats for cats—what has CL got? He's probably workin' in a barbershop or something.

B: He got out the game cuz he didn't want to deal with the bullshit.

S: He's watchin' Jerry Springer in the morning. What the fuck is he doin'?

B: He's doin' his thing on the low.

S: Pete's still doin' his thing! Your man was rhyming about Tony Randall and Faye Dunaway. What the fuck do their monkey-asses have to do with hip hop? Your man's career is Dunaway.

WINNER: SATCHMO

FINAL OUTCOME:
Four rounds to "Satchmo," four rounds to "Belafonte," one round even. IT'S A DRAW—EVERYONE WINS! Stand proud and walk tall because it doesn't matter what shade you represent within the wonderful, varied spectrum of humanity. (Unless you're the devil.)

PROFESSOR GRIFF'S FAVORITE JEWISH PEOPLE, SOME OF WHOM ALSO HAPPEN TO BE FRIENDS.

1. BEN COHEN
   One half of Ben & Jerry's Ice Cream

2. DR. BEN (JOHANNAN)
   Author and researcher

3. RONALD L. SKOLER
   Head of Lethal Records and my attorney

4. BILL ADLER
   Former director of publicity, Rush Artist Management

5. MARK FREID
   Former director of writer/publisher relations, BMI

6. RICK RUBIN
   Co-founder of Def Jam Records and founder of American Records

7. CARA LEWIS
   Head chick-in-charge at William Morris Agency

8. HAILE SELASSIE
   Emperor of Ethiopia

9. LYOR COHEN
   Head of Island Def Jam

10. SAMMY DAVIS JR.
    World-class entertainer

Professor Griff is the Minister of Information for one of hip hop's greatest groups, Public Enemy. He caught some flack from some Jews a few years back. But all we are saying is give Griff a chance.

RACIAL (AND ETHNIC) RAP NAMES.*

HONORABLE MENTIONS:

*Excludes all exclusively "Black" names (see our last book, dummy).

**Included because they are white.

RACIAL (AND ETHNIC) ROCK BAND NAMES.

HONORABLE MENTION:

YOU GIVE RACIAL UNITY A BLAND NAME: 10 MILQUETOAST INTERRACIAL GROUPS.

BACKSTREET BOYS
You'd think that one Latin guy would spice things up. Blah blah Backstreet.

BLACK EYED PEAS
Eazy duz it, but they're doin' it too easy.

BRAND NEW HEAVIES
Funk lite just ain't right.

COLOR ME BADD
Exactly.

EDEN'S CRUSH / O-TOWN
Two TV dinners with no flavor.

HOOTIE AND THE BLOWFISH
Better idea: blowjobs at Hooters.

LINKIN PARK
'NSync wit' attitude.

DAVE MATTHEWS BAND
Dave Matthews Bland.

QUO
Michael Jackson's rapping duo duds. Quo hum.

SUGAR RAY
Shit ain't sweet.

EGO TRIP'S TOP INTERRACIAL BANDS.

THE ALLMAN BROTHERS BAND
Despite recording a song called "Whipping Post" (as in "tied to the . . ."), these honky-tonk cowboys found room in their bluesified rock rodeo for Black funky drummer Jai Johanny Johanson.

BOOKER T. & THE MG'S
Composed of two Blacks (organ grinder Booker T., stickman Al Jackson Jr.) and two whites (guitarist Steve Cropper, bassist Donald "Duck" Dunn), this pioneering, way 2 fonkay Memphis quartet rolled like Kid 'N Play: 2 hype.

CAN
Consecutive incarnations of this Krautrock outfit featured not just one, but *two* lead-singing brothas from anotha color—raspy Black American Malcolm Mooney and former Japanese street singer Damo Suzuki. Ah, sookie-sookie, now.

DEAD KENNEDYS
John, Bobby, and John-John may be gone, but Ted and Jello (Biafra, bey-otch) live on. (And they're both down for affirmative action—behold DK's second edition stickman D.H. Peligro, a Black man.)

DOOBIE BROTHERS
They rocked and rolled (and rolled—that cheeba-cheeba, y'all) with odd (and honorary) soul brothers in tow, including the original blue-eyed funky M&M, Michael McDonald.

GUNS N' ROSES
The history of the Black man in America: racism, firearms, loud-singing, and flower-bringing.

JANE'S ADDICTION
Dave Navarro: sounds Latin, *looks* Latin, acts, uh . . . axe up! Boy, he can really work that guitar like the best Johnny Winter–looking white boys out there. Only a Jew like Perry Farrell would stand for some kind of Spaniard showboating onstage like he's on a Puerto Rican Day parade float.

THE JIMI HENDRIX EXPERIENCE
A Black man telling two English muffins what to do: What could be better, bloke?*

LOVE
Before Andre "OutKast" Benjamin and Pharrell "No one Ever Really Douches" Williams made it popular to be a weirdo brotha, Black bandleader Arthur Lee was making the Los Scandalous scene (and probably making it with white babes), while making it count with psychedelic opuses like 1967's *Forever Changes*. Original Arthur wasn't going out on no three-fifths-of-a-man shit. (That's change you can count on, you honky.)

METALLICA
James Hetfield is the kind of name that you see on mailboxes way deep in the South. Kirk Hammett is the kind of name you'd see on a frosted beer mug in Düsseldorf, Germany. But the dude looks like a timid Latin frog. (Turns out good ol' Kirk is part Imelda Marcos!) Some say that James H. is a redneck rocker with a dastardly plan to whitewash white boys with white pride poems set to music. Not so—he even allowed former Danish ten-nis star Lars Ulrich (a man with a very un-American accent) to speak (broken) English during awards-show press confer-ences. *That's* America.

THE PIXIES
Black Francis, a helluva white man, loved to sing about Puerto Ricans and Mexicans. No wonder Joey Santiago (who is of Filipino heritage) was the band's lead guitarist. ¡Olé!

QUEEN
Fresh Freddie Mercury always knew what you wanted to hear at a sporting event. *We* are the champions? No, *he* was a champion: a North African–born

*Except maybe Jimbrowski bossing around three flavaless crumpets.

Parsi who knew how to command the attention of thousands of crazy pale soccer hooligans and hockey brutes years before Interpol or restricted beer sales.

RAGE AGAINST THE MACHINE
Guitar god Tom Morello and major throat Zack de la Rocha's parents said, hey, let's go half on a baby! (Morello is half Black, half white; de la Rocha is three-quarters Chicano, one-quarter Irish-German.) Together, with garden-variety whites bassist Tim Commerford and drummer Brad Wilk holding down the rhythm section, they dropped science on otherwise deaf, dumb, and blind Oz Fest–going pinball wizards and mulletheads alike.

SANTANA
Carlos is Mexican. There was a Black singer at some point, and a bunch of whites who went separate ways and morphed (presto!) into Journey. Carlos should've kept it Black. (We guess that's why he got down with Haitian Wyclef.)

SLAYER
White heat combined with a hot-blooded Latin equals bloody piñatas. And Anton Szanzor LaVey was damn proud.

SLY & THE FAMILY STONE
Sly was one baaad mutha. He was only messin' with the baddest of the bad. (Ever see that footage of his wife? She was the numba one stunna of her day.) Any nonbrotha in Sly's camp had to be—that's right—a baaad mutha, too. A white boy on drums (Greg Errico), a white boy on sax (Jerry Martini)—a lot of Black musicians could have used the work, but those two were funky and that's a fact, Jack.

SMASHING PUMPKINS
"Billy" and his band of gypsies—which included Japanese-American supastar fretworker James Iha, an allegedly crack-smoking, single, bass-playing white broad (fuck, yeah, baby!) named D'arcy, and a heron-lovin' white drummer boy named "Jimmy"—put the suburban lullabies of Jordanland in jukeboxes everywhere.

SOUNDGARDEN
Guitarist Kim Thayil is one tall, talented East Indian man. Chris Cornell's solo album was wack—even white people will tell you that. (Maybe that explains CC's attempts to work with Tom Morello.) So, it makes you wonder: Was brother Kim whipping that ass into shape in the studio? (Dude was probably kicking a Black hole, son, in his bottom.)

THE SPECIALS
The English have always been progressive. (That's why they offered African slaves in America freedom if they joined the redcoats.) So it ain't no surprise that it took five whites and two Blacks to bring ska—a Black thing, a Jamaican Ting™—back to the future. (Peace, Rancid.)

WAR
Funky bunch o' brothas from the city they call Long Beach merged with two others from Caucasoid mothers (former Animal Eric "Sippin' Burbon" Burdon and Afroed Dutch mouth harpist Lee Oskar), and came up with some real Chicano-sounding shite: sounds like *Arriba* Franklin, smells like beans 'n' fried chicken.

5 RECORDING ARTISTS MARK RAMOS-NISHITA (A/K/A MONEY MARK) LISTENS TO WHEN HE'S FEELING MEXICAN . . .

1. Esquivel
2. Astrid Haddad
3. Quetzal
4. Plastilina Mosh
5. Domingo Siete

. . . AND 5 HE LISTENS TO WHEN HE'S FEELING ASIAN.

1. The Boredoms
2. Buffalo Daughter
3. Ryuichi Sakamoto
4. Fred Ho
5. Sadao Watanabe

Singer, songwriter, one-man band, and sometime Beastie Boys' keyboardist Money Mark is half Mexican, half Japanese, and 100 percent dynamite.

THE WAYNE KRAMER OPINION:

MADE-IN-DETROIT JEWELS FROM THE FORMER MC5-ER, WHITE PANTHER, AND PIONEERING CAUCASIAN AFROMAN.

A lot of folks say that punk started over the pond yonder where the food is terrible and the rap music isn't much better. (Hmmm, KFC in the shadows of Big friggin' Ben might be the ticket.) Well, you shouldn't believe those wankers. Punk started in Detroit in the late 1960s, motherfuckers, where a band called the MC5—shorthand for the Motor City 5—used to kick out the jams, motherfuckers. ('Nuff respect to fellow rock city punk pioneers The Stooges, motherfuckers.) Robin Tyner sang, Dennis Thompson hit skins, Michael Davis was bassman, Fred "Sonic" Smith and a gentleman named Wayne Kramer played the guitars.

Dude, these guys worshipped the Black Panther Party! That's why they helped launch the White Panther Party! (The Black Panthers actually gave the albino version of their politically bold clique the thumbs up. Well, sorta. Read on.) The 5 even sported Afros! They were like a white Public Enemy!

Brother Wayne's world has love for all colors. Listen to this man. Learn from this man. Love this man.

WAYNE KRAMER ON INTEGRATION:

As a musician in the '60s, I could go to any club in Detroit and feel welcome and safe. I could go to the 20 Grand, which was the home of Motown acts, I could go to a nitty-gritty blues club on the East Side, or I could go to a club like the Checkmate, which was kinda like a bluesy, beatnik joint. It was nothing for there to be a dance at Christ the King Church Hall in Taylor, Michigan, that would feature on a given Friday night Jack and the Stranglers, the MC5, Marvin Gaye, Stevie Wonder, and Bobby Goldsboro. It happened all the time—which isn't to say there wasn't any Black neighborhoods or Black clubs. But there really was integration—just an acceptance of each other. We know we're different, but we accept that.

Culturally speaking, the MC5 never drew any distinctions [between musical genres], because we were just looking for the source of the energy. We came to the realization that a lot of white music was pretty . . . limp [laughs]. It was simple enough to follow the source of music—from rock music back down through the blues, down the Mississippi to the fields to the slaves to Africa to singing to chanting to the drum—the very first instrument. All music comes from Africa. But we never felt like it was "their music" or "our music"—we just went for the music that meant the most for us—that had the most significance to us.

WAYNE KRAMER ON THE WHITE PANTHERS:

Bobby Seale and Huey Newton (of the Black Panther Party) put out a call that there should be a White Panther Party to do parallel work in the white community that the Black Panthers did in the Black community. We idolized the Black Panthers. They were our heroes. They were ready to put their lives on the line for their beliefs, and that's the people that we wanted to be, too. So, we were ready.

But when we had some contact with them, they really didn't like us [laughs]. I think they wanted us to be a lot more serious than we were. It wasn't like we were sitting in an abandoned warehouse in the West Side of Detroit, cleaning our shotguns, waiting for the revolution. We were maniacs. And we spent most of our time—if we

weren't rehearsing, doing a gig, or recording—sitting around a kitchen table smoking massive amounts of marijuana, laughing our asses off at the world—really laughing to keep from crying. And so the Black Panthers called us "psychedelic clowns."

But we were serious about our principles, and we adopted the rhetoric of the day: by any means necessary. We were frustrated with the slow pace of change. You know, we were strong young men who saw tired old men ruining the world around us, and we wanted to do something about it. So, we formed our organization, and we looked at it as a way to help us carry a message to young people—that you don't have to go along with the program, that you can break the rules and things might turn out better than you think.

WAYNE KRAMER ON BIG BROTHER:

As time went on, the White House and the Justice Department took us seriously. I'd read an interview with G. Gordon Liddy where he said he'd read our propaganda, and said, "These people say they're gonna tear down the country, so I will use everything at my disposal against them." So, we got pretty paranoid—on top of the weed, and the acid, and occasional methedrine comedowns. But it was beyond drugs—this was really happening.

Our phones really were being tapped. They really were sliding agent provocateurs in on us. In the MC5 documentary, the filmmakers got their hands on United States Army surveillance footage of the MC5 from when we played in Chicago at the Democratic Convention in '68. And the funny thing is it was shot *really* well! The ins and outs are good, the color is good, the angles are good. Whoever the Army had doing their photography was pretty talented!

WAYNE KRAMER ON WHITE AFROS:

The Afros were cutting-edge fashion statements, man. That was a forward-moving kind of look. Truth be told, the Afros were really the final result of accepting how the hair comes out of your head, as opposed to trying to flatten it down and try to make it look like the Beatles' or the Rolling Stones'. It

just happened that me and [MC5 singer Rob] Tyner's hair was curly. His had little tight curls—it was *kinky*. We'd both used to use Dippity-do and all this shit to try to make our hair look like the Beatles', you know? And finally, I think we took enough acid to where we realized, you know, that natural was beautiful. I don't think Afrosheen had come out then.

WAYNE KRAMER ON HIS FAILED INTERRACIAL ROCK EXPERIMENT:

I have a dear friend in Detroit named Melvin Davis. He was a drummer at Motown and a wonderfully talented vocalist and songwriter. We put a band together after the 5 broke up. I had this idea for a band that was an interracial band that played completely interracial music—music that had rock guitar on top with a Motown rhythm section that was soulful and funky.

So, we formed this band, we wrote some songs, and we did the stuff that bands do to get started. And I went to my agent in Detroit, who was a decent man who I had known for years. I played him a tape and he said, "Yeah, I like it. It's good, Wayne." Then I showed him a publicity photo that we had done and he said, "Wayne, man, I can't book the band." And I asked, why not. And he said, "You've got a brother in the band."

This was 1973. I said, "We're in the modern age now. What are you talking about?" He said, "Well, Wayne, you know, if I book you guys into a white club, the girls are gonna like the Black guy, cuz he sings so well, and then the white guys are gonna want to start fights, and then it's gonna be a big problem. I can't book the band." I was fuckin' dumbstruck. I couldn't believe that a guy I knew and actually respected was coming so far out of left field at me. I was gob-smacked.

I went back and told Melvin about it. Melvin said, "Wayne, maybe this is the first time this has ever happened to you, but this ain't the first time it ever happened to me. This is normal." I said, "But this is outrageous. It's unbelievable that this is what we're up against today." And, in fact, the guy never did book the band. That's the other side of it. Everything wasn't completely happy-valley in the city of Detroit. Detroit's a tough place, man.

THE TRUE RACE ADVENTURES OF THE ROLLING STONES.

1962
▶ Appropriating their name from the song "Rollin' Stone," by blues legend and great Black man Muddy Waters, five skinny white guys (one with unusually large lips) form the Rolling Stones in England.

1963
▶ The group releases its debut single, a cover of rock 'n' roll pioneer (and great Black man) Chuck Berry's "Come On."

1964
▶ The group's cover of New Orleans soul singer (and great Black woman) Irma Thomas' "Time Is on My Side" becomes its first U.S. top-ten hit.

▶ Stones manager Andrew Loog Oldham urges the band to write original material and stop "sparring with [other cover bands] for some Black guy's song that hadn't been recorded to death."

1966
▶ The group releases one of its early smashes that isn't a tune written and originally performed by a Black artist. Ironically, it is entitled "Paint It Black."

1968
▶ Despite previously showing all signs of being down for darkies, the Stones show all signs for being down for the dark side with the release of the ditty "Sympathy for the Devil."

1969
▶ Drunken disorderliness by Hell's Angels working as security at the Stones' free concert at Livermore, California's Altamont Speedway leads to the murder of Black concertgoer Meredith Hunter. Keith Richards later says of Hunter's killing, as recounted in the anthology *The Book of Rock Quotes* (Delilah Putnam, 1982), "The underground suddenly leaps up in a horrified shriek when some spade hippie gets done, which is a terrible thing, but they never get uptight if some cop gets done . . ."

▶ *Let It Bleed* is released. The album features the provocatively titled "Monkey Man." Twenty-four years later the song is sampled by Public Enemy's white rap spin-off group Young Black Teenagers for their banger "Soul Wide Open."

'70s

1970

November 4. Karis Jagger, the love child of Mick and Black singer/actress Marsha Hunt, is born. A few years later, Hunt successfully files suit against a deadbeat Mick for child support.

1971

Mick marries Nicaraguan model Bianca Perez Morena de Macia, a female, brown-skinded dead ringer for Fat Lip himself. Their daughter, Jade, is born later that year.

The single "Brown Sugar" becomes an FM radio staple. It will remain so for decades despite the fact that its storyline celebrates a white slaveowner's sexual appetite for Black slave girls. Though some assume the song was inspired by Marsha Hunt, others believe singer Claudia Linnear is the chocolate ingenue being bigged-up.

Keyboardist Billy Preston becomes one of the only musicians (and definitely the only Black) to record with both the Beatles and the Stones when he guests on *Sticky Fingers*. Preston continues to perform and record with the band through the remainder of the decade.

1972

Exile on Main Street is released. The album, which was recorded in the South of France at a house that once served as the Gestapo's HQ during the Nazi occupation of France, features "Sweet Black Angel," an homage to (sweet, Black) political activist Angela Davis.

The Stones tour North America with opening act Stevie Wonder.

"No."

1974

Racially ambiguous guitarist Shuggie Otis is invited to join the band after Mick Taylor quits. Otis declines.

1976

Black and Blue is released. The album features "Hey Negrita" (which translates to "Hey Little Black Girl" *en Español*), a proposition for brownside sex that contains the object of affection's retort, "Going to get your boss, boy / Going to tan your hide."

Bassist Bill Wyman releases his solo album, *Stone Alone*. It features an homage to Native American poontang called "Apache Woman," which includes the refrain, "We know we did your people wrong / Let's try to get it back together / Let's get it on, get it on, get it on."

1978

Some Girls is released. The title track includes the lyrics "Black girls just wanna get fucked all night / I just don't have that much jam / Chinese girls are so gentle / They're really such a tease / You never know quite what they're cookin' / Inside those silky sleeves." The album's hit single, "Miss You," also contains the line "We gonna come by around twelve with some Puerto Rican girls that's just *dyin'* to meet you!"

Ex-Wailer (and great Jamaican Black man) Peter Tosh releases a hit duet with Mick—a cover of the Temptations' "Don't Look Back."

COC 59100

THE ROLLING STONES
STICKY FINGERS

1. BITCH (3:42)
   Mick Jagger–Keith Richard

STEREO   SIDE TWO

2. I GOT THE BLUES (4:00)
   Mick Jagger–Keith Richard
3. SISTER MORPHINE (5:34)
   Mick Jagger–Keith Richard
4. DEAD FLOWERS (4:05)
   Mick Jagger–Keith Richard
5. MOONLIGHT MILE (5:56)
   Mick Jagger–Keith Richard

PRODUCED BY JIMMY MILLER

(ST-RS-712190 PR)

1980

▶ *Emotional Rescue* is released. The album features "Indian Girl," a song about how war and political turmoil makes life hell for mud people, and includes the lyric "Please Mister Gringo, please find my father."

1981

▶ Mick and Keith are seen chillin' with Rastas on a stoop in the "Waiting on a Friend" video. The song is one of three from the *Tattoo You* LP (the others being "Neighbors" and, uh, "Slave"—hmmm . . .) that features jazz legend (and great Black man) Sonny Rollins on saxophone.

▶ Prince opens for the group at the L.A. Coliseum. Unfortunately, the Stones' largely white following can't get with the deep, Purple One's Black-rock Revolution, and he is mercilessly booed off the stage.

1984

▶ Mick sings on "State of Shock" with Michael J. and the Jacksons.

1985

▶ The Live Aid concert features a risqué duet between Mick and Tina Turner doing "State of Shock" and "It's Only Rock 'n' Roll." Their interracial simulated sex romp is broadcast across the globe for the benefit of starving Ethiopians who can't eat at Red Lobster for free.

1986

▶ Keith is a presenter at the first ever Rock 'n' Roll Hall of Fame induction. Handing Chuck Berry his award, he reverentially announces, "I lifted every lick he ever played." Keith will later pay further homage to his hero by leading the band for Berry's sixtieth birthday celebration as documented in the film *Chuck Berry: Hail! Hail! Rock 'n' Roll.*

▶ The Stones go back to their roots—pillaging old songs by forgotten Blacks—with their hit cover of Bob and Earl's R&B oldie "Harlem Shuffle" from *Dirty Work.*

'00s

'90s

1988

Keith Richards releases his first solo album, *Talk Is Cheap*. The album is entirely co-produced and co-written with former *Late Night with David Letterman* band drummer Steve Jordan—a Black. Other Blacks who appear on the album: Bootsy Collins, Bernie Worrell, Maceo Parker, Sarah Dash, Charley Drayton, and Ivan Neville (Aaron's seed).

December 17. Author Stanley Booth sits with Keith's daughter, Theodora, after the final show of the *Talk Is Cheap* tour—a performance highlighted by Keith's band, the X-pensive Winos (comprised of many of the Black musicians that played on the LP), being joined onstage by Johnnie Johnson, Chuck Berry's old piano player, for a cover of "Run Rudolph Run." Booth writes in his book *Rythm Oil* (Vintage Books, 1993):

I found myself . . . talking to the four-and-a-half-year-old Miss Theodora, who'd seen her father work that night for the first time. "Did you enjoy the show?" I asked her. "I wanna be a Black girl," she said.

1989

A Black artist finally turns the tables on the Stones' career of artistic thievery when Los Angeles rapper Tone-Loc surreptitiously samples "Honky Tonk Women" on his mega-hit "Funky Cold Medina."

1994

Black bassist Darryl Jones replaces Bill Wyman after the cradle-robbing old fart finally retires.

1996

Keith Richards releases an album with the Wingless Angels, the Nyabinghi Rasta dudes who crash on his estate in Jamaica. The album's liner notes refer to "Brother Keith" as "the self-styled 'albino' of the group . . . an Englishman guitarist [the Rastas] trust enough to invoke the spirit with, through music."

1999

May 17. Lucas Morad Jagger, Mick's love child with Brazilian model, Luciana Giménez Morad, is born.

2001

Mick releases the solo single "God Gave Me Everything"—a collabo with half-Black sensation Lenny Kravitz.

2039

Long since dead, lying in their luxury sarcophagi, the embalmed corpses of the greatest rock 'n' roll band ever to grace the earth make their final transition. As their flesh slowly rots away, as their bones turn to dust, their once ghostly skin tones turn to blue, then gray. Then, at last, to a deep, dark black. Say word.

EGO TRIP'S TOP 40 RACIAL HIT PARADE.

"BELSEN WAS A GAS (LIVE)"
SEX PISTOLS (WEA, 1979)
(Ge)Stop(o) in the name of (no) love: Sid Vicious rock-shockin' the house, y'all.

"BLACK GIRL"
LENNY KRAVITZ (VIRGIN, 1993)
Lenny's ode to beautiful Black women (even though he's not really fucking with them no more).

"BLACK GIRLFRIEND"
PORNO FOR PYROS (WARNER BROS., 1993)
Perry Farrell's post–L.A. riots paen to forbidden love between booty-full Black chicks and the white fellas who luh 'em.

"BROTHER LOUIE"
THE STORIES (KAMA SUTRA, 1973)
When Louie, who's "whiter than white," falls for a chick as "Black as

the night," the couple's families flip out and nix the mix. Boo hoo, boo.

"CLEAR BLUE SKIES"
THE JUGGAKNOTS (FONDLE 'EM, 1996)
"Brother Louie" revived for the backpack rap generation. In a fine performance, ebony emcee Breeze acts like he knows (whitey) by portraying two Caucasoid roles—a jungle fever–struck Caucasian boy and his intolerant dad.

"COLOR BLIND"
FRANKIE BEVERLY'S RAW SOUL (GREGAR, 1971)
Before he let go of his edge with mild-mannered Maze, Frankie Beverly favored deep funk beats and liberation-minded lyrics like, "I've often heard that white is right / You better believe Black is all right, too / And so is blue and green and yellow."

"DIRTY WHITE BOY"
FOREIGNER (ATLANTIC, 1979)
Hey ladies, according to this ditty, a dirty white boy knows "what's good for you all day" even though he "don't drive no big Black car." (FYI, he's riding with the bigots on a backwoods bus.)

"DON'T CALL ME NIGGER, WHITEY (DON'T CALL ME WHITEY, NIGGER)"
SLY & THE FAMILY STONE (EPIC, 1969)
Here's the anthem, get your damn hands up.

"(DON'T WORRY) IF THERE'S A HELL BELOW WE'RE ALL GOING TO GO"
CURTIS MAYFIELD (CURTOM, 1970)
Curtis said it best: Your skin ain't no sin.

"ERASE RACISM"
KOOL G RAP FEATURING BIZ MARKIE AND BIG DADDY KANE (COLD CHILLIN', 1990)
This half-assed plea to bridge racial divides nonetheless pleases once Biz belts out an off-key interpolation of Three Dog Night's "Black & White."

"EVERYONE'S A BIGOT"
THE OFFS (415, 1978)
Fuck "Ebony and Ivory."

"HALF-BREED"
CHER (MCA, 1973)
Life's a bitch. Especially if you're one that's half Native American and living amongst racists.

"HERE'S TO THE STATE OF MISSISSIPPI"
PHIL OCHS (ELEKTRA, 1965)
Old folkie fuck disses hick bigots down South. Burn, Mississippi, burn.

"HONG KONG"
SCREAMIN' JAY HAWKINS (OKEH, 1957)
Q: How would "I Put a Spell on You" sound with lyrics sung in garbled pidgin Cantonese?
A: Rude-icrous.

"HONKY CAT"
ELTON JOHN (UNI, 1972)
Classic wigger storyline. Despite being repeatedly told, "Get back, honky cat," whitey vows to dismiss his "redneck ways" and get down with hip happenings in the big (colorful, alternative lifestyle–tolerant) city.

"I FEEL LIKE A WOG"
THE STRANGLERS (A&M, 1977)
UK punks' message goes for the throat: Alienation is so dismal, it makes you feel like a darkie.

"ILLEGAL ALIENS"
CONVICTS (RAP-A-LOT, 1991)
Mexicans, Asians, Middle Easterners, and even educated Nigerians, all get touched by two Texans (one of whom went on to greater fame as acclaimed rapper Big Mike) who just want their 'hood back in Black: "I want beans and rice, cornbread and hamhocks / Keep your flour tortilla, fried beans and steel woks / Man, I'm so mixed up I don't know left from right / Bad enough we had to worry 'bout these muthafuckin' whites."

"IMMIGRANT SONG"
LED ZEPPELIN (ATLANTIC, 1970)
"We come from the land of the ice and snow / From the midnight sun where the hot springs blow / How soft your fields so green, can whisper tales of gore / Of how we calmed the tides of war / We are your overlords." The first white power anthem?

"INDIAN GIRL"
SLICK RICK (DEF JAM, 1988)
Wasn't the raunchy story of Davy Crockett sexing up a fetching, but frightened, Indian hottie in fact an allegory for the other man's fucking over of the Native American people? Yes.

"IS IT BECAUSE I'M BLACK?"
SYL JOHNSON (TWINIGHT, 1970)
One more time: yes.

"I WANNA BE BLACK"
LOU REED (ARISTA, 1978)
Punk's grandpappy puts up a middle finger to middle-class collegiate vanillans who just wanna be down.

"KUNG FU FIGHTING"
CARL DOUGLAS (20TH CENTURY, 1974)
Leave it to an East Indian producer and a Jamaican singer to come up with a disco homage to "funky Chinamen from funky Chinatown."

"LIVING FOR THE CITY"
THE DIRTBOMBS (IN THE RED, 2001)
A Stevie Wonder classic is reinvented (by a Black-led band, no less) into a lowly Mexican's tale of brown domestic-worker woe. This is for la raza.

"NO MASTER PLAN NO MASTER RACE"
3RD BASS (DEF JAM, 1991)
Two white rappers (and their Black DJ) wanna know: Why can't we live together? (Probably cuz the Black doesn't get to say shit.)

"THE PARASITE"
EUGENE MCDANIELS (ATLANTIC, 1971)
Folky, acoustic guitar-led narrative follows pioneering whites as they land on this country's shores and are greeted by friendly Native Americans. Everything's hunky-dory until the carnage kicks in, along with an explosion of screams and instrumental cacophony.

"PUERTO RICAN"
ADAM AND THE ANTS (STRANGE FRUIT, 2001)
Though their '78 recording is *muy* hateful toward PRs ("I'm gonna light up a beacon on a Puerto Rican / Strike a matchstick on his head . . . / You gonna watch me smile if he drops down dead"), these English Ants were buggin' with all the "¡Arriba!"s up in this bitch. If you're gonna be racist, at least get your ethnic exclamations right. Can we get a *"¡Wepa!", familia?*

"THE RACIST"
BOOGIE DOWN PRODUCTIONS (JIVE, 1990)
KRS-One, in one of his more populist moments before going insane, breaks the struggle down to its very last compound: "If Black and white didn't argue the most / They'd see clearly that the government's screwing them both."

"REDBONE IN THE CITY"
BAD BRAINS (CAROLINE, 1996)
Recorded in '79, D.C.'s finest's rewrite of the Sex Pistols' "God Save the Queen" shows no love for stuck-up light-skinded beyotches with attitude. Back up off 'em

"RUN TO THE HILLS"
IRON MAIDEN (METAL-IS, 1982)
Classic U.K. metal rundown of the white man's Indian extinction agenda.

"SETH"
BIG BLACK (RUTHLESS-FEVER, 1984)
Steve Albini and crew relay the timeless story of a cuddly canine with one minor character flaw: He's been trained to kill Black people. Must have been a white guy who started all that.

"SEXY MEXICAN MAID"
RED HOT CHILI PEPPERS (EMI, 1989)
Fuck French maid outfits. The real live clean-up women are young, gifted, and brown.

"SPEAK ENGLISH OR DIE"
S.O.D. (MEGAFORCE, 1985)
Or at least speak enough English to take our super-sized Big Mac meal order.

"WE DON'T DIG NO BUSING (THE BUSING SONG)"
GREER BROTHERS (DUKE, 1972)
Five shorties (all fourteen years old and younger) caught in the busing system send a message to the board of ed: "If I were the President / Tell you what I'd do for us / I'd make a hot dog stand / Out of every yellow bus . . . just let us walk!"

"WHAT IF I WAS WHITE?"
STICKY FINGAZ FEATURING EMINEM (UNIVERSAL, 2001)
You'd still be a mediocre poseur. But you'd probably be more popular.

"WHITE MINORITY"
BLACK FLAG (SST, 1982)
Message to the white man: Forecast calls for a whole lotta dark days (and hella dark knights). Get used to it, crackerjack(s).

"WHITE PEOPLE CAN'T DANCE"
WAS NOT WAS (4TH & B'WAY, 1989)
We're not sure exactly who was supposed to dance to the robotic rhythms of this faux rap clunker, albeit one with insightful lyrics: "White people can't dance / If they move to the beat it's just by chance / They wiggle and squibble and dress for the part / But they dance from the head, not from the heart."

"WHITE RIOT"
THE CLASH (EPIC, 1977)
Class of '77 punk's finest are sick of colored folks hogging all the revolution.

"WHITEY ON THE MOON"
GIL SCOTT-HERON (FLYING DUTCHMAN, 1970)
GSH is sick of Caucasians hogging all the everything.

"WHY CAN'T PEOPLE BE COLORS, TOO?"
THE WHATNAUTS (STANG, 1972)
Digitally looted by everyone in the rap game circa 1994 for its obese drum break, this banger from the Baltimore soul trio also features a moral: Don't judge a (Black) book by its cover.

"YELLOW FEVER"
BLOODHOUND GANG (REPUBLIC, 1996)
"China Girl" never sounded like this: "She's like an oriental rug 'cause I lay her where I please / Then I blindfold her with dental floss and get down on my knees / I'm a diving Kamikaze eating out Chinese / Chinky chinky bang bang I love you / Sing, chinky, sing."

PLAY IT AGAIN, SAMBO:
20 SONGS THAT, CONTRARY TO THEIR TITLES, ARE NOT ABOUT RACE.

"Black"—Pearl Jam (Epic, 1991)
"Black Is Black"—Los Bravos (Press, 1966)
"Black Water"—Doobie Brothers (Warner Bros., 1975)
"Chinese Rock"—The Ramones (Sire, 1980)
"Colour My World"—Chicago (Columbia, 1971)
"Don't It Make My Brown Eyes Blue"—Crystal Gayle (United Artists, 1977)
"Free Man"—Southshore Commission (Wand, 1975)
"I'm a Slave 4 U"—Britney Spears (Jive, 2001)
"I Need a Slave"—The Vibrators (Epic, 1977)
"Mellow Yellow"—Donovan (Epic, 1966)
"Mixed Bizness"—Beck (Geffen, 1999)
"One Monkey Don't Stop No Show"—Honey Cone (Hot Wax, 1971)
"The Paw Paw Negro Blowtorch"—Brian Eno (Island, 1973)
"Running with the Devil"—Van Halen (Warner Bros., 1978)
"Southern Cross"—Crosby, Stills & Nash (Atlantic, 1982)
"Turning Japanese"—The Vapors (Liberty, 1980)
"Very Ape"—Nirvana (DGC, 1993)
"Whip Appeal"—Babyface (Solar, 1990)
"White Room"—Cream (Atco, 1968)
"Yellow Submarine"—The Beatles (Capitol, 1966)

EGO TRIP'S RACE ALBUM REVIEW.

THE AUCTION
DAVID AXELROD (DECCA, 1972)

This veteran, Caucasian composer and producer enjoyed a resurgence in popularity in the '90s when sample-seeking rappers rediscovered good grooves aplenty on nearly every album with his credit emblazoned on it. (If you thought Lou Rawls was always old, check his Axelrod-produced joints, jughead.) But Axe, who was raised in South Central Los Angeles, not only had the funk in a smash, he also had a lot on his mind (plus, he freely admits to having experimented with "every [drug] known to mankind"). This probably

explains his predilection for wigged-out, challenging concept projects that no major record label in their right (or white) mind would roll the dice on today. Having already dedicated full-lengths to such heavy mental topics as the literary work of William Blake, the world's pending ecological disasters, and interpretations of Handel's *Messiah*, the shaggy D.A. based his fifth album on turn-of-the-century Black poet Paul Laurence Dunbar's writings on the slave trade.

True, *The Auction*'s heady mix of Dunbar-inspired lyrics, traditional spiritual material, and spoken-word monologues ain't exactly the blueprint for bouncin'. (What'd you expect from an album exploring the evils of slavery, anyway?) Fortunately, the weight of the subject matter is balanced out somewhat by the music's all-around funky elegance. Axelrod's producing and arranging smarts (in collabo with longtime colleagues, saxophonist Cannonball Adderley and drummer Earl Palmer) are in fine form here, as is his strong choice in '70s session musicians. Tunes like "The Leading Citizen" (an indictment of white lawgivers of the slavery era) and the elegiac "Freedom" ride trademark rocksteady backbeats as the bluesy guitar leads by David T. Walker, nimble electric piano runs by the Crusaders' Joe Sample, and a soulful chorus one dozen voices strong marinates in the mix. Meanwhile, the message stays pertinent to Black and white affairs of any era, with or without an Emancipation Proclamation. Take "Freedom," for instance, which poses the rhetorical question, "If you don't feel the chain when it makes a brother pain / Are you not slaves indeed / Slaves unworthy to be freed?" Well? Chew on that shit.

THE DIALECT OF BLACK AMERICANS
(WESTERN ELECTRIC, 1970)

This ancient school "Community Relations Presentation" is required listening for anyone who thought the late-'90s controversy over ebonics as a language of its own was some recent phenomenon, or simply anyone who can't get enough of that offensive stuff. The liner notes read, "At a time when interracial communication and understanding are assuming enormous importance, this record hopes to help explain for listeners of all races what Black dialect is and how it functions." But however good its intentions, this stab at untying African-

American tongues comes off pretty racist itself from the giddy-up, dramatizing examples of how Black people talk through coonish scenarios like a woman scolding her (apparently lazy) man for not getting up when the alarm clock rings, an irate (probably single) mom screaming "shut up" at her uncontrollable houseful of kids, and another woman warning her smooth-talking (but supposedly unreliable) husband not to get into "no jive, off-the-wall stuff" and come straight homo after work.

Much of the remainder of the album is narrated by a Black character who's left the 'hood and gone on to success in the proper English-speaking world. Problem is, most of the time he comes off like a self-hating jerk. "The old neighborhood hadn't changed much," he says of a trip back to his old stomping ground. "What a lousy, miserable place. I walked around some old garbage and got the almost forgotten whiff of what it was like . . . It was good to be on my way."

Elsewhere, between more minstrel-caliber dramatizations—a Black applicant's painful job interview, random street chatter, etc.—our guide spews out strict generalizations: "The middle-class Black must be careful of the language he is using, or rather, *which* language he is using. . . . On the streets of Black America, there is no choice. Life and its meanings *only* come alive with the dialect." Even attempts to validate and dissect Black speech patterns come off hopelessly condescending, using examples like "Leroy at home" and "Debra have free brova." The program's ultimate recommendation—to have ghetto children taught both standard English and Black dialect—concludes with a typically smarmy remark from our narrator: "Under no condition should the speaker's use of the dialect be considered something inferior. . . . Actually, he doesn't need to learn [standard English] at all—until he has to make a living!" Guess the joke's on you, (Black) Jack.

FEAR OF A BLACK PLANET
PUBLIC ENEMY (DEF JAM, 1990)

We know what you're thinking, smart-ass rap young'n. How can we choose just one Public Enemy album as being "racial" when P.E.'s entire catalog rings and sings Blacks and blues, right? Well, yes, and no. The super superb *FOABP* distinguishes itself from the two masterpieces that preceded it (*Yo! Bum Rush the Show* and *It Takes a Nation of Millions to Hold Us Back*) by widening its scope of colorful topics from previous

installments. In addition to the expected calls to mobilize Nubian minds ("Brothers Gonna Work It Out"), articulation of inner city ills ("911 Is a Joke"), and examination of Uncle Sam's scams ("Who Stole the Soul?"), P.E. boldly ventures into the uncharted areas of jungle fever ("Pollywanacraka")

and miscegenation (the title cut), exhibiting a humorous, humanist lyrical bent most of the group's critics didn't believe Chuck D and Co. had in 'em. As the latter song asks, "Man, c'mon now, I don't want your wife / Stop screamin', it's not the end of your life / But suppose she said she loved me / What's wrong with some color in your family tree?"

All this over some of the hardest, densest, and most sagely sequenced aural collages its production battalion, the Bomb Squad, could muster before the spectre of sample clearance litigation eventually moved in and shut 'em down. Track work like the looped guitar crescendo of "Brothers Gonna Work It Out" (pilfered from a chunk of Prince's "Let's Go Crazy"), or the JBs wail-of-sound of "Fight the Power" are as revolutionary for their music as their content. You want more drama? Fuck a skit. Check "Contract on the World Love Jam"'s tension-building introductory meshing of samples, scratch-cuts, and speech bytes. Better yet, listen as the charged talk-show discourse of "Incident At 66.6 FM" (which includes one caller's priceless barb, "When I see someone wearing one of [Public Enemy's] shirts, I think they're scum, too") brilliantly segues into the still astounding "Welcome to the Terrordome," Chuck's state-of-the-group address on P.E.'s internal struggles with charges of anti-Semitism, infamous for the lines, "Crucifixion ain't no fiction / So-called chosen frozen / Apology made to whoever pleases / Still they got me like Jesus." It's a fitting centerpiece for one of hip hop's true platters that matters. And if ya don't know, now ya know, Negroes.

RACIALLY YOURS
THE FROGS (4 ALARM RECORDS, 2000)

Indie rock ain't so hard to figure out. What is it? A bunch o' college-town, coffee-house-managing, sock-tie-wearing whiteys who have a hard-on for Elvis Costello, Marianne Faithfull, pre-Allah Cat Stevens, and of course, the bloody Beatles! Hey, what do you expect? The stringy-haired parents of these reservoir-sipping cave dogz pissed and got pissy to the Beatles, and then let their kids play in their backyards

and kill beetles while listening to the Beatles. Simply put, every indie rock album sounds like the Beatles. You pick the LP.

So this cultish indie rock group called The Frogs goes and records an album called *Racially Yours* back in 1993 that doesn't see light till 2G. Lucky for them, Al Sharpton

wasn't at the album release party, because somebody would have taken a few strong ones to the grill. *Racially* features twenty-five Beatles-Waits-Stevens-esque compositions (backward clock noises, scary circus pianos, lightly amplified acoustic guitars . . .) worth of white man's burden, no holds barred. Songs like "Sorry I'm White" flirt with crusty stereotypes ("All this gold you flash about, I'm not envious / And if I dropped my drawers, you'd win"), but the Frogs' balls-out words of warning are for fellow white men. On "Whitefully Dead" one Froggy Frog ironically belts out, "Now that the blue-eyed devil's gone, we can only have some fun—watch as the Black man reigns!" A *Battle for the Planet of the Apes*–like uprising is told on "Full of Monkeys" where humankind (a/k/a the white man) is squashed and down-pressed by you-know-who in a Caucasian-dreamed switcheroo: "In the Oval Office, president swings from his tire / He's got an idea / He'll make this place match his face / The Black House is full of monkeys." How could cute, rubbery little guys like frogs—the most laid-back creatures ever to chill in an eco-system near you—be so damn racist? Maybe Miss Piggy knows.

Like typical hip white men, the Frogs have to represent with at least a few P.C. hymns. Hence, there's "An Unwanted Child and a Wanted Man": "Brought up in the ghetto where nothing changes much / Souls are sold for money / Love is out of luck." (Awww.) This false sensitivity continues with "You're a Bigot." "You hurt me," Froggy quips, "Be big about it." If *Racially* is the wild, wild West, then these two ditties are like the Lone Ranger twins riding off into the sunset. But the two Tontos ain't givin' a fuck. Besides, this is just some Beatles rip-off shit. And who did the Beatles rip off? Little Richard. A Black man!

WHITE TRASH, TWO HEEBS, AND A BEAN
NOFX (EPITAPH, 1992)

Fine. So there are two Hebrews, a trailer urchin, and some kind of bastardized Spaniard offshoot in this SoCal punk band. The inside artwork reveals a photo in which the white-trash drummer's mug is replaced by a can of Schaefer malt liquor; the Jew singer's mug is replaced by a box of Manischewitz brand Passover matzos; the Jew guitar player's mug is represented by a clear jar of pickled gefilte fish; the

trumpet-playing "Spaniard" guitarist is seen as an opened can of Sun-Vista black beans. Get it? They're sooo Dead Kennedys! They're sooo not racist! They're sending a message to the hate mongers who hate what punx stand for. . . .

Guess again. *White Trash, Two Heebs, and a Bean* is teeming with sub-liminal racism (which, FYI, is even worse than overt racism). Bad enough that these guys play that cookie cutter, Circle Jerks meets Bad Religion, harmonic Caucasoid/sing-along punk steelo with the occasional ska breakdown for backward baseball-cap-sporting palefaces from Orange County. But then there's shit like "Soul Doubt": "Sometimes I feel my life is going 'round in circles," sings throatman Fat Mike. "Beneath my eyes are blueish black." Listen, fat boy: There are millions of Black people with blueish-Black beneath their eyes. Black is a beautiful thing. But Fat Mike the "nonracist" punk wants to make Black an ugly thing. Even uglier is "Buggley Eyes": "Have you ever gone to sleep with Bo Derek and woke up with Bo Diddley? . . . Woke up in the morning / To your surprise / A couple of melons in tube socks, and buggley eyes?" Basically, Fat Michael is saying, A) Bo Diddley is ugly (not true, not cool), and B), "bugged" eyes are funny. *Birth of a Nation*, then, must be fuckin' hilarious to you, homes.

"Straight Edge"—a cover of the classic jammie recorded long ago by Washington, D.C.'s Coca-Cola-swilling legends Minor Threat—walks the line, then burns the line like a cruci-fix blazing brightly on a Black Atlantian's front lawn. Here, fatso decides that he's gonna sing the no-drinking-and-drugging manifesto in the voice of the late, great Louis Armstrong, as ragtime-flavored horns swagger underneath. Yuck! First of all, get a grip—the Plastic Man–cheeked brother loved to smoke his trees. Secondly, a white man tryin' to flow like Satchmo is gonna sound racist every damn time. Even if Tom Waits is kickin' it. Ya heard me?!

El Heffe (the band's beaner guitarist): You should know better than to make "music" (and trouble) with these *hon-quistadors. Odelay!*

THE MINSTREL MAN FROM GEORGIA
EMMITT MILLER (SONY/LEGACY, 1996)

Macon, Georgia native son Emmitt Miller was an accom-plished entertainer wigga who loved to smile big and wide while wearing Blackface. But his shade-y fascination was no passing fancy. As the first light-skinded emcee with clout, E-Mil knew the importance of street cred. Friends remember how he'd spend several hours a day in the dark-est reaches of town in order to soak up authentic "jive

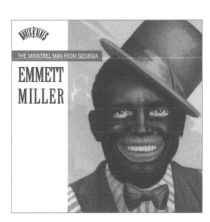

talkin.'" His home-work and dedication was rewarded with a large following of fans. For a time, much like our Savior (you Christians know who I'm talkin' 'bout), Emmitt Miller was every-where.

Em's career would be engulfed by a raging storm-front when the Devil's Supermarket

(a/k/a the New York Stock Exchange) crashed back in '29. Suddenly, for the first and last time, the Mr. and Mrs. Whitefolks of the land got an up close, personal and dan-gerous look at the dark existence of those with permanent Blackface and thought, "That's fucked up! That's us!" Minstrel artists everywhere were suddenly out of work. Of course, our unsung hero Emmitt just kept on keepin' on.

Yes, this Em, the original Em—sorry, Marshall "Family Matters" Mathers—had to suffer in order for the special art of the minstrelsy to survive. It not only survives, it flourishes into the digital age with *The Minstrel Man From Georgia*, a long player that illustrates the genius of this Southern man. Now, without skipping a beat, we can all sing the hits of brotha Em's forgotten catalogue: I'm talkin' about hot joints like "I Ain't Got Nobody"—you know, the shit that (star of) David Lee Roth sang, post-Van Halen; and "Lovesick Blues"—you know, that shit that hanky-panky-lovin' honky-tonk hillbilly Hank Williams made famous yet again. One listen to this buttercup of a comp will have you open like fallopian tubes. Some people say that Emmitt just wanted to be Black. I believe them. Emmitt Miller was no racist—he was just extra race-con-scious. Which just goes to show you: white people sure am versatile!

CHAPTER 4

LIGHTS, CAMERA, AFFIRMATIVE ACTION.

ego trip's™

FIRST ANNUAL
MIDDAY AFTERNOON
Bawnoplex Times Square, NYC

FILMS-FOR-RACE-FANS FESTIVAL.
Buy tickets online at www.mooliesluvmovies.beyotch

MONDAY — "HUMAN GUMBO" DOUBLE FEATURE

Black and White (1999)

The *New York Post* of race films and not just because Page Six fixture Bijou Phillips swings a Central Park sexcapade within the first five minutes. Like the popular tabloid, James Toback's audacious ad-libbed adventure is a vehicle bent on hitting you in the gut rather the brain. Watch in fascinated horror as "cum guzzler" Robert Downey Jr. attempts to pick up Mike Tyson only to almost get knocked the fuck out in a scene that ranks as one of the most compelling moments in movie history. See a focused Brooke Shields (as a document-Aryan) quiz Method Man about Black life; catch Wu-Tang affiliate Power running through Claudia Schiffer after she quits bungling b-baller Allan Houston (who's set up for a point-shaving fall by a serious Ben Stiller and his big-ass feet). In other words, watch it for the white chicks analyzing Black dudes or the Black dudes anal-izing white chicks. The bottom line: It ain't good, it ain't bad, it just is. To paraphrase Fiona "Don't Fuck with Me" Apple, this movie is a mess we don't want to clean up. (And we don't do windows either, motherfuckers.)

The Thing with Two Heads (1972)

An Oscar winner and an all-pro lineman surgically joined at the neck. Next to champagne kisses and caviar dreams, we can't think of a better combination. Actor Ray Milland is a racist M.D. who finds out he's about to buy the farm. Faster than you can say HMO ("Hey Moolie, Operation"), his dome is attached to foxy Pam's evangelical *cuzzo*, Rosie Grier, a death row inmate who ain't takin' no crap from some old-ass prejudiced peckerwood. The grisly moment in which each party discovers his new neighbor reminds us of the feeling we get every time we read a royalty statement from our former publisher. Clunky, messy, and surreal, you'll like the way it's going down. Give us some head(s).

TUESDAY — "CIAO, CHOW" DOUBLE FEATURE

China Girl (1987)

New York City's Chinatown and Lil' Italy have been rubbing shoulders (and punching each other's faces) for generations. Demented Italiano auteur Abel Ferrara pays homage to the two things cinema nuts truly can't get enough of——love and racism (which always equals violence, naturally)——with this nutty spin on *Romeo and Juliet*. Rival chink and wop gangs take each other out, but all the lovers want is some nice, quiet duck sick time, fettuccine style.

Year of the Dragon (1985)

Mickey Rourke plays a white cop named Stanley White who's white-hot about Asians. See, he tamed his name (of Polack origins) to be mo' 'Merican and toured 'Nam, too. To this unpleasant guy, all them gooks is sure flippant for not altering their own hard-hell-bent on cleaning up Chinatown and its corrupt underbelly. (Rourke's own belly is still years from blowing up.) Italian glutton Michael Cimino directs from a script he co-wrote with Ollie Stone, the ex-vet we bet has got some anti-Asian feelings of his own.

The Spook Who Sat by the Door (1973)

Lawrence Cook portrays Dan Freeman (you goddamn right!), a Black CIA agent who gets no respect and is being used by superiors so they can say, "C, I ain't no racist." Fed up, he leaves, retiring to a quiet life as a social worker. In reality, at least that's what he has everybody thinking. In reality, he's employing the techniques he learned from the sneaky white man to train Black guerrillas to kick-start a race war! Talkin' 'bout a revolution at twenty-four frames per second, thirty-three r.p.m. (and that starts at 3:30 P.M. so don't be late, darkie).

Three the Hard Way (1974)

Drinking water has no color. But the water in this flick is far from colorblind since evil scientists have designed it to kill the coloreds. Jims Brown and Kelly as well as Fred Williamson ain't wet behind the ears, though, when it comes to kicking racist ass and, before you know it, it's three feet high (up an Aryan rectum) and uprising time. Fuck Kevin Costner, this is the real *Waterworld*.

Star Maps (1997)

It's hard figuring out who's more screwed up in this crazy Mexican *familia*: The pops who pimps his son, the deranged mon who chats with the ghost of comedic legend Cantinflas on the 'regular, or the grown brother who rocks wrestling outfits and makes unsu table hand gestures at the dinner table. What is certain is that the young male hustler, who has Hollywood dreams, ain't gonna have it easy in Tinseltown. Yet another case of a Puerto Rican (director Miguel Arteta is Boricua) controlling the Mexicans in movies, but we forgive him cuz this is one dope flick.

Popi (1969)

Alan Arkin is Puerto Rican. At least he is in this family tale about a single father with two young sons and his desperate schemes to make a better life for them. Predating the Elián González episode by thirty years, Arkin's character dreams up a plot where he can get his offspring out of the slums by having them appear as if they're Cuban immigrants fresh off the raft. This way, wealthy whites will adopt the "orphans." Do you think he had one too many rum and Cokes?

American Me (1992)

Rappers Fat Joe and Ice Cube have seen this movie, but we don't know about their mutual buddy Mack 10 (though that *vato loco* does look kinda Mexican, don't he?). We do know the narration mostly rhymes in this bleak in-and-out-of-prison drama directed by and starring Edward James Olmos. A young Castillo drops couplets but not the soap. Still, somehow, he gets poked in juvey, an incident that angered the real-life Mexican Mafia gang (also called "La Eme"), upon whom the film is based. (They actually put a contract on Eduardo's *vida loca*.) With the Black Gorilla Family and the Aryan Brotherhood also vying for control of San Quentin Prison, the racial tension runs high in this riveting, if depressing, joint.

The Education of Sonny Carson (1974)

Rap producers RZA and Pete Rock have seen this movie, one filled with choice samples of memorable dialogue every five minutes. Based on former gang-leader-turned-activist Carson's autobiography (we know Lauryn Hill read it), this finely acted, yet also depressing, film follows the defiant protagonist in and out of the pen as he tries to deal with a future where the odds are stacked against him. (Man. the way he's tortured by the two pasty pigs in that one scene will have you holding your own *huevos* in pain.)

PUTNEY SWOPE

GET YOUR TICKETS TODAY!

Putney Swope (1969)

Through their own backfired devices, white ad execs elect the sole Black to run the company when the old boss croaks. Written and directed by Robert Downey Jr.'s dad, this cult classic is still cutting edge—just ask director Paul Thomas Anderson, who cribbed a scene in *Boogie Nights* from it (FYI, the one at the '80s music-loving coke dealer's pad where a barely dressed Asian houseboy lights firecrackers indiscriminately). Extra bonus: Antonio Fargas as "the Arab."

The Man (1972)

When the leaders of America start dropping like flies, the next in line to hold the highest position in the country is Darth Vader. That's right, CNN lovers, James Earl Jones, the voice behind the evil empire (Verizon), is the first Black President. And only the formidable Mr. Jones could pull off this historic feat considering every pale-skinned politico wants to impeach our man. Adapted by *Twilight Zone* creator Rod Serling and featuring a memorable job by Burgess "the Penguin" Meredith as a hateful senator, this drama goes places Colin Powel I can only dream about. (And he gets around.)

The Klansman (1974)

The words from the prophets were written on the subway movie poster: RED NECKS. WHITE HOODS. AND RAPED BLACK GIRLS. O.J.'S GRABBING A GUN AND GOING TO WAR. Sounds too good to be true, doesn't it, white people? But here it is on the cold-blooded silver screen. Orenthal is innocent. Or at least "Garth," the running Black O.J. portrays, is. Garth is falsely accused of raping a white lady in this sometimes-hard-to-watch, Sam Fuller–scripted-but-not-directed tale of bloodthirsty crackers out for justice. What follows must be seen to be believed: Richard Burton (tipsy off the juice) karate-chopping a redneck foe with ease, the Juice intermittently picking off Klan-dudes sniper style (and eventually turning up distraught and armed in the back-seat of a Jeep—whoa!), Lee Marvin being Lee Marvin, and, unfortunately, a nightmarish scene with the sultry Lola Folana max. t's on fire. Cross our hearts.

White Dog (1982)

What's worse than Lassie with a bad case of rabies? Try White Dog, a canine trained to attack Black folks on sight. (No, he didn't escape from the LAPD's K-9 unit.) Kristy McNichol loves the prejudiced pup to death until she discovers Fido's unsavory attitude. Trainer Paul Winfield thinks he can reprogram the dog. (What is he thinking?) Only Sam Fuller (here back in the director's chair) could pull off this type of shit, doggone it.

LANDMARK STEREOTYPES.

Breakfast at Tiffany's (1961)
Mickey Rooney as the bucktoothed, mush-mouthed, Japanese oddball landlord Mr. Yunioshi. Rooney, you got a karate chop to the neck coming. (That is, if you're still alive.)

Daughter of the Dragon (1931)
Anna May Wong creates and popularizes the Asian "dragon lady" in this old school flick. So hot, so dangerous, so stereotypical. The flames still burn.

Full Metal Jacket (1987)
2 Live Crew take notice and sample the Vietnamese hooker's "Me so horny" pleas only to get sued years later. Long afterward the idea is sown: Foreign ladies of the night versed in broken English like to say "sucky fucky" as much as they can.

The Godfather (1972)
A masterpiece made during a golden era in American filmmaking. This family epic also reinforces the negative image that all Italian clans are somehow mob-related. Word to Luca Brasi.

Scarface (1983)
Cuban refugees coming to this country will forever fall under the shadow of filthy-tongued Tony Montana. Who put this thing together? Two Italians (Pacino and De Palma), that's who.

Treasure of the Sierra Madre (1948)
The Mexican *bandido* posing as police who jacks Bogart and company had the unfortunate name of Gold Hat and the following unforgettable lines: "Badges? We ain't got no badges. We don't need no badges. I don't have to show you any stinking badges." The shit-talking, slightly bilingual baddie is born (in the U.S.A.).

West Side Story (1961)
Natalie Wood's turn as the hot-blooded Puerto Rican Maria, who falls for the leader of the gang her brother's gang hates, forever gets white boys hot for Spanish tail. Keep them woodies in your pants, whitey.

MOVIE FRANCHISE STEREOTYPES.

Amos and Andy
Charlie Chan
Dr. Fu Manchu
Ernest
"The Latin Lover"
Mr. Moto
Stepin Fetchit
Tonto

NEVER JUDGE A MOVIE BY ITS TITLE: STARRING STRICTLY WHITE FOLKS.

Amazon Women on the Moon (1987)[*]
The African Queen (1951)
The China Syndrome (1979)
Chinatown (1974)
The Indian Runner (1991)
The Mexican (2001)
Minority Report (2002)
Out of Africa (1985)
The Purple Rose of Cairo (1985)
Salvador (1986)

NOT-SO-NICE MOVIE TITLES.

Chin Chin Chinaman (1931)
The Eternal Jew (1940)
Greaser's Palace (1972)
Jap Zero (1943)[*]
Kiss Me Guido (1997)
Mexican Spitfire (1940)
Mulatto (1949, made in Italy)
Old Gringo (1989)
Ozone! Attack of the Redneck Mutants (1986)
Russkies (1987)
The Spook Who Sat by the Door (1973)
Tony, the Wop (1915)
Wetbacks (1956)

BONUS:
NOT-SO-NICE CARTOON TRAILER TITLES.

Chinaman's Chance (1933)
Gyped in Egypt (1930)
Hill Billys (1935)
Injun Trouble (1938, 1951, 1969)
Little Black Sambo (1935)
The Mexican Problem (1913)
Redskin Blues (1932)
You're a Sap, Mr. Jap (1942)

FADE TO BLACK:
10 MOVIE TITLES FEATURING THE N-WORD.

Baldwin's Nigger (1968)
Boss Nigger (1975, a/k/a *The Black Bounty Hunter*)
The Legend Of Nigger Charley (1972)
A Nigger in the Woodpile (1904)
The Nigger (1915, a/k/a *The New Governor*)
Nigger Lover (1973, a/k/a *The Bad Bunch*; a/k/a *Mothers, Fathers, and Lovers*; a/k/a *Tom*)
Run Nigger Run (1974, a/k/a *The Black Connection*)
The Six Thousand Dollar Nigger (1980, a/k/a *Super Soul Brother*)
The Soul of Nigger Charley (1973)
Tossing a Nigger in a Blanket (1898)

*Starring white folks and Arsenio.

*Starring Ronald Reagan.

THE BIGGA PICTURE, NIGGA: CINEMATIC ALLEGORIES.

Alien Nation (1988)
In this sci-fi feature's future world, it's like the integration-mad 1950s all over again. Except no one in the prop department had the sense to make "Humans Only" water fountains.

Chan Is Missing (1982)
Two SF Chinatown cabbies search in vain for an elusive fellow Asian, "Chan," who owes them $4,000 in this parable for the identity crisis of the yellow man in white America.

Chicken Run (2000)
Don't let the claymation fool ya. The saga of farm fowl being raised for slaughter is more *Schindler's List* than *Wallace and Gromit*.

Night of the Living Dead (1968)
Despite saving a group of whites from the evils of their own kind's mindless savagery, the Black hero can't survive the police, who shoot him on sight. The End.

Planet of the Apes (1968), and subsequent sequels
Next time you watch these movies, substitute the word "Black" every time you hear "ape," and we bet you'll go Blackshit.

Pokémon: The First Movie (1998)
Believe it or not, this polyethnic creature-fest is all about tolerance. And not just how long you can tolerate watching this film with your little rugrat in tow.

The Time Machine (1960)
Sci-fi flick based on H.G. Wells' novel explores a future world in which a race of blond, beautiful people live above ground in fear of a scary, dark-skinded, subterranean-based race of monsterlike creatures who want to enslave and eat them. A literal projection of white paranoia.

The Time Machine (2002)
In the re-flipped future, a mo'-pigmented evolved race of people take control above the earth's surface and try to maintain a peaceful paradise while a hideous, pasty race of evildoers who've been forced into underground dwellings scheme to eat them. Not recommended for white supremacists with self-image issues.

MAY THE FARCE BE WITH YOU.

Bamboozled (2000)
Spike Lee's story of a bourgie-brotha who sells out the race in order to make it big as a television executive. Contrary to popular belief, the title doesn't intentionally refer to how most people felt about the film after seeing it.

Blazing Saddles (1974)
Cleavon Little stars as the unlikely, newly elected African-American sheriff of an all-white town in this Old West satire by Jewish funnyman Mel Brooks featuring campfire fart jokes, illicit miscegenation, and geriatric beatdowns. Note to ex-LAPD chief Bernard Parks: *This* is how the West was won.

Bonfire of the Vanities (1990)
Talk about selling wolf tickets: The cinematic adaptation of Tom Wolfe's bestselling novel about race relations in New York City is a cartoonish, tangled waste of celluloid guaranteed to burn unsuspecting viewers. Ring the alarm.

Bring It On (2000)
White suburban high school cheerleaders endure massive loads of white guilt after discovering they inadvertently stole their innovative dance routines from Black cheerleaders in Compton. So they steal from other sources instead . . . and still lose the big competition. (Cheer up, pom-pom pilots. At least you'll never have to worry about sickle cell anemia.)

Bulworth (1998)
Bullshit. *Next.*

Coonskin (better known as *Street Fight*) (1974)
Adults-only animated tale by counter-culturalist Ralph Bakshi that fucks with the already racist characters from Disney's *Song of the South* (1946). Featuring the voices of Scatman "Hong Kong Phooey" Crothers, Philip Michael "Tele-Tubbs" Thomas, and Barry "Sho' Ya Right" White, this gritty urban fable was rawer than Rudy Ray Moore eating steak tartare, baby.

Drop Squad (1994)
ER's Eriq La Salle stars as a Black advertising exec who's lost touch with his roots. He's abducted by a band of Blacker-than-thou crusaders for the purpose of "Deprogramming and Restoration Of Pride." Sounds suspiciously close to the subplot in *Bamboozled*. Oh dear, when will the scourge of Black-on-Black crime end?

The Great White Hype (1996)
Go round for round with this send-up of the sweet science and watch for the hook: as this film slyly conveys, no matter how hard you hit 'em, stereotypes won't stay down for the count.

Hairspray (1988)
The rapport between daytime-talk-show diva Ricki Lake and the Black people who love her can be traced to this John Waters coming-of-age comedy set during the civil rights era. Good hair, good movie.

Livin' Large! (1991)
Black man fears selling out in order to become a news reporter. At one point he even actually becomes Caucasian. This just in: *Livin' Large!* is deplorable.

Whiteboyz (1999)
Danny Hoch's hip hop wiggers in Iowa satire is desperately in need of some Black star power—and gets it in the form of scene stealer Bönz Malone. Unfortunately, when he's not on screen, it's a (white) wash.

WHITEY GON' WHIP 'DEM NIGGAZ ('N' SPICS) INTO SHAPE.

Bananas (1971)
Dangerous Minds (1995)
Fast Break (1979)
Finding Forrester (2001)
Hardball (2001)
The Lords of Discipline (1983)

SHOW ME THE WAY, MUD PERSON.

Assault on Precinct 13 (1976)
Driving Miss Daisy (1989)
Gung Ho (1986)
Jerry Maguire (1996)
An Officer and a Gentleman (1982)
The Patriot (1998)
Philadelphia (1993)
Remember the Titans (2000)
Rudy (1993)
To Sir, with Love (1967)

HELP ME WHOOPI,* I'M WHITE.

Clara's Heart (1988)
Corrina, Corrina (1994)
Ghost (1990)
Girl, Interrupted (1999)
Sister Act (1992)

*Grow some eyebrows, girl. Ya scarin' us.

10 FILMS ABOUT COLOREDS IN WHICH WHITES VALIDATE THE MOVIE.

Amistad (1997)
Slaves got it bad, y'all. Licks, licks, licks on their backside (and it ain't no fun cuz their homies got some). But imagine the plight of the poor (but rich) white lawyers defending the fifty-three Africans who in 1839 overpowered their captors aboard the not-so-friendly Spanish ship *La Amistad*. Their migraines musta been something terrible, Jack, as they tried to convince the (unkinky) bondage-practicing judges that the Black renegades were men and not estate's property. This fact-fueled retelling of rebellion by Steven Spielberg sinks to familiar whitewashed terrain as it absorbs itself with the troubling nuances of the law rather than focusing on the people in a whole lotta trouble. Like *Jaws*, *Amistad* is another flick about "great white(s)."

Come See the Paradise (1990)
An Irish-American union man (Dennis Quaid) and a young, easy-on-the-eyes Japanese-American woman (Tamlyn Tomita) fall into forbidden love in 1930s Los Angeles. Defying miscegenation laws and the girl's father's disapproval, the couple flee to interracial paradise (Seattle) where they wed and have a daughter. World War II erupts and all Japanese living in the States are contained in internment camps. Audiences then experience the racial discrimination against Asians through Anglo eyes. Go see something else.

Cry Freedom (1987)
Denzel Washington is activist Steve Biko, who stirs it up in segregated South Africa during the mid '70s. Kevin Kline is a bleeding heart journalist who befriends the anti-Apartheid-ist. After the cops brutally murder Biko (with lots of time left in the movie), this twisted tale takes on a lighter shade of pale as the story shifts its focus to Kline's inclinations to honor the fallen hero in a controversial book. Directed by that limey Dicky Attenborough and based on a true story (the same ol' one where whitey's feelings are more important than the darkie's daring courage and endeavors). Cinematic insults like these are enough to make you cry.

Glory (1989)
The history books give few props to the 54th Regiment of Massachusetts, an F(ree)-troop of Black soldiers who knew what time it was

("Fuck you, Massa" time). It took the cocreator of TV's *thirtysomething* to bring their bravery to the big screen. That would explain why so much attention is given to yuppie-fo'-life Matthew Broderick as the affluent white commander who must lead the squad in the savage Civil War. Though Ferris Bueller gets a lot of shine, Denzel doesn't take no day off and acts his ass off, overshadowing his "boss" and eventually copping critical glory and his first Oscar. Miracles do happen.

The Killing Fields (1984)
Though most critics of this highly praised film based on a true story poo-pooed the overly sappy inclusion of John Lennon's "Imagine" in the final reel, real heads were keen on how much better the movie was when it merely focused on the hectic life during civil wartime of Cambodian interpreter Dith Pran (the late Dr. Haing Ngor, who actually suffered through similar experiences in his lifetime) rather than Pran's dealings with *New York Times* journalist Sydney Schanberg (Sam Waterson). In a telling postscript, lead Ngor snagged an Academy Award for Best Supporting Actor while the actual supporting thespian Waterson received a nomination for Best Actor. A white-collar crime, no doubt.

Mississippi Burning (1988)
In the powder keg summer of 1964, Blacks wanna rock the vote but can't cuz whitey won't let them. Three civil rights proponents are slain by backwoods baddies in the process and it's up to . . . the *FBI* to save the day? Lost in Alan Parker's translation is the real deal on how the government dragged its feet to track the bigots, or how Black folks united to help themselves and get some equality. Ole Miss was burning all right, but it was those with the ashy skin that helped the soul men win.

'Round Midnight (1986)
He's got the jazz—the dearly departed Dexter Gordon that is. This film's semibiographical storyline is set in late '50s Paris and follows the last months of a gifted but weathered saxophonist (Gordon) addled by substance abuse as he tries to put his life back together. But of course, there's a young, adoring, and altruistic French (vanilla) artiste lurking in the background, waiting to help the aged tenor player.

Time is wasted on the fan's fam when all moviegoers want is some mo' Gordon and the all-the-way-live musical stylings of Herbie Hancock, Freddie Hubbard, Bobby Hutcherson, Ron Carter, Billy Higgins, and the golden-voiced Lonette McKee.

Seven Years in Tibet (1997)
Brad Pitt stars as Austrian Nazi Heinrich Harrer (and with a name like that, how could he be anything else?). Harrer is bananas over huge-ass mountains, so he and a buddy head out to the Himalayas. During their big adventure World War II breaks out and Harrer goes from a British POW camp to Tibet where he encounters a teenaged Dalai Lama—a rather interesting chap, if we do say so ourselves. But evidently he's not as interesting as a Nazi who's abandoned his pregnant wifey to go rock climbing because Harrer's character hogs the plot like it's nobody's business. As a result, the Dalai Lama is reduced to playing second fiddle to the man he calls "Yellow Head" (and we call "pus-head").

Three Seasons (1999)
A dreamlike look at a modern-day Vietnam, this film follows the lives of ordinary denizens in Ho Chi Minh City dealing with life's hardships. But the inconsequential subplot involving an ex-marine vet (Harvey Keitel, also one of the movie's executive producers) looking for his long-lost daughter bogs things down since little character development is given to Keitel's role. Apparently, one white face among the rice paddies was the seasoning the financiers demanded.

A Time to Kill (1996)
The adaptation of ex-lawyer John Grisham's first novel electrifies whenever Samuel L. Jackson is in action. Here he portrays a father who avenges his ten-year-old daughter's rape at the hands of two evil pieces of white shit. Matthew McConaughey is the cocky Caucasoid attorney who takes the case. While the book made the lawyer's motives and thoughts more ambiguous, director Joel "I've Just Wasted Two Hours of Your Life" Schumacher makes McConaughey more of a hero. As expected, more time is spent on how the courtroom battle affects the lawyer's clan as they deal with things like burning crosses on their front lawn instead of exploring the effects the brutal violation has on the Black family. C'mon, you know the devil don't play fair.

6 (WHITE) FISH OUTTA WATER FLICKS.

Ace Ventura: When Nature Calls (1995)
Jim Carrey goes to Africa to fight for animal rights.

The Air Up There (1994)
Kevin Bacon goes to Africa to find basketball players.

Black Rain (1989)
Michael Douglas goes to Japan to find a member of the *yakuza*.

Cadence (1991)
Charlie Sheen goes to an all-Black POW camp in Germany to find out how to march to Sam Cooke's "Chain Gang" in rhythm.

Dances with Wolves (1990)
Kevin Costner goes to Sioux Indian country to find himself.

I Dreamed of Africa (2000)
Kim Basinger goes to Africa to fight for animal rights; does not run into Jim Carrey.

PEOPLE HELPING PEOPLE: THE STRANGE / GAY / MYSTICAL / COLORED SAVIOR-SIDEKICK.

Alice (1990)
Mystical Chinese doctor (Key Luke)

Chasing Amy (1997)
Gay Black comic book creator (Dwight Ewell)

Crossroads (1986)
Mystical Black bluesman (Joe Seneca)

The Family Man (2000)
Mystical Black angel (Don Cheadle)

The Green Mile (1999)
Mystical Black prisoner (Michael Clarke Duncan)

Happy Gilmore (1996)
Strange Black golfer (Carl Weathers)

Indian in the Cupboard (1995)
Mystical Native American plaything (MC Litefoot)

The Karate Kid series (1984, 1986, 1989, 1994)
Mystical Japanese master (Pat Morita)

The Legend of Bagger Vance (2000)
Mystical Black caddy (Will Smith)

Living Out Loud (1998)
Gay Black jazz singer (Queen Latifah)

Mannequin (1987)
Gay Black assistant (Meshach Taylor)

The Matrix (1999)
Mystical Black oracle (Gloria Foster)

The Shining (1980)
Mystical Black groundskeeper (Scatman Crothers)

The Toy (1982)
Strange Black babysitter (Richard Pryor)

Unbreakable (2000)
Mystical Black comic book collector (Samuel L. Jackson)

What Dreams May Come (1998)
Mystical Black angel (Cuba Gooding Jr.)

Woman on Top (2000)
Gay Black matchmaking drag queen artist (Harold Perrineau Jr.)

WHITES AS COLOREDS . . . A SELECTIVE LIST.

Alan Arkin, the Russian/German Jew, as . . .
a Latino ("Abraham Rodriguez") in *Popi* (1969)
a Latino ("Bean") in *Freebie and the Bean* (1974)
an East Indian shrink ("Wellness Guide") in *America's Sweethearts* (2001)

Antonio Banderas, the Macho Spaniard and Mr. Melanie Griffith, as . . .
a Mexican ("El Mariachi") in *Desperado* (1995)
an Arab poet turned fighting machine ("Ahmed Ibn Fahdlan") in *The 13th Warrior* (1999)

Robby Benson, the sensitive '70s teen dream, as . . .
a Latino gang member ("Emilio Mendez") in *Walk Proud* (1979)
Native American Billy Mills (who won the Olympic 10,000-meter run) in *Running Brave* (1983)

Marlon Brando, the Marlon Brando of his generation, as . . .
Mexican revolutionary Emiliano Zapata in *Viva Zapata!* (1952)
an Asian ("Sakini") in *The Teahouse of the August Moon* (1956)
an East Indian guru ("Grindl") in *Candy* (1968)

Charles Bronson, the toughest big-screen S.O.B. and S.O.L. (son of Lithuanians), as . . .
Native Americans ("Hondo") in *Apache* (1954), ("Chief Blue Buffalo") in *Run of the Arrow* (1957), and ("Pardon Chato") in *Chato's Land* (1971) just to name a few

Yul Brynner, the exotic bald Russkie, as . . .
Siam's HNIC King Mongkut in *The King and I* (1956)
Mexican revolutionary Pancho Villa in *Villa Rides* (1968)

Marlene Dietrich, the German-accented sex *frauline,* as . . .
a Mexican madame ("Tanya") in *Touch of Evil* (1958)

Brendan Fraser, Canadian, as . . .
a Colombian drug lord ("Jefe") in *Bedazzled* (2000)

Valerie Harper, Mary Tyler Moore's around-the-way homegirl, as . . .
a Latina wife ("Consuela") in *Freebie and the Bean* (1974)

Charlton Heston, the square-jawed gun fetishist, as . . .
a Mexican district attorney ("Ramon Miguel 'Mike' Vargas") in *Touch of Evil* (1958)

Linda Hunt, the diminutive Oscar-winning New Jerseyite, as . . .
a (male!) Indonesian photographer ("Billy Kwan") in *The Year of Living Dangerously* (1982)

Kiel Martin, the alcoholic cop on *Hill Street Blues*, as . . .
a really light-skinded Black ("Johnny 'White Folks' O'Brien") in *Trick Baby* (1973)

Al Pacino, Bananarama's first choice for their song "Robert DeNiro's Waiting" but his name didn't sound quite right, as . . .
a Cuban drug lord ("Antonio 'Tony' Montana") in *Scarface* (1983)
a Puerto Rican ex-con ("Carlito Brigante") in *Carlito's Way* (1993)

Jack Palance, the former Mr. Vladimir Palanuik (believe it . . . or not!), as . . .
a Mongol ("Ogatai") in *The Mongols* (1961)
"the bloodiest cutthroat in Mexico" ("Jesus Raza") in *The Professionals* (1966)
Cuba's big boss man Fidel Castro in *Che!* (1969)

Peter Sellers, the Brit popularly known as bumbling French Inspector Clouseau in the *Pink Panther* films, as . . .
an Indian physician ("Dr. Ahmed el Kabir") in *The Millionairess* (1960)
a singing Spanish matador ("Juan Bautista") in *The Bobo* (1967)
a "fish out of water" Pakistani ("Hrundi V. Bakshi") in *The Party* (1968)
a Chinese private investigator ("Sidney Wang") in *Murder by Death* (1976)
an Asian ("Dr. Fu Manchu") in *The Fiendish Plot of Dr. Fu Manchu* (1980)

Ringo Starr, the fourth, "fun" Beatle, as . . .
a Mexican ("Emmanuel") in *Candy* (1968)

Fisher Stevens, the Former Steven Fisher, as . . .
an East Indian scientist ("Ben Jabituya") in *Short Circuit* (1986) and *Short Circuit 2* (1988)

Marisa Tomei, the Brooklyn-bred Italian hottie, as . . .
a Cuban ("Dottie Perez") in *The Perez Family* (1995)

John Wayne, a true white American who made movies about America's wars while other people actually fought in them . . .
the Mongolian ruler Gengis Khan in *The Conqueror* (1956)

Catherine Zeta-Jones, the UK-bred glamour-puss, as . . .
a Latina ("Elena Montero") in *The Mask of Zorro* (1998)

PASSING FAD:
COLOREDS PLAYING OTHER ROLES.

Giancarlo Esposito, Black Italian, as . . .
a Latin drug dealer ("Esteban") in *Fresh* (1994)
Puerto Rican writer Miguel Algar in *Piñero* (2001)

Andy Garcia, Havana-born Cuban, as . . .
an upstart Italian rookie cop ("George Stone") in *The Untouchables* (1987)
an Italian mafioso ("Vincent Mancini") in *The Godfather Part III* (1990)
Italian mobster Lucky Luciano in *Hoodlum* (1997)
a white Casino owner ("Frank Conner") in *Ocean's Eleven* (2001)

Persis Khambatta, former Miss India, as . . .
a bald female alien ("Lieutenant Ilia") in *Star Trek: The Motion Picture* (1979)

John Leguizamo, Colombian comedic tour de force, as . . .
an Italian plumber damsel-saver ("Luigi") in *Super Mario Bros.* (1993)
an Italian-American hairdresser ("Vinny") in *Summer of Sam* (1999)

Jennifer Lopez, Bronx-bred Boricua, as . . .
a white social worker ("Catherine Dean") in *The Cell* (2000)
an Italian-American ("Maria Fiore") in *The Wedding Planner* (2001)

Ricardo Montalban, rico *and* suave Mexican, as . . .
a Japanese Kabuki dancer ("Nakamura") in *Sayonara* (1957)
an Arab ("King") in *Cannonball Run II* (1984)

Anthony Quinn, the Mexican-Irish movie legend, as . . .
a French humpty-hump ("Quasimodo") in *The Hunchback of Notre Dame* (1956)
an Arab ("Auda abu Tayi") in *Lawrence of Arabia* (1962)
a Greek ("Alexis Zorbas") in *Zorba the Greek* (1964)
a tough Italian New York top cop ("Captain Mattelli") in *Across 110th Street* (1972)
a Libyan guerrilla leader ("Omar Mukhtar") in *Lion of the Desert* (1980)

Vanessa L. Williams, half-Black, half-white, all sizzling, as . . .
a Puerto Rican cop ("Carmen Vasquez") in *Shaft* (2000)

Jeffrey Wright, remarkable Black thespian phenomenon, as . . .
a Dominican drug lord ("Peoples Hernandez") in *Shaft* (2000)

TRADING PLACES:
RACIAL ROLE REVERSAL.

Black Like Me (1964)
Down to Earth (2001)
Soul Man (1986)
True Identity (1991)
Watermelon Man (1970)
White Man's Burden (1995)

WHEN AFRICAN-AMERICANS AND ASIANS COLLIDE.

SPIKE LEE'S GREATEST RACIAL RHUBARBS.
A DIRECTOR WHO HOLDS HIS TONGUE FOR NO ONE. HE MUST BE FROM BROOKLYN.

Spike Lee versus Whoopi Goldberg
Thrust into the limelight with the success of his first independently-produced feature, 1986's *She's Gotta Have It*, Shelton Jackson Lee quickly becomes one of filmmaking's most vocal and opinionated personalities. In a *New York Times* interview from the same year, the man called Spike chastises Whoopi Goldberg (among other Black celebrities) for wearing blue contact lenses and possessing a "vicious crossover mentality." Whoopi replies in the *Orange County Register*, "Spike . . . stay off my eye color because if I want to change it I will." But four years later Spike enjoys the last laugh in a *Playboy* interview when he says, "[Whoopi] don't wear them blue contacts no more, do she?" Rest *azured*—Whoopi's no betta blues were no mo'.

Spike Lee versus Eddie Murphy (and Arsenio Hall)
Though by 1989, Lee is making movies in Hollywood, he doesn't endear himself with Tinseltown's "Black Pack" with his widespread criticism of superstar Eddie Murphy, who Spike feels isn't doing enough to create jobs for Blacks at Murphy's home studio, Paramount Pictures. Guesting on his pal Arsenio Hall's late-night talk show, Eddie responds by clowning Spike, saying he looks like "a cricket." Arsenio also takes it upon himself to defend Murphy when Lee appears on his show. Says Hall, "Even someone with Eddie's box-office power can't change Hollywood overnight. And that change doesn't occur any quicker if you go to a Caucasian journalist looking to stir up conflict by telling him what you think of your Black brother." Shortly thereafter, Spike labels Arsenio an Uncle Tom.

Spike Lee versus Wim Wenders
Spike sets Hollywood afire in 1989 with *Do the Right Thing*, a film about race, which critics either highly praise or condemn for fueling racial acrimony. At the Cannes Film Festival, acclaimed German director Wim Wenders—who presides over the panel that dishes out awards—calls "Mookie," the Lee-portrayed character who turns on his Italian employers and hurls a garbage can through their pizzeria (thus starting a riot), "unheroic." Perturbed, Spike strikes back: "Wim Wenders had better watch out 'cause I'm waiting for his ass. Somewhere deep in my closet I have a Louisville Slugger bat with Wenders' name on it." The world quickly learns that Lee might rep Crooklyn, but he ain't no dodger.

Spike Lee versus Matty Rich
Spike often espouses the need for more African-American filmmakers, but gets red over green when raw-as-hell Matty Rich comes on the scene. The upstart's no-budget debut, *Straight Out of Brooklyn*, generates a critical buzz in 1991 and is set for release around the same time as Lee's *Jungle Fever*, thus threatening to cut in on the crucial opening weekend box office intake for Spike's interracial drama. When Spike warns Rich to change *Brooklyn*'s release date, the young buck mouths off and refuses.

It ends up not mattering, since *S.O.B.* does lackluster business. However, during a 1999 interview with Nasser Metcalfe, Spike reveals that he still holds a grudge, calling Rich "Matty Poor" and stating: "He knew nothing about film. He used to say, 'Spike Lee, he went to college. I'm from the streets!' That's just some ignorant shit, man. That type of thinking . . . where Black people equate . . . being real and being Black with just being stupid . . . has got to stop. Where if you're intelligent, and you speak well, and you go to school, then you're considered [trying to be] white. We've got to stop that stuff." Sho' 'nuff.

Spike Lee versus Norman Jewison
Spike raises a stink when it's announced that his dream project, a Malcolm X biopic, is already under way at Warner Bros. with seasoned (as in the color of salt) shot-caller Norman Jewison attached. So in early 1991 he promptly informs the *New York Times* of his "big problem" with the decision: "That disturbs me deeply, gravely. It's wrong with a capital 'W.' Blacks have to control these films." A short time later, Jewison steps down, Lee takes over, goes over budget, gets bailed out by donations from Black celebs and, besides the part where he casts himself as Detroit Red's best friend, makes a great movie. Xcellent!

Spike Lee versus Quentin Tarantino (and Samuel L. Jackson)
Despite casting Tarantino in a bit part in *Girl 6*, Mr. Lee cools on Mr. T for his refusal to nix the n-word from his vocabulary. "Quentin is infatuated with that word," says Spike in a 1997

interview with *Daily Variety*. "What does he want? To be made an honorary Black man?" He goes on to offer some free advice: "I want Quentin to know that all African-Americans do not think that word is trendy or slick."

Tarantino responds by saying that Lee would have to stand on a chair to kiss his ass, and that nobody goes to his movies. Surprisingly, Lee's frequent collaborator Sam Jackson (the Black man who can't stop spitting the n-word in Tarantino's flicks) also joins the verbal sparring. Jackson responds to Lee's criticism of Tarantino by pointing out that Spike also uses the word in his films, then mocks Lee by telling the *Toronto Sun*, "George Lucas didn't let me say 'nigga' once on the *Star Wars* [*Episode 1: The Phantom Menace*] set, and yeah, I was mad." Lee tells the *Washington Post*: "I don't have nothing against Sam . . . if he wants to defend Quentin Tarantino, he can. But for me, it's a lot like the house Negro defending the massa." A/k/a massa appeal.

Spike Lee versus The Academy of Motion Picture Arts and Sciences
Though he's been nominated, Spike has never won an Oscar—and he knows why. "I know that stuff a lot of times is not based on merit," he tells the *Washington Post* in 1998. He goes on to explain in the same article that even though his documentary *4 Little Girls,* about the tragic 1963 Birmingham church bombing, was up for consideration, the actual winner, *The Long Way Home,* which details the plight of European Jews after the second world war, was a lock. Why? "When the film is about the Holocaust and one of the producers is a rabbi and it comes from the Simon Wiesenthal Center, there are not many sure things in life, but that was a sure thing when you consider the makeup of the voting body of the Academy of Motion Picture Arts and Sciences. I'd have rather been the New York Knicks in the fourth quarter, down ten points [to the Bulls], [with] a minute left in the United Center, than have the odds we faced of winning the Oscar against the Holocaust film."

A year later, he writes an article for the *New York Times* in which his view of the AMPAS hasn't changed: "African-American artists and technicians are passed over again and again, while the Academy of Motion Picture Arts and

Sciences rolls out the usual dark suspects as presenters—and the master of ceremonies, Whoopi, in whiteface. They throw in some Debbie Allen choreography, have Whitney Houston sing, and try to pretend there's diversity in Hollywood." Call us crazy, but we bet that Spike will never win an Oscar.

Spike Lee versus Jonathan Demme
Producer Oprah Winfrey manages to get Black author Toni Morrison's supernatural novel, *Beloved,* to the big screen. But the Pulitzer Prize–winning project is given to Caucasian director, Jonathan Demme. Well, guess who goes to see the movie and doesn't like it? You're right! Says Spike, "In my opinion, [Demme], a white director, failed to get it." Oh no, Demme got it, all right—another victim of Spike's opinion.

Spike Lee versus Black Film Audiences
In the same *New York Times* article in which he lambasts the Academy, Lee proves himself an equal opportunity attacker: "When an independent Black filmmaker tries to [make] a serious film, don't count on the fickle Black audience to come. That is the most disturbing thing about the prospect for Black film. Black people complain about Black films, but nobody shows up to support a different type of film. Where was the Black audience for *Daughters of the Dust, Rosewood, Eve's Bayou?* Where? Packing theaters to see *Set It Off* and *Booty Call*." (For the record, *ego trip* saw *Rosewood*. At a free press screening.)

Spike Lee versus Eddie Murphy, Part 2
Far from PC, Fox's *The PJs,* the animated inner-city comedy series executive-produced by Eddie Murphy, is heavily criticized by Spike. In January 1999, Lee tells *USA Today,* "I am not a big fan [of the show]. When you have crackheads and cockroaches coming out of toilets, and you're making fun of the whole pathology of lower-income African-Americans living in the projects, I don't see any humanity in that." CNN also quotes Lee as saying, "I'm not saying [African-Americans] are above being made fun of, but [the show's] really hateful, I think, toward Black people. Plain and simple." C-I-L-L my landlord. Or a network programming exec.

Spike Lee versus Will Smith
Throughout a 2001 college lecture tour Lee

voices his dissatisfaction with cinema's reigning number one Black star, Will Smith, and his decision to appear as a coonish, mystical caddie for Matt Damon in the Depression-era South period piece, *The Legend of Bagger Vance* (or as Spike calls it, *Driving Mr. Damon*). Lee is quoted by the *Boston Globe* as saying: "In real life, Black men were being castrated and lynched left and right. With all that going on, why are you fucking trying to teach Matt Damon a golf swing?" Good question.

The answer to Spike's genuine anger, however, may lie even deeper. Whispers abound that Lee was still pissed at Smith for helping Michael Mann get the directing gig for *Ali,* a job Spike wanted and probably could have gotten had Smith sided with him. But Lee later dismisses those rumors, calmly chalking it up to he and Smith just not sharing the same vision of Muhammad Ali's story. Spike avoids any casting problems on his next flick by doing a documentary on gridiron great Jim Brown, a brown man who played for the Browns. Stay Black, Spike.

HONORABLE MENTION:
Charlton Heston versus Spike Lee
In 1999 while promoting *Summer of Sam* (a story set amid the killings of David Berkowitz), Lee is asked by a reporter what steps he would take to curb violence in America. "We've got to dismantle the NRA," states Lee. Well, what about National Rifle Association president Charlton Heston? "Shoot him with a .44-caliber Bulldog," jokes Lee with a laugh. (The Bulldog was the type of gun Berkowitz used in his killing spree.)

In response, Heston at first goodnaturedly downplays the incident. But then, in a June 5 letter to the editor printed in the *Los Angeles Times,* Heston gets philosophical on that ass: "I feel some irony. In '63, when I was marching for the freedom of Black Americans, I was threatened by white men. In '99, active now for the freedom of all Americans, I'm threatened by a Black man. When Lee was still in diapers, I was working with Dr. Martin Luther King to break down the racist code in the Hollywood technical unions that denied Blacks any place behind the cameras, paving the way for young filmmakers like Lee. I want no apology from him; my character speaks for itself." And so does his big-ass gun. Duck down!

ONE MISCEGENATION UNDER A GROOVE:
60 NOTABLE FILMS FEATURING INTERRACIAL LUV 'N' LUST.

Aaron Loves Angela (1975)
Black male (Kevin Hooks) and Latina female
(Irene Cara)

Angel Heart (1987)
white male (Mickey Rourke) and Black female
(Lisa Bonet)

Bad Company (1995)
Black male (Laurence Fishburne) and white
female (Ellen Barkin)

The Bad News Bears Go to Japan (1978)
white male (Jackie Earle Haley) and Asian
female (Hatsune Ishihara)

Behind the Green Door (1972)
Black male (Johnnie Keyes) and white female
(Marilyn Chambers)

Black and White (2000)
Black males (Power, Allan Houston) and white
females (Bijou Phillips, Claudia Schiffer)

Blood and Wine (1997)
white male (Jack Nicholson) and Latina female
(Jennifer Lopez)

The Bodyguard (1992)
white male (Kevin Costner) and Black female
(Whitney Houston)

Boogie Nights (1997)
Black male (Don Cheadle) and white female
(Melora Walters)

Bottle Rocket (1996)
white male (Luke Wilson) and Latina female
(Lumi Cavazos)

Bronx Tale (1993)
white male (Lillo Brancato) and Black female
(Taral Hicks)

Corrina, Corrina (1994)
white male (Ray Liotta) and Black female
(Whoopi Goldberg)

crazy/beautiful (2001)
Latino male (Jay Hernandez) and white female
(Kirsten Dunst)

Do the Right Thing (1989)
Black male (Spike Lee) and Latina female
(Rosie Perez)

The English Patient (1996)
East Indian male (Naveen Andrews) and white
female (Juliette Binoche)

Fort Apache, The Bronx (1981)
white male (Paul Newman) and Latina female
(Rachel Ticotin)

Freeway (1996)
Black male (Bokeem Woodbine) and white
female (Reese Witherspoon)

Guess Who's Coming to Dinner (1967)
Black male (Sidney Poitier) and white female
(Katherine Houghton)

Heavy Traffic (1973)
white male (Joseph Kaufmann) and Black
female (Beverly Hope Atkinson)

He Got Game (1998)
Black males (Denzel Washington, Ray Allen) and
white females (Milla Jovovich, Jill Kelly, Chasey
Lain) and Latina female (Rosario Dawson)

High Fidelity (2000)
white male (John Cusack) and Black female
(Lisa Bonet)

Jefferson in Paris (1995)
white male (Nick Nolte) and Black female
(Thandie Newton)

Joey Breaker (1993)
white male (Richard Edson) and Black female
(Cedella Marley)

The Joy Luck Club (1993)
white male (Andrew McCarthy) and Asian
female (Rosalind Chao)

Jumping Jack Flash (1986)
white male (Jonathan Pryce) and Black female
(Whoopi Goldberg)

Jungle Fever (1991)
Black male (Wesley Snipes) and white female
(Annabella Sciorra)

The Karate Kid, Part II (1986)
white male (Ralph Macchio) and Asian female
(Tamlyn Tomita)

Love Field (1992)
Black male (Dennis Haysbert) and white female
(Michelle Pfeiffer)

The Lover (1992)
Asian male (Tony Leung) and white female
(Jane March)

Made in America (1993)
white male (Ted Danson) and Black female
(Whoopi Goldberg)

Mighty Peking Man (1977)
Asian male (Danny Lee) and white female
(Evelyne Kraft)

Mission: Impossible 2 (2000)
white male (Tom Cruise) and Black female
(Thandie Newton)

Mississippi Masala (1992)
Black male (Denzel Washington) and East
Indian female (Sarita Choudhury)

Money Train (1995)
Black male (Wesley Snipes) and Latina female
(Jennifer Lopez)

Monster's Ball (2002)
white male (Billy Bob Thornton) and Black
female (Halle Berry)

"O" (2001)
Black male (Mekhi Phifer) and white female
(Julia Stiles)

One False Move (1992)
white males (Billy Bob Thornton, Bill Paxton)
and Black female (Cynda Williams)

100 Rifles (1969)
Black male (Jim Brown) and Latina female
(Raquel Welch)

One Night Stand (1997)
Black male (Wesley Snipes) and white female
(Nastassja Kinski) and Asian female (Ming-Na Wen))

A Patch of Blue **(1965)**
Black male (Sidney Poitier) and white female
(Elizabeth Hartman)

Play It to the Bone **(1999)**
white male (Woody Harrelson) and Asian female
(Lucy Liu)
Pulp Fiction **(1994)**
Black male (Ving Rhames) and white female
(Uma Thurman); white male (Quentin Tarantino)
and Black female (Venessia Valentino)

The Royal Tenenbaums **(2001)**
Black males (Danny Glover, Alem Brhan Sapp)
and white females (Anjelica Huston, Gwyneth
Paltrow)

Rushmore **(1998)**
white male (Jason Schwartzman) and Asian
female (Sara Tanaka)

Save the Last Dance **(2001)**
Black male (Sean Patrick Thomas) and white
female (Julia Stiles)

Sayonara **(1957)**
white male (Marlon Brando) and Asian female
(Miiko Taka)

The Score **(2001)**
white male (Robert DeNiro) and Black female
(Angela Bassett)

Shadows **(1960)**
white male (Anthony Ray) and Black female
(Leila Goldoni)

The Shrimp on the Barbie **(1990)**
Latin male (Cheech Marin) and white female
(Emma Samms)

The Siege **(1998)**
Arab male (Sami Bouajila) and white female
(Annette Bening)

Snow Falling on Cedars **(1999)**
white male (Ethan Hawke) and Asian female
(Youki Kudoh)

Star Maps **(1997)**
Latin male (Douglas Spain) and white female
(Kandeyce Jorden)

The Story of a Three-Day Pass (1968)
Black male (Harry Baird) and white female
(Nicole Berger)

Storytelling (2002)
Black male (Robert Wisdom) and white female
(Selma Blair)

Total Recall (1990)
white male (Arnold Schwarzenegger) and Latina
female (Rachel Ticotin)

Wayne's World (1992) and *Wayne's World 2* (1993)
white male (Mike Myers) and Asian female (Tia
Carrere)

The Wedding Banquet (1993)
Asian male (Winston Chao) and white male
(Mitchell Lichtenstein)

White Men Can't Jump (1992)
white male (Woody Harrelson) and Latina
female (Rosie Perez)

The World of Suzie Wong (1960)
white male (William Holden) and Asian female
(Nancy Kwan)

Zebrahead (1992)
white male (Michael Rapaport) and Black
female (N'Bushe Wright)

BARREL FULL O' MONKEYS:
11 MOVIES FEATURING MULTIETHNIC GROUPS.

The Bad News Bears **(1976)**
D.C. Cab **(1983)**
Hook **(1991)**
Kids **(1995)**
Light It Up **(1999)**
Major League **(1989)**
The Matrix **(1999)**
Moscow on the Hudson **(1984)**
The Muppet Movie **(1979)**
The Replacements **(2000)**
The Warriors **(1979)**

MORGAN AND ME (A WHITE).

Along Came a Spider **(2001)**
Morgan Freeman and Monica Potter

Driving Miss Daisy **(1989)**
Morgan Freeman and Jessica Tandy

High Crimes **(2002)**
Morgan Freeman and Ashley Judd

Kiss the Girls **(1997)**
Morgan Freeman and Ashley Judd

Nurse Betty **(2000)**
Morgan Freeman and Renee Zellweger

Robin Hood: The Prince of Thieves **(1991)**
Morgan Freeman and Kevin Costner

Se7en **(1995)**
Morgan Freeman and Brad Pitt

The Shawshank Redemption **(1994)**
Morgan Freeman and Tim Robbins

Unforgiven **(1992)**
Morgan Freeman and Clint Eastwood

WHEN THE SHIITE HITS THE SCREEN, PART 1:
10 POPULAR FILMS IN WHICH MIDDLE EASTERNERS MUST DIE IN ORDER FOR THE GOOD GUYS TO WIN.

The Delta Force (1986)
We'll bet that woolly tough-dude relic Chuck Norris has never heard the Cure's "Killing an Arab," but he's sure done it a lot in his action-packed movies—especially this one. Hairy Charlie might fear the barber, but he's not the least afraid of the hygiene-challenged, don't-know-who-they're-messin'-with Palestinian and Lebanese terrorists who hijack an American jumbo jet and hightail it to Beirut. When the Delta Force touches down behind enemy lines it ain't pretty, fight fans. One annihilation later and it's hundreds of du(med)-rags dead compared to only one stateside superfriend killed in the line of duty. Bankrolled by the completely unbiased Israeli production team of Golan/Globus and featuring two-dimensional Islamic extremists (hey, they let the women and children hostages go) as portrayed by Israeli actors and extras.

Executive Decision (1996)
Palestinian radicals overtake a flight to Washington, D.C., demanding that their imprisoned leader be released. The U.S. government complies, but it turns out that the head sneaky terrorist on board was lying all along and plans to drop 'nuff tons o' nerve gas on that ass to wipe out a third of the country. (One of the Arab henchmen is shot by his own when he learns of the actual plot and protests loudly, "This has nothing to do with Islam!") Goldie Hawn's loverboy, Snake Plissken, leads a rag-tag bunch of anti-terrorists to bring the 747 to safety before the prez exercises the "executive decision" to blow the plane up in midair. In a weird twist, protests against the film's stereotypical characterizations are halted and all is immediately forgiven when it's learned that universally hated costar Steven Seagal plays a character who flies out of the plane to his death in the film's first twenty minutes.

G.I. Jane (1997)
An Officer and a Gentleman with estrogen . . . and intolerance. Demi Moore shaves her head, buffs up, and proves she has the balls to become the first-ever female Navy SEAL. Without warning, the film's final act shifts to Libya where Demi and her commando crew celebrate her graduation by participating in that favorite all-American pastime of slaughtering A-rabs. Fuckin' A.

Iron Eagle (1986)
A Queen-loving sixteen-year-old steals an F-16 with the help of air force colonel Chappy (Louis Gossett Jr.) in order to save his pilot pops who was gunned down by a nameless Middle Eastern country and taken prisoner. The Footloose of shoot-the-sheiks flicks.

Navy SEALs (1990)
Time to wipe out the rags—again. Whores-d'oeuvre-loving Charlie Sheen is a punk, goofball military leader of a posse that's given a second chance to correct a past work-related fuck-up: they didn't kill all the fucking camel jockey terrorists on their last mission and let the biggest meanie escape (with Stinger missiles no less). But no worries, Uncle Sam's clan won't make the same mistake twice. If you're happy (that a bunch of A-rabs are gonna get bombed to pieces) and you know it, clap your hands (like one of them cute-as-hell baby seals they got at the zoo).

Rules of Engagement (2000)
The American-Arab Anti-Discrimination Committee called this "probably the most racist film ever made against Arabs by Hollywood." You bet it was a box-office bonanza. When the U.S. Embassy in Yemen is violently attacked by protesters (for reasons that are never clearly explained), a marine colonel (Samuel L. Jackson) is called in to restore order. He does so by ordering soldiers to fire into the Middle Eastern mob after three marines are gunned down. The aftermath: 83 deaths, including women and children. The National Security Advisor suppresses the videotape showing that the civilian crowd was armed and dangerous (watch for the supposedly crippled little girl on crutches who pulls out a gat) so the Black colonel can take the fall in court. (Even mo' racism?)

The Siege (1998)
A story with shades of 9/11 sure to leave Middle Eastern viewers as cold as Slurpees from 7-Eleven. The Big Apple is being bombed left and right by a radical Muslim organization after United States forces capture their zealot leader. Arab-Americans are consequently rounded up by the army and herded into internment camps. The filmmakers feature an upstanding Arabian FBI agent (his son is detained) as if to say, "See, we ain't stereotyping. There's good and bad sand niggaz." The most aggravating thing about this movie, however? The typical, bullshit Hollywood ending.

Swordfish (2001)
The unveiling of Halle Berry's breathtaking hooters in this hi-tech thriller (easily the Most Eye-Popping Special Effects of that year) distracted many from the ruthless anti-terrorism activities of John Travolta's demented cell leader, an Israeli madman fighting fire with fire. When it comes to Arabs, Swordfish swims in no sea of love.

True Lies (1994)
Unbeknownst to his bored (thus cheating) wife, Austrian hormone Arnie Schwarzenegger is not the dull computer salesman he pretends to be, but rather a suave super-secret agent. Arnold must put the thrill back in his marriage while at the same tracking down nuke-carrying Mid Easterners who really hate America, loudly cuss a lot, have no regard for human life (or soap) and never smile (not even at Arnie's brilliant touché-filled dialogue). Of course, it's a comedy.

Wanted: Dead or Alive (1987)
Ex-CIA-er-turned-bounty-hunter must stop the sadistic games of Malak Al Rahim, an evil, "I Don't Give a Fuck" international terrorist (played by KISS bassist Gene Simmons) who is blowing shit up with a remote-controlled contraption in broad daylight for no apparent reason other than he likes it (and that he's Arab). Let's give away the ending, shall we? Gene goes out like he's auditioning for Scanners when his head explodes. Obviously, the producers were playing mind games with the movie's title, cuz ain't no way Dr. Love was ever wanted alive.

OFFEND AN ARAB NIGHT:
7 MOVIES YOU SHOULD NEVER SEE WITH A MIDDLE EASTERN DATE.

Best Defense (1984)
This horrible offense, set in Kuwait, places camels in the backgrounds of almost every single shot. Trust us. You won't be humping later.

Exodus (1960)
An Arab Jew lover gets a noose around his neck in this epic about the Arab/Israeli conflict in Palestine. Exit stage left.

Ishtar (1987)
This ish won't get you laid like Warren Beatty. It'll just make you wonder who you hate more: an ancient chocha-monger or a rank-and-vile people?

Lawrence of Arabia (1962)
A classic that nevertheless features Obi-Wan Kenobi and Zorba the Greek in brown face. Not a cock-block-buster.

Network (1976)
A deranged veteran newscaster is "mad as hell" and he's not gonna take it anymore. That could also describe those offended by the no-nonsense and uncivilized Saudis planning a hostile takeover of the TV network. Rated R (Rag-bashing).

Sphinx (1981)
'Cuz it stinks.

Things Are Tough All Over (1982)
Off-the-hook Cheech and Chong put on some hook noses and tell off-color jokes. Not the comedy oasis that you're looking for. Highly unrecommended.

9 FILMS FEATURING ARABS KIDNAPPING (USUALLY WHITE) WOMEN.

Harem (1985)
Harum Scarum (1965)*
Mondo Bizarro (1966)
Not Without My Daughter (1991)
Protocol (1984)
Rosebud (1974)
Sahara (1983)
The Sheik (1921)
The Wind and the Lion (1975)

*Features Arabs kidnapping Elvis Presley.

WHEN THE SHIITE HITS THE SCREEN, PART 2:
10 FAMILY FILMS THAT TEACH KIDS TO STEREOTYPE, MOCK (AND PROBABLY HATE) ARABS . . . AND WHY.

Aladdin (1992)
The dark-skinded Arab villains with thick accents and the light-skinded heroes who speak perfect English in this animated Disney flick subliminally suggest to tots everywhere who they can and can't trust. More blatant are select song lyrics (which were partially deleted from the video version) like: "Oh, I come from a land, from a faraway place / Where the caravan camels roam / Where they cut off your ear, if they don't like your face / It's barbaric, but hey, it's home." It's a small (minded) world after all.

Back to the Future (1985)
Marty McFly's best friend, the lovable and goofy Doc, gets done in by terrorists. Ask any kid any age that's seen the movie and they'll tell you, "The Libyans did it." Not even time travel can outrun racism. (Ain't that a long-ass-but-real-short trip?)

The Black Stallion (1979)
Vicious and mean Arab is cruel to animals and kids. Whoa, Nelly! Ride or die.

Father of the Bride, Part II (1995)
Eugene Levy is the filthy-rich-yet-still-money-hungry, thickly accented Mr. Habib, who acts just plain filthy whether he's screaming at his wife and son or disrespecting wholesome white dad Steve Martin. Mothers, don't let your girls grow up to marry Arabs.

In the Army Now (1994)
It's debatable whether children would be more damaged by being exposed to Pauly Shore or racist views toward Arabs. Enlist parental discretion either way.

Jewel of the Nile (1985)
Welcome to the jungle. This exotic Indiana Jones rip-off offers plenty of savage, back-stabbing Arabs controlled by religion and a thirst for dominance at all costs. A cubic zirconium representation.

Kazaam (1996)
Get anything you want from the black market from Malik, an Arabian sleazeball in this urban fantasy flick starring Shaq as an overgrown genie. Offensive to genies as well.

The Mummy (1999)
American culture vultures address a character of Arab descent as "our smelly little friend" and "a stinky fellow." Foul language has no place in family fare, you big dummies.

The Prince of Egypt (1998)
Animated Moses must lead the Hebrews to freedom while angry God punishes and kills. Egyptian massacre at the bloody Red Sea is the film's climax. Based on a true story and rated PG (Punish Gentiles).

Raiders of the Lost Ark (1981)
Stand-out scene played for laughs in which Indy reacts to the elaborate sword-wielding of a turban-rocking bad guy by merely shooting him is cold-blooded murder. Lore has it that actor Harrison Ford had the runs that day so the quick kill was improvised. Shit happens.

EGO TRIP'S CINEMA AWARDS.

Best Assumption of a Slave Name When He Didn't Even Have to Do It
Nicolas Cage (né Coppola), who changed his surname to that of Black comic book superhero "Luke Cage" (a/k/a "Powerman") so that he'd be accepted for his acting talents, not his Hollywood pedigree.

Worst Rationale for Banning a So-Bad-It's-Good Rap Movie
Apartheid-era South Africa, which banned the Run-D.M.C. vehicle *Tougher than Leather* (1988) on the grounds of obscenity (vis-à-vis D.M.C.'s post-coital pose with a platinum blonde cocaine-colored floozy), and because "whites are portrayed as moronic bunglers while Blacks are the heroes."

Best Black Buck in a Nonporno Porn Flick
Hal "227" Williams as "Big Dick Blaque" in *Hardcore* (1979). This film has a tight cast—Tracey Walter (a/k/a "Miller" from *Repo Man*) as a porno shop worker, as well as an appearance by *Bewitched*'s "Darren" 2.0, Dick Sargent. But it's another "Richard" that steals the show in an audition scene with George C. Scott. Roll the clip:

> **HW:** "I'm Dick Blaque. You doin' a porno movie, right?"
> **GCS:** "Right."
> **HW:** "Then I'm the man for you."
> **GCS:** "Well, I'm glad to meet you, Mr. Blaque. But I'm afraid you're not exactly the type we're lookin' for."
> **HW:** "You mean because I'm Black."
> **GCS:** "No. You're just not the type."
> **HW:** "What do you mean not the type? Man, don't you know who I am? I'm Big Dick Blaque. I've done more porno movies than you ever saw. I worked with Harry Reems, Johnny Wadd. Not the type [grabbing crotch]?! I can cum ten times a day. I can keep it hard for two hours at a time. I'm a woman's dream. I got a dick hung on me nine inches long."
> **GCS:** "I'm sorry, Mr. Blaque. I'm sure you're very good. But at the moment I just don't have anything for you. If something comes up, I'll be happy to give you a call."
> **HW::** "Sheeeit. You don't want to hire any niggers, that's all. I knew this was a scam! This is bullshit!" [Exits pissed.]

Best Example of a Negro Thinking Awards Grow on Trees
Ving Rhames, who at the 1998 Golden Globe Awards, gave away his Best Actor in a TV Movie award to his idol Jack Lemmon.

Lifetime Misery Award
Native American actor/activist Russell Means, who in a 1992 editorial for *News from Indian Country* recalled the trauma of going to the movies while growing up:
On Saturday afternoons in Vallejo, California, my younger brother, Dace, and I would go to the Esquire Movie Theater and watch those damn cowboy-and-Indian flicks of the forties, the ones where the bugle sounds and the cavalry charges in and starts killing Indians willy-nilly while everyone in the audience cheers. Dace couldn't watch; he'd bury his head in his hands. When you're eight or nine years old, as we were, you think that maybe this time the Indians are going to win, that this movie will be different. Then, afterward, we'd leave the theater, and honest to God, we had to fight back-to-back, just the two of us, against Mexicans, Filipinos, Chinese, and Blacks as well as the whites. All these neighborhood kids saying, "Hey, Indians, we're going to whip your ass."

Worst Uproar over Nothing New
PC critics of *Black Hawk Down* (2001), who voiced shock at the flick's depiction of Somalis as vicious, never-ending hostile hordes pumped up on haterade, and the racist epithets for them ("skinnies" and "sammies") regularly used by onscreen U.S. soldiers. Soldiers at war dehumanizing their enemy with name calling and bad words? Say it ain't so!

Best Event Proving That Blacks Can Never Be Satisfied
The dual Best Actor/Actress victories of Denzel Washington and Halle Berry at the seventy-fourth annual Academy Awards in 2002. While many Blacks rejoiced, many others charged "tokenism," and still others complained that Washington and Berry's winning roles weren't "positive" enough. Shut up already.

Best Special Effect
Pearl Harbor (2001) has a lot of big costly explosions, but none compares to the sparks between the two army air pilots and a navy nurse caught in an amorous triangle. That's right, *Pearl Harbor* is a love story, papa-san! But the real news is how the sneaky producers with a yen for yen altered offensive dialogue and action to make the movie more palatable to audiences in Japan. Either way, we can't believe the film's best line—"Girl, you got some bomb-ass pussy"—was left on the editing room floor.

Worst Lip Service Award
It truly is sad to go back and watch the beautiful and talented songstress Aaliyah, who perished in a plane crash in 2001, in her *Romeo Must Die* (2000) acting debut, partly because a promising career was cut tragically

short. She deftly holds her own against romantic interest and charismatic Asian icon Jet Li, who plays the dude everybody's trying to merk, in this tongue-in-cheek action flick. However, rest assured that no tongues or lips even came close to some cheeks at the conclusion of this story. That's because in keeping with Hollywood's unwritten emasculation rule regarding Asian men (even those who just survived attacks from one-hundred-plus would-be assassins to save the girl) our homeboy Jet can't even get a peck from his pretty costar. He can flex, but no sex for Mr. Li.

Best Reason to Hate Disney One Mo' Time

Throughout its history the Walt Disney corporation has been criticized for its insensitivity toward non-Anglo cultures. But Disney's about tradition. So, for three straight years in the late '90s, those Micks explored the "savage" life with disturbing results. 1997: While visiting his ex-wife in the African bush, everyone's favorite ex-con Tim Allen is forced to look after his newly discovered white-'n'-wild child son in *Jungle 2 Jungle*. And boy, the brat sure does cause quite a commotion back in New York City! 1998: In *Krippendorf's Tribe*, anthropologist Richard Dreyfuss "discovers" a lost New Guinea tribe that actually doesn't exist in order to get some lucrative grant money. When asked for proof, Dick's fam winds up "aping" the restless natives for the check writers. 1999: Disney releases the animated *Tarzan* with no Black people in it, despite the fact that, like most *Tarzan* films, it's set in Africa. It's all your fault, Walt.

Best Unassuming Performance by a Black Who Has No Business Being in the Movie

It's been said that only white people would refuse to leave a haunted home. But that's even more reason to applaud Ernie Hudson's courageous, going-against-type role as a laid-back, going-with-the-flow phantom exterminator in *Ghostbusters* (1984). True, Ernie's character got minimal screen time, delivered no good lines, and had nothing to do with any key plot points. But he did it well enough that the whites-in-charge brought him back to re-create the Black magic for the sequel, *Ghostbusters II* (1989).

Most Unlikely Cinematic Inspiration for an Ignorant Rap Lyric

You thought Jay-Z wrote all the ethnic stereotypes for his smash "Girls, Girls, Girls" on his own? Think twice. The pride of Brooklyn's Marcy projects obviously paid close attention to the scene in *Good Will Hunting* (1997) in which human calculator Matt Damon kicks knowledge to Robin Williams about the remarkable life and times of East Indian mathematical genius Srinivasa Ramanujan. When Mork the dork can't seem to grasp the ethnic background of Ramanujan, Damon's character coyly explains, "Indians—as in dots, not feathers." Real edumacated.

Worst Blatantly Racist Visual Joke in an Otherwise Classic Comedy

The famed frat house romp *Animal House* (1978) is loaded with memorable scenes. The raciest is the one in which Black band Otis Day and the Knights cold rock a party to the A.M. in an all-Black club the white (frat) brothers and their scared-ass sorority sisters (not sistas) unwittingly enter. Most filmgoers remember the immortal line "Do you mind if we dance with your dates?" spoken by one of the big-and-tall ebony ladykillers eyeing Amadeus and them's chicks. But then there's also the following shady visual pun: When one of the nervous white girls is asked her major by one of the nervous white guys, she shakily answers, "Primitive cultures." Cut immediately to Head Knight in Charge Otis ripping some "Shamalama ding dong"–style alliteration and dancing a two-step on stage with mucho gusto. Savage.

Worst Racist Plot Device in a Romantic Comedy

Who says minorities don't get good roles in major motion pictures? In *The Wedding Planner* (2001), if it wasn't for a bumbling Asian cabbie recklessly getting his 31 Flavors on while driving and setting off a freak accident, J.Lo and midnight toker Matt McConaughey (who saves her ass) would never meet and fall in lust and, thus, no damn picture. See, there really is no love without hate.

Worst Absolute Ending

For most of its 107 minutes, *Absolute Beginners* (1986) is a bubbly, breezy, highly stylized modern musical in which a couple of young, pre-mod white kids run around late '50s London looking for love, fame, and a piece of the jazzyfatnastee action. But then near its conclusion, director Julien Temple decides to bust up the party and remind everyone how much racism sucks by setting off a huge race riot. Bloody hell.

Best Forgotten Random Racist Moment

From the terminally adolescent mind of Chicago's beloved Caucasian celluloid dream weaver John Hughes came *Weird Science* (1985), a box-office hit about virginal brainiac misfit teenagers who create the perfect woman by using a computer and wearing bras on their heads. Genius as the premise was, African-American viewers were undoubtedly left dumbfounded by the picture's out-of-nowhere blues bar scene in which a tipsy Anthony Michael Hall breaks into some spontaneous and seriously stoopid (though admittedly amusing) jive talk. Of course, it doesn't take a rocket scientist to figure out what's really going on here: Hughes don't love them hues.

IN FILM . . . White **"INSPECTOR CLOUSEAU"** (Peter Sellers) and Asian **"CATO"** (Burt Kwouk) in the *Pink Panther* films (1963–1993) ● Black **"VIRGIL TIBBS"** (Sidney Poitier) and white **"BILL GILLESPIE"** (Rod Steiger) in *In the Heat of the Night* (1967) ● White **" 'DIRTY' HARRY CALLAHAN"** (Clint Eastwood) and Latino **"CHICO GONZALEZ"** (Reni Santoni) in *Dirty Harry* (1971) ● Black **"AL HICKEY"** (Bill Cosby) and white **"FRANK BOGGS"** (Robert Culp) in *Hickey & Boggs* (1972) ● White **" 'DIRTY' HARRY CALLAHAN"** (Clint Eastwood) and Black **"EARLY SMITH"** (Felton Perry) in *Magnum Force* (1973) ● White **"FREEBIE"** (James Caan) and

WE CAN ALL GET ALONG: NOTABLE

Latino **"BEAN"** (Alan Arkin) in *Freebie and the Bean* (1974) ● Black **"GROVER MULDOON"** (Richard Pryor) and white **"GEORGE CALDWELL"** (Gene Wilder) in *Silver Streak* (1976) ● White **"HAN SOLO"** (Harrison Ford) and Wookie **"CHEWBACCA"** (Peter Mayhew) in *Star Wars* (1977) ● White **"PETER LOWENSTEIN"** (Ted Danson) and Black **"OSCAR GRACE"** (J.A. Preston) in *Body Heat* (1981) ● White **"DEKE DASILVA"** (Sylvester Stallone) and Black **"MATTHEW FOX"** (Billy Dee Williams) in *Nighthawks* (1981) ● White **"SHARKY"** (Burt Reynolds) and Black **"ARCH"** (Bernie Casey) in *Sharky's Machine* (1981) ● White **"JACK CATES"** (Nick Nolte) and Black **"REGGIE HAMMOND"** (Eddie Murphy) in *48 Hrs.* (1982) ● White **" 'DIRTY' HARRY CALLAHAN"** (Clint Eastwood) and Black **"HORACE KING"** (Albert Popwell) in *Sudden Impact* (1983) ● Black **"RAY HUGHES"** (Gregory Hines) and white **"DANNY COSTANZO"** (Billy Crystal) in *Running Scared* (1986) ● White **"TONY COSTAS"** (Jay Leno) and Asian **"FUJITSUKA NATSUO"** (Pat Morita) and Black **"SHORTCUT"** (Ernie Hudson) in *Collision Course* (1987) ● White **"MARTIN RIGGS"** (Mel Gibson) and Black **"ROGER MURTAUGH"** (Danny Glover) in the *Lethal Weapon* films (1987–1998) ● White **"MATTHEW SYKES"** (James Caan) and Newcomer **"SAMMUEL 'GEORGE' FRANCISCO"** (Mandy Patinkin) in *Alien Nation* (1988) ● White **" 'DIRTY' HARRY CALLAHAN"** (Clint Eastwood) and Asian **"AL QUAN"** (Evan C. Kim) in *Dead Pool* (1988) ● White **"JOHN MCCLANE"** (Bruce Willis) and Black **"AL POWELL"** (Reginald VelJohnson) in *Die Hard* (1988) and *Die Hard 2* (1990) ● White **"NADA"** (Rowdy Roddy Piper) and Black **"FRANK"** (Keith David) in *They Live* (1988) ● Black **"DENNIS CURREN"** (Forest Whitaker) and white "Alex Kearney" (Anthony Edwards) in *Downtown* (1990) ● Black **"JAMES 'JIMMY/JIM' ALEXANDER DIX"** (Damon Wayans) and white **"JOE HALLENBECK"** (Bruce Willis) in *The Last Boy Scout* (1991) ● White **"NATHANIEL (HAWKEYE)"** (Daniel Day Lewis) and Native American **"CHINGACHGOOK"** (Russell Means) in *The Last of the Mohicans* (1992) ● White **"JOHN CONNOR"** (Sean Connery) and Black **"WEBB SMITH"** (Wesley Snipes) in *Rising Sun* (1993) ● Black **"RON HUNTER"** (Denzel Washington) and white **"FRANK RAMSEY"** (Gene Hackman) in *Crimson Tide* (1995) ● White **"JOHN MCCLANE"** (Bruce Willis) and Black **"ZEUS CARVER"** (Samuel L. Jackson) in *Die Hard with a Vengeance* (1995) ● Latino **"RODRIGUEZ"** (Tupac Shakur!) and white **"DIVINCI"** (Jim Belushi) in *Gang Related* (1997) ● Black **"JAMES DARRELL EDWARDS III"** (Will Smith) and white **"AGENT KAY"** (Tommy Lee Jones) in *Men in Black* (1997) and *Men in Black 2* (2002) ● Black **"SCOTT ROPER"** (Eddie Murphy) and white **"KEVIN MCCALL"** (Michael

Rapaport) in *Metro* (1997) ● Black **"JAMES CARTER"** (Chris Tucker) and Asian **"LEE"** (Jackie Chan) in *Rush Hour* (1998) and *Rush Hour 2* (2001) ● Black **"MILES LOGAN"** (Martin Lawrence) and white **"CARLSON"** (Luke Wilson) in *Blue Streak* (1999) ● White **"ETHAN HUNT"** (Tom Cruise) and Black **"NYAH NORDOFF-HALL"** (Thandie Newton) in *Mission: Impossible 2* (2000) ● Black **"MONTELL GORDON"** (Don Cheadle) and Latino **"RAY CASTRO"** (Luis Guzmán) in *Traffic* (2000) ● Black **"ALONZO HARRIS"** (Denzel Washington) and white **"JAKE HOYT"** (Ethan Hawke) in *Training Day* (2001)

INTERRACIAL CRIME-FIGHTING DUOS.

...AND ON TELEVISION. White **"LONE RANGER"** (Clayton Moore) and Native American **"TONTO"** (Jay Silverheels) in *The Lone Ranger* (1956) ● Black **"ALEXANDER SCOTT"** (Bill Cosby) and white **"KELLY ROBINSON"** (Robert Culp) in *I Spy* (1965–1968) ● White **"GREEN HORNET"** (Van Williams) and Asian **"KATO"** (Bruce Lee) in *The Green Hornet* (1966–1967) ● White **"STEVE MCGARRETT"** (Jack Lord) and his crew including Asian **"CHIN HO KELLY"** (Kam Fong) in *Hawaii Five-O* (1968–1980) ● Black **"TERRY WEBSTER"** (Georg Stanford Brown) and white **"WILLIE GILLIS"** (Michael Ontkean) in *The Rookies* (1972–1976) ● Black **"SMITTY"** (Hal Williams) and white **"HOPPY"** (Howard Platt) in *Sanford & Son* (1972–1977) ● Black **"RON HARRIS"** (Ron Glass) and white **"ARTHUR DIETRICH"** (Steve Landesberg) in *Barney Miller* (1976–1982) ● White **"QUINCY"** (Jack Klugman) and Asian **"SAM FUJIYAMA"** (Robert Ito) in *Quincy* (1976–1983) ● White **"JON BAKER"** (Larry Wilcox) and Latino **"FRANCIS LLEWELLYN 'PONCH' PONCHERELLO"** (Erik Estrada) in *CHiPs* (1977–1983) ● White **"THOMAS REMINGTON SLOANE III"** (Robert Conrad) and Black **"TORQUE"** (Ji-Tu Cumbuka) in *A Man Called Sloane* (1979–1980) ● White **"THOMAS SULLIVAN MAGNUM"** (Tom Selleck) and Black **"THEODORE 'TC' CALVIN"** (Roger E. Mosley) in *Magnum P.I.* (1980–1988) ● Black **"E.L. 'TENSPEED' TURNER"** (Ben Vereen) and white **"LIONEL WHITNEY"** (Jeff Goldblum) in *Tenspeed and Brown Shoe* (1980) ● Black **"BOBBY HILL"** (Michael Warren) and white **"ANDREW RENKO"** (Charles Haid); white **"JOHN LARUE"** (Kiel Martin) and Black **"NEAL WASHINGTON"** (Taurean Blacque) in *Hill Street Blues* (1981–1987) ● White **"JAMES 'SONNY' CROCKETT"** (Don Johnson) and Black **"RICARDO TUBBS"** (Philip Michael Thomas); white **"GINA CALABRESE"** (Saundra Santiago) and Black **"TRUDY JOPLIN"** (Olivia Brown) in *Miami Vice* (1984–1989) ● White **"SPENSER"** (Robert Urich) and Black **"HAWK"** (Avery Brooks) in *Spenser: For Hire* (1985–1988) ● Black **"VIRGIL TIBBS"** (Howard E. Rollins) and white **"BILL GILLESPIE"** (Carroll O'Connor) in *In the Heat of the Night* (1988) ● White **"TIM BAYLISS"** (Kyle Secor) and Black **"FRANCIS 'FRANK' XAVIER PEMBLETON"** (Andre Braugher); Black **"MELDRICK LEWIS"** (Clark Johnson) and white **"STEVE CROSETTI"** (Jon Polito) in *Homicide* (1993–1999) ● Black **"J. C. WILLIAMS"** (Malik Yoba) and Latino **"EDDIE TORRES"** (Michael DeLorenzo) in *New York Undercover* (1994–1998) ● White **"NASH BRIDGES"** (Don Johnson) and Latino **"JOE DOMINGUEZ"** (Cheech Marin) in *Nash Bridges* (1996–2001) ● Asian **"SAMMO LAW"** (Sammo Hung) and Black **"TERRELL PARKER"** (Arsenio Hall) in *Martial Law* (1998)

FOREIGN DOMESTICS: 50 DOCUMENTED LATINA HOUSEKEEPERS ON THE BIG AND SMALL SCREENS.

CRIADAS DE CINE . . .

1. "Arizona Housekeeper"
   Almost Famous (2000)
2. "Carmen"
   Down and Out in Beverly Hills (1986)
3. "Clara"
   Curdled (1996)
4. "Cleaning Lady"
   John Carpenter's Vampires (1998)
5. "Aurora de la Hoya"
   Seems Like Old Times (1980)
6. "Gabriella"
   Curdled (1996)
7. "Gage's Maid"
   Indecent Proposal (1993)
8. "Graciella, the Bowdens' Maid"
   Cape Fear (1991)
9. "Hotel Maid"
   Flashfire (1993)
10. "Housekeeper"
    The Big Picture (1989)
11. "Housekeeper"
    The Man with Two Brains (1983)
12. "Inez"
    Bottle Rocket (1996)
13. "Lady Jessica's Maid"*
    Dune (1984)
14. "Maid"
    American Gigolo (1980)
15. "Maid"
    Basic Instinct (1992)
16. "Maid"
    The Big Fix (1978)
17. "Maid"
    California Suite (1978)
18. "Maid"
    Fletch (1985)
19. "Maid"
    Fraternity Vacation (1985)
20. "Maid"
    MP Da Last Don (1998)
21. "Maid"
    Suburbia (1984)
22. "Maid"
    Universal Soldier (1992)
23. "Maid"
    Wolf (1994)
24. "Maid #2"
    8 Heads in a Duffel Bag (1997)
25. "Mathilda"
    The End of Violence (1997)
26. "Maya" (and the supporting characters of . . .)
    Bread and Roses (2000)
27. "Nora"
    As Good as It Gets (1997)
28. "Rosa" (and the supporting characters of . . .)
    Bread and Roses (2000)
29. "Rosa"
    Down to Earth (2001)
30. "Rosa"
    Troop Beverly Hills (1989)
31. "Rosalita"
    The Goonies (1985)
32. "Spanish Maid"
    Loverboy (1989)
33. "Spanish Maid"
    The Man Who Wasn't There (1983)
34. "Stella"
    What Women Want (2000)
35. "Taft Hotel Maid"
    Best in Show (2000)

. . . Y CRIADAS DE TELEVISION

36. "Dora Calderon"
    I Married Dora (ABC, 1987)
37. "Carmela"
    Dream On (HBO, 1992)
38. "Celia"
    Dharma and Greg (ABC, 1998)
39. "Mrs. Chavez"
    Hagen (CBS, 1980)
40. "Evie"
    Seinfeld (NBC, 1991)
41. "Lisa Flores"
    The Ted Knight Show (ABC, 1986)
42. "Maria Conchita Lopez"
    What a Country (Syndicated, 1986)
43. "Louisa"
    Veronica's Closet (NBC, 1997)
44. "Maid"
    Charlie's Angels (ABC, 1976)
45. "Maid"
    The Incredible Hulk: Death in the Family
    (CBS, 1977)
46. "Maid"
    Misfits of Science (NBC, 1985)
47. "Maria Conchita Navarro"
    One of the Boys (NBC, 1989)
48. "Marta"
    Dudley (CBS, 1993)
49. "Rosario Salazar"
    Will & Grace (NBC, 2000)
50. "Tia"
    The Hughleys (ABC, 2000)

* ¡Una criada en espacio!

TRIBUTE TO A MEXICAN.
GOMEZ ADDAMS: KILLER OR REJECTED ICON OF CHICANISMO? BY ESTEBAN ZUL

In the crowded world of eccentric Mexican-American millionaires, one name still resonates with distinction—the late, great Gomez Addams. Born Adam Gomez to a modest Mexican-American family in California's San Joaquin Valley, Gomez rose from poverty to become one of the 1960s' highest-paid television stars. His program, *The Addams Family,* was the first docu-comedy on TV, and is still considered by many to be the first Latino sitcom in U.S. history, as it explored universal Latino themes such as social alienation, deranged uncles, hairy cousins, and outdated fashion sense.

Gomez grew up in the orchard town of Dinuba, California. "We were very poor Chicanos!" Gomez would remark decades later. "We had to scrimp and save tooth and nail! Sometimes all we had to eat was tooths and nails!" Yes, the Gomezes were a poor family, but a happy one. Mama Gomez was a homemaker and amateur taxidermist, known for her experimental styles, often mixing and matching animal parts from the partially obliterated carcasses of dead mapaches, rodents, and other wild roadkill. Young Gomez's fascination with taxidermy may have been inspired during this time.

Papa Gomez was a hardworking farm worker with a taste for the wild life. Young Adam would often be awakened from his bed and hauled off for some good ol' family mischief that, more often than not, would end up in hog-tying greedy ranchers belly-to-belly with their own livestock during mating season. Eventually, the Gomez *familia* were forced to flee Dinuba after Papa Gomez and cousin Demetrio abducted several union-busting strikebreakers and were caught basting the plump, glistening goons of the imperial Lettuce Company in Demetrio's secret ranchero sauce—a closely guarded recipe in the Gomez family to this day.

Years later, the Gomez family regrouped in San Jose, California. Adam, now a teenager, would often attend the lowrider car shows and hairdo pageants so popular in fashion-conscious San Jose.

It was at one such event that **Coors executive Heinrich von Klanmueller's death occurred [1].** (It has been confirmed that a one Adam Gomez was indeed registered as a participant in the hydraulic car-hopping contest.) Klanmueller was in attendance that day offering free samples of his company's beer. Some say that Klanmueller became enraged and allegedly made many anti-Mexican comments when Gomez slapped some Coors out of the startled exec's hand. **He was later found under Gomez's still bouncing '59 Chevrolet Impala smashed into a bloody pulp [2].** Gomez had fled the scene, and the case was never solved.

It wasn't until Gomez Addams' death that it was discovered that his birth certificate had been faked. Addams apparently used his wealth and power to cover up his secret identity, a revelation that has angered the surviving Klanmueller clan. "We'll settle for nothing short of every cotton pickin' peso the filthy beaner has ever earned!" snorts Claus von Klanmueller, the deceased victim's grandson.

The reclusive Gomez Addams, never comfortable with all the attention that his stint in Hollywood brought to him, would often remark in his later years, "My *raza,* they just don't understand me." Though many progressive Latinos viewed Gomez as someone who left his community and never looked back, many have no idea of the humanitarian contributions made by this great philanthropist. The famous, albeit peculiar, Chicano icon made huge annual donations anonymously to the Mexican-American Legal Defense Fund and the United Farm Workers. Gomez Addams also provided the seed money for the Mutated Chicano Fund, an organization he established to help disadvantaged Chicanos and train them for careers outside the agricultural field. Some beneficiaries include Edward James Olmos, Paul Rodriguez, and **famous Chicano flyweight Mosca de la Hoya [3].**

Esteban Zul is the former coeditor of the gone-but-not-forgotten Pocho *magazine, Aztlan's Rudest Political Satire Publication.*

MEMORABLE MEXICANS AS PORTRAYED BY PUERTO RICAN ACTORS.

"CHICO RODRIGUEZ"
FREDDIE PRINZE SR. (*CHICO AND THE MAN*, 1974–1977)

"FRANCIS LLEWELLYN PONCHERELLO" B/K/A "PONCH" ERIK ESTRADA (*CHiPs*, 1977–1983)

"BOB MORALES"
ESAI MORALES (*LA BAMBA*, 1987)

"PILAR DOMINGO"
ROSELYN SANCHEZ (*AS THE WORLD TURNS*, 1996–1997)

Back in the day, Boricua and Chicano public relations were strained due to the fact that self-described "Hunga Rican" Prinze was portraying a Mexican-American character from East L.A. That he was a grown-ass *hombre* called "Chico"—basically "boy"—threw another monkey wrench in the premise of this classic auto shop situation *comedia* on NBC (Never Big-up Chicanos). So when the show's creators appeased everyone by changing Mr. "Eet'z Not My Jawb" into a half–Puerto Rican/half-Chicano from New York, it was a beautiful thing. Either way, Prinze paved the way for future Latin primetime stars like, uh, . . . um, . . . oh yeah, Frankie Muniz (the little *papi*'s *papi* is Puerto Rican, you know).

Whether or not "Ponch" was a Chicano we may never know since info on his actual ethnic heritage remains undocumented on the Web or anywhere else (though his middle name guarantees he was mixed). But does it really matter? Well, not to the millions of E Double fans south of the border who loved *Señor* Estrada in the hit Mexican soap *Dos Mujeres, Un Camino* made a dozen years or so after he stopped fucking with his no-fun co-officer "Jon 'I'm Supposed to Be Arresting These Spics, Not Working with Them' Baker." (Los Neilsones even forgave Erik's shaky Spanish.) On *CHiPs*, the hunky (not to mention horny) healthy-haired hero from Harlem was so damn likable he made cops seem cool to minority rugrats everywhere. As far as the mystery of "Ponch's ethnicity," we are only left with a few valuable clues: Despite steady work, he lived in a mobile home, was no stranger to being placed on probation, and owned a used, beat-up Trans Am that he bought for cheap. But, then again, he could hang glide his ass off. Yeah, he was definitely mixed.

While Lou Diamond Phillips (as Ritchie Valens) was slanging an axe and serenading white girls in the hugely popular *La Bamba*, Esai Morales (as Valens' half-brother Bob, an aspiring cartoonist) was boozing it up and drawing his ass off in his trailer home. Bobby was jealous of all the admiration his ma showed his bro and, as a result, tore his place up every five minutes. Believe us, this was some real deep Mexican shit. *Bravo!**

Honestly, none of us has ever dared sit through an episode of the forty-plus-year-old *ATWT*, so we have no idea if "Pilar" (the first spicy sister served in the soap's history) was Mexican, Manilan, or Mongolian. But after seeing Roselyn in *Rush Hour 2* (2001), well, *Goddamn!* This banging beauty can play a Chicana any time she likes. But from what she said in an interview, she might not have to. Apparently, her character "Lili Arguelo" on the short-lived TV series *L.A. Fame* (1997–1998) was originally written as a Mexican-American homegirl from East Los but changed to a native PR hottie when she snagged the role. Rosie, we forgive you. It wasn't you, it was the *Fame*. Holla back!

*Esai also appeared as the gang-affiliated "Chuco" in the *Gone with the Wind* of Puerto-Ricans-playing-Mexicans flick *Mi Familia* (1995).

"AZTECA"
JENNIFER LOPEZ (ANTZ, 1998)

The Bronx bombshell shaped like a bottle was a smash as the slained *Tejana* Chicana superstar singer Selena Quintanilla back in 1997.* We still can't forget Ms. Lopez as "Maria Sanchez" crossing a raging river (while carrying a beanie baby) as she crossed the border in *Mi Familia* (1995). There was also her unexpected turn in *U-Turn* (1997) as the sizzling "Grace McKenna," the Mexican-Apache siren with heavy-duty sexual hang-ups and an Anglo surname. But the closest Jennifer's ever come to realistically repping Mexicanos is when she voiced the animated "Azteca," a "sassy," "seductive," and "spunky" *worker* ant. (Can you say "sweatshop," boys and girls? That's how hard ants work.) Hollywood gossip columnists might brand her a royal Queen B, but we'll work on Aunt J.Lo's hills anytime. *¡Arriba!*

"DR. GONZO"
BENICIO DEL TORO (FEAR AND LOATHING IN LAS VEGAS, 1998)

Oscar-winning del Toro became only the seventh Latino actor to be nominated for an Academy Award for his universally talked-about role as the incorruptible TJ patrolman "Javier Rodriguez" in the over-hyped *Traffic* (2000). Even though he became the seven hundredth Puerto Rican in a row to steal a Mexican role from an actual Mexican actor, the homie deserved to win. Still, we prefer Benny the Bull as the "Samoan" attorney "Dr. Gonzo" (based on infamous Chicano rebel Oscar "Zeta" Acosta) in Terry Gilliam's cinematic adaptation of Hunter S. Thompson's infamous rebel story. On some DeNiro shit, del Toro put on more than forty pounds for the flick in which he ingests drugs like free Jujubes, menaces anybody with a gun or knife who looks at him funny, and lusts after every woman he comes across. A fine Mexican indeed.

"ED ROEL"
LUIS GUZMÁN (THE LIMEY, 1999)

Because he was in the gripping prison drama *Short Eyes* (1977), played the shiesty "Pachanga" in *Carlito's Way* (1993), and fulfilled his porn aspirations as "Maurice T. Rodriguez" in *Boogie Nights* (1997), we will always love Big Luis. The only thing is that none of those characters was Mexican. No problemo. He was a tough yet lovable Mexican-American ex-con (this time with regular thespian aspirations) in *The Limey*. And as usual he was great. C'mon, it's "Pachanga" we're talking about.

"MIGUEL ALVAREZ"
KIRK ACEVEDO (OZ, 1997–2002)

The HBO prison drama *Oz* ain't no fucking fairy tale. (Well, there are some fairies behind these bars, but they're the kind who will stick a knife in your ass like *American Me*.) And it ain't no illusion that nutcase "Miguel 'Put Him in the Hole' Alvarez" is one of the most popular inmates on the disturbing cable series. We know actor Acevedo is Boricua, but so far as Alvarez is concerned we presume his membership in the El Norte gang (a thinly veiled reference to Norteños, the members of the real life Northern California prison gang Nuestra Familia) makes him Mexican-American. We also know that "M.A." is a third-generation jailbird, which makes him a cell-blocked Chicano candidate, and that he was heading toward Mexico when he escaped Emerald City. Since plenty of on-the-run cons would try to skip out of the U.S.A., we can only add in his defense that Alvarez's pregnant wife was arrested and incarcerated at the same time he was. And that sounds like one *vida loca*, playboy.

*The musical *Selena Forever* (2001) stars Veronica Vazquez, the Nuyorican sultry R&B songstress.

THEY ALL LOOK ALIKE ANYWAY: BLACK TV CHARACTERS PORTRAYED BY TWO DIFFERENT ACTORS.*

CHARACTER: "GORDON"
SHOW: *Sesame Street* (PBS)
ORIGINAL ACTOR: Matt Robinson (1969–1971)
REPLACED BY: Roscoe Orman (1973–present)
HOW THEY WERE DIFFERENT: Robinson had hair. Orman was bald. (He also portrayed the title pimp character in the 1974 Blaxploitation staple *Willie Dynamite*.)

CHARACTER: "LIONEL JEFFERSON"
SHOW: *The Jeffersons* (CBS)
ORIGINAL ACTOR: Mike Evans (1975, 1979–1981)
REPLACED BY: Damon Evans (1975–1978)
HOW THEY WERE DIFFERENT: Mike was light-skinded and had an Afro. Damon was dark-skinded and rocked a close natural. (And no, they weren't related.)

CHARACTER: "VIVIAN BANKS"
SHOW: *The Fresh Prince of Bel-Air* (NBC)
ORIGINAL ACTOR: Janet Hubert-Whitten (1990–1993)
REPLACED BY: Daphne Reid (1993–1996)
HOW THEY WERE DIFFERENT: Hubert-Whitten was dark-skinded. Reid was light.

CHARACTER: "RON FREEMAN"
SHOW: *True Colors* (FOX)
ORIGINAL ACTOR: Frankie Faison (1990–1991)
REPLACED BY: Cleavon Little (1992)
HOW THEY WERE DIFFERENT: Faison was heavy. Little was slimmer.

CHARACTER: "CLAIRE KYLE"
SHOW: *My Wife and Kids* (ABC)
ORIGINAL ACTOR: Jazz Raycole (2001)
REPLACED BY: Jennifer Freeman (2001)
HOW THEY WERE DIFFERENT: Raycole was dark-skinded. Freeman was lighter-skinded.

*None of them soap stars here neither. Sorry, girlfriend.

MUST-NOT-SEE-TV: 10 FAILED NETWORK ATTEMPTS AT RACIAL BREAKTHROUGHS.

1. **"KELLY'S KIDS" EPISODE OF** *THE BRADY BUNCH*
   AIRED: January 1974 (ABC)
   BREAKTHROUGH PREMISE: The Brady Bunch's neighbors adopt a white orphan and then adopt his best friends— one Black, one Chinese.
   WHY IT SHOULD'VE WON: It was a spin-off of *The Brady Bunch*—a muthafuckin' sitcom phenomenon; the plot was optimistic, integrationist, and family-oriented (and also a precursor to FOX's '90–'92 *True Colors*).
   WHY IT PROBABLY FAILED: Complacency. Who needed to see the colored *Kids* when the *blanco Bunch* were white hot?

2. **MR. T AND TINA**
   AIRED: September 1976–October 1976 (ABC)
   BREAKTHROUGH PREMISE: A Japanese inventor ("Mr. T") relocates his family from Tokyo to Chicago, where his traditional homeland values hilariously conflict with the American values of his Nebraska-born housekeeper ("Tina").
   WHY IT SHOULD'VE WON: Mr. T as a brilliant Japanese inventor.
   WHY IT PROBABLY FAILED: It wasn't *that* Mr. T.*

3. **HARRIS AND COMPANY**
   AIRED: March 1979 (ABC)
   BREAKTHROUGH PREMISE: "Mike Harris," Black (and blue-collar) widower/family man, uproots his Detroit clan to the sunny slums of Los Angeles.
   WHY IT SHOULD'VE WON: It was arguably the first attempt to seriously portray Black family life on a dramatic series; Bernie "Hit Man" Casey as "Mike" was a fine dramatic actor.
   WHY IT PROBABLY FAILED: A weekly primetime televised hour about Blacks being serious? You gotta be kidding.

4. **PINK LADY . . . AND JEFF**
   AIRED: March 1980–April 1980 (NBC)
   BREAKTHROUGH PREMISE: Saturday morning potheads Sid and Marty Krofft produce a variety show starring two non-English-speaking Japanese pop-tarts (Pink Lady) paired with comedian Jeff Altman (who cracks jokes the girls don't understand).
   WHY IT SHOULD'VE WON: Pink Lady.
   WHY IT PROBABLY FAILED: Jeff.

5. **THE NEW ODD COUPLE**
   AIRED: October 1982–June 1983 (ABC)
   BREAKTHROUGH PREMISE: Blacks are just as good as whites. At least good enough to rehash old scripts from the original sitcom and present them in Blackface.
   WHY IT SHOULD'VE WON: The inspired casting of light-in-the-ass Ron Glass as finicky "Felix Unger."
   WHY IT PROBABLY FAILED: Blatantly ripping off white shows didn't really hit paydirt until BET got the ball rolling years later.

6. **A.K.A. PABLO**
   AIRED: March 1984–April 1984 (ABC)
   BREAKTHROUGH PREMISE: Paul Rodriguez stars as a struggling Latino comic (now there's a stretch) who finds inspiration for much of his material from the exploits of his traditionalist family and friends.

*It was self-proclaimed "hip nip" Pat Morita.

WHY IT SHOULD'VE WON: Not one token cast member.
WHY IT PROBABLY FAILED: Despite the abundance of K-Mart jokes, producer Norman Lear's surefire racial formula couldn't do for Mexicans what *Good Times* did for Blacks. (It did much better when it was overhauled years later and retitled *Seinfeld*.)

7. **I MARRIED DORA**
   AIRED: September 1987–August 1988 (ABC)
   BREAKTHROUGH PREMISE: A single white father enters a marriage of convenience to save his illegal Salvadoran maid/nanny/budding-love-interest from deportation.
   WHY IT SHOULD'VE WON: Illegal acts are always provocative; INS humor; one of the kids was played by the creepy, teenaged Juliette Lewis.
   WHY IT PROBABLY FAILED: The neighborhood Applebee's reputedly made "Dora" an offer she couldn't refuse: an assistant managerial position—plus medical.

8. **ALL-AMERICAN GIRL**
   AIRED: September 1994–March 1995 (ABC)
   BREAKTHROUGH PREMISE: Almost twenty years after *Mr. T and Tina* bit the dust, ABC gives Asians another chance with self-proclaimed "fag-hag" Margaret Cho as an assertive, assimilated, Caucasian-lusting Korean-American chick at odds with her multigenerational family.
   WHY IT SHOULD'VE WON: Lots of Americans have yellow fever; lots of Asians are looking for love (and representation) on the tube.
   WHY IT PROBABLY FAILED: No one really likes Koreans. Especially other Asians.

9. **HOUSE OF BUGGIN'**
   AIRED: January 1995–March 1995 (FOX)
   BREAKTHROUGH PREMISE: John Leguizamo presents a Hispanic *In Living Color* comedy sketch show.
   WHY IT SHOULD'VE WON: Puerto Rican–Jew jokes, Catholicism satire, and more eager-to-work Latinos than the parking lot entrance at your local Home Depot.
   WHY IT PROBABLY FAILED: Perhaps too spicy for white-bread America, Leguizamo's early salvo was a few years premature for the lucrative "Latin Explosion." Sorry, Charlito.

10. **THE SECRET DIARY OF DESMOND PFEIFFER**
    AIRED: October 1998 (UPN)
    BREAKTHROUGH PREMISE: Absurdist farce set in the slavery-era Lincoln White House, seen through the eyes of Lincoln's Black butler and chief confidant, "Desmond."
    WHY IT SHOULD'VE WON: Allusions to oval office hanky-panky and other Clinton-like snafus; a Black man is the only sane person in the cast.
    WHY IT ACTUALLY FAILED: Overly sensitive Black groups hated on it before the show even aired. That, and the accompanying bad publicity, caused UPN to quickly cancel the program. No one here at *ego trip* ever saw it—our guess is that the satire probably went over people's heads—but it sounds like our kinda show. Anybody got bootleg videos? Get at us.

THE *SEINFELD* PROPHECIES.

Way back in the '90s, if you really believed that *Seinfeld* perpetuated a Woody Allen–esque NYC devoid of people of color you were probably watching *Martin*. Untrue! Not only did the top-rated sitcom employ mud people in such meaty roles as salesclerks, servants, and delivery boys, yadda yadda yadda, but it was also—in light of subsequent real-world events—an eerily prophetic barometer of race relations. Who knew "Jerry," "George," "Elaine," and "Kramer" were veritable boob tube Nostradamuses? No one. Except maybe Ms. Cleo.

PROPHETIC EPISODE: "THE ENGLISH PATIENT" (MARCH 1997)

When stogie aficionado Kramer thinks he's receiving illegal "Cubans" from his connection in Miami, he means cigars. What he gets instead is a trio of real live cigar-rolling Cuban people (who actually later turn out to be Dominican). Despite getting them jobs and educating them about communism, Kramer's best intentions to provide the illegal immigrants their place in America escalates to absurd proportions.

REALITY (NOVEMBER 1999):

When estranged Miami relatives of Elián Gonzalez receive the Cuban cherub from a Florida fisherman, they think he's an innocent refugee. What they get instead is a real live media frenzy surrounding the boy (who actually later turns out to be a political football). Despite taking him to Disney World and denouncing his father as a commie pawn, Elián's Miami fam's best intentions to provide him his place in America escalate to absurd proportions.

PROPHETIC EPISODE: "THE PUERTO RICAN DAY" (MAY 1998)

Finding themselves in the middle of Manhattan's annual traffic stoppa, the Puerto Rican Day parade, Jerry and gang ditch their car but incite the ire of Boricuas when a clumsy Kramer accidentally sets a Puerto Rican flag on fire. An unruly mob of hot-blooded Puerto Rocks enact payback by overturning Jerry's abandoned Saab convertible.

REALITY (JUNE 2000):

Though at the time of its airing it was loudly condemned by New York City's Latino community, *Seinfeld*'s P.R. riot pales in comparison to the actual Boricua-day brouhaha that occurs when more than forty parade-going young women are attacked and stripped of their clothing by a mob of unruly, hot-blooded Puerto Ricans.

PROPHETIC EPISODE: "THE WIZARD" (FEBRUARY 1998)

Elaine dates Darryl, whom she suspects is Black because she hears rap music coming from his apartment. Darryl suspects Elaine is Latina because she's always taking him out for Spanish food. They both acknowledge the scorn of people who "have trouble with an interracial couple." As it turns out, they're both white. They lose interest in each other and stop dating.

REALITY (FEBRUARY 2001):

P. Diddy and J.Lo break up, proving to the world that Black/Latin romances are tough to pull off—especially if you're both shallow and phony.

PROPHETIC EPISODES: "THE TAPE" (NOVEMBER 1991)/"THE VIR-GIN" (MAY 1992)/"THE VISA" (JANUARY 1993)

Jerry's gang endures a series of mishaps with Chinese people. The strained relations culminate in Elaine's literal run-in with bike-riding Chinese food delivery guy Ping Wu. The accident, Ping insists, was caused because Elaine jaywalked, forcing him to run into a parked car. Elaine denies jaywalking.

REALITY (APRIL 2001):

Uncle Sam's already tricky relations with Big Red worsen when an American Navy spy plane collides with a Chinese fighter jet over Chinese airspace, killing the fighter pilot and bringing a lot of subsequent back-and-forth accusations. Guess that's how the fortune cookie crumbles.

PROPHETIC EPISODE: "THE CIGAR STORE INDIAN" (DECEMBER 1993)

Joking "we smoke-um peace pipe," Jerry offers Elaine a cigar store Indian as a gift to end an argument and simultaneously impress one of her visiting friends. But his plan backfires when the girl he likes turns out to be Native American. She finds the gift distasteful and denounces his remarks as culturally insensitive. Jerry continues to try to woo her, although he can't seem to stop making offensive comments.

REALITY (APRIL 2001):

The U.S. Commission on Civil Rights officially denounces the longtime usage of Indian mascots, imagery, and nicknames by universities and pro sports teams as insensitive and demeaning. Despite the condemnation, Atlanta Braves fans can't seem to stop doing the "tomahawk chop," and no major pro sports team changes its racist mascot, imagery, or nickname.

PROPHETIC EPISODES: "THE CAFÉ" (NOVEMBER 1991)/"THE VISA" (JANUARY 1993)/"THE FINALE" (MAY 1998)

A friend of Jerry's, Pakistani immigrant Babu Bhatt, is deported when Jerry does not receive his mail (which includes Babu's immigration papers). A vindictive, finger-waggin' Babu returns in the show's final episode to testify against Jerry 'n' friends in a court case that forever alters their lives.

REALITY (SEPTEMBER 11, 2001):

Pissed off at U.S. foreign policy, swarthy, vindictive Middle Easterners from a once-CIA-sponsored terrorist group forever alter the lives of millions of Americans with their attack on the World Trade Center.

PROPHETIC EPISODE: "THE CHINESE WOMAN" (OCTOBER 1994)

Jerry meets a woman over the phone whom he assumes is Asian, and why shouldn't he? She always introduces herself as "Donna Chang," suggests dining at a Chinese restaurant, takes an acupuncture class, at one point says "ridicurous" instead of "ridiculous," and even dispenses over-the-phone Confucian wisdom to George's feuding parents. Turns out she's really "Donna Changstein," a regular Jewish chick apparently livin' off the durian vapors.

REALITY (JANUARY 2002):

After the arrest of "American Taliban" John Walker Lindh, it's revealed that he frequently masqueraded on Internet newsgroups as an African-American, droppin' science, and schoolin' the www.masses on wack rhymes and Islam in his pre–al Qaeda daze. Turns out he was just a regular rich white kid from Mill Valley, Cali, with dreams of Jihad. Guess that's how the cracker crumbles.

ARSENIO HALL: A RACIAL ORATOR DE FORCE.*

"It's an uphill battle, being Black, but if a Black can do it —I can do it!"

"We've always partied separately in this country. White kids had Bandstand. Black kids had Soul Train. The only thing we did together was riot. Now I'm inviting everyone over to my house to jam—and they're coming."

"One of the first jokes I ever wrote was, 'My name is Arsenio. That's a very unique name for a Black man. In Greek it means Leroy.' There was a night when some white people laughed too hard for me. And it was like: you all enjoyed that too much. Thank you. Good night."

"I was a drummer and a magician, like Johnny [Carson]. All the kids wanted to be like [Jim] Brown. I wanted to be some little old white guy. I didn't think, as a Black man, I was living in the right time."

"I change every day. One day I have a heart of gold. The next day, I want to march with Al Sharpton the rest of my life."

"I'm the Martin Luther King Jr. of comedy."

"They're laughing because you touched that racist bone that they can't fuck with because they might get their ass beat. But since you did it for them, thank goodness—'because I love that kind of stuff and I think y'all are named Leroy anyway.'"

"**People think I'm the Black Alan Alda. When you see me clean-shaven and with a suit on, I think you see something very commercial and brown bread.**"

"There's a subconscious racism that's been driven on Blacks so hard that it's become part of their attitude about everything. But you cannot become part of the oppression. I want to hear Black people say, 'I can do anything!' I'm not one of those guys who uses the word *nigger* for fun. And I don't use it onstage to entertain. Never."

"Why were they pulling so hard for Pat Sajack to succeed [against Carson], instead of me? Why? Is it because I'm Black?"

"My show is not a Black show, it's not a show to take over the airwaves, it's a show to say, 'Let's share the medium now.' . . . Beaver's dead, baby. Beaver's gone. And it's time to let some Blacks move into that neighborhood."

"I was told by Black people, 'Hey, I watch you and I love you, man, but lemme tell you, the white man ain't gonna give it up to you.' But America— *white* America—is watching me."

"To be successful as a Black man in this country you have to be bicultural. White people can function in a white world and only concern themselves with white things. But a Black man has to know it *all*."

* From his biography, *Arsenio Hall*, by Norman King (Morrow, 1993).

WHAT'S UP, BABY DOC?
BENSON DUBOIS' BALLAD OF FU-GEE-LA. BY NIGEL SPIVEY

Milk is chillin'. Benson is chillin'. What more can I say? A lot, actually. There's much to say about the head ninja-in-charge brother who put it down for years on ABC's ground-breaking situation dramedy, *Benson*. Here are the facts for those uncivilized non-Blacks who know little or nothing about this great Haitian (or Haitians in general, you living-through-the-eyes-of-a-tourist, witch-and-warlock-actin' savages). Who cares about Zimbabwe Legit? Haitian BD is too legit to quit.

Forget about the negative images of darker-skinded, moolied movers and pepper shakers stirred up by Marion "Crack It Up" Barry—Mayor/President-for-Life of Chocolate City. Motherfuckin' Benson was everything that Barry, the One-Nutted One, wanted to be: well dressed, well read, well fed, and generally fed up with the bullshit system that America's white, big foreheaded forefathers created while high on reefer in the cornfields of Richmond, Virginia (while their wives were busy fucking around with Ouija boards in Salem, Massachusetts . . . I read those same lessons, Ghostface. Peace, God). Sure, Benson worked for Whitey Ford, governor of Iceland, but this Haitian was the true overlord, landlord, and vocal springboard for that stupid puppet sap.

WELL DRESSED: Benson, like a true corporate Haitian of wealth and taste, stayed rockin' the fat brown three-piece suits. The stuff could've been from Calvin or Caldor—no one knew. And it didn't matter, cuz like El DeBarge once sang, "You wear it well." He was repping for Haitians the world over, right there. A Haitian without a brown suit is like Albert without the fat, ya dig, nig?

WELL READ: Benson wasn't a player, he just read a lot. On the late-night tip. Even before he spun-off of that special spacey soap opera sitcom, *Soap*, Benson was reading. As a young boy of the privileged class, Benson walked tall through Haiti's endless shantytowns with a book tucked into his money clip. He didn't have time to play kick the tumbleweed with the peasant children because he couldn't work his legs and read at the same time. Decades later, however, B-son did figure a way to make nasty sex-love to the governor's wart-riddled German maid, Ms. Kraus, while reading. It was a technique that would please him immensely. A stress reliever.

WELL FED: Benson had a little gut. After a night of *Twister* games with Lady Kraus, Benson DuBois would be mad hungry. So Lady would prepare stunning pork shoulder sandwiches and scratch his ass when it itched. That's the life, *bay-beh bay-bay!*

Well dressed, well read, well fed (and well sexed)—the four attributes of success. Yo, Benson, you've made it! You are continuing the powerful tradition of Haitian butt-kicking. (Remember, prehistoric Haitians kicked Napoleon's midget mug off their island, earning their freedom the way whites earn their riches—through bloodshed). The illest brother takes respect. Benson is one ill Haitian.

WHAT I LEARNED ABOUT NONWHITE PEOPLE FROM WATCHING SATURDAY MORNING CARTOONS.

BY KEVIN BURKE

In the good old days of Saturday morning television, the average white-kid viewer could count on an almost exclusively Caucasian cast in his animated entertainment. And were it not for vocal activists and misguided psychologists in the late 1960s hell-bent on "increasing the quality" of children's television, it might have remained that way forever.

Action for Children's Television (ACT, but also known as "the Mothers from Boston") insisted that Saturday mornings were a vast wasteland of vapid, soulless crap and that it was not at all reflective of the complex racial and cultural makeup of the United States.

With the exception of the occasional diminutive ethnic sidekick, à la Hadji from *Johnny Quest*, they were quite right on the latter charge. Saturday morning cartoon characters were, by and large, extracted from pure honky stock.

ACT was determined to make Saturday mornings a time for educating young white Americans about other cultures and races. And damn them if they weren't right on. As much as it pains me to admit, there really was a lot to be learned from Saturday morning television in the 1970s about all the "other" people in the world. Thank God, too, because the future of white America hung in the balance. A good way to avoid a race war is for everybody to get to know each other real well and what not. What better time to do that than during the innocence of childhood?

Thanks to ACT, here are just a few of the things white children like me learned about all the nonwhite people of the world.

From *The Super Globetrotters*' Sweet Lou Dunbar, I learned that Black people keep useful tools like hammers or other things in their hair. Sweet Lou was always reaching into his Afro and getting himself and the other Globetrotters out of a jam with the crazy gadgets he kept up there. It made me realize that Black people are *amazing!* I was always jealous of this and used to put things I needed in my hair. I tried to keep a copy of John Knowles' *A Separate Peace* in there when I was in seventh grade, but it

kept falling out. (I never did read that book.) I'll bet Sweet Lou had a whole library in his Afro.

I learned many valuable lessons about the culture and people of the island state of Hawaii from Honolulu's most prominent citizen, Hula-Hula. Hula was Plasticman's buddy on *The Plastic Man Comedy/Adventure Show*. Hawaii is a strange and sad place. Here's what I learned: Hawaiians are fat and clumsy. They are also jovial although they suffer from a terrible condition that brings them and the people around them bad luck. It rains a lot in Hawaii because every time a Hawaiian has bad luck a dark cloud appears over his head. On the plus side, however, Hawaiians are able to give very good practical advice. Unlike the dreary safety spots on *Superfriends* where Aquaman would warn you about going into the water too soon after eating or some boring crap that you'd never pay attention to, Hula dispensed really useful wisdoms. There are two things that I will never forget that Hula said at the end of *Plastic Man* episodes:

1. "A bargain is only a bargain if it's something you can use." Hula learned this after buying a box of yo-yo strings at half-price.

2. "Never send cash through the mail." I don't remember what he was buying, but I sure wish Hula had gotten this piece of advice to me a little earlier. Unfortunately, I never got the footlocker full of army men I ordered from the ad in the back of my favorite comic book.

There were many things to be learned from *The Amazing Chan and the Chan Clan*. China is an ancient culture. And in spite of the rumors that I had always heard growing up, *The Chan Clan* taught me that Chinese people don't drown their children after all. At least Charlie didn't, 'cause he had, like, fifty kids and a semiretarded dog. I learned that white people make better Chinese people than Chinese people do. After the first year of *The Chan Clan*, all of the clan's original voice actors were let go and replaced with Anglo voices, including that of Oscar-winning actress Jodie Foster! The producers of the show said they did it to make them "easier to understand." I don't know why they said that. They really did it because it made the show much funnier! Remember Mickey Rooney in *Breakfast at Tiffany's*? (Editor's note: Sure you do, you read about him elsewhere in this chapter.) I often wondered to myself if Jodie wore comically large, false front teeth just to get her in the mood. I hope so. I also learned that Chinese men have the ability to reproduce without a female. To be honest, that was a source of much comfort to me at the time because I was a little bit confused about how that happened anyway. I also learned that there are some similarities between Hawaiians and Chinese people—both are clumsy and make terrible judgments when solving mysteries, but only at a very young age. Chinese adults, by contrast, have super-duper kick-ass mystery-solving skills.

There is no end to the knowledge I cultivated from *Superfriends*. At first the Superfriends were all white, depending, that is, what country the Wonder Twins were from. I knew they were supposed to be aliens, but they seemed like they came from Korea or the Philippines or something. They were definitely foreign-looking. What was really exciting was when the Superfriends hired four new buddies from different races and cultures. They weren't as important as the white Superfriends and didn't bust as many criminals, but they were pretty special and could teach you a lot if you paid attention.

Black Vulcan was the Black guy in the group. You knew he was Black because his name identified his skin color pretty smartly. Which is the first lesson I learned from him. Super heroes of color need to have something in their name that identifies where they are from or what their skin color is. It doesn't have to have anything to do with their superpowers as long as you know what kind of minority they are. I found at least one other person who shares my opinion on this at seanbaby.com's excellent *Superfriends* Web site, which also pointed out that "Black Vulcan talked

almost exclusively in electricity puns: 'I'll electrify you with the shock of your life!' " The lesson being that Black people love electricity. It's their main weakness.

From Samurai I learned that all it takes to make a Japanese person is to have your accountant disguise himself by tying his hair up and wearing a mustache. Also, Japanese people suffer from spontaneous combustion and can, if the climate is just right, turn into a tornado with their head on it. Basically, Japan is a dangerous country. Don't go there if you're not Japanese.

Before we inoculated their blankets with smallpox and drowned their initiative with heap big firewater, Native Americans were a proud people that could grow fifty times the size of a normal human. Apache Chief was one of the few remaining giant Indians left in this country. We were very clever to defeat the Native Americans with smallpox. How else do you fight a nation of thirty-story-tall giants? The pioneers weren't as dumb as I thought they were I guess. But if you watched Apache Chief closely you realized that really his size was no big deal because the Native Americans weren't particularly smart, as they had still been unable to learn English properly. Apache Chief rarely hung out with the other Superfriends because they couldn't fully understand him and were very afraid that he would lose control inside the Hall of Justice, turn into a giant Indian, and bust open the roof. Marble is expensive and the Superfriends didn't really have normal-paying jobs. Most of the time they made him sleep in the Teepee of Justice out back.

Having grown up in Southern California, El Dorado probably taught me the most valuable lessons out of any of the ethnic Superfriends. El Dorado is an important figure in Mexican culture. Cadillac named a car after him and a lot of Latinos in Los Angeles airbrush his picture on their Chevy vans. Mexican-Americans have an understanding of the English language but still like to spice it up a bit in conversation by replacing really simple words with the Spanish equivalent. They do this to keep the white people

on their toes. El Dorado also taught me that the Mexican people can teleport themselves, but only over very short distances. El Dorado was often missing from the Hall of Justice but that's because he was standing out in front of the building in his undershirt, smoking cigarettes with his buddies.

Tragically, since the golden age of 1970s children's television, programs have taken a big step backward. What used to be an educative process about other cultures for knowledge-starved suburban white children is now just plain old dull television. Today, characters of color are no different from the white ones! It's a real shame and quite troubling for future generations that won't know about the dangers of standing too close to Japanese men during bad weather or how Black people might be able to fix their flat tires with their hair.

Kevin Burke is the coauthor of Saturday Morning Fever *(St. Martin's Press). If you ever meet him, ask him what he learned about nonwhite people watching* Cops.

WHO ARE THE BLACK MUPPETS?

Back in the '50s when the Gepetto-from-the-ghetto Jimmy "Jam" Henson (R.I.P.) first stuck his fingers up some green glutes, he knew he was on to something. Something *big*. Something Black. Something white. And something yellow, too.

Word on the Sesame Street is that his fur-'n'-felt friends infested PBS's piece of fo' real estate—the first, true, on-the-tube melting pot " 'hood" in AmeriKKKa. Henson's muppet-regime held a Pinochet (fuck Pinocchio)-like grip on the country's households, exposing fertile young minds to the joys of singing, counting, spelling, and

ROWLF

Uptown's Panamanian dark Gable played the piano and had more snaps than ginger. Like Sammy Davis Jr., Liza Minnelli, and Jackie Joyner Kersey, he was an all-around entertainer, repping Harlem and ripping down stages all across 1–2–5 while rolling with Alpo (the infamous Uptown "pharmacist" *and* the canine canned Spam). Rowlf, an Apollo legend.

FOZZIE THE BEAR

This hack Hebrew ha-ha boy honed his skills in the Catskills while making no bills—yeah, that's paying dues. However, a chance encounter with Henny Youngman at his father's thriving gefilte-fish processing plant in the heart of Newburgh, New York, set this cub's career back on track. And it's been a bear market ever since.

MISS PIGGY

A career JAP (Jewish American Pork), she's got a serious love jones for French dudes—a/k/a "frogs." Her vices: shopping, jazzercising, and hot anal sex.

KERMIT

No, it's not easy being green. Not when you regularly canvas for Greenpeace and you're good friends with Mr. Green Jeans. But inside he's all white. Lily (pad) white.

DR. BUNSEN HONEYDEW

This soft-spoken Asian science wizard's real moniker is, in fact, Hoon Yee Du Bun-San. His ethnic makeup is a Pan-Asian delight: part Korean, part Japanese, part Vietnamese, part Chinese, part Guyanese, and part Mayonnaise (that's one happy family). Blinded by science, he wears his glasses so he can see.

THE SWEDISH CHEF

He's actually Canadian.

ERNIE & BERT

Ernie's Puerto Rican, Bert's Dominican (check the latter *hombre's platano* eyebrows). And just because they live together don't mean they love together (not that there's anything wrong with that, all you *papi culos*).

ELMO

He's an American Indian. He's lived on a reservation his whole life. It's been rough. But the kids love him. He's an inspiration.

picking boogers. That's why the United States is #1 in education, baby—puppets, baby, puppets. But not just any ol' hand in sock—*Muppets* (mulattos + puppets).

So in the spirit of higher education, live a little and learn a lot, you lazy Snuffleupagus. Open up your crusty eyes and smell the old coots Statler and Waldorf in the balcony. It's a multiethnic world you didn't even know about. And that's word to Big Bird.

OSCAR THE GROUCH

Often mistaken for Bulgarian, but actually Russian, Oscar was a devoted fanatic of "the Life." Boos, booze, and breaking heads were his favorite pastimes while he passed time for years as a bouncer at Scores in midtown. That is, until he met Janice (stage name: Nexxxu$ Lexxxu$). Then he lost it all. ("The bitch set me up," he still growls to whomever will listen.) Now he's homeless. He's homeless.

GONZO

Born Demetrius Gonzodopolous to Greek immigrants in Astoria, Queens. *Opa!* Loves smashing plates while listening to Smashing Pumpkins. *Opa!* Does interesting things with shish kebab sticks. *Opa!* Hot-tempered, but, contrary to popular belief, he's not quick to get in that Onassis. *Opa!* He's addicted to daytime TV talk shows. *Oprah!*

THE COUNT

Sesame Street's own numbers man turned muppet Myer Lansky turned Atlantic City casino magnate turned Mr. Vivian Vance turned four bottles of Robitussin a day junkie turned Jewish mob turncoat turned protected witness turned beloved neighborhood mathematician and cape-adorned weirdo shops at Levitz, sips Manischewitz, not Bailey's—and he's Israeli.

COOKIE MONSTER

Take a close look at this wild-eyed Iraqi loose cannon's mitts—just four fingers per hand. See, in Iraq, if you get your hand caught in the cookie jar they cut off a finger. So, after repeat offenses in the land of Saddam, CM screamed, "Chips Ahoy!" and stowed away on a tanker to the States. Now, he rakes in the dough and leaves the crumb-snatching to the Gypsies.

ANIMAL

Drunk, inarticulate, and wilder than Tijuana on a *Jerry Springer* celebrity spring break—naturally, he's Mexican. Having first learned to play drums by mashing *masa* for his dear old *madre*, Animal eventually headed up *norte* in search of maize. Instead, he ended up a session player in Maze. But due to "creative differences" between he and Frankie Beverly, he soon found himself down and out in San Francisco's Mission District before being saved by his own personal Manson, Dr. Teeth.

BIG BIRD

A Vietnamese drag queen. Act like ya know.

GROVER

Though pigeonholed as a Pakistani-born virgin with low self-esteem (and an even lower sperm count), Grover's actually got it going on on the low. Mr. Sensitivity has a sweet disposition, great sense of humor, and a nice chunk of savings (for all your shopping needs, ladies).

ROOSEVELT FRANKLIN

Bingo, he's Black. Just check out his smash hit "The Skin I'm In" (Columbia, 1970), featuring fellow Black 'n' proud muppet Baby Ray. It's awesome.

STAR JONESES: GREAT BLACKS IN OUTER SPACE: AN APPRECIATION.

"Mars Blackmon." Michael Jackson's moonwalk. *Amateur Night at the Apollo*. Read between the lines. Black earth people love outer space. Considering their cruel treatment at the hands of the other man and their own elite brothers down here on this terrible *mundo*, it's no small wonder like Vickie or Stevie. In a galaxy far, far away, shit must be better than the cosmic slop earthlings are dishing out.

But even in TV and movie-lands, Blacks rarely get to go beyond sky high (experiments with space dust notwithstanding). It's no secret that mighty whiteys like Ruth Buzzi and Buzz Lightyear eclipse the Black stars of the stars, but some of them still shine on regardless. They got the Black Star Power of the Force and we salute them.

The sexy Nichelle Nichols was light-years ahead of her time—just ask *Star Trek*'s William Shatner, who as "James 'T.J.' Kirk" locked lips with N.N.'s calm, cool, and collected "Lieutenant Uhura" in 1968, the first interracial smooch on the boob tube. As it turns out, Nichols would have rather been administering tongue lashings on Billy Shat—offscreen she couldn't stand Willie's mammoth ego.

Her 1994 autobiography, *Beyond*

Uhura: Star Trek and Other Memories (G.P. Putnam), revealed other infinite jewels: due to a lack of lines and unfair treatment (she was the only cast member without a contract and her fan mail was regularly kept from her), Neecee, a single mom, almost left the show after the first season. But a pep talk from none other than Martin Luther King Jr. convinced her to keep on trekking. Dr. Mae Jemison, the first African-American woman in space, would cite the "Uhura" character as an inspiration. Whoopi Goldberg (who played "Guinan" on *Star Trek: The Next Generation*) would too, but we're not sure whether the Whoopster was referring to Nichols' brief offscreen dalliance with male milky ways. (No lie, people: she had a real life "close encounter" with show creator Gene Roddenberry.)

Nichelle, our belle, is simply out of this world. "Uhura" will always be Queen of the Cosmos—the missing link between Egypt and the dead air up there.

Roddenberry's journeys throughout the spheres included more dark sun riders. Who could forget the friendly soul controller of *Reading Rainbow*, LeVar Burton, who as the blind "Lt. Geordi LaForge" on *Star Trek: The Next*

Generation was anything but le miserable? In fact, he was excellent. His presence on the program must have prompted L.A. Laker legend / *Trek* lover James Worthy to make a 1993 appearance on the series as "Koral," an extremely low-key artifacts smuggling Klingon sporting more rings (championship and otherwise) than Saturn.

ST: TNG was followed by *Star Trek: Deep Space Nine* and it starred "Hawk" from *Spenser: For Hire* (not to be confused with "Hawk" from *Buck Rogers* who had a thing for crazy feathered bathrobes and hailed from Bogota, Colombia, home of black coffee). No, this "Hawk" was Avery Brooks, the first African-American to graduate with a Master of Fine Arts in acting and directing from Rutgers University, as Cap'n "Benjamin Sisko," who when not collecting ancient African art and having visions like some sort of Black Jesus, was fighting evil aliens in astro turf wars as commander in charge of his own motley crew.

Speaking of battles, who can forget Louis Gossett Jr. as the reptilian celestial creature "Jerry" going against Dennis Quaid in *Enemy Mine* (1985)? Even with a serious saliva-gland prob-

MAJOR UNCLE TOMS: NOT-SO-GREAT BLACKS IN SPACE.

lem he stilled schooled Quaid in the ways of harmony, finally embracing the ways of War and not war.

Why can't we all be friends? Well, as great African Yaphet Kotto found out the hard way in *Alien* (1979), in space no one can hear you scream. That's something to remember not only if you're Black, but if some giant ferocious female cockroach is trying to exterminate you (proving no matter how far he goes, the Black man can't escape someone hunting him down). Kotto was able to bring a don't-mess-with-me-sucka attitude to his character "Parker," and let's be honest, the second you saw him on that space ship you thought he was going to die first. (Special shout out to extra Bolajo Bolaji, the seven-foot Masai tribesman who wore an alien suit in some scenes for staying Black and paid.)

A Black man on Pluto is one thing. Try being *The Brother from Another Planet* like Joe Morton in 1984. A runaway slave (talk about an underground RR time warp), he crash lands in the Rotten Apple and must deal with some asteroid-sized culture shock while avoiding the bounty hunters on his tail. But it's worth it when he discovers

earth girls are easy.

No countdown of stupendous shaded star-travelers is complete without gorilla pimp Darth Vader, a dude so bad emphysema couldn't beat him. A cat brought to life by the deep throat of thespian overlord James Earl Jones, a man with a voice so commanding that even God says, "Damn him, he got a good voice." D.V. alias Jones breathed E.Z. and didn't sweat his name not being in the *Star Wars* credits. (He knew he wasn't going out like no Haley's Comet.)

Of course, his omission confirmed what we'd always suspected: that equality the universe over is still eons away. The final frontier has always been nearer for the paler-skinned space traveler. But the big foot strides of every Wookie counts for something. From using Comet to scrub floors to chasing comets, Nubians have come a long way. Outer space is their destiny because outer space ain't nothin' but Black faces. That's right. The nighttime sky is a sea of dark-skinned mugs with stars for eyes, black holes for colons, and zits for an eternity. And they're speaking real words: "Let my people go . . . up into space."

"DODGE" IN *PLANET OF THE APES* (1968)
Nubian NASA man ends up a stuffed zoological exhibit after smart-ass monkeys do him in. You should have gotten the fuck out, Dodge.

O.J. SIMPSON IN *CAPRICORN ONE* (1978)
The former gridiron great plays an astronaut on the run from government killers after he and two cohorts attempt to expose that the Mars landing that NASA has televised to the world is actually a hoax. Like the Juice at his own murder trial, his character must be pleading the Fifth cuz he hardly utters a peep. (Oh yeah, he gets squeezed, too.)

"LANDO CALRISSIAN" IN *THE EMPIRE STRIKES BACK* (1980)
Billy Dee Williams plays a backstabbin' snitch. Apparently, bad guys don't just wear black, they are Black.

HOMEBOYS IN OUTER SPACE (UPN, 1996)
Spaceballs (in a darker shade) gets the bozack.

DON CHEADLE IN *MISSION TO MARS* (2000)
The virgin landing on a hostile planet goes all wrong, and a Black man is left stranded. White people must rescue him. They could have at least sent Luis Guzmán to chill with him.

6 PM **2** **4** **7** News (CC) *1:00*
3 Jews
5 *Jaws*—Drama *:30*
(1975) Great white shark versus great white man. White man wins (of course). (Edited for television)
9 The WonderBread Years (CC) —Dramedy
Kevin faces the sting of discrimination and alienation when he learns that he's 1/64th Greek. His revelation rocks the town to its very foundation.
13 Family Don't Matter—Comedy
Wayward father sires seven children in the projects. (Repeat)
25 Married...With Immigrants—Comedy
47 Noticias (CC) *1:00*
A&E Mahmoud P.I. *1:00*
Mahmoud, pungent Arab private investigator, sets up practice in Hawaii, and turns paradise into Stankonia. (Repeat)
CAR Uncle Tom and Jheri—Cartoon
HBO *D.G. Cab 2:00*
(1998) Danny Glover runs a Black-owned cab service that's strictly for the niggaz— even the ones that don't pay.
HIS Davy Crockett: Remember the Asshole *2:00*
LIF The Gold Front Girls—Comedy
Four elderly Boricuas get on some Black shit.
MTV Total Reparations Live—Fantasy *1:30*
PBS Master P's Theater (CC)—Drama *1:00*
SCI *Tianenmen in Black*—Comedy *2:00*
Super secret team of INS workers keep an eye on thousands of illegal yellow aliens that populate the country without anyone knowing it.
TRV World's Best Segregated Beaches *1:00*
TVL Sanford and San—Comedy
Black junk bondsman and his half-Japanese son serve up big hijinks in Little Tokyo.
6:30 PM **3** Hassidim Yoga
5 Let's Judge Judy—Baby Mama Drama
Latinas sit on the stoop and gossip about the neighborhood hussy.
9 Half-Black Alice—Comedy
Light-skinded single mom slangs hash-browns (and works on MLK Day) at Arizona BBQ eatery, Melquan's Diner.
13 ¡That's Our Pepe! (CC)—Comedy

25 The Boat Peoples' Court
32 Magic Johnson
CAR Speed Racist—Cartoon
LIF One Dago at a Time—Comedy
TVL What's Hapa-ning?—Comedy
Three Amer-Asian teens vascillate between privileged slacker-hood or inevitable careers as brilliant mathematicians.
7 PM **2** **7** World News *1:00*
3 Jew's the Boss—Comedy (Repeat)
4 Orientertainment Tonight (CC)
5 Potato CHiPs—Drama *1:00*
Cantankerous Celtic cops-on-choppers Jon and McPonch take down a dope-peddling punk rocker prone to weeping (Sinead O'Connor) hiding out in a convent. Conan O'Brien guests. (Repeat)
9 The Invisible Maid—Horror *1:00*
Her name is Consuela, and she gets treated like shit.
13 In Search Of...
Promises kept by white people in power.
25 Enslaved by the Bell—Comedy
Overworked Caribbean butler moonlights as night-school principal.
47 Dos Equis Presenta el Super Piñata y Horchata Bomba Mas Grande (¡Mira, Mira!)—Variedad *2:00*
A&E Call & Order—Drama *1:00*
Chinese takeout arrives late . . . again! (Goddamnit!)
CAR Ezekial and Jeckyll—Cartoon
DSC This Old House Nigga (CC) *1:00*
LIF Gene Anthony Ray's "Chill Out" Corner—Discussion *1:00*
MAX *The Nazi Professor 2*—Comedy *2:00*
Nasty German prof fucks around with mo' experiments (this time with germs) and accidentally resurrects Germs singer Darby Crash. Eddie Murphy stars in multiple roles.
PBS Tony Brown's Journal (CC) —Discussion
The Black struggle for equality. (Repeat)
SCI Black Starliner Trek: Back to Africa Voyager *1:00*
TRV Great Vacations, Homes: Cheap Chicano Getaways (CC) *1:00*
TVL Tha JefferSons—Comedy
Thomas Jefferson's illegitimate Black kids run rampant at Monticello.
VH1 Pop-up Coochie—Videos *3:00*
7:30 PM **3** Makes Me Wanna Challah! —Cooking
4 Access Bollywood (CC)

13 In Search Of...
Alabaster booty cuties.

25 Guinea a Break—Comedy
Corpulent, but succulent, Sicilian maid moves in with double-chinned Polish police chief, and they mate.

CAR Massa, You's a Friendly Ghost (Now That I Done Killed Ya)—Cartoon

MTV Jacques Ass
French fucks make fools of themselves.

PBS (CC)
Off the air.

TVL Chino and the Man—Comedy

PM 2 Martha Stewart's Living (a Lie): Prime Time Special (CC)

3 America's Funniest Home Brisses —Reality

4 3rd World from the Sun (CC) —Comedy
They're here: Poor people are invading your space.

5 Mister Charlie in Charge (Repeat)

7 Who Wants to Be a Mulignane? (CC)—Game
Final episode. (Canceled)

9 Gooks and Spooks (CC) —Reality 1:00
Korean convenience store owners and the African-American customers they don't trust one bit caught on video.

13 Sabrina the Privileged Bitch —Comedy 1:00
Despite her low grades, lazy WASP debutante is accepted into Princeton. After a raging kegger, daddy has to cover up an embarrassing MDM overdose.

25 Gordo and the Fatman—Drama 1:00
Two fat-fuck cops—one Mexican, one not.

79 Fuzzy Image and Scratchy Noises

A&E Call & Order—Drama 1:00
Hi. Yes, I'd like to—Yes, I'll hold.

CAR The Woody Woodpeckerwood Hour — Cartoon 1:00

DSC Irrational Geographic Explorer: Porch Monkeys and Baboon Hearts (CC) 1:00

ESN Honkey (CC)—Sports 3:00
Whoops, we meant *hockey.* (Live)

HBO Jewe$$ (CC)—Drama 1:00
Ex-Scarsdale JAP has to work for a living.

HIS From Columbus to Colombine: When Whites Get Busy (CC) 2:00

LIF Latin Lapdance Championships —Dance Competition 1:00
(Live on Stage)

MTV Crips (BK)

SCI The Clarence 13X-Files (CC) —Drama 1:00
FBI agents investigate suspicious pork ingestion within the ranks of the Five Percent Nation.

TRV Forgotten Inner City—Travel 1:00
Manute Bol's favorite New England township, Bridgeport, CT.

TVL The Münchees—Comedy
Here they come, goose-stepping down the street. Krauts rock? Yes they Can.

8:30 PM 2 Everybody Loves Damon (CC) —Comedy
Slice-of-life sitcom starring the only Wayans family member anyone can really stand.

3 The Jews Brothers (CC) —Comedy 2:30
(1999) Chi town ex cons/record execs on a mission from Jehovah. Directed by the Hughes Brothers.

4 Just Shoot 'Em (CC)—Tragedy
Oh, fuck . . . it was only a wallet. Shit.

5 Token Black Gay Friends—Comedy
"Carter" from *Spin City,* "Keith" from *Six Feet Under,* and "Michel" from *Gilmore Girls* share a fabulous Chelsea loft that they can't afford. "Anthony" from *Designing Women* guests.

7 The Weakest Chink (CC)—Game
Five Asian males answer questions to determine who is most masculine.

MTV Blood Rules (CK)

TVL Wait Till Your Mom's Boyfriend Gets Home—Comedy

9 PM 2 Malcolm X in the Middle (CC) —Comedy
Malik Al-Shabbaz finds himself in the middle of some shit in the wake of the JFK assassination and his "chickens come home to roost" remarks.

4 Will & Race (CC)—Comedy

5 Padlock—Drama 1:00
Old white geezer lives in fear as he watches his lily white neighborhood go all "colored."

7 Spic City (CC)—Comedy

9 Happy McMeal 1:00
Skinny white heifer needs to get her emaciated ass to McDonald's.

13 Touched by a Hell's Angel —Drama 1:00

25 TJ Hookah—Crime Drama 1:00
Adventures of an Arab cop who stays high all the time.

Wednesday

47 **Todos Mis Niños Ilegîtimos** **—Novela** *2:00*

(A&E) **Call & Order—Drama** *1:00*
Hello?...Fuck!

(CAR) **Spade Ghost—Cartoon**

(DSC) **The Caucasoid Hunter** **—Adventure** *1:00*
See you later, alligator. (Season finale)

(HBO) **The Cocolos (CC)—Drama** *1:00*
Dominican crime boss Tony Cocolo suffers a panic attack after his mistress hurls a plate of fried *platanos* at his fat head. ¡*Dios mio*!

(LIF) *The Color of Purple*—**Drama** *2:00*
(1986) Black woman pool hustler schools young homosexual white man on ways of the pool hall and kitchen. Stars Whoopi Goldberg, Tom Cruise, Oprah, and Paul Newman's gourmet salad dressing.

(MAX) *HoodwinKKKed* **(SS)** **—Dramedy** *2:30*
Director Spike Lee does the white thing in this brighter sequel to the beleaguered *Bamboozled*. Pasty TV exec airs Klan fare to much fanfare.

(MTV) **Dairy**
Milky white celebs talk about themselves endlessly at a breakfast table in the Midwest.

(SCI) **Star of David Trek: Business Enterprise** *1:00*

(TRV) **Lonely Plantation** *1:00*

(TVL) **The Duck Sauce of Hazzard** *1:00*
Cantonese hillbillies drive souped-up customized Hondas and contemplate hitting off their hot cousin.

9:30 PM **2** **The Shah of Queens (CC)—Comedy**
Exiled Persian ruler moves to Jackson Heights, gets a job at UPS, and is never heard from again.

4 **(Joe) Frazier (CC)—Comedy**
Retired boxing legend pioneers hoagie therapy in bigot-friendly Philadelphia.

7 **Shwarma & Greg (CC)—Comedy**

(CAR) **Denny's: The Menace—Cartoon**

(MTV) **Diarrhea—Cartoon**
Lactose-intolerant mulatto high schooler struggles with her Strawberry Quik addiction.

10 PM **2** **Temptation Riker's Island (CC)** **—Reality** *1:00*
Multi-culti inmates (and their mates) drop the soap and swab the poop deck.

4 **ERR (CC)—Drama** *1:00*
Doctor covers up a racially motivated slip of the scalpel. (Repeat)

5 **Dawson's Crack—Drama** *1:00*
A chronicle of the inner city's pregentrified "lean" years.

7 **7th Eleven (CC)—Drama**
Little Medina's rumor mill is rife with camel fodder, thanks to Khadija's situation. The gossip takes its toll on Akbar and A'isha. Infidels!

9 **The West Wang (CC)—Drama** *1:00*
Series premiere. The United States' first Chinese president enters into brief affair with White House intern that leaves him and the nation hot and sour. David Carradine stars.

13 **Hate American Style (SS)—** **Comedy**

25 *Valhallaween 2* *1:30*
(1978) Jamie Lee Curtis, Irene Cara, Thor.

(A&E) **Call & Order—Drama** *1:00*
Hello? . . . Hello? Damn.

(CAR) **The Iraqi and Bullwinkle Show** **—Cartoon** *1:00*

(DSC) **No Sleep Till Giza: The True Story of Egypt's Cocaine Mummies** *1:00*

(HBO) **Sex and the City of Compton**
Four career 'hoodrats agree: A good man is hard to find, *okaaay*?

(HIS) **Gypsy Eyes on the Prize, Part 1** *2:00*

(MTV) **Real Ward Marathon (CC)** *8:00*
Black roomies in a big-ass house in a Deep South 'hood squabble over who gets to kick out the lightest darkie.

(SCI) *The Island of Dr. Yacub* **—Thriller** *2:00*
Evil mad scientist Yacub (Marlon Brando) creates white people. Civilization (no longer civilized) permanently fucked.

(TRV) **Idi's Gourmet** *1:00*
General Amin cooks up a mean genital. (Live from Uganda)

(TVL) **Lovebug Starski & Hutch** **—Crime Drama** *1:00*
Old school rap legend gets ripped off by white partner. (Repeat)

(VH1) *Moroccan Roll High School* **—Musical Comedy** *1:30*
(1979) Mayhem erupts when the Ramones rock the Casbah at Casablanca High, much to the chagrin of the principal, the parents . . . and the students.

10:30 PM **13** **Hate American Style (SS)** **—Comedy**

(HBO) **Oz. (CC)—Drama** *1:00*

Juan Valdez's nephew gets into some serious trouble.

11 PM **2** **4** **7** **Mo' News—All Bad (CC)**

3 *An Officer and a Gentile* **(CC)**
—Drama *2:00*
(1982) Romance between Israeli Army lieutenant and a goy slut. Features hit song "Up Where We Shalom."

5 **Black Men Are From Africa, White Women Are From Europe (CC)**
—Discussion
The first show to seriously discuss the battle between the races. Tonight's topic: Those shifty Arabs.

9 **Kleinfeld—Comedy of Errors**
Neurotic *New York Times* reporter writes acclaimed piece about race, but gets the real story all wrong.

13 **Colorblind Date (CC)**
Desperate singles will date anybody—even races they normally wouldn't share a water fountain with.

47 **Noticias (CC)**

A&E **L.A. Law (CC)—Drama** *1:00*
O.J. on trial. Subplot: Ofay on trial—and it's about time. (Repeat)

CAR **Animated Porn Marathon**
—Cartoon *8:00*

DSC **Behind Blue Eyes: The Spitting Image of Satan—Documentary** *1:00*

LIF **Best of Bliss: Interracial Facials** *1:00*

TRV **Bloodsucking Jews: The Palm Springs Mosquito Epidemic** *1:00*

TVL **T*R*A*S*H (CC)**

11:30 PM **2** **The Hate Show (CC)** *1:00*
Guests: Pat Buchanan, Grouchy Smurf.

4 **The Ta-dow! Show (CC)** *1:00*
Guests: Boo-Yaa T.R.I.B.E.

5 **Car 54, Where Are Your Hubcaps?**
—Comedy (*En Español***)**

7 **Racially Incorrect—Discussion**
Bill Maher, Robert DeNiro, Roger Ebert, Ron Perlman, and Peter Norton (of Norton Utilities fame). Tonight's topic: Black chicks.

9 **It's Showtime at the** *Pollo Loco* *1:00*
Guests: A Lighter Shade of Brown, Foghorn Leghorn.

13 **The Haitian Game—Game**

25 **Tom Vu's Erotic Rendezvous—Paid Programming**

47 *Risky Negocio: Crossing el Border*
—Comedia de Sexo *2:00*
(Mexican; 1983) Problemas occuren cuando un joven estudiante (Tomás Cruz) comienza controlando una "chica house" en el lado equivocado de las rieles (San Diego). Apariencia especial: Guido "El Killer Pimp."

HBO **Black Man's Taxicab Confessions (CC)** *1:00*

MAX *Cannonball! Run Nigga! 2:30*
See Close-Up.

TVL **W-H-I-T-E-C-O-P in Cincinnati**
—Black Comedy
Young hick cop joins the wacky police force that *could* shoot straight (at brothas, anyway) in tha 'Natty and fits right in. (Repeat)

VH1 **Behind the Mormons**
—Documentary *1:00*
The Osmonds testify.

CLOSE-UP

CANNONBALL! RUN NIGGA!
WED. 11:30 PM **MAX**

Starring Max Julien, Richard Roundtree, Richard Burton, Roscoe Lee Brown, bell hooks, Michael Winslow, Kellen Winslow, Gene Wilder, Lonette McKee, Vonetta McGee, LaWanda Paige, Dennis Page, Reginald VelJohnson, Whitman Mayo, Garcelle Beauvais, Leonard Nimoy, Sally Struthers, Cantiflas, Sparky D, and Tawana Brawley, this slice of African-Americana is the bomb diggy, no question. (Actually, there is one: What the hell is T. "Wappinger's Falls" Brizzy doing in this movie?)

A runaway slave (Julien) finds himself in the thick of a heated Revolutionary War fire fight. He discovers that a cannonball (VelJohnson) aimed at our nation's first president (Burton) is gunning straight for his spine (Wilder) instead. He hears in the distance, "*Cannonball!*" and jumps on a Siamese horse (Winslows) to escape the megablast. Next, there's a wacky chase. Check it out. Written, produced, and directed by Michael Schultz, the 1981 film is rated R for blue language, violence, raunchy situations, and rap music.

CHAPTER 5

RACE 4 DA SPORT UV IT.

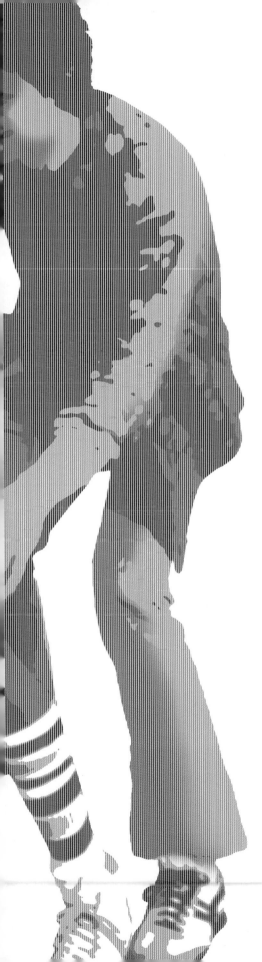

BORN TO RUN:
ARE BLACK ATHLETES REALLY BETTER THAN WHITE ATHLETES?
BY CHRIS HOUGHTON

If someone were to point out that Asians make the best Ping-Pong players, or that Pakistanis dominate field hockey, no one would blink. However, pointing out the similarly obvious fact that Black athletes dominate sports that involve running and jumping makes a lot of people uncomfortable. To understand why is to know history.

For decades pseudosciences like crainiology and phrenology were used to "prove" that Blacks were inferior, thereby justifying slavery, colonialism, and segregation. Even today there are scientists who concoct models showing that Blacks are less intelligent. As a result, any sentence that combines the words "race" and "genetic tendency" makes many people wary. Still, the subject of Black dominance in track, boxing, football, and especially basketball does come up, with the argument breaking down along these lines.

THREE MAIN REASONS
WHY BLACKS ARE BETTER NATURAL ATHLETES

1) CHECK THE STATS
Really, all you have to do is buy a television and turn it on, but to put some numbers behind what you're seeing . . . there are 800 million Blacks in the world, which works out to one-eighth of the world population, but they hold all the major world records in running, from the 100-meter dash to the marathon. In the U.S.A., Blacks, who make up 13 percent of the population, constitute 90 percent of pro basketball players and 70 percent of the NFL. A Black man in America has a 1 in 4,000 chance at playing in the NBA; a white man 1 in 90,000. It isn't an American thing either—in England, Blacks are less than 2 percent of the population and 20 percent of pro soccer.

2) UNDENIABLE DIFFERENCES EXIST BETWEEN RACES
Blacks have a predisposition to carry genes for sickle cell anemia. Mediterranean people are more likely to get Beta-thalassemia, another type of anemia. Research has also shown Chinese people tend to have straight black hair. The point is, different population groups (races) have different physical and physiological differences. Skeletal structure, lung capacity, and distribution of muscle fiber types are not evenly distributed, not any more than hair color or susceptibility to certain diseases.

3) YOU'RE AN EVOLUTIONARY PRODUCT OF YOUR ENVIRONMENT
The theory goes like this: Bipedalism began in Africa, as did toolmaking, language, and pretty much everything else that makes us human. The adaptations that made us human were determined by the African climate. So when man migrated from Africa there were adaptive changes to accommodate for the colder weather, like higher body fat and shorter limbs (to better conserve heat). These changes

are great if you're trying to survive an Iberian winter, but not much good when sprinting for 400 meters.

THREE REASONS
WHY THE ABOVE REASONS ARE PROBLEMATIC

1) WHO ARE YOU CALLING BLACK?
The problem is with mixing cultural and scientific definitions. Let's take NBA all-star Jason Kidd, the man who took the New Jersey Nets from worst to first. Kidd is biracial. The guy who counted the number of Blacks in the NBA undoubtedly categorized Kidd as Black—which is fine, most census takers (and New Jersey state troopers) would draw the same conclusion. But from a biological point of view, he's as much of a European as an African. You could say the same about other biracial all-stars like the NFL's Rod Woodson, and about light-skinded dominators like Tim Duncan. How do you prove that Blacks have a biological advantage when some of the Blacks you're citing as proof have all this "white blood" flowing through their veins?

2) WHO ARE YOU CALLING DIFFERENT?
There are far more differences within any race than between races. The typical Black athlete is no more Michael Jordan than the typical white athlete is Pee Wee Herman. Any NBA fan who's watched lead-footed Mark Jackson go against much quicker Steve Nash, or any track-and-field fan who's watched Greek sprinters and Swedish high jumpers win gold medals can tell you that athletes come in many different packages. It wouldn't be that way if there were these grand differences between the races. You don't see Thoroughbreds losing to Clydesdales.

3) IT AIN'T WHERE YOU'RE AT, IT'S THE AUTO CATALYTIC FEEDBACK LOOP!
No, it's not between the carburetor and the pistons. (Ha, ha, ha!) An ACFL is a situation where variables influence each other to drive a system forward. In our debate topic it works like this: High-profile '60s success stories like Jim Brown or Deacon Jones provided inspiration for other Blacks to enter pro football. Some of these men had similar success, which led still more young Black men to enter, to the point where they now dominate the field. It's not like white men have evolved shorter limbs or higher body fat since, say, the early 1970s when the NFL's all-pro squads were pretty evenly split between Black and white athletes. (Although, you have to wonder about the body fat.)

ONE BIG REASON ANY THINKING PERSON SHOULD
BE SKEPTICAL OF EITHER OF THE ABOVE LISTS

This is a "nature versus nurture" debate, a "chicken or the egg" argument, which means the damn thing will never end. Finding conclusive proof would mean all sorts of scientific crap like tests, control groups, and vivisections—fine for lab rats, not so fine for millionaire athletes. Plus, you gotta wonder about anyone who might get too emotional about the debate. There's nothing wrong with discussing sports minutiae for hours on end—such behavior ought to be considered healthy and admirable. But when you use sports—normally escapist entertainment—to prove theories about racial superiority, you need to grow the fuck up. Or evolve.

WHITE MEN WHO CAN JUMP (AND DUNK, TOO).

Brent Barry
Austin Croshere
Jeff Foster
Pau Gasol
Dirk Nowitzki
Peja Stojakovic
Charles Stuart
Wally Szczerbiak
Them flubber cats
Keith Van Horn

TEED OFF: 10 REASONS RICH BLACK MEN LOVE TO PLAY GOLF.

10. Need to get close to the greeny-green by any means.
9. Finally get to trade in nine millimeter for nine iron.
8. Used to gettin' up early in the morning to sell drugs.
7. The chicken fried steak at the country club house cafeteria is off the heezie!
6. Big fans of *Caddyshack* on the low.
5. White women (healthy, wealthy, and wide).
4. Rich monkey see, rich monkey do.
3. "You mean I get to grab this big stick and smack the shit outta this tiny white ball? Where do I sign?"
2. Tiger Tiger Woods, y'all.
1. Blacks are used to low scores.

COURT IS IN SESSION: TEAM FLUBBER GETS LIFTED IN *THE ABSENT MINDED PROFESSOR.*

"JUST A FRIENDLY GAME OF RACEBALL": MATCH THE ETHNICALLY AMBIGUOUS ATHLETE WITH HIS/HER ACTUAL RACIAL COMPOSITION!*

1. **ROY CAMPANELLA**
BASEBALL

2. **JOHNNY DAMON**
BASEBALL

3. **RON DARLING**
BASEBALL

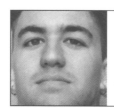

4. **ANTHONY ERVIN**
SWIMMING

5. **DOUG FLUTIE**
FOOTBALL

6. **FRANCO HARRIS**
FOOTBALL

7. **JEROME IGINLA**
HOCKEY

8. **REGGIE JACKSON**
BASEBALL

9. **DEREK JETER**
BASEBALL

10. **PAUL KARIYA**
HOCKEY

11. **JASON KIDD**
BASKETBALL

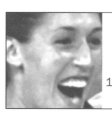

12. **REBECCA LOBO**
BASKETBALL

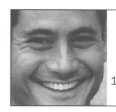

13. **GREG LOUGANIS**
DIVING

14. **YANNICK NOAH**
TENNIS

*Some of the answers will appear more than once. (It's tricky.)

15. **DAN O'BRIEN**
DECATHLON

16. **JIM PLUNKETT**
FOOTBALL

17. **JUNIOR SEAU**
FOOTBALL

18. **JIM THORPE**
BASEBALL, FOOTBALL

19. **PETER WESTBROOK**
FENCING

20. **TED WILLIAMS**
BASEBALL

21. **TIGER WOODS**
GOLF

A. 1/2 Asian (Chinese-Hawaiian),
1/2 white (Canadian)

B. 1/2 Asian (Japanese),
1/2 white (Scotch)

C. 1/2 Asian (Thai), 1/2 white

D. 1/2 Black, 1/2 Asian (Japanese)

E. 1/2 Black, 1/2 white (Finnish)

F. 1/2 Black, 1/2 white (Irish)

G. 1/2 Black, 1/2 white (Italian)

H. 1/2 Black (Camaroonian),
1/2 white (French)

I. 1/2 Black (Nigerian), 1/2 white

J. 1/2 Native American (Sac and Fox
Indian), 1/2 white (French, Irish)

K. 1/2 Pacific Islander (Samoan),
1/2 white (Swedish)

L. 1/2 white, 3/8 Black,
1/8 Native American

M. 3/4 white (French, Welsh),
1/4 Latin (Mexican)

N. 3/4 white (Irish, German, Polish),
1/4 Latin (Cuban)

O. A self described "Black kid with
Spanish, Indian, and Irish blood."

P. Mostly white, but says of his makeup:
"I think I have 1/32nd Arab blood
in me."

Q. 100 percent Cablinasian

R. Pacific Islander (Samoan)

S. Some cool coalesce of Latin
(Mexican), and white (German, Irish)

ANSWER KEY:
[1.] G. [2.] C. [3.] A. [4.] L. [5.] P. [6.] G.
[7.] I. [8.] O. [9.] F. [10.] B. [11.] F. [12.]
N. [13.] K. [14.] H. [15.] E. [16.] S. [17.]
R. [18.] J. [19.] D. [20.] M. [21.] Q.

FAUX FIELD NEGROES: 8 WHITE BASEBALL PLAYERS WITH "BLACK"-ISH NAMES.*

BONUS SWITCH HITTER: BLACK BASEBALL PLAYER WITH A "WHITE"-ISH NAME.

Kevin Brown
Marcus Giles
Gary Glover
Shawn Green
Darren Holmes
Derek Lowe
Herbert Perry
Jarrod Washburn

Troy O'Leary

*Additional research by Ben Osborne.

CHIEF WAHOO'S REVENGE:
WHAT'S HE REALLY SMILING ABOUT?

ILLUSTRATIONS BY DEVIN FLYNN

DISSIN' FRANCHISES:
IT'S NOT WHETHER YOU WIN OR LOSE,
IT'S WHAT YOU NAME YOUR TEAM. BY CHRIS HOUGHTON / LOGOS BY (((STEREOTYPE)))

It wouldn't be fair to hate Washington NFL fans because the team's coach, Steve Spurrier, is an arrogant, vindictive, smirk of a man, just as you can't blame the fans for the sins of owner Daniel Snyder, bar none the worst owner in sports. (And given the competition that's a pretty amazing title.) Hell, you can't even fault the fans for Joe Theisman's inability to shut up and go away. None of that is their fault.

But it's very fair, and just, and required, to blame those hog nose–wearing, cross-dressing, Enron-donation–collecting ass-holes for their complicity in allowing Washington ownership to give their team the ugliest name in sports—the Redskins. This isn't a relatively innocuous title like "Seminole" or "Indian" (or "Celtic"), it's a slur. "Redskin" is as nasty an ethnic slur as any-

NOTRE DAME DRUNKEN IRISH
Whenever the team scores a touchdown, the team mascot drinks a pint of stout. If they score more than three
touchdowns, he punches his wife in the mouth and falls
into a gutter.

NEW YORK DIAMOND MERCHANTS
When the other team scores a touchdown, they browbeat
them until they knock it down to five points instead of seven.

CHICAGO MARINARAS
When the opposing team takes a commanding lead, Chicago
can always be counted on to surrender and switch sides.

CLEVELAND POLACKS
Opponents regularly psyche out Cleveland with trash talk
like, "It's starting to rain, if you don't get your family out of
that locked convertible they'll drown."

thing you could come up with and the only reason the team brass hasn't changed the name (besides the fact that they're ass-holes) is because Native Americans don't have enough clout to make them do it. It's the nation's capital and if you don't have the votes, or the money, get lost.

Washington fans and ownership would never admit that, of course. They blather on about tradition, how the Redskins are one of the NFL's oldest franchises. Yeah, sure. You have to wonder how much tradition would matter if it were another, more powerful ethnic group being slammed, such as . . .

NEW ENGLAND WHITEBREADS

Their team color is Ralph Lauren's eggshell™, their theme song is "Bad, Bad Leroy Brown," and they're always a threat to bore the other team half to death with arguments about what's better, *The Waltons* or *Dawson's Creek*.

CINCINNATI GESTAPO

You'll beat them, but then you're stuck supporting them financially for the rest of the season.

MIAMI BALSEROS

It takes four guys to kick a punt for Miami: one to snap the ball, one to kick it, and two to talk about how in Cuba everything was better.

SAN DIEGO BEANERS

By season's end the fifty-two-man roster has exploded to 120 . . . and they all still fit into the team station wagon.

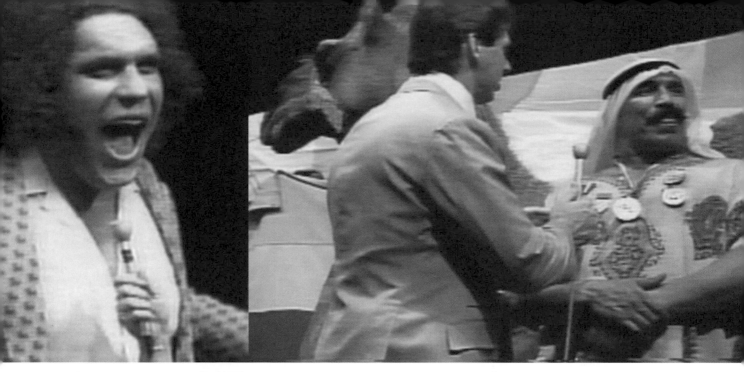

WRING-LING BROTHAS: GREAT ETHNICS IN WRESTLING.

Somewhere in a trailer park, Anyshittown, U.S.A., circa 1978. Wilbur and his deaf-in-one-ear sister's baby boy, Bubba, encounter their very first Black man—on their terminally-on-the-fritz B&W Hitachi idiot box. He was probably strongman Tony Atlas, raising some helpless Caucasoid above his beefy, bronze shoulders and slamming him down hard onto the mat. Ramblin' man and boy nearly choke on their charred-up Jiffy Pop popcorn.

You see, race-mixing has for years been an effective tool in the marketing and promotion of this unique alchemy of sports and entertainment known simply as wrasslin': Divide, conquer, and prosper is the m.o. Shit, even current heartthrob, The Rock (a Black P.I.—Pacific Islander), began his career in a "Bean pie, my brother?"–inspired crew called the Nation of Domination. And who can ignore the long-standing tradition of Captain America–inspired poster boys— from crybaby Richie Cunningham–lookalike Bob Backlund to steroid-abuser Hulk Hogan to real-life Olympic gold medalist Kurt Angle? It's true. You bet your bum it's true, you pencil-necked geeks.

Boxing may only have great white hopes (on the ropes). Wrestling has stars from the darkest reaches of the universe. Peep this list of the squared circle's credits to their races and places they dwell.

ANDRE THE GIANT
Everyone knows that ring-addicted Francophile athletic supporters are really down with the king of wrestling, a friendly Frenchman born Andre Rene Roussimoff. For years, this ambassador of bloodsport was undefeated until the powers that be forced him to lay the fuck down like Jake LaMotta, losing to Thunder Lips (a/k/a Hogan) in Wrestlemania 3. It's a shame, a damn shame, *mon frere.*

THE HAITI KID
Arguably the most popularest buckshot shorty to ever strap on little tights, Haiti Kid (a real live midget) inspired a young Wyclef "Joy of Cola" Jean. Okay, maybe that's not true, but that lil' fella could wrestle. Oh, and he was in *Penitentiary III.*

IRON SHEIK
At the height of the USA-Iran conflict (1979—early '80s, or some shit), Iron Sheik defied all odds by ending the lengthy reign of WWF champion Bob Backlund right in the mecca of wrestling, Madison Square Garden. Unfortunately, his reign at the top was shorter than Ronnie Reagan's memory as he quickly handed the belt back to Uncle Sam's then-new pin-up boy, the incredible Hulk Hogan.

KAMALA THE UGANDAN GIANT
Although he never won the big one, Kamala was the toughest son of a beast to ever rock a grass skirt. Just one look at his massive, dark-chocolate frame, white-war-painted face, and dangling nose rings instilled fear in the hearts of all who dared tangle with the big mute with a brutish attitude. Like Phyllis Hyman, he never got the props that he deserved.

IVAN PUTSKI
With all due respect to Michael "Meathead" Stivic, Ivan Putski was the only Polack who ever made a difference in popular culture. Short, stocky, and with more muscles than Diana Ross on X tabs could handle, Putski punished anyone who stood in his path and brought it straight to your Kool-Aid-pumping Jarvic 7. Ouch! And he liked to sing, too!

BRUNO SANMARTINO
Inspired by cauliflower-eared KO artist, Rocky Marciano, Bruno "Broccoli-head" Sanmartino was a proud, no-shit-takin' Italian Stallion who would toss turnbuckle-gobbling opponents from pillar to post. They ass was toast. Tossed salads? Sanmartino-no.

TITO SANTANA
Easy on the ladies' eyes (if they were toking that cheeba-cheeba) and reviled by current Minnesota People's Viking, Jesse "the Body" Ventura (who often referred to him as "Chico"), Tito Santana was a hot-hemoglobined *vato loco.* He could go toe-to-toe with you by the books (hot Greek action style) or off-the-books (jailhouse [Puerto] rock style). Santana was hotter than a Peruvian hooker with gonorrhea.

CHIEF JAY STRONGBOW
No minority gets more disrespected than AmeriKKKa's original original man, so it ain't surprising that there hasn't been a wrestler from A Tribe Called Best since the mighty Chief Jay Strongbow. Stompin', walkin' in his tan suede boots, Jay was droppin' native 'bows on palefaces from distant places—even caves. John Wayne couldn't understand the reign dance of this Redman, who'd cold bust your windpipe with a peace pipe. Peace.

NIKOLAI VOLKOFF
Repping the hammer and sickle to the fullest, Nikolai insisted on beginning every match by huskily humming the Russkie national anthem much to the jingoistic chagrin of mullet-coifed Yankee doodle pasties. Still and all, Nikolai did his thing-thang, especially when tag-teaming with the Iron Sheik to form an awesome alliance that immortalized the not-very-nice mantra, "Iran #1!, Russia #1!, U.S.A., *hag-puhhh!*"

THE WILD SAMOANS
Managed by Cyndi Lauper's ex-pimp, Captain Lou Albano, blood brothers Afa and Sika were a pair of Afro-rocking, nose-picking, barefooted renegades who put tag-team action on the map. After years of ass-kicking and takin' names, the duo disbanded. They would officially drop out of the spotlight when Afa was fired by that old stickler for rules, wrestling econo-Christ Vincent K. McMahon, for taking a day off to see the birth of his child. Fuck you, my man (McMahon).

WHITE HOPES AND BLACK BASTARDS:

BOXING'S BIGGEST CARD IS THE RACE CARD.

BY R.A. THE RUGGED MAN

Racism makes boxing exciting. Most people watch fights to root for their own kind. Mexicans root for Mexican fighters, Blacks root for Blacks, and a roomful of white boys root for anything that's white even if it's a fat retard like Butterbean. That's just how it is.

When it all started at the end of the 1880s, boxing was dominated by white fighters: whiskey-guzzling Irish guys like John L. Sullivan (a/k/a the "Boston Strong Boy"), the guy who declared, "I will fight any man breathing," and usually did in long, bloody, messy matches just as long as the other guy wasn't Black. Or the fancy-footed "Gentleman Jim" Corbett, who did fight Blacks, but was also described as sometimes "arrogant, moody, and bigoted."

That all changed when Jack Johnson became the first Black heavyweight champion in 1908, a title he held until 1915. The controversial Johnson was the all-time king of pissing off hateful Caucasians. Jack would knock the shit out of America's white idols—and laugh in their faces while doing it—back when a Black guy making a living beating up white people wasn't going to win him any popularity votes. In fact, Congress banned film footage of Jack beating white boxers, claiming it could incite race riots. (Actually, Jack beating white boxers *did* cause race riots, like when he beat the "Great White Hope" Jim Jeffries on the fourth of July, 1910, in Reno, Nevada.)

Johnson was also a trendsetter, being the first Black ath-lete to marry a white woman (an act that changed America and is still being practiced today). But this was almost a hundred years before the O.J. Simpsons and Chris Byrds of today, during a time when Black men would be lynched just for looking at a pale-skinned female.

Rivals once tried to poison Jack. When that didn't work, they tried to bribe him into taking dives against white fight-ers. But when he wouldn't, white folks eventually pinned him in 1913 with violating the Mann Act (or the "White Slave Traffic Act"), for transporting a white woman across a state line. (Never mind the fact it was actually his wife.) Jack got a bum rap. He ended up moving to France to avoid the long arm of the law.

While away, Johnson was forced to defend his title in other countries, including Cuba, where he was finally con-vinced to lose the title in exchange for money and the charges back home being dropped. He got the dough (which they tried to front on), but still couldn't come back to the United States until five years later because the case was not closed as he had been led to believe. Jack still ended up doing a one-year bid in federal prison upon his return.

After Jack Johnson, there was nothing but white champs. And no promoters would do fights that featured Black challengers.

It wasn't until 1937 that boxing would have its next Black heavyweight champion, Joe Louis. The "Brown Bomber" always devastated white rivals with a straight face because his management told him that if he smiled in the ring it could start up some racial beef.

But in 1938—instead of Black versus white—it became America versus the Nazis. Louis, who two years earlier had been shockingly KOed by German Max Schmeling, humiliated Hitler and his forces (who, in case you didn't know, were on some racial superiority shit) by destroying Schmeling in one round. (Louis broke Schmeling's spine.) The radio broadcast was instantly taken off the air in Germany. The fight, which took place on June 22 at Yankee Stadium in front of 70,000 spectators, made Louis an international hero.

Joe Louis retired in 1949, after an eleven-and-a-half-year reign as champion (the longest in boxing history). But nagging tax problems forced him to fight again. He lost against Black champ Ezzard Charles in 1950 and was knocked out in 1951 by the man white America desperately needed, Rocky Marciano.

The victory put Marciano in line for a September 23, 1952, title shot against Black champ "Jersey Joe" Walcott. In front of 40,000 fans in Philly, Rocky beat Walcott to become the only white heavyweight champion in fifteen years. This made him God.

Besides being white, what made Rocky so appealing to Caucasian fans was that he was the real thing—a good fighter who was tough as hell. He was so tough that he'd have cuts cemented shut and then have the cement surgically removed within twenty-four hours. On top of all that, he believed that he couldn't lose. But was he the best ever? No. Was he one of the top five all-time greatest fighters? Probably not. The top ten? Definitely.

Still, Joe Louis at his peak would've most likely punished him. Larry Holmes in his prime was too talented and had too perfect a jab, so he probably could have smacked him up. And had Marciano boxed in the Liston/Ali/Foreman era, there is no way he would have had his undefeated record of 49–0 (a record that has yet to be matched by any heavyweight champion). Of course, in today's era where the "champions" are guys like the glass-jawed/half-girl Lennox Lewis, the very-average Hasim Rahman, and a terribly overrated Evander Holyfield, Rocky Marciano's pale ass would be king of the ring.

Since "The Rock" retired in 1956, there hasn't been any dominant white heavyweights. Ingemar Johansson from Sweden won the belt by knocking out the heavily favored Floyd Patterson in 1959, only to be KOed twice in rematches.

Jerry Quarry was a white guy who fought professionally from the mid-'60s to the mid-'70s that should have been champ. But standing in his way were guys like Joe Frazier, Muhammad Ali, and George Foreman. Tough luck.

In the early '90s, who better than Tommy "the Duke" Morrison to become the next great white heavyweight? He wasn't just white, he was John Wayne's real-life nephew. He was an all-American star in the making, except for the fact that if your kid sister hit him clean on the chin, he'd probably hit the canvas faster than a coke-happy Pablo Picasso.

My favorite white hope versus Black bastard feud is the one I saw live on television as a kid and which took place on June 11, 1982, in Las Vegas—Gerry Cooney versus Larry Holmes.

Cooney was a solid white fighter—good jab, good power, and talented—but, most important, he was Irish. Even though Holmes was the undefeated heavyweight champion of the world, the white challenger was getting paid the same amount for the fight and getting all the press coverage, posing with celebrities like Sly Stallone on the covers of magazines.

Holmes, who throughout his career never got the respect he deserved and was greeted by racial slurs from white fight fans before and after the match, is one of the top three greatest heavyweights of all time and on his best night might have beaten any fighter in history. He eventually knocked Cooney out in the thirteenth round, which made Cooney a bum overnight. White America was depending on him and in their eyes he let them down. To this day he is considered a bum and his reputation is that of a fighter who always got the shit kicked out of him, which actually wasn't the case. His only losses were to Michael Spinks, Larry Holmes, and George Foreman, all respected champions.

A few years after the Cooney fight, Larry Holmes was one win away from tying Marciano's 49–0 record when the judges robbed him by giving a bogus decision to Michael Spinks on September 21, 1985. At the postfight press conference, an angry Holmes said, "Rocky Marciano couldn't carry my jockstrap," which turned most of the sports world against him and angered white people worse than not having a white champ (or not having a white fighter win any big fights) in almost fifty years.

R.A. the Rugged Man is not only a big-time pugilism nut, but is the undisputed lord of controversy and the mad genius of underground hip hop. When not producing and directing dirty music videos or writing seedy screenplays, he's working on his fifteen-years-in-the-making, will-probably-never-come-out, legendary album, American Lowlife.

*Evander Holyfield made his money pathetically going the distance with two forty-two-year-old men (Holmes and Foreman), losing two out of three with Riddick Bowe, losing to nothing-special Michael Moorer, getting beat up or looking like shit against below-average guys like Bert Cooper, Michael Dokes, and Vaughn Bean, winning titles by beating an out-of-shape Buster Douglas and losing to—but getting the decision in their first fight—John Ruiz, a man who got knocked out in nineteen seconds by David Tua.

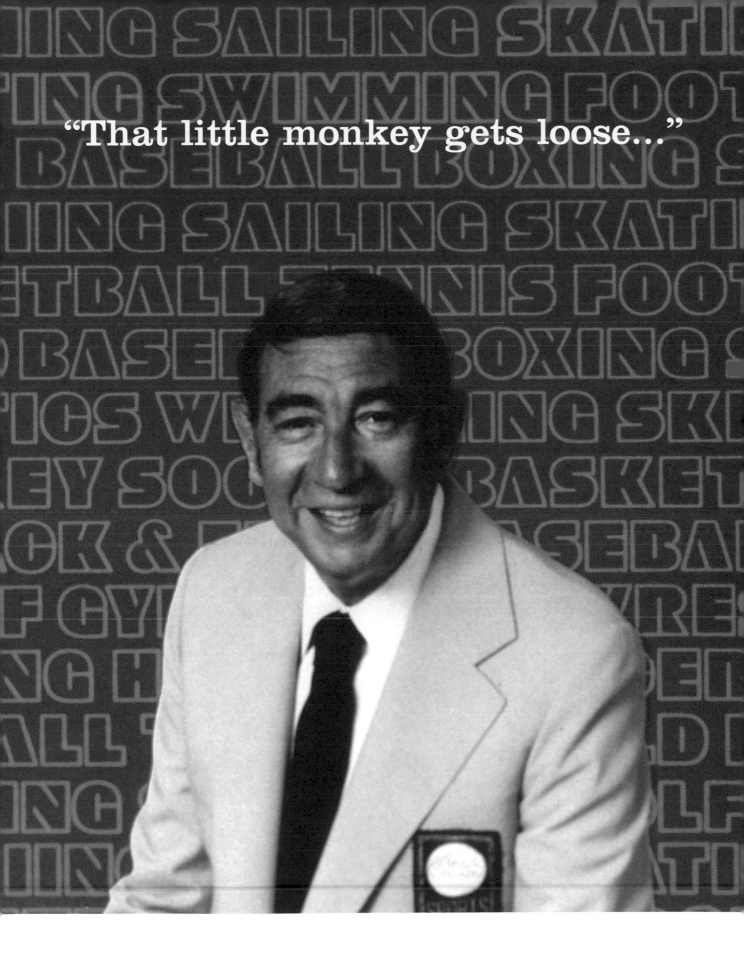

"That little monkey gets loose..."

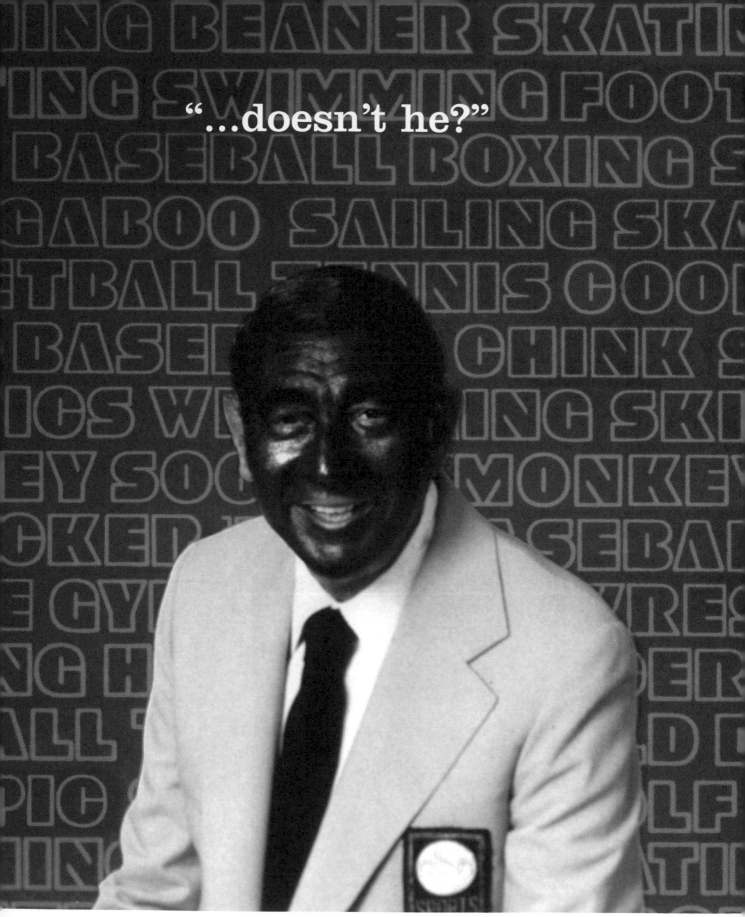

"...doesn't he?"

As we often do when discussing our twin national obsessions, we turn to Sir Charles ¶ "The best thing about sports is that it's color blind. In the locker room, we're all the same. Sports bring us together. I mean, if you can play, you gonna play, no matter what color you are." ¶ So says Mr. Barkley, who in his sixteen-year NBA career, and in his current job as a TNT talking head, has shown more common sense, honesty, and just plain balls on the topic of race than any other athlete, ever. ¶ Too bad he's wrong. ¶ Okay, not completely wrong. The athletic field is a meritocracy, the purest one we have. That's the main reason why Blacks were able to make such relatively rapid progress in sports, as opposed to larger society. When Jesse Owens ran faster than the field, when Joe Louis knocked everyone out, there wasn't anything to debate. They were the best, and no Jim Crow laws could legislate that away. ¶ And, sure, because of that, sports has for the most part been a positive influence on race in this country. It wasn't *Brown vs. Board of Education* that kick-started civil rights in this country, it was Jackie Robinson. ¶ But sports isn't color blind and Mista Chuck knows it. The games are played by and (especially) covered by some of the same ignorant fools you'll find in any Ku Klux Klan meeting or Fox News Channel boardroom. ¶ Most hide their bile beneath a screen of clichés and code-speak, but every so often one will loosen his lips and earn a place in *ego trip's* . . .

SPORTS RACISM HALL OF SHAME.

BY CHRIS HOUGHTON

"THE OLD AND STUPID WING"

SOME HALL INDUCTEES WERE SO FOSSILIZED IN THEIR WAY OF THINKING THAT THEY ACTUALLY THOUGHT THEY WERE HELPING. ALL THESE DUST FARTS CONSIDERED THEMSELVES CHAMPIONS OF THE BLACK ATHLETE.

AL CAMPANIS AND JIMMY "THE GREEK" SNYDER

Back in the late '80s, whenever he appeared on a talk show (which was with surprising frequency), Jimmy "J.J." Walker's opening joke was, "I just got done having dinner with Al Campanis and Jimmy the Greek!" The point is not how desperate talk shows were for guests back then, but that Campanis and Snyder are forever linked in the public consciousness—two fat, dumb old clowns who couldn't handle their booze.

Al came first. It was Opening Day in 1987, and to commemorate the fortieth anniversary of Jackie Robinson's breaking of the color line, *Nightline* interviewed Campanis, an executive for the Dodgers and a minor league teammate of Robinson's. He told an incredulous Ted Koppel that Blacks "may not have some of the necessities to be a field manager or perhaps a general manager." He went on to ask, "How many are good swimmers? . . . [T]hey don't have the buoyancy."

A few months later, just before Black QB Doug Williams was about to tear up the field (and the record books) with his performance in Super Bowl XXII, "the Greek," CBS's gambling shill, Dean Martin's childhood pal, the man who was right 52 percent of the time, heaved out a long-winded, beer-soaked dissertation on why Blacks are better athletes than whites. It was a little hard to follow, but it had to do with slave owners breeding Blacks to have "high thighs and big size."

Both men were fired as a result of the media hoopla and are largely forgotten today. Except by "J.J." Walker, who's probably still using that joke.

HOWARD COSELL

It was the first *Monday Night Football* game of the '83 season—the Dallas Cowboys and the defending champion Redskins. Washington receiver Alvin Garrett was having a great first half, prompting Cosell's comment, "That little monkey gets loose, doesn't he?" TV viewers across the country did spit takes with their beer, but somehow no one in the ABC booth seemed to notice the slur. When the complaints started pouring in, Cosell, who was apparently unfamiliar with the concept of videotape, made a bad situation worse by initially denying everything.

There was controversy but it didn't amount to much, and Cosell kept his job. (In his defense, a posthumous HBO documentary actually reveals Cosell calling a light-footed white football player "little monkey" back in 1972, well before the Garrett incident.) In his book, *I Never Played the Game*, Howard wrote that Garrett thanked him for the compliment (yeah, right) and that the print media was out to get him (if so, they deserved a medal). He also wrote, "Nobody, but nobody, in the history of sports in this country has served the cause of Black athletes as I have," a show of hubris more objectionable than a barrel full of monkeys.

"THE CURIOUS BUT STUPID WING"

THE PEOPLE IN THIS WING ARE, IN THEIR OWN CLUMSY WAY, TRYING TO MAKE SENSE OF THIS WORLD. THEY'RE ALSO PRO ATHLETES, AND THESE GUYS AREN'T RICH AND FAMOUS FOR THEIR SOPHISTICATED INTELLECT.

KERRY COLLINS

Now better known as the poor S.O.B. who got run over by the Ravens' defense in Super Bowl XXXV, Collins used to be famous for his ability to drink. Back when he played for the Carolina Panthers he was well known in the Charlotte area for his public drunken rampages. It was during one of these boozing sessions, at a team party, that he called teammate Muhsin Muhammed a "nigger." He later said he meant it as a joke.

Usually, "I was only joking" is a crock, but in this case Collins may deserve the benefit of the doubt. The word in question was undoubtedly kicked around by Blacks on the team in conversations with each other, and, hey, it was a party, we're all friends here, right? Kind of a stupid way to think, but when you're blood-alcohol level is sky high and you're not that bright to begin with, it's understandable.

"I WOULD NEVER HIRE A NIG TRAINED MONKEY WORK

MARGE SCHOTT, FORMER OWNER OF THE CINCINNATI REDS.

Collins apologized to his teammate the next day, went in to rehab the next year, and now the incident is pretty much over. Though Ravens' sack-happy Black linebacker Ray Lewis still seemed pretty pissed off at Collins in the Super Bowl.

CHARLIE WARD AND ALLAN HOUSTON

"Jews are stubborn." "They had [Christ's] blood on their hands." "There are Christians getting persecuted by Jews every day."

These are the now infamous words of New York Knicks' guard Charlie Ward, showing off his FSU education to a reporter for the *New York Times Magazine*. Teammate Houston got some ink for quoting scripture saying Jews, "spit in Jesus' face and hit him with their fists."

At first glance it seemed that Ward had joined the Lost Tribe of Israel, those guys who wear costumes and scream at people in Times Square. A reading of the article, however, makes Ward and Houston seem less like raving anti-Semites and more like sheltered souls who'd never talked to an actual Jew before. The reporter in question was at a Bible study group, and the players asked him about the Old Testament and other aspects of Jewish life before pulling that "Jews are stubborn" stuff out of their pockets. Ignorant to be sure, but not hatefully ignorant. There's a difference.

REGGIE WHITE

Ward's friend Reggie White, while still a defensive lineman for the Green Bay Packers, made a speech to the Wisconsin Legislature in March of '98, because that's what you do when you're a Packers star. White was no bigot, not at all. The man wanted to celebrate ethnic diversity. He liked *all* people, he spoke of how we all have different gifts.

Here are some of the words of praise from the hour-long speech:

Blacks are gifted at worship and celebration. If you go to a Black church, you see people jumping up and down because they really get into it.

[Whites] do a good job of building businesses . . . [they] know how to tap into money.

Hispanics are gifted in family structure . . . they can put twenty, thirty people in one home.

[Asians are inventive and] can turn a television into a watch.

[Native Americans, unlike Blacks, were never enslaved because] they knew the territory and knew how to sneak up on people.

White, nice guy that he is, probably wanted to praise Germans for their ability to follow orders, Italians for being gifted at singing opera, and Russians for being able to drink gallons of vodka, but it was only a one-hour speech, some things had to be edited for time.

DENNIS RODMAN AND ISIAH THOMAS (BUT PROBABLY NOT ISIAH)

The '87 Eastern Finals between Detroit and Boston had more drama than an entire season does today, and after losing a tough game seven, Rodman said of Larry Bird and his three MVPs, "He's white. That's the only reason he gets it."

Like piranhas to a bleeding goat, the reporters swarmed to team captain Thomas. His comment: "I think Larry Bird is a very, very, good basketball talent, but I have to agree with Rodman. If he were Black, he'd be just another guy." The media, which was busy putting the Legend in Larry, went nuts, and Thomas held a press conference a few days later. He discussed media stereotypes about Blacks, saying, "When Bird makes a great play, it's due to his thinking and his work habits. It's all planned out by him. [To the media] it's not the case for Blacks. All we do is run and jump. We never practice or give a thought to how we play. It's like I came dribbling out of my mother's womb." This perceptive criticism of the media was, of course, largely ignored by everyone in the room.

There's a mystery attached to this story. At the same press conference, Thomas maintained that he was kidding about Bird. He played a tape of the locker room interview, and when Thomas made his remark about Bird being just another player he said it with a sarcastic laugh. Reporters, however, swore up and down that Thomas was dead serious in the locker room. This raises questions: Did Isiah create

GER. I'D RATHER HAVE A NG FOR ME THAN A NIGGER"

the tape just for the news conference? Was there a second tape recorder perched on a grassy knoll in Boston Garden? Did they mix the tape at the same studio where they faked the Apollo moon mission? Or did these reporters, the same ones who ignored Thomas' comments about stereotypes, miss the fact that he was kidding? No one will ever know and it's enough to make you laugh. Sarcastically.

"THE GRAND DRAGON WING"

MARGE SCHOTT

With her fat-guy-in-a-dress look and prodigious consumption of alcohol, some might call Large Marge a female version of Jimmy "the Greek," but she's a lot meaner. The Cincinnati Reds' former owner, the proud possessor of a Nazi arm-band, has said, "I would never hire a nigger. I'd rather have a trained monkey working for me than a nigger." She's also referred to outfielder Eric Davis as a "million dollar nigger" and made similarly insulting remarks about Asians and gays.

It was too much for even baseball to ignore, so in 1993 they banned her from day-to-day operations of her club for one year and fined her $25,000. Her response was, "If I have ever said anything to offend anyone, it was never my intention and I apologize for any hurt I may have caused." It's easy to see how she would be unaware that the word "nigger" could cause pain. I myself was shocked to find that people took offense at my calling them "butt-ugly, alcoholic old sows."

TY COBB

Some have said that baseball legend Ty Cobb wasn't so much a racist as he was a product of his era, and, yes, he was born less than ten years after the Reconstruction. Others say that Cobb hated everybody, which is also some-what true. This was a man who slept with a loaded pistol on road trips because he thought his own teammates would try to kill him in his sleep. But even factoring in his time and disposition, Tyrus Raymond Cobb was the most virulent racist the sports world has ever seen.

In 1907 he slapped a Black groundskeeper because he was "too informal," and choked his wife when she objected. In 1908 he kicked a Black chambermaid in the stomach and knocked her down a flight of stairs because she objected to being called "nigger." He stabbed a Black hotel worker in Cleveland in 1909, punched a Black man in Detroit the same year. He also hated Roman Catholics, Cubans, and probably everyone else who wasn't a white Southerner. Which means he would've gotten along fine with . . .

JOHN ROCKER

Again, some say Cobb was a product of his era. Major league reliever John Rocker, born in 1974, raised in the era of

Sesame Street and *Fat Albert*, has no such excuse. In this day of aggressive lawyers and affordable handguns, he doesn't indulge in actual violence, he keeps his abuse verbal.

Like calling his Latino ex–Atlanta Braves teammate Randall Simon "a fat monkey." Or, "Look at this idiot [driver]. I guarantee you she's a Japanese woman. How bad are Asian women at driving?" (Editor: Okay, maybe he had a point there.) The gold standard, however, will forever be, "Imagine taking the #7 train to the ballpark looking like you're riding through Beirut next to some kid with purple hair next to some queer with AIDS right next to some dude who just got out of jail for the fourth time right next to some twenty-year-old mom with four kids. It's depressing."

Rocker doesn't even have the brains/career sense to fake it like Schott. He's completely unrepentant. Some peo-ple admire his stubbornness; that's why they applaud when he runs out on the field. At least that's the reason the fans give. A more cynical soul would say they're cheering because they agree with Rocker and want him to know he's not alone in his way of thinking, but such suspicions are, to quote John-John, "depressing."

WHAT THE FUTURE HOLDS

It's hard to predict who will be the next inductee into the Hall. Many initially thought the NBA's Latrell Sprewell and coach P.J. Carlesimo were shoo-ins, but their dust-up had nothing to do with race and everything to do with P.J. being a dick.

No, late-addition fan favorites like Denver Nuggets' coach Dan "Drink another beer you fuckin' Mexican piece of shit!" Issel aside, the future of the Hall isn't in the sports that have been integrated for decades, but in the ones where Blacks are still a radical new concept—like golf and tennis. Actually, Black faces aren't new at the golf course. But seeing a Tiger Woods swinging a club instead of carrying one led Fuzzy Zoeller to call him "that little boy," and make cracks about him serving fried chicken and collard greens. (Tiger Woods, by the way, likes to tell dirty jokes about Buckwheat's use of the word "dictate.")

Tennis, that whitest of games, played by the youngest, most sheltered, and least educated of athletes, seems to have a racially charged incident every other day. Anna Kournikova describes Venus and Serena Williams as "mas-culine Amazons," the Williamses' father calls someone a "white turkey," and Lleyton Hewitt accuses a Black linesman of making calls to help a Black player beat him. Before long, tennis just might have its own wing in the Hall of Shame. Till then, sports fans, be patient. Gather your batteries and work on your serve for the next time knuckleheads like John Rocker run onto the field.

CHAPTER 6

DA YELLA PAGES.

The classic comic barb on corpulence goes, "You're so fat you've got more chins than a Chinese phone book." But ever wondered what kind of hot Chin action a U.S. phone book from a random metropolis near you might yield? Well, much like your local, trusty Hunan Garden, we here at *ego trip* are qualified to satisfy. Check the vital stats below on America's most Chin-dense and deprived cities and create your own well-researched punchline the next time you're in the mood to insult that overweight lover (of any race) that's in *your* house. (Insert gong crash here.)

CHIN CHECK:
A PHONE BOOK ANALYSIS.

CITY	CHIN COUNT	CHINSIGHTFUL COMMENTARY
BATON ROUGE, LA	1	To the pioneering Mr. (or Mrs.) Kit L. Chin: you're a regular Chinese Jackie Robinson. Keep hope alive!
GULF COAST, MS	2	It takes more than two to make a Chin thing go right.
DETROIT, MI	5	Crouching Tigers, hidden Chins. Where ya at?
ST. LOUIS, MO	9	And you know, there's no Tsing Tao in the land of Anheuser-Busch either.
CHARLOTTE, NC	11	NC = No Chins. (Unless you count those eleven.)
LAS VEGAS, NV	14	The house odds are that at least two of these Chins are blood-related. Ante up!
NEW ORLEANS, LA	28	Very few ragin' Asians amongst the Cajuns.
PHILADELPHIA, PA	39	Chins gets no love in the City of Brotherly Love.
ORLANDO, FL	42	*Someone's* gotta fit into those snug Mickey Mouse outfits.
ISLAND OF OAHU, HI	55	Surf's up. Chins down.
ATLANTA, GA	64	ATLiens? Or just plain aliens?
PORTLAND, OR	66	These trailblazers are just doing it. One Chin at a time.
LOS ANGELES, CA	96	Tinseltown needs some plastic surgery to enhance its Chins.
CHICAGO, IL	104	Chi-town = Chin-town as the Windy City breaks the century mark!
BOSTON, MA	153	Ain't nuthin' but a Boston Chin Party, y'all. (RSVP only.)
MIAMI, FL	158	*Everybody*—retired Jews, vacationing music industry fucks, Elián Gonzales' rich relatives, Will Smith, and a gang of Chins—loves the Sunshine State's beachin' boomtown.
SEATTLE, WA	186	Good numbers, but Sea-town's predispostion for race-mixin' makes you think some wayward Chins went missin'.
SAN FRANCISCO, CA	435	The West Coast favorite makes a predictably strong showing. We left our hearts (and our laundry) in San Francisco.
NEW YORK, NY (MANHATTAN ONLY)	517	And there you have it. Once again, New York is king of the hill, top of the list, A#1 (A is for Asian). If a Chin can make it here, he can make it anywhere! Even Mr. (or Mrs.) Kit L. Chin of Baton Rouge, LA.

LET'S GET DIRTY: SURVIVING CHINATOWN.

BY SHERMAN MAYO / PHOTOS BY ROSS SCHWARTZMAN

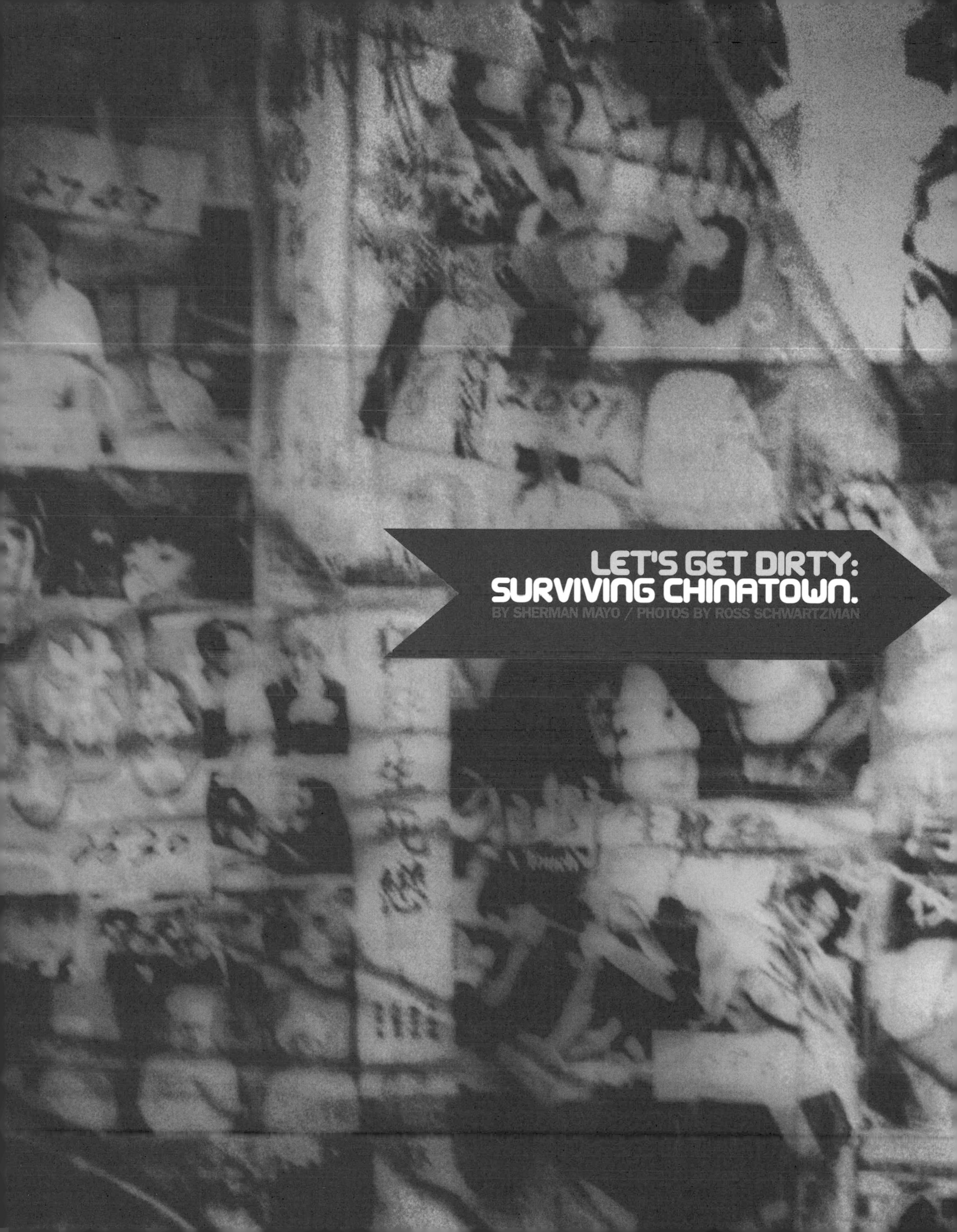

You can't front on any C-town, U.S.A. It's the adopted hot spot for more Chinese immigrants than you can shake a chopstick at—all of them searching for a better life (though one still filled exclusively with Chinese people). If you live in or around any major city in America, there's a good chance a Chinatown is nearby. Like the mystical East itself, its allure and mystery perpetually draws Gypsies, tramps, and thieves alike to indulge in the pleasure of its cheap thrills. Once you're there, everybody have fun tonight: The cuisine's affordable and authentic; the grocery shopping is on fire (even sans curry powder); gold and jewelry bargains abound; and every street corner provides a fine selection of bootleg first-run feature films on video, or a chance to grab an unofficial copy of the latest Jigga CD a good month before it hits the racks at your local Coconuts.

But despite its merits, Chinatown isn't nearly as user-friendly as it should be. In fact, Chinatown is often downright difficult, even disgusting. There's a reason Asian extras ran amuck in the bleak, polluted, dimly lit, claustrophobic metropolitan squalor of everyone's favorite '80s sci-fi flick, *Blade Runner*. That's because the knowers behind that cinematic bonanza based their depiction of futuristic urban blight on some Chinatown shit—except that the chaos of your typical C-town on a busy business day makes *BR* look positively *Joy Luck*-like. Thinking of patronizing this slanty-eyed wonderland? By all means, give your green to the A-team. But take precautions. Or at least some aspirin.

SCHEDULE WISELY

Like vintage MJ, all good Chinese people are working day and night. Hence, their 'hood is a hub of constant activity, and perpetually hectic with visitors—especially during big-splash hootenannies like the dragon parade on Chinese New Year. But like most immigrants, Chinese folks don't give a flying fuck (or fist) about U.S. holidays—they'll stay open on said dates in the hopes of making an extra buck even though they know most Americans will stay away. That's where sage scheduling comes in. Shrewd New York City Jews traditionally go downtown for a taste of Szechuan on Christmas night because they know they can probably get a table at whatever restaurant they want, and extra plum sauce, while all the gentiles are dreaming of sugarplums.

Informed heads do as the Hebrews do. If you wanna check out Chinatown with less stress, go on a national day of rest.

DON'T DRIVE

Every weekend when I was a wee bowl-cut lad, my non-Chinatown-residing nuclear Chinese family would pack itself into the Dodge Dart and head into Boston's Chinatown for a full schedule of eating, greeting (other families), and garnering groceries. It was an all-day affair, so we'd leave early in order to find a really good parking spot. If you're planning to drive to Chinatown, I guarantee that you're not gonna set out as early as my family did or, more important, as early as any similar contemporary familial expedition will. So, inevitably you're gonna wind up getting stuck in traffic for hours behind

bad, tardy Chinese drivers circling the myriad, narrow, winding, one-way streets looking for a space that doesn't exist, only to eventually have to pay out the ass at some overpriced lot or garage. Unless you're willing to pay the cost to be the boss, or double-park, do like Melle Mel says: Forget it, forget it, take the train, take the train.

ABANDON RUSH HOUR
So you're not driving in Chinatown. You're a pedestrian. You even came on President's Day. You should be able to move about freely and fluidly now, right? Wrong. You thought those yellow bastards were slow drivers, ever tried walking amongst a crowd of them at anything quicker than a snail's pace? It's just not possible. Everybody's all over the side-

walk, either looking at stuff for sale, or yelling at you to buy something, or haggling in Cantonese with someone else over fake Polo pullovers, or trying to keep track of their kids, etc. Ease back and accept the fact that you're not gonna get where you want any time soon and go with the flow (of the slow-moving Chinese mob).

DESENSITIZE YOURSELF / DON'T LOOK IN THE BUCKETS
An unfortunate fact of Chinatown life—it is an assault on the senses. The most repulsive sights and smells known to humankind call this place home: mountains of restaurant refuse; streets made slippery by layers of greasy filth; cockroaches the size of water bugs; water bugs the size of rats; rats the size of Michelle Kwan. It's as though every-

thing dirty and unappealing has been exponentially enlarged. Of course, packing this much Hunanity into a next-to-nathan space without it smelling like sanitation is virtually impossible. But you can alleviate your disgust by investing in some nose plugs, or avoiding visits on garbage pick-up days and during the warm weather months. (Everything stinks more in the heat.)

And if you're hanging near the fish markets and don't feel like losing your lunch special, do yourself a huge favor: Don't look inside the barrel-sized buckets regularly housed at these establishments, for you may subject yourself to the sight of hundreds of barely living frogs as they limply writhe atop one another, slowly suffocating in their collective march toward death. No matter what the sign says,

that's *not* fresh. Word to Kermit.

BE ALERT TO "LOOGIES"

If spitting was an Olympic sport, China would be taking home the gold every four years like clockwork. No question. But it's not. So Chinese people spit at their leisure in the street. It's no big deal, sometimes we just gotta let some phlegm fly. But people unfamiliar with this common cultural trait get really grossed out. If that person is you, slow your roll, stop trying to walk so damn fast, and stay out of the spitlane—that area between the center of the sidewalk and the gutter—when you notice that bamboo huckster revving up, and let him clear his throat like DJ Kool. Your shoes and pantlegs will be glad you did

BEWARE D'EVILS

In almost every movie of the past twenty years with scenes set in Chinatown, there's a big, violent shootout—even at the end of *48 Hours*, and there wasn't even a single Chinese muthafucka in that flick. Though such episodes are trite, they're also no coincidence. Chinatowns have always had a seedy side to them, whether, as in the cases of Beantown and San Francisco, it's due to their close proximity to the local red-light district, or simply because Chinese tong warlords are like real regular Chinese folks—content to stick with (or stick it to) their own. These days, the realistic likelihood that you'll be an unwitting victim of gang violence in Chinatown is slimmer than it was back in the days of SF's infamous Golden Dragon Massacre of 1977 when rival gangs opened fire on each other in a restaurant full of innocent victims. But you never fuckin' know. So err on the side of caution. Unless you've got reliable local guides, stay out of that scary Sino-section movie theater. (Besides, you can get all the Jet Li, Jackie Chan, and Samo Hung classics you want on the Web.) Stick to quality noodle shops on the radar. Stay secure in your outsider status no matter how real you aspire to keep it.

FINALLY, SAVOR THE NOVELTY

Just as you don't have to be Black to love the blues, you don't have to be Chinese to love Chinatown. In fact, here's a little secret: If you grew up second-generation Chinese-American any time in the last thirty years, you're probably

sick of stupid-ass Chinatown. You'd probably be pleased as punch never to set foot in a Chinatown anywhere ever again. That's because somewhere between the first time your parents took you there (probably minutes after your birth) until the last time they dragged your ass there (sometime after earning your learner's permit), the novelty wore off. I remember one year, my dad drove us from Boston down to New York City for a "vacation." The itinerary: go to Chinatown to eat lunch, go to the motel on the other side of the Holland Tunnel in New Jersey for an afternoon nap, go back to Chinatown for dinner, back to the motel, drive home in the morning. With irreparably psyche-damaging experiences like that, is it any wonder the magic no longer lingers for some of us beneath those faux pagodas?

But you, wide-eyed, double-lidded Occidental tourist, know nothing of this. Armed with your newly acquired neighborhood navigation knowledge, go forth and frolick amidst the neon, firecrackers, custard pastry, and pork buns. Let the good times (egg) roll. And when you spot that cynical soul like yours truly for which these dirty, dispossessed streets conjure only conflict, you can make like Walsh told Gittes and deliver the final word on this godforsaken garden of grime: "Forget it, homie, it's Chinatown."

Sherman Mayo's guilty pleasure is Koreatown.

"THE CHINESE EXPRESSION IS LIKELY TO BE MORE PLACID, KINDLY, OPEN; THE JAPANESE VERSATION, LAUGH LOUDLY AT THE WRONG TIME. JAPANESE WALK STIFFLY ERECT, HARD

MORE POSITIVE, DOGMATIC, ARROGANT. JAPANESE ARE HESITANT, NERVOUS IN CON-
HEELED. CHINESE, MORE RELAXED, HAVE AN EASY GAIT, SOMETIMES SHUFFLE."
TAKEN FROM "HOW TO TELL YOUR FRIENDS FROM THE JAPS," ORIGINALLY PUBLISHED IN *LIFE*, DECEMBER 22, 1941.

NOT-SO-MODEL MINORITIES: ASIANS THAT ASIAN-AMERICANS AREN'T NECESSARILY PROUD OF.

ANNABEL CHONG
Porn star once held the record for the biggest gang bang of all time after having intercourse with 251 men on camera in 1995. Four years afterward in the documentary *Sex: The Annabel Chong Story*, Chong deadpanned, to the horror of her adult-film-industry peers, that she did not practice safe sex with all her gang bang buddies. Elsewhere in the film, she visits her family in Singapore and reveals the nature of her fame to her unsuspecting mother who is predictably devastated.

DENNIS FUNG; JUDGE LANCE ITO
The former was the criminologist widely blamed for botching the collection of evidence during the O.J. Simpson police investigation. The latter was the justice heavily criticized for dubious decision making while presiding over the circus that was the criminal trial (and became a national laughingstock as evidenced by the *Tonight Show*'s recurring "Dancing Itos" skits).

BYUNG-HYUN KIM
Arizona Diamondbacks' Korean reliever nearly set Asians in stateside professional sports back decades when he served up World Series game-blowing meatballs to the Yankees on consecutive nights. (He was saved from permanent Bill Buckner goat status by the game-seven heroics of teammate Luis Gonzalez.)

DONG-SUNG KIM; APOLO OHNO
2002 Winter Olympic speed skaters that have each incurred the wrath of a different Asian ethnic group. Though he technically crossed the finish line first in the men's 1500-meter finals, South Korean Kim did so by performing a cross-tracking move that fans of Japanese-American competitor Ohno saw as unsportsmanlike. Kim's conduct was ruled illegal, the gold medal was awarded to second-place finisher Ohno, and thousands of e-mail threats poured into the U.S. Olympic Committee from sources in—where else?—South Korea. In a twist, Ohno himself was later disqualified in the 500-meter semifinals for colliding with Japanese national skater Satoru Terao. (Can anyone please put a stop to this tragic cycle of yellow-on-yellow crime?)

MAO TSE-TUNG / HO CHI MINH / POL POT / FERDINAND MARCOS / WHATEVER DESPOT MADE LIFE HELL BACK IN THE MOTHERLAND
Like elephants, your parents, grandparents, and other now-naturalized kin never forget (the horror, the horror).

THEO MUZUHARA
Velvet-voiced longtime West Coast radio personality's schtick is faux Barry White. Unfortunately, this Japanese cornball's game is perpetually played like a piano.

SUCHIN PAK
MTV's token on-air Asian = on-air airhead.

BETTY TING PEI
Copious use of medicines is *very Asian*. Giving Bruce Lee the painkillers that inadvertently triggered his death in 1973, however, is *very wack*. Pei, a Taiwanese actress who was to costar in Lee's next film, earned many a fan's disgust for not calling an ambulance quickly enough after the kung fu hero fell into his final, fatal sleep.

SALMAN RUSHDIE
This East Indian author got no love from the Islamic community (which includes some Asians, by the way) after releasing his fantasy tale, 1988's *The Satanic Verses*. A few riots and death threats later, Iran's Ayatollah Khomeini—citing the book's criticism of fundamentalism—put a bounty on his head, sending Salman upstream on the run and into hiding.

"HOSHI SATO" (UPN'S *ENTERPRISE*)
Whiny and annoying, it's only a matter of time before they beam her ass into orbit.

"SHORT ROUND" (*INDIANA JONES AND THE TEMPLE OF DOOM,* 1984)
Why did the sequel to 1981's *Raiders of the Lost Ark* suck so bad? Look no further than Harrison Ford's irritating kid sidekick, who nearly outscreamed the equally irritating white lady Kate "Mrs. Spielberg" Capshaw.

TOM VU
Judging from his early '90s infomercials, this Vietnamese immigrant-turned-real-estate-mogul was living the "American Dream": luxury automobiles, palacial mansions, and a yacht full of more g-stringed bimbos than you'd find on *Temptation Island.* Turns out Vu made his fortune the real old-fashioned way—he stole it—and was eventually sent to prison for fraud and a ton of other charges.

GEDDE WATANABE
Watanabe's role as the pathetic, nerdy, broken-English-spewing exchange student Long Duk Dong in the film *Sixteen Candles* (1984) has made him pop culture enemy number one among Asian-Americans for almost twenty years. He's since rounded out his acting resume with parts as a swishy waiter in *Booty Call* (1997) and a tourist in *Armageddon* (1998). We feel sorry for his career.

SHANG HAI'D: GREAT ASIAN SCAPEGOATS.

JAPAN
Nation blamed for America's economic downturn during the '80s. They blinded us with science, we bombed them (again) with resentment. (There's some free trade for ya.)

WEN HO LEE
Scientist blamed in 1999 for removing nuclear secrets from a U.S. weapons lab and selling them to China or Taiwan. Who cares if he was cleared of any wrongdoing? Asians have no business being in New Mexico.

DR. THOMAS NOGUCHI (A/K/A "THE CORONER TO THE STARS")
Coroner blamed for shattering the myths revolving around the deaths of beloved public personalities like Robert F. Kennedy, Marilyn Monroe, and Natalie Wood. So what if his reports were on the money and he was just telling it like it was—Asians are best seen, not heard. (And if you're the "dead people's doctor," no one wants to see your morbid ass anyways.)

YOKO ONO
Widow of John Lennon blamed for instigating the breakup of the Beatles in 1970. All right, so those wankers already hated one another before she showed up. It was still the Beatles, not no Funky Four + 1.

I.M. PEI
Architect blamed for the inferior engineering of Boston's glass-sheathed monolith, the John Hancock Tower, when many of its ten thousand windows habitually dislodged themselves and fell to the ground during the early '70s. It didn't matter that it was another architect at his firm, I.M. Pei & Partners, and not Pei himself, who actually designed the damn building.

OSHIN'S 11: 11 THINGS YOUNG JAPANESE-AMERICAN WOMEN LEARNED FROM WATCHING THE 1983 NHK SYNDICATED SERIAL DRAMA *OSHIN.**

1. The destiny awaiting young girls forced into apprenticeship is harsh and cruel.
2. You will have to work even at the tender age of five as a live-in housemaid.
3. The first bus outta town ain't a bus. It's a raft.
4. Rice is as good as money.
5. Grandma will give away her share of the coveted rice in order to save other family members from starvation. Grandma rocks! *Hai!*
6. Postwar prostitution pays.
7. Even if you relocate to the big city, get a job at a salon, get married, and think it's all good, an earthquake can still fuck your shit up. *Sayonara!*
8. Stank mother-in-laws will not recognize your marriage.
9. Parents just don't understand—unless you're talking about emigrating to Brazil.
10. You will lose your baby if no one helps you during pregnancy.
11. All the suffering you endure is worth it because one day you will open a big local supermarket chain. Piggly Wiggly? *Ichiban! Hai!*

*A true worldwide phenomenon, this miniseries was like *Roots* for Japanese gals. Based on the life of the mother of the Yaohan supermarket chain founder, this drama was all about joy and pain. But mostly pain. Lots and lots of it. (No wonder Japanese girls need love, or at least lots of cute Sanrio toys.)

HOME INVASIAN.
SUBURBAN CRIME SPREES SHATTER SUBSERVIENT STEREOTYPES.
(OR, NGUYEN THINGS GO WONG-WEI WONG.)
BY LUC E. PHUC / ILLUSTRATION BY TODD JAMES

It is a violent crime delivered to your doorstep that leaves people traumatized, left in disbelief to ponder the state of humanity. No, we speak not of your local Jehova's Witnesses peddling their fanatical fanzine (though we highly recommend their special Black Jesus issue [*All Along*] *The Watch Tower*). Law enforcement officials describe it as the most horrible, vicious and intrusive form of attack threatening our communities—and it is spreading across America quicker than illegal aliens moonlighting as porn stars. It is not anthrax, the latest Creed album or another Bush seeking office. It is the home invasion robbery.

This method of assault—according to a September 2000 *Los Angeles Times* article—was first reported in Canada thirty years ago back when America honestly didn't give a shit about what happened north of the border. (Actually, we still don't.) Further research reveals that the disturbing trend emerged in the U.S. during the mid-'80s, although an even more disturbing trend—poofy-haired white people in spandex jazzercising—largely overshadowed it. Eventually, Southeast Asian gangs would make this (and the Fonzie look) their trademark, preying on what they saw as

the easiest targets—fellow Asians, especially recent immigrants, who are usually hesitant to report crimes to the police. More importantly, because most of the newcomers mistrust the big pimpin' (or Yankee doodling) done by the U.S. banking system, they often opt to keep their valuables at their own houses ("fat pads" we like to call 'em), leaving them vulnerable to a violent ambush.

The profile of the crime is usually the same. Someone posing as a delivery person knocks on a staked-out victim's door. As soon as the door is opened, the perpetrator, along with several more accomplices, storms the residence and immediately ties the occupants up. Helpless, the victims are either beaten or raped until they reveal the location of the hidden family valuables. The wanton (not to be confused with wonton) violence that occurs during these attacks is considered to be one of the most horrendous types in all robberies committed. Victims have been hung out of windows, have had their heads repeatedly dunked into toilets, and have even been made to choose between seeing their children tortured or watching BET original programming.

This, of course, contradicts the long-standing Asian

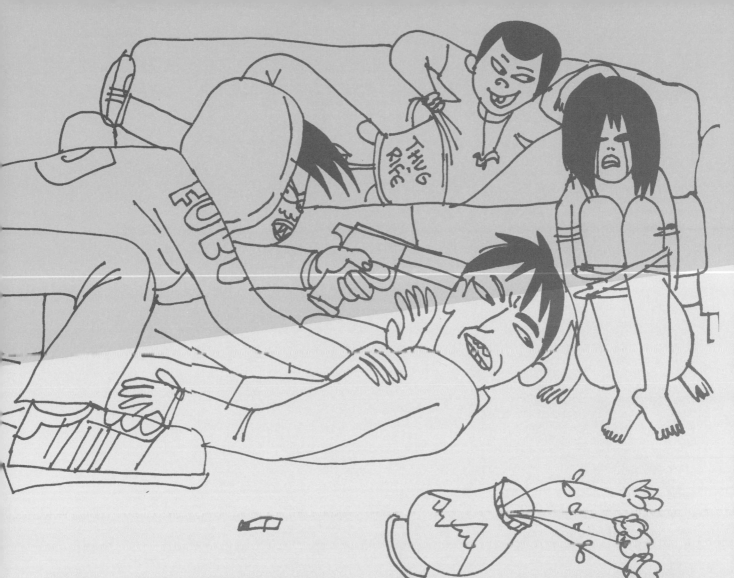

stereotype of the "model minority." While other ethnic groups are commonly portrayed as unruly low-life criminals, when it comes to violent behavior committed by Asians, you're more likely to see it in a chop-socky flick than on the nightly news. Ask Connie Chung. She knows.

Or ask Thumper, a twenty-two-year-old Asian gang member from Orange County, California. "People think we're all docile college students," he says with a tone of disgust. "Or kung fu experts. Well, man, I got tired of people calling me Bruce Lee and shit!"

Since his family's arrival to this country over a decade ago, Thumper has not made the cultural transition as easily as many of his countrymen. Unable to assimilate into the "American Dream," his life has been marred by drug abuse, gang warfare and participation in numerous criminal activities. Like other troubled adolescent and young adults who claim an Asian and Pacific Islander heritage Thumper joined a gang to empower himself against a society who sees "Orientals" as nothing more than push-over Charlie Chans.

"People think they can pull whatever they want on Asians and get away with it," he says. "We proved them wrong."

Asian gangs ain't nothing new. Organized Chinese and Japanese crime syndicates have existed for centuries. Opium, missing fingers and ancient secrets are the images conjured up by these shady organizations. What makes these younger, Americanized Asian gangs different from the older clans is that they have adopted the domestic mentality of gangbangin'. Even though their main illegal enterprises center around microchip heists, credit card fraud, prostitution and home invasions, they still find time to fly colors, write graffiti and throw up signs. Plus, they'll "set trip" quicker than a vintage Hideo Nomo fastball.

Filipino-American gang members, in particular, as well as *La Bamba/Stand and Deliver* actor Lou Diamond Phillips, have styled themselves after traditional Latino street gangs. It is now common to see them wearing oversized "baggies" or Dickies, blaring white T-shirts, and baseball caps monogrammed with Old English lettering that represent their "klicka" or clique.

"A lot of our traditions and style came from bangin' in the same neighborhoods with [Latino gangs]," explains Joker, a Filipino gang member. "The Vietnamese became more known for traveling around the country committing major heists while we became known for bangin' in our 'hoods."

Because they are territorial, or "neighborhood oriented" as the wiry gangster claims, much of the violence associated with Filipino gangs is a result of conflict between warring factions. While the majority of their crime sprees include burglary, car theft and drug dealing, the act of home invasion is not regularly practiced, unless you consider "raiding" or "crashing" house parties where rival neighborhood youth are thought to be in attendance. This commonplace activity often leaves a trail of brutalized party goers, destroyed cars or, in the worst case scenarios, victims of flying lead.

Although most Asians despise the weak-and-humble stereotype, the *veteranos*, or experienced gang members, do take advantage of it when the time is right. "You know the deal. When one-time [cops] pulls you over, you give them the naive and innocent routine," discloses Joker, who speaks through a dark blue rag wrapped around the lower part of his face, *bandido* style. "That makes it easier for us to move around in our 'hood without being sweated as much. A lot of our weapons are hidden in secret compartments in our cars. They're less likely to rip our cars apart trying to find them, since they think we're just on our way to make it to class in college."

That ain't no ancient secret, big poppa-san, that's street smarts. And like any gangbanger of any race knows, you can't leave home without it.

Luc E. Phuc is Asian. He don't bang, he writes the good articles.

10 ITEMS FOUND IN EVERY ASIAN HOME NOT WORTH STEALING.

1. **PORCELAIN LUCKY CAT.**
Tempting because the little critter is cute as hell, but stealing it will result in instant bad karma.

2. **BETAMAX.**

3. **DOS 5¼ FLOPPY DISKS.**

4. **MEMBERS ONLY JACKETS.**
Because in the twenty-first century, membership doesn't have its privileges.

5. **MINIATURE LAUGHING BUDDHA STATUE.**
Note to home invaders: Looks like gold, but it's really metallic yellow. Keep on passin' it by

6. **BACKLIT WATERFALL AND LANDSCAPE PAINTING.**

7. **FLUORESCENT LIGHTS IN THE LIVING ROOM.**

8. **TAMAGOCHI KEYCHAINS.**
Not even the limited edition gold-colored ones

9. **PLASTIC FLOWERS.**

10. **TIGER BALM.**
The cops will smell ya a mile away.

VERY SUPERSTITIOUS:
HAWAIIAN DON'TS YOU DON'T WANNA FORGET.

RESEARCH BY JEN TADAKI

Hawaii's serene beauty and sunshine lure thousands of melanin-challenged tourists each year to the tiny Pacific islands. But *haoles** beware, this poly-Asian (and Polynesian) paradise is rife with old-world superstition. There's a reason why the *Brady Bunch* kept catching bad breaks (and we don't mean waves) in that trip-to-Hawaii episode after "discovering" the taboo tiki statue: They didn't listen to the locals or respect their legends until it was too late. So when you come to the "Five-O" (and fiftieth) state you better come correct. That is unless bad luck, removal of soul, wrath of gods, sickness, unexplained injury, disease, or death is your idea of fun. We don't expect you to understand, just stay in line, bright eyes.

DO NOT UNDER ANY CIRCUMSTANCES . . .

. . . TAKE PORK UP THE PALI HIGHWAY.
Finally, Jews, Muslims, *and* Hawaiians can agree on one thing: Swine is a hazard. Traveling over the Pali with pork in your car will surely stall or stop the vehicle until the offending white meat is tossed out like a cheap hooker. (Proof positive that Spam really can clog arteries.)

. . . REMOVE ROCKS FROM A VOLCANO.
There are thousands of documented cases of bad luck and illness, along with letters of apology and returned stones found at the National Park Post Office on the Big Island of Hawaii. Why? 'Cause conquer-minded *haoles* don't respect boundaries. Do us all a favor and go "claim" something in the gift shop.

. . . PICK THE LEHUA BLOSSOMS.
If a Lehua blossom is plucked from the Ohi'a tree, it will rain the tears of the "lovers" being separated. Again, *haole*, if you can't keep your hands to yourself, go tiptoe through some tulips.

. . . LOOK A "NIGHT MARCHER" IN THE EYE.
Spirits of the dead, usually chiefs or gods, are believed to march in processions around the island. Unless one of your *aumakua*, or family spirit, is in the procession to protect you, a spearsman will swiftly kill you. Wipeout!

. . . PLACE A BED FACING A DOORWAY.
The "Night Marchers" will walk right through your sleeping body and carry your spirit away, killing you softly (with their song—"Tiny Bubbles").

. . . TRY TO LOOK FOR THE MENEHUNE.
These magical "little people" will torment you with mischievous behavior if they are caught. (Full service with "happy ending," however, is negotiable.)

. . . WHISTLE AT NIGHT.
The spirits go where they are called. Plus, that shit is annoying. This ain't *The Andy Griffith Show*.

. . . GIVE LEIS TO EXPECTANT MOTHERS.
If a pregnant woman wears a lei, her child may be choked by its umbilical cord. Keep that shit on lei-away. Ha ha!

. . . BRING BANANAS ON A FISHING TRIP.
No fish will be caught that day and fishing conditions will worsen. And don't bring any "bananas" with you either (you know, "yellow" on the outside, "white" on the inside)—we hate them. Sellouts.

. . . DENY PELE A RIDE.
If you see a woman walking by the side of the highway, pick her up. It could be a prostitute, but then again it might be the goddess Pele who rewards kindness and brings bad luck to those who abandon her. Or it could be Pelé, the Brazilian *futbol* god, in drag. Pick him up. It'll make for an unbelievable vacation story.

*BTW, If you haven't figured out what this word means by the time you've finished reading this, you are one dumb ass *haole*.

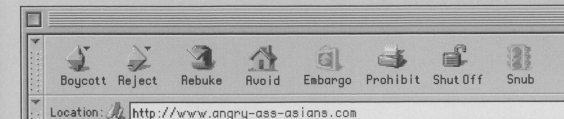

Location: http://www.angry-ass-asians.com

WHO'S THE MAC?
THE ASIAN E-MAIL CIRCUIT WINS AGAIN. BY JEFF CHANG

Asians with a law degree call it "retail racism." The rest of us call it fucked up. It's when you want to go buy something and they flip on you like the KKK. Nothing in the world—not famine, pestilence, segregation, war, not even Steven Seagal—gets us yellows more pissed. It makes us want to steal your parking spot at the outlet mall. It makes us want to scream, "Pay respect to the yellow fist or we'll fry your T3 lines down to a crisp!" Hell hath no fury like an Asian-American with disposable income and an email address. Just ask these corporate running dogs:

5. ADOBE
An Asian-American couple called the Adobe support line to ask about software. They were greeted by Robert, an employee who apparently skipped diversity training. After suffering through his Bull Connor customer service—which ended with Robbie Racist telling them, "Orientals are cheap"—they emailed friends about their experience. The email reached 5,000 people in four days. Adobe fired the worker and released a public apology—something to the effect of, oh shit, Charlie ain't playing.

4. ACURA
It was a typical day at a San Francisco Bay Area Acura dealer. Asian walked in, wanting to upgrade from his Honda. Unfortunately, the salesman, a failed stand-up comedian, told the customer, "There are no Chinese salespeople here, so you have to speak English. No speak Chinese. We fired all Chinese salespeople because they were giving away the cars too cheap." (There's a Tom Metzger-approved sales pitch!) The Asian's jaw dropped, he went home, and emailed his friends. Funny guy got the pink slip. The world was safe once again for Acura-coveting Asians.

3. SKYY VODKA
Adweek called the vodka ads "brash and spicy." Asian-Americans called them racist and degrading. The point of contention was Skyy Vodka's "Inner Peace" ads, in which a white woman receiving a massage was shown being poured vodka by an Asian woman in a kimono. (Guess who's at peace here?) Here comes AsianAvenue.com to the rescue. After hundreds of protesters post slogans on AsianAvenue's bulletin boards—including one appalled barkeeper who stopped ordering Skyy—the embarrassed vodka company pulled the stupid ads. "Prior to AsianAvenue.com, most corporations had no way of getting feedback from the very important consumer group represented by Asian-Americans," said CEO Ben Sun in the company's official press release. Monetize that struggle, comrade!

2. *EGO TRIP'S BIG BOOK OF RACISM!*
Come on, you know it's gonna happen.

1. ABERCROMBIE & FITCH
The suburban outfitter unveiled a line of T-shirts with illustrations of buck-tooth laundrymen, wok-carrying bowlers, and six-armed Hindu bodega clerks. The resulting flood of angry Asian-American email, followed by impromptu protests at A & F stores across the country (sample chant: "2-4-6-8! We refuse to buy your hate!"), quickly turned the T-shirt line into cleaning rags. Spokesman Hampton Carney (his real name!) told the press, "Everyone here at the company thought it was funny. I even polled the Asians around the office today of what they thought of the shirts, and they thought the shirts were hilarious." Look, dude, asking your trophy girlfriend and your cute intern doesn't count.

Respected journalist and author Jeff Chang makes the best damn fried rice in the fifty states.

THE ART OF WHIRL: ENTER THE SPIN CYCLE OF ASIANS WHO TWIRL PENS AND FLEX FIVE FINGERS OF DEX(TERITY).

BY JEFF CHANG

Asian-American men have had it worse. It used to be that you couldn't amble into Truckee, CA, to do a load of laundry without worrying about Denis Kearny's hoodie parade interrupting you during the rinse cycle. But what a difference a century makes. In the 1990s Asian men won all the DJ contests, were declared A-OK to date ("Trophy boyfriends!") by *Newsweek Magazine*, and watched Jet Li kick much white ass on the big screen. It was a good time to be an Asian dude—cheap noodle shops, karaoke centers, powerful computers, anatomically correct thumbstick pads, and Aki Ross from *Final Fantasy VII*. Even William Gibson was on the dilz.

He had probably seen the future in some Vancouver high school computer lab: all these moody dudes in black turtlenecks at the back of the class, staring at the ceiling while Mr. Basic earns his pension. They are leaning back, they are wearing shades, and they are twirling their pens. The authentic hardcore shit. You can fake chopsticks, but who the hell knows how to twirl pens?

It looks easy, of course. Like you're picking up a rock cod eyeball to slurp up at the end of a nine-course dinner, triad-style. But instead you're sending that pen into a wicked horizontal spin. The pen just flies, as if you're juggling M-1 missiles. Twirling has been carefully passed from person to person, an apparently secret art.

Toys begin with jumbo pencils. One twirling expert, a twenty-year-old named Wellington* who is studying to become a civil engineer, says, "When you start with a big fattie, it's really easy. You can get the right amount of centrifugal force and the velocity is slower. If you try to go straight to Bics, you put too much force and it flies off your hand. And if a girl catches you losing your pen, it's kinda like pissing in your pants or something.

"But if you can't do this shit after a couple tries, you're probably a damn banana," he snorts.

Most pen-twirlers point to Bruce Lee as the originator, although no actual evidence has ever been caught on film. His flying *nunchaku* skills are an acknowledged influence on today's generation. "Oh, he was a twirler," says Wellington, who has since had "I am Bruce" tattooed below his thumb on his basal joint. "Just ask Kareem Abdul-Jabbar."

Some anthropologists have favorably compared pen-twirling to Rocky Aoki's Benihana knives show. "It's a typically scintillating display of Oriental ingenuity," remarks Dr. Cleophilus Bradley, a craniologist at Lowell University. But others disagree. As Ho Chi Lin writes in a recent issue of *Yellow Man*: "Clearly, such performative activity is constructed within spaces of aggrievement as a demonstrative symbolic retort to 'otherizing' forces. You may spin me around, but you will not knock me off."

While the cultural mainstream continues to align more and more with Asian males, the most pressing question now facing twirlers is whether to sell out or keep it underground. Some openly compete with others in hand-to-hand combat, seeing who can spin the fastest and longest. Money and fame, they hope, may soon follow. "It's not like the old days," complains one veteran, who declined to give his name. "It was fun back then. These new kids don't have any respect. They just do it for the glamour and glitz."

But the fad may be spreading. One recent martial-arts film, *Thumbs of Death*, which featured brief clips of pen-twirling, reportedly sent non-Asian audiences into a frenzy. Cops were said to have broken up a massive twirling battle on a Chicago street corner after a showing of the movie.

Thumbs of Death director Bucky Freen immediately apologized, saying, "Clearly, we showed the pen-twirlers to be evil, inscrutable nerds bent on taking over the planet. We figured most people would think that was pretty uncool."

So then the fundamental question remains: Why twirl in the first place?

"Why do we do it? I don't know. Asian dudes just have hand skills," Wellington says, as he takes a sip from a carton of Calpis, puts down his Playstation 2, and picks up a copy of *Thai Chicks*. "I'm a twirler for life."

---

* Not his real name

1

PINCH THE PEN BETWEEN YOUR THUMB AND YOUR MIDDLE FINGER AND BRACE IT AGAINST THE BACK OF YOUR RING FINGER. YOUR INDEX AND PINKIE DON'T REALLY COME INTO PLAY EXCEPT TO PROVIDE MORE BALANCE, BUT THAT THREE-FINGER PINCH IS THE BASIC STANCE TO LAUNCH.

2

WITH YOUR THUMB, PUSH THE PEN OFF THE BACK OF YOUR RING FINGER. DON'T PUSH TOO HARD OR THE PEN WILL SPIN RIGHT OFF YOUR HAND. YOU DON'T HAVE TO BE HELLA LIGHT EITHER—CENTRIFUGAL MOTION WILL KEEP THE PEN SWIRLING AROUND YOUR HAND EVEN WITH A GOOD PUSH.

3

THE PEN WILL VERY QUICKLY MAKE A 360—KEEP YOUR THUMB AND INDEX FINGERS APART TO LET IT LAND IN THE GROOVE IN BETWEEN.

4

WHEN THE PEN ENTERS THAT GROOVE, QUICKLY PINCH YOUR THUMB AND INDEX FINGER TOGETHER. THIS MOVE SHOULD CAPTURE THE PEN. IF IT DOESN'T, THE PEN WILL JUST SLIP OFF OF YOUR HAND ONCE IT STOPS TWIRLING. ONCE STOPPED, ALL YOU NEED TO DO IS MOVE THE PEN BACK TO THE STARTING POSITION—YOU CAN DO IT IN ONE EASY MOVE—AND YOU'RE READY TO TWIRL AGAIN.

HANDSOME BOY HAND MODEL: OLIVER WANG.

"THE LAND BRIDGE":
TO BE RECITED TO THE BEAT AND CADENCE OF MC SHAN'S "THE BRIDGE."

Ladies and gentlemen, we got *ego trip* in the house tonight
They just came from off their book tour
They wanna tell a little story about where America's indigenous
people came from

THE BRIDGE, LAND BRIDGE
THE BR-, THE BR-, THE BRIDGE
THE BR-, THE BRIDGE
LAND BRIDGE
THE BR-, THE BR-, THE BRIDGE
THE BR-, THE BRIDGE
LAND BRIDGE
THE BR-, THE BR-, THE BRIDGE
THE BR-, THE BRIDGE
LAND BRIDGE

You love to hear the story again and again
Of how Asians got it started way back when
The monument is gone with no trace
But sit and listen for a while to the name of the place

THE BRIDGE, LAND BRIDGE
THE BR-, THE BR-, THE BR-, THE BRIDGE
LAND BRIDGE
THE BR-, THE BR-, THE BR-, THE BRIDGE
LAND BRIDGE
THE BR-, THE BR-, THE BR-, THE BRIDGE
LAND BRIDGE

North America was barren and stark
It used to look like Jurassic Park
But then the mercury started to fall
Ice so frigid it would not thaw

The temperature was cold as crap
Across the map
The Ice Age had arrived at last
Dinosaurs were a thing of the past

Woolly mammoths were ruling the roost
They were down with the climate cuz it got them loose
Classic example of extended winter
This was a world no man could enter

But to the East some folks had a plan that made them grin
If they could cross the Bering Strait, then they might just make it in
Sea level fell hundreds of feet, then everything was peace
That's why this region's time as unknown had to cease
Cuz Asians used

THE BRIDGE, LAND BRIDGE
THE BR-, THE BR-, THE BRIDGE
THE BR-, THE BRIDGE
LAND BRIDGE
THE BR-, THE BR-, THE BRIDGE
THE BR-, THE BRIDGE
LAND BRIDGE
THE BR-, THE BR-, THE BRIDGE
THE BR-, THE BRIDGE
LAND BRIDGE

Why don't you wise up show all the people in the place you know what's right
Make sure you tell 'em those who got here first weren't white
Cuz Columbus was nothin' but a filthy, greedy bum
And if you give him props your ass had better run
Cuz we're talkin' 'bout

THE BRIDGE, LAND BRIDGE
THE BR-, THE BR-, THE BRIDGE
THE BR-, THE BRIDGE
LAND BRIDGE
THE BR-, THE BR-, THE BRIDGE
THE BR-, THE BRIDGE
LAND BRIDGE
THE BR-, THE BR-, THE BRIDGE
THE BR-, THE BRIDGE
LAND BRIDGE

Asians as a people, they were great
Running dynasties from state to state
Civilized in so many ways
Eating pasta, rocking silk and jewels jade

They never dreamed they'd see the day
When an invention of theirs would make their own kind pay
Gun powder was the thing, you see
That made their descendants run and flee

The "Indians"—they held their head
But Puritan guns threatened showered lead
Religious nuts out to get loose
On the "savage" native folk for whom they had no use

This was the way America was born
Straight stolen from a people of color torn—apart
While every red man, woman, boy, and girl
Reminisced of a better time in the world
And of

THE BRIDGE, LAND BRIDGE
THE BR-, THE BR-, THE BRIDGE
THE BR-, THE BRIDGE
LAND BRIDGE
THE BR-, THE BR-, THE BRIDGE
THE BR-, THE BRIDGE
LAND BRIDGE
THE BR-, THE BR-, THE BRIDGE
THE BR-, THE BRIDGE
LAND BRIDGE

This land, bought and sold
For bags of worthless beads and alcohol
How ever it happened, this charade "trade"
Don't ever go by what history books say

Cuz in the chronicles of shitty deals
This one beat Orlando letting go Shaquille
Asian descendants sadly misled
By benevolent thoughts running through their heads

They weren't conniving, they couldn't see
Genocide masquerading as "manifest destiny"
By the time this routine was known
Their peeps in South America had lost their homes

Europeans were inflicting pain
On the Aztecs and Incas without restrain
Their bloody conquests left millions dead
All cuz them cats were trying to get ahead

Today you say that you're not with it
Mention racism, you're talkin' 'bout "Quit it!"
But as you let Old Glory fly
Have you ever thought about what its colors signify?

Red for blood shed now and later
White for the man who believes he's greater
Blue for the mood of those whose fate
Is to be victimized by all this hate

The whole reason for this story we've told
Is not reparations, but to let you know
Stop walking through life as if you were blind
And acknowledge this continent's debt to crime
After

THE BRIDGE, LAND BRIDGE
THE BR-, THE BR-, THE BR-, THE BRIDGE
LAND BRIDGE
THE BR-, THE BR-, THE BR-, THE BRIDGE
LAND BRIDGE
THE BR-, THE BR-, THE BR-, THE BRIDGE
LAND BRIDGE

Our mixed-race first born
　　Blessed fruit of our union
Let's raise her as white.

Hey, see that Black man
　　Note how gracefully he walks
Throw a rock at him.

No doubt it's true love
Fate has brought us together
　　My mail-order bride.

Yellow chink bastard
　　China man, oh China man
"Two shirts, no starch please."

岩戸神樂/起題

HAIKU! (GESUNDHEIT?)

DRAGON LADY IN A KIMONO ROBE. SEXY IS YOUR WAY. HOW DO WE SEDUCE THEE? AHH! HAIKU!—(PRONOUNCED "HIKOO") AN UNRHYMED VERSE FORM OF JAPANESE ORIGIN HAVING THREE LINES CONTAINING USUALLY FIVE, SEVEN, AND FIVE SYLLABLES RESPECTIVELY.

AND YOU KNOW WHAT GETS YOU *REALLY* HOT? WASABI? NO. *RACIST* HAIKUS! YEAH, THAT'S RIGHT, WE GOT YOUR NUMBER, SWEETIE-SAN.

I live in terror
   I don't trust those sand niggaz
Still, I love Slurpees.

Oh mighty white man
   Builder of bridges and steel
Don't touch my daughter.

"Kill that nigga dead,
Fuck them niggaz, kill niggaz"
   Our first gold record!

Yo, yo, I'm Black, yo
   Rap music and basketball
If only I danced.

Norte del border
They look down at us all day
   Canadians, die.

Straighten your hair out
To look like the white man's wife
At least you got ass.

DA HIGH YELLA PAGES.

SCENARIO I: You own the most talented professional basketball team in the NBA. But your best player happens to be light-skinded, and you know what that means: Thanks to his temper tantrums, he's regularly tossed from games for arguing with the refs.

SOLUTION: Tough love. When he's hitting the showers early, let him know how important he is to the team's success (by any means necessary). If he doesn't respond, pick a scapegoat. Blame it on the reign . . . of the white coach. Close that festering wound with a human Band-Aid: a Black coach who can appeal to his "niggerlect." (that's intellect for ignorant Blacks).

SCENARIO II: You're the wealthy white publisher of a lucrative rap magazine. But your stubborn, light-skinded Black music editor won't lavish your rapper chums with glowing editorial praise that they don't deserve. And that's bad for business.

SOLUTION: Journalism is an ethical profession. So give that disgruntled chap some dap, and come to grips with the fact that agreeing to disagree will not deflate your pockets one bit. (Besides, you have other light-skinded Blacks in your empty life to worry about.) Don't be a 'fraidy cat.

SCENARIO III: You're a high-ranking member of a government law-enforcement agency. But a light-skinded Black revolutionary leader with a surfer-dude accent is stirring shit up in a very bad way—exercising his group of rebel rousers' right to bear arms, setting up free breakfast programs, and exposing the malpractices of Uncle Sam. When he flees the country, be patient. You see, you know his weakness—coke is it, especially the affordable rock version. Finally, when he's

SOLUTION: Have local police authorities harass that ass. Put him on trial for trumped-up charges. When he flees the country, be patient. You see, you know his weakness—coke is it, especially the affordable rock version. Finally, when he's Roy Jonesin', (shadowboxin' and sweatin' profusely) for a fix, just wait for another Black to buck him down. Problem solved!

HOW TO PROPERLY DIFFUSE LIGHT-SKINDED RAGE.

From the womb to the tomb, presume the predictable: Light-skinded Black folks are full o' fire like Al Green's jilted snookie-wookie. In other words, they're perpetually pissed-off. (Grrrgggrhhh!) Their Blackness is always being questioned. So, LFOs (Light Funky Ones) stay ready, willing, and able to prove at a moment's notice that they can be just as "real" as any pigment potent, pig-feet-chompin', chocolate soul brother.

How'd it come to this, you might be wondering. They can't help it if they wanted to. (They couldn't help it even if they could.) For fair-complexioned ebony folk, it's them against the world.

If Black rage is harder to handle than the ghost of Otis Redding haunting (and hunting) Black (Jim) crows, then light-skinded Black rage will burn your fingers like a crackhead with poor pipe-palming skills. But don't hate. Regulate. Here's how to keep a level head when it happens.

MELLA YELLA FELLAS:
ONE DOZEN LIGHT-SKINDED MEN WHO AREN'T ANGRY.

SAVION GLOVER
"The Glove" is tap dancing for the love. Not the hate.

CUBA GOODING JR.
So agreeable, he'll make a crappy movie with anyone, even talking dogs.

GREG GUMBEL
The humble Gumbel doesn't mind living in brother Bryant's shadow.

HEAVY D
Still overweight. Still a lover, not a fighter.

ALLAN HOUSTON (NEW YORK KNICKS)
Can't take it to the hole, but nonetheless takes home $100 million. He's happy.

KID (OF KID 'N PLAY)
Fallen rapper even brought the *House Party* vibe as host of the *Star Search* rip-off *Your Big Break* in the late '90s. Unfadeable.

CURLY NEAL (HARLEM GLOBETROTTERS)
His dribble will make you drool—with glee!

SMOKEY ROBINSON
His Irish eyes are always smiling. Here's to you, Mr. Robinson.

SINBAD
Black comedy's gentle giant. Don't fight his comedic powers.

WILL SMITH
Big Willie style: a thank you and a soft shoe.

JAKE STEED
Porn star lives by one simple slogan: A nut a day keeps his melanin at bay.

DJ YELLA
He's the calm one, but his crew is sorta sick. N.W.A's nigga with the least attitude.

FANATIC OF THE N-WORD.
HE'S GOT SO MUCH TROUBLE ON HIS MIND. *EGO TRIP'S* RESIDENT HALF-BLACK, HALF-LATIN YELLA FELLA, ELLIOTT WILSON, WAGES A WAR OF WORDS WITH HIMSELF

It's been goin' on since the beginning of time and it's gonna continue on and on until Erykah Badu runs out of hair weaves and somebody shuts the lights out on this muthafucka: Black folks just can't stop using the n-word. In recent times, however, the issue of whether the race formerly known as "Negroes" should or should not use the word has been replaced by the recent increase of its usage by the Latino community. To put it simply, the spics have taken over like Jay Hova. In these troubled times, what's a bro to do—especially when he's one of mixed descent? *BBOR!'s* own tragic mulatto has a by-himself meeting to sort through his true feelings on the world's most dangerous word.

BLACKHAND SIDE: Shit, I used to say it—a lot. Much to the dismay of my partner-in-crime, Sacha Sebastian Jenkins. I remember the dirty looks he would hit me with when the word would slip out of my mouth. Sometimes I would feel self-conscious about it, but for the most part I didn't give a fuck what he thought (and I *still* don't give a fuck). I just felt his sensitive half-Haitian ass was just bein' bourgie. Lookin' back, how ignorant was that?

I now fully understand the science: Those white cracker-barrel whip-crackers used to call us that when they was carvin' their initials in our backs like our name was Toby. But we forward thinking dark folk took the term, flipped it, and gave that n-word power—as in "That's right, I'm a nigga. I'm that nigga that'll bust your racist ass." Among us former "Negroes," "nigga" meant "friend." "Nigga" also meant being thug, being thorough. And it tightly hugged the end of our sentences to emphasize our points—"I'll see you later, *nigga*."

But now things done changed. Black folks have replaced the n-word in their daily convos with more up-to-date slang like "son," "kiko," "dawg," etc. You'd think that its usage by famed rap singer Afroman would substantially decrease the word's popularity, too, but that's not the case, baby paw.

Thanks to muthafuckas like the other side of me (my Ecuadorian side, to be specific), the word is stronger than ever. Our Latino brothers and sisters have been usin' the n-word flagrantly. If I had a bitch for every time I saw two spics on the A train spittin' that "nigga this and that," I'd be the Bishop Magic Don Juan of Money-Makin' Manhattan. (Hell, even the Boricua *mamis* can't help but get their Angie Martinez on as they describe their men to their fellow baby mothers: "That nigga ain't call me in two days." Yada, yada, don dada.)

You *panas* and your partners need to dead that shit like your pork intake. What right do you Goya bean snackers have to say this shit? Hello? I'm talkin' to you, muthafucka.

LATINO HEAT SIDE: Yo, why don't you go fuck yourself! Ever since your Black ass started clockin' six figures you've gotten softer and softer. You're makin' a big deal out of nothing with this fake Black-pride shit. You're a mulatto, man. Don't forget it.

I listen to hip hop—all day, everyday. And as far as I can tell almost every other song has the word "nigga" in it. It ain't goin' nowhere. It's hip hop, fool. It's slang. It's how we talk. No Black person should get offended when a Latino says the n-word. We're just like you. We grow up in the same neighborhoods, get hassled by the cops for pissin' off the subway platform, and go through the same shit as you. Feel me?

There's thousands of muthafuckin' Dominicans darker than your light-skinded ass. Who the fuck are you to say that they can't say the word? You need to give up this born-again Richard Pryor shit. Our mother is Ecuadorian and she doesn't know how to speak Spanish, so I don't neither. This is how I speak, you slang editorial Oreo.

Spanish people are not your enemy, bro—because Spanish People In Control, *maricon*. Whitey Ford is thy ememy, *pa pa*. 'Member when you was little and hangin' out with all those pimply-faced future gym teachers on your Little League baseball team and every once in while they'd forget you was Black and say "nigger" in front of you? Now *that's* fucked up. Hate on them. Don't hate on me, bro.

BLACKHAND SIDE: Stop coppin' pleas, please. Maybe there'd be fewer white boys sayin' that shit if we hadn't been givin' you cats a free ride for so long. They see Spanish cats sayin' it and they think it's cool for them to say it as long as there's no dark-skinded dude around.

You're right, Black people—yours truly included—come in all shades and colors. But Latinos will never, ever, ever know how much that word hurts. One time I saw two Puerto Rican teenagers on the train arguing using the word and there was an old Black guy sittin' across from them visibly upset that those two guys felt the need to use the word in every other sentence. Imagine how that old fucker felt. How would you feel if two Black guys were on the train next to you saying, "Spic this, spic that"? It wouldn't happen, right? I don't think y'all even realize how much you use it and how wrong it sounds.

The only reason Spanish people used the word originally is 'cause they was just bitin' off us—copyin' the way we talk like they copy what we wear, how we walk, all that shit. Black people are the innovators of culture. Whatever we do, others (Spanish, whites, Asians, Hindus—you name it) make like Grand Pu and copy, copy, copy, copy, copy. As Ice Cube once said, you're all on our nutsac.

LATINO HEAT SIDE: There you go again with your fake-ass Professor X, Million Man March shit. You make it sound like those two Puerto Ricans were callin' the old Black man "nigger." That doesn't happen. You never see a Spanish person callin' a Black person "nigger" in a derogatory manner. Anyone can tell we are not usin' it in a bad way. You have to be an idiot to think otherwise. I seen Black guys say it to other Spanish dudes. They don't seem to have a problem with it

It's just become like any other so-called dirty word. Like "fuck." Everyone uses it. You tryin' to censor my ass like the great George Carlin. People have the right to say whatever they want. There's no law against saying "nigga." There never will be.

Words have power, so it's all in the context of how you say it. "Bitch" can mean several things in different contexts. You got girls saying, "I'm that bitch," meaning strong woman. But if *you* call them that, they're ready to whyle out on you. You say we just bitin' off y'all—but then some of y'all consider it a compliment that we use it. We're payin' homage.

BLACKHAND SIDE: Whatever . . . ignorant-ass nigga.

CHAPTER 7

LUST.

for dating w/possiblity of relation-ship. No head games. ☎ 2305

Are you a thuggish Hisp or light-s-kinned Black guy? I'm GWM, very gdlkg, strt acting, brn hair,gold eyes,34, 5'9, 160, lkg for something real. Like sports, outdrs. Grt catch if I'm what you're lkng for. ☎ 2116

BLACK F WANTED
WM business exec, 40's, handsome sks F for sensual discreet relation-ship. Take a chance. ☎ 2361

Seeking Extremely HAIRY Man 34, Italian, 5'4", br/br, mustache, slim build, cute. Enjoy movies, dining out. Seeking Indian, Pakistani Iranian, Italian, Arab men.
☎ 1829

Pretty, full-figured, black girl, 35, sks white sugar daddy.
☎ 7234

Long legs on a magnif IVORY W
YOU
Long legs on a magnif Ebony Man 49+, N/smkg, mustache a+ ☎ 7230

CHOCOLATE SEEKS
PLUS SIZE VANILLA
Attractive SBM 41, has a sweet tooth for an attractive, affectionate, & pas-sionate Hispanic or White full figured woman, 18+, for poss LTR. ☎ 7141

MWM 35 sks kind caring attractive
SBF who would like to get involved in a role reversal with my white wife. You could take her place, she would love it. ☎ 2745

Oriental Men Wanted
Smooth soft sweet orientals wanted by 52yr old Italian to kiss all over and kiss me all over, front & back.Oral for hours. ☎ 2394

Cute Israli, total bottom, 5'5, 138 lbs, 34, waist 29; really nice, clean, healthy, friendly bottom. Seeking well-endowed masculine Black Bi top man. Easygoing & slim for hot time. Peace. ☎ 2316

---

the same time. No baggage pls! ☎ 2404

BiWC ISO BiM tops please be safe sane educated sweet passionate & have a gd sense of humor. Bi's only. No Gay,Straight or Republicans any race. Black is a+. ☎ 2081

Savvy, sexy BiWM, 39, tall, Italian, artistic type sks daytime fun with femme petite Asian or Indian bottom. Long term, no strings, NYC only, your place, squeaky clean only. Cross-dress +. ☎ 1915

A Voyeur's Delight
EXPLOSIVE INTERRACIAL COUPLE
FOR VOYEUR. ☎ 1899

BORED
40yo. married WM, 6'3, 210, sks merry Black Female 40-55yo. for discrete relationship. ☎ 1653

Sexy English Black F
Home attendant seeks White gentleman for good times.
☎ 1741

Nubian Queen
seeking a King to spend time with & to have fun with. Any race, 30-36.
☎ 1305

A CHEROKEE DREAM
PALE SPIRIT WOMAN WANTS WIND IN HAIR CHEROKEE MAN.
☎ 7515

Pass this by
UNLESS
You are tall Black NS gorgeous over 48 financially stable guy and wish to meet a redhead Diva. ☎ 6965

Different Kind of India Man.
A different kind of man, prof., 42, intellectual, college-grad with a wicked sense of humor, seeks a lusty SF for a fantasy-like relationship. ☎ 7119

---

rangement. Dinner, travel, & MORE. SERIOUS inquiries only. ☎ 2306

Non-Traditional Mixed Couple in an open relationship. I'm white, she's dark. Looking for mature, sen-suous, open-minded, SUBMISSIVE WOMAN for EROTIC PLEASURES/LTR ☎ 1957

Black Men Desired
Couple NYC area, 30. She is busty, voluptuous Latina. We are looking for a black, bald thuggish type who is very well endowed to fulfil a fantasy. Be clean & discrete. ☎ 2652

BE MY B*TCH!
Firm but loving, intelligent, exper'd 33 y.o. DOMINANT BM sks smart & sexy wh*re of color in need of discipl-ne & obedience training. NO flakes, men or white women, pls! ☎ 1728

INDIAN COUPLE
From the Caribean looking for an-other couple or a Bi-curious F. Race unimportant. ☎ 1404

Lets Try Three The Hard Way
Blk cpl in early 30's seeks Bi or Straight F. Race not import. Looking to fulfil our fantasies. We'll be waiting at the phone for your call. ☎ 1982

A BLACK MALE
EXTREMELY WELL-ENDOWED ISO
HOT FEMALE. ☎ 1460

MIXED FEMALE THE ACTRESS LISA BONET TYPE LOOKING FOR TALL, MUSCULAR, RUSSIAN M 20s w/BLONDISH, BROWN HAIR OR RAPPER EMINEM TYPE FOR FRIENDSHIP/RLTNSHP. ☎ 6778

CHOCOLHOLICS
Get your taste buds ready. SBF Sexy 5ft 8. Longing to be pampered by SWM 30-45, handsome/financially stable.Reply if you are serious 2355

AFFLUENT LOVABLE ASIAN
Guy seeks cute, fun-loving, buxom WF, 18-35, to fulfill fantasies. I am sweet, caring and generous. Be spoiled and pampered by me. I will drive anywhere to meet you. No pros, please. Call Box 5779.☎

QUALITY FROM TAIWAN. Are you a special Caucasian guy with good quality? I'm 5'1", 105, young 48, healthy, fit, artistic, love nature, ca-reer, well-educated. Seeking same quality, 5'11"-6'2", athletic, sincere, humorous, professional, n/s, to share life with. (Glendale) Call Box 5407.☎

DON'T TAKE IT PERSONAL.
Believe it or not, these are actual, legitimate listings of assorted-flavored skin searching for sin.

SWF SEEKS SECRET ASIAN MAN
5'2", brown/ blue, curvy, irreverent, inquisitive, dolphin-girl seeking SAM, 28-42, for hanging out and discovering LA via tours and spy mis-sions. N/s, no heavy drugs, no kids (your's or mine!). (LA) Call Box 5482.☎

for dating w/possiblity of relationship. No head games. ☎ 2404

the same time. No baggage pls! ☎ 6949

rangement. Dinner, travel, & MORE. SERIOUS inquiries only. ☎ 2306

BLACK F WANTED
MWM 40s 6' handsome bus exec sks BF for sensual, warm rltnship. You won't be sorry. ☎ 1395

1 BI WOMAN OF COLOR SOUGHT
By sexy, fun, smart, dredlocked B couple into the arts/culture. He: 6'3, grn eyes, she: 5'6, 130. Well-read, natural hair & busty are +++! Brooklyn in the house? ☎ 7620

A1 HOT COUPLE
STACKED ASIAN & WELL ENDOWED BLACK MALE ISO HOT BLACK COUPLE FOR FINAL SWAP ☎ 2408

Black Male seeking
White Female for relationship. ☎ 1374

ASIAN FEMALE & WHITE MALE
seek Bi or Bi-curious F to seduce Asian wife. Husband likes to be present. Asian Bi a plus. Limits respected. Discreet. ☎ 7421

BLACK DREAM
White male, tall, trim, good looking, EMPLOYED, 52, seeks A Youthful (33-47) NYC Black female for serious relationship. Try Me - U will Like Me. ☎ 2301

INTER-RACIAL
SBM, open minded searching for a SWF for friendship & possibly more. ☎ 1528

...I'M IN CONTROL...
Tall, biracial, beautiful, hung, dredlocked DOM seeks OBEDIENT F of color 18-35 (thick/busty a +!) into roleplay, bdsm, 3somes...experience the joy of SUBMISSION. ☎ 7616

INTERRACIAL RELATIONSHIP WTD
I am a coll educ Mulatto M, 5'10", 175lbs & handsome. I'm extremely lonely & ISO a SWF btw 25-40 who I can love, cherish & share life's experiences with, good & bad. ☎ 2473

WANTED SWF
who is into Luciferian for friendship with Black Luciferian. Let's get together and bring out the stars. I am waiting, sweetie. ☎ 1739

SBM & SWM, students seeks female closet freaks 4 fun. Black, Asian, Latino, White, thick bbw, buxom - no matter. We'd love to meet you. D & D free. Very, very discreet!
☎ 2305

DEAR SEXY, I'M AN OK LOOKING
Asian Male, into loud music & hot hard sex. Friendly, good sense of humor, professional. Looking for sexy women with like tastes. ☎ 7001

White or Latina sought by a SBM. If you're slim athletic, I'm a shy, tall, muscular, considerate SBM, w/shaved head, hazel eyes and dimples. :-). Let's explore New York. ☎ 1328

THE MIGHTY THOR
Dom Norse god SWM 36, 6', 185, blue/long blond hair sks attr in-shape sub F vixen to kneel before the power of my magic hammer. ☎ 7028

Bi Black Man Wanted
by Bi WM Married 40's, 6', 240, handsome, sks discreet Bi bottom or switchable for sensual fun. Don't be shy. ☎ 2193

THREE TIMES A CHARM
Blk & White cple looking for Bi F. petite, blonde & blue eyes for a ton of fun. ☎ 1593

ORAL FOR BLACK MEN
BI BM 31 CONSTRUCTION WORKER Discreet sks profl Bi BM, own car, no gays. ☎ 7448

MWM seeks kind caring thick cutie SBF to become involved in a threesome relationship. My willing white wife hopes you become the wife one day and she, tho third wheel. ☎ 1750

HUNGRY WILY 21 yr old Blk Attr F
5'9 195lbs sking attr aggressive M who can handle this thick sensual chocolate. Bronx a +/Blunts a +. ☎ 7157

BLACK BEAUTY SKS WHITE KNIGHT Attractive SBF, 32, seeks tall (6'), athletic, sincere, educated SWM for LTR. Be my lover & my best friend! I am 5'8", athletic, sexy. D & D free only! ☎ 2536

100% MALE,
Healthy prof'l, very oral, 49, seeks trim, virile, White/Asian/Latino Male 18-34, for discreet encounters. Sit back, relax & enjoy. ☎ 1831

WILD BLACK FREAKY F (30's)
WAITING 4 U.
☎ 7311

WEST INDIAN Female,
dark skin, 20s, 125 lbs. sks handsome, Russian or Greek White Male, 25-31, financially secure, for relationship. D&D Free. ☎ 1324

Looking For Mr Right
Cuban/Black M 40 yo 6' 225 lbs aver build, lkg for good lkng fit Bi M straight Guy, White, Lite skinned Hisp Or Asian 23-55 for encounter or fshp. Will pamper right guy. ☎ 7418

Sexy, professional, chocolate chick, who digs Rock-n-Roll, would love to make a "vanilla swirl" with a mentally stimulating man in his 30's. FOREIGNERS A PLUS!! ☎ 7274

BLACK BEAUTY WITH BIG BOOTY sought by VGL professional WM for discreet afternoon/ evening adventure. You have cute face, any body type. I'm d/d free, you too. Let's talk/ meet. (Westside) Call Box 5860. ☎

JUNGLE FEVER ORGIES
Tall, dark and handsome, well-endowed WM, 40, 6'0", 190, shaved head, mustache, goatee, loves sloppy seconds, wants thin, attractive girlfriend, any age or race, who loves to party who well-endowed Black guys on a regular basis, one-on-one or groups. (SFV) Call Box 5195. ☎

HIP-HOP ZEN CHIC. Seeking only sirius-minded Afrocentric. R U a tall, vegan, agnostic traveler looking to kick flava with one homez on all dimensions? This Afro-Asian artist, writer, filmmaker and metaphysician is ready to root. (Westside) Call Box 5857. ☎

ASIAN LOOKING. He: WM, 45, over 6'0", and She, Asian, under 5'0". seeking other couples to watch, be watched and be part of the act. We are new to this style of fun. (OC) Call Box 5618. ☎

WHEN A (BLACK) MAN LOVES A (WHITE) WOMAN.

Even we here at *BBOR!* must wholeheartedly agree with KRS-One: "Love's Gonna Get'cha." And when it does, it don't matter which cross-colors characterize your strange relationship. Love may be blind, but society at large isn't. Just

1 PRECONCEPTIONS

Break those mental chains. If, while looking into the eyes of your mate lovingly, you're thinking less than loving thoughts, then things aren't gonna go so well.

2 DATES

Hanging out in groups of three or more can deflect a lot of unwanted attention on your social habits. While the saying goes, "Two's company, three's a crowd," in your case, "Three's company and two . . . is . . . dangerous. So dangerous, so dangerous."

3 THEFT

Too often overlooked within the courtship process, thievery makes a great first-date activity. However, if you are gonna steal, please make sure that your ivory mate makes those moves. The darker shade in the relationship may be utilized as a rather good decoy.).

4 ROMANCE/FINANCE

It's true, there isn't one without the other. But don't spend all of her money, money. Let her save up some emergency cash for:

- Food
- Cabs to your side (a/k/a the wrong side) of the tracks
- Unplanned parenthood
- Bail

EGO TRIP'S 8 STEPS TO INTERRACIAL DATING PERFECTION.

ask your man, Steven "Black Amistad" Spielberg. Interracial dating can be a beautifully orchestrated love movement if you handle the following issues properly:

5 BEEF

Anything goes, but don't hit below the belt. Chill on the racial epithets or you'll have to settle your differences physically. That's our word.

6 PDA. (PUBLIC DISPLAYS OF AFFECTION)

Watch your PDA. *Jungle Fever*, the Spike Lee loin-tingler, can teach you a little something-something about PDA: Wesley Snipes' girl, the Italian broad from Bensonhurst, BK, gets the beatdown of her life by her not-havin'-it tough-guy brothers after it is discovered that her man is Blacker than a dirty lump of coal. (Ouch!) Disguises are an indispensible accessory in enjoying those truly tender moments.

7 FAMILY AND FRIENDS. (HOW MANY OF US HAVE THEM? NOT MANY IF YOU'RE IN AN INTERRACIAL COUPLE)

Don't let redneck cousins or McDonald's-working Blacks disapprove of your personal B.I. If they do, feel free to let some heads get flown.

8 SEX

Always practice safe sex. It doesn't matter if you're Black or white. Ask Lisa Marie. Or Bubbles. (But don't ask Tommy Mottola—4 shit.)

WHEN WHITEY MET MUDDY:
20 CAUCASIAN CELEBS AND THE COLORED FOLKS THEY'VE MARRIED (AND SOMETIMES DIVORCED).

David Bowie + scintillating nubian runway queen Iman

Lorraine Bracco + Chicano acting/directing sensation
and activist Edward James Olmos

Edgar Broufman Jr. (owner of Universal Studios and Universal
Music) + a civilian sista (and guess what? She's paid!)

Tyne Daly + equally talented, all-Ivy- League-christened
brother man Georg Stanford Brown

Vic Damone + the always ravishing ebony supa duchess
Diahann "Julia/Claudine/*Dynasty* chick" Carroll

Robert DeNiro + '80s downtown NYC Black fashion empress
Toukie Smith

Roger Ebert + a civilian sista (who's always seated in Rog's
front row. Thumbs up!)

Carmen Electra + Dennis Rodman

Woody Harrelson + a civilian Asian woman

John Lennon + avant-garde Japanese artsy-fartsy icon Yoko Ono

Peggy Lipton + perpetually celebrated African-American music
impresario Quincy Jones

Tommy Mottola + Latina songbird Thalía
Tommy Mottola + troubled mulatta songbird Mariah Carey

Peter Norton (computer virus detection czar) + a civilian sista

Maury Povich + pioneering Asian news broadcasting
personality Connie Chung

Steven Seagal + a civilian Japanese woman

MC Serch + a civilian sista
(and presumably a Brooklyn Queen)

Shadoe Stevens + dynamic Black disco diva Donna Summer

Billy Bob Thornton + fair-skinded Black actress
Cynda Williams

Lindsay Wagner (television's *Bionic Woman*) +
the Black/Native American actor/stuntman Henry Kingi Sr.

John Wayne + a civilian Mexican woman*

*We can't believe it either.

THE PEARLY BIRD GETS "THE WORM": DENNIS RODMAN AND HIS ELECTRA COMPANY.

20 FAMOUS BUT AVERAGE-LOOKING WHITE GIRLS WHO WHITE PEOPLE THINK ARE HOT JUST BECAUSE THEY ARE WHITE.

Gillian Anderson
Jennifer Aniston
Lara Flynn Boyle
Laura Dern
Kirsten Dunst
Carmen Electra
Bridget Fonda
Sarah Michelle Gellar
Melissa Joan Hart
Elizabeth Hurley
Nicole Kidman
Heidi Klum
Anna Kournikova
Courtney Love
Jenny McCarthy
Gwyneth Paltrow
Tara Reid
Meg Ryan
Britney Spears
Tori Spelling

20 FAMOUS WHITE GIRLS WHO *EGO TRIP* ADMITS ARE HOT.*

Brooke Burke
Laetitia Casta
Jennifer Connelly
Megan Ewing
Claire Forlani
Nelly Furtado
Natalie Imbruglia
Angelina Jolie
Milla Jovovich
Ashley Judd
Vanessa Paradis
Amanda Peet
Piper Perabo
Natalie Raitano
Gwen Stefani
Charlize Theron
Shania Twain
Liv Tyler
Estella Warren
Catherine Zeta-Jones

*See, we're not that racist.

INTERRACIAL DATE HATE: SEEING MIXED UP LOVE IN BLACK AND WHITE.

BY SANFORD JENSON

It just doesn't make any sense. I know.

It started in '88—back when Public Enemy told a nation of millions that the Nation of Islam had some things to say. In those days, this brotha was soul searching—literally trying to navigate my way through seventeen years of *blanco* popular television memories; looking to make sense outta the various jumping jack (mental) flashes of happy white families with long-haired daughters who, on those very bad days, worried about the nose swelling that a stray football done caused. But P.E. (fuck phys. ed!) was the Lil' David that woke this sleeping Goliath up. It was as if emcee Chucky D and his main homie Flavor Flav dropped a medicine ball—one filled with a whole lotta pro-Black science—on my chocolate-covered coconut.

Knowledge of self comes with many a string attached. Yummy-flavored dome or no, the one thing that I did pick up when I entered the junior varsity world of nouveau Blaque pride was that interracial dating—the gateway drug that leads to interracial *mating*—would only weaken my beloved race. And so no matter how *caliente* I thought Marcia Brady or Heather Thomas was, or how crazysexykool I thought the Greek, Italian, or Yugoslavian babes at my Queens, New York, high school were, there was no way in hell that I'd allow myself to even dream about stuffing their fresh cherry pies with original Cool Whip. Then again, during the late 1980s a brotha had no use for whiteys: the home of the brave was an expanse where great Noir Amerikans like Jesse Jackson, Bill Cosby, Spike Lee, Robin Givens, and various other buffalo roamed. Like a wonderful Japanese automaker who shall remain nameless once asked via some singing ritzy cracker's voice (*sorrynora,* Mr. Roboto—no gratis exposure here), who could ask for anything more?

In my mind, them salt 'n' peppa couplings didn't look right—word to George and Weezy. I didn't have a problem, per se, with the East Indian woman who fancied some booming Egyptian lover, or the Chinese MIT grad student who fell for her nutty, Harrison Ford–looking philosophy professor because, you know, I'd seen that stuff on TV and nobody ever had a problem with it. From my kinte-cloth-shrouded vantage point, however, within your standard ebony-on-ivory duo, the female portion of the pairing was essentially this slightly portly trailer park queen with dreams strapped into a pair of 2-tight, stone-washed overalls; "Missy" would always have mousy, dirty-blonde hair, pack of crush-proof Newports in tow. Chronic mayonnaise breath. *Sexy.*

On the flip, Mayonnaise Breath's man, Big Barry, is a former playapimp who pumps more iron than all of Full Force. His mustache/beard combo is on point just like Teddy Riley's circa 1988. He hangs at Heavy D's barbershop in the heart of Mt. Vernon, New York, on Sunday afternoons—his only day off. Playa's root-beer-flavored Maxima is old, but in impeccable shape. He fantasizes about Dallas Cowboys' cheerleaders lap-dancing at Harlem's Apollo Theater. He's got a decent job in the mailroom of a prominent midtown law firm—Berserkowitz, Berserkowitz, Chandler and Gully. He sports rather mild, latter-day Jheri Curls. He's maaad phat, yo.

Man, was I down for my sistas back in the Olde English daze. No Nivea in my coffee, bro. It was strictly about head wraps, incense, random foot massages, baby mommas with hustler baby daddies. Yeah, I lived it. It was really real. I ain't mad at my time spent as the coal-Black revolutionary who swore off stringy-haired cave dwell-ettes.

Then the '90s came skipping in. Rap's hard jams at this point weren't like Chuck D's good ol' kulcha seminars anymore. Party joints came back strong, only with mo' cleverer lyrics. Everyone was questing for the Tribe vibes. Right around this time, I met a white girl with a spanking new Afrikan name. She was "finding herself." And I found myself getting to know her. I figured, hey, she's shittin' on the white man's heritage—and sharing with the brothaman—she can't be all bad, aight? At any rate, I didn't have any great expectations here; I was pretty sure that no love would develop between myself and this, or any, albino-skinded girl. I was wrong, of course. But Chucky D and his boys are to blame, for if Public Enemy were still on top . . . this would never have happened. That's my word up! Because they told me what to do.

My homeboys will be the first to tell you that I went on to date more than two pelicans in my day. Admittedly, none of 'em were down with that creamy mayonnaise breath thang. But don't front on personal growth, y'all. I've learned that people should love people for who they are, not *what* they are. Feel me? To judge the Lord's creatures on the basis of their genetic and cultural identity be a dirty sin.

Well, I guess I'm a sinner something ugly because an interracial-dating hypocritter like myself still somehow hates interracial dating. No, wait, let me rephrase that. I hate GROUP interracial dating. *Hate.* Groups of mix masters, in my opinion, should go right to the back of the Ikea bus.

Some Black folks don't like hummus; some don't like backgammon. For me, going for a stroll with two other mangled-up couples—at the mall or anywhere where there are scores of everyday people—is seriously not da mooove. That's a Lakers-esque three-peat that I'm not trying to meet. Granted, we mammals have more important things to tangle us up in a tizzy—just go to www.google.com and type in "beef," "Pakistan," "Enron," "L. Ron," or "dirty bomb" and make a wish. On paper, I guess we could all use all the peace, unity, love and having fun there is to go around. But who really wants to be at the mall with a bunch of cross-breeding happy jacks? Only P.T.L. Club weirdos and fellow Kool Aid-sniffing sorry-saps, I say! Listen, one interracial couple in your crew? Shit happens. Two? We've all heard of twins. But triplets?! Never that! Any crew with more than two Afro / Anglo mixed bags is not the kind of culture club I wanna belong to.

You see, I've done the three the hard way thing; it's usually three white brides for three brothas. I rolled to the movies like this once. Went to see wrinkly-ass Tommy Lee Jones do his thing in *U.S. Marshals.* The six of us in the theater's lobby, three Black men lamping with three you-know-whats, catching stares from pairs of portly Black grandparents snacking on popcorn, diggin' deep into their buckets, scooping puffy kernels with dingy fingernails, synthetic butter dripping onto the burgundy, decorative peacock print carpet. I could hear 'em calling us three Jovan-musketeers Uncle Tommys with their dark brown eyes; it was as if I heard 'em singing, waaay loud: "Tommy, can you hear me?" Then, in real time, they're mumbling nonsense and pointing at us like

we're a cross-dressing Ben Vereen on a float gliding down Fifth Avenue.

The funny thing about this story is, of course, the white girls didn't notice any of this. None of us said anything to our birds as the Black-on-Black hate was happening. But as soon as we got outside—it was like, "You guys are just paranoid. Nobody was thinking about you." (Yeah? Well, If nobody's ever thinking about me, then how come every time I go to a store I've got white *and* Black shadows—shame on y'all Senegalese brothas—trailing me?) Sometimes white girls just don't understand.

Whatever. Gramps and 'em are from a different time—that's how I've had to look at it. Plus, these O.G.s have been through some shit, just like my grandparents, just like all of my American Black people from generation's past. That's when the disapproving popcorn eyes start to move me. That's when I start to feel like the Rolling Stones at Madison Square Garden after the Black scalpers have all gone home: Sold the fuck out.

The white folks? Most of them will just try to pretend that they don't see the six of y'all. That's how it is. Even when you're at the mall and your white girl walks over to one of them McCoys to find out what floor the Gap outlet store is on. You're standing next to your shorty, your boys and their WGs are within ear shot (your lady, again, never picks up on the force field of hate that surrounds interracial daters in general). Thy girlfriend is the bravest of the fonkay bunch, so she asks away. "Excuse me miss, do you . . ." Next thing you know the coffee-stained snaggle-tooth of a white mommy, lugging her three spoiled bastards, cuts into my girl's dialogue, ignores her, and asks me where the fuck Funcoland is, knowing damn well that I'm not no Beverly Hills rent-a-cop. Holly-Mae just doesn't want to acknowledge me and my cookie's bond—James fucking Bond—and it's the fucking bond that really troubles her husband, Reginald, who's sipping latte a few feet away at Dairy Queen; he watches our conversation while squeezing his daughter hella tight. He whispers, "Not my daughter, Blackie!" and makes his way towards us.

I've had to put up with this crap whenever I've walked the streets with two additional pairs of interracial-dating "friends." I don't go to the mall or anywhere else with those creeps anymore. Things are getting hectic out here and I've got health considerations: three couples on the Black and white tip just hangin' out might make Ted Nugent-types wanna pull out their bows and arrows and start the spraying now, and leave the explaining to white mall security officers (the Black ones wouldn't do a damn thing) for later. Don't make you and your smiling, color cone-free loved ones marks. It's a hazzard. Either the dirty bomb people will get you or Ted Nugent-types or me. All of us will get you.

But I'm the least of your worries because I'm easy to spot: I'm the big Black dude at Ikea with the white girl on his arm who's lookin' at you twisted.

Sanford Jenson loves to visit the pandas, zebras, and penguins at his local zoo.

CHOCOLATE CHEESECAKE: KING OF PINUPS, JET'S LAMONTE MCLEMORE PUTS BLACK BEAUTY (AND BOOTY) IN FOCUS.

In 1789, half-bald mullet-man Benjamin Franklin wrote that "in this world nothing is certain but death and taxes." If Benny were alive today he could've added, ". . . and page forty-three of *Jet* magazine." For over thirty years, LaMonte McLemore has been the primary photographer of dark and lovelies for *Jet*'s venerable "Beauty of the Week," which almost always appears on said page of the aforementioned Black newsweekly. Despite being a cofounding member of pop music group The 5th Dimension, McLemore's name is widely recognized for the cheesecake photo forum that's helped set off the careers of celebrities such as the stunning Marilyn McCoo and the scandalously delicious Jayne Kennedy. (He's even shot ya girl Suzanne Sommers on the side.) And much to the chagrin of some of the "church members" at *Jet*, who patrol his submissions for too-skimpy bikinis, McLemore acknowledges that the page remains more popular than lemonade. Right on! Read on!

HOW DO YOU DEFINE BEAUTY AS FAR AS BLACK WOMEN ARE CONCERNED?
I think that everybody's pretty in their own right. I don't try to make nobody look like nobody else—I try to bring out the best in them. So if somebody asks me, "What kind of women do you like?" I say, "I have two favorite types of women . . . foreign and domestic."

But Black people, we have our own standard anyway. It intertwines with what other people think, but we like a little more meat on our bones—a little more grease—than other folks do. So *Jet* would get away with showing somebody with a few more pounds than you'd see in other magazines. We known for our *ass*ets. Pun intended!

"BEAUTY OF THE WEEK" NEVER DOES A STRAIGHT-UP ASIAN WOMAN OR—
No. I mean, they may do a Puerto Rican or maybe a Mexican or something. But see, the white people have their magazines and they got so many outlets. [Black people] only have this one little one. So [*Jet*'s] not prejudiced, but they want to give the Black kids a chance.

WELL, AS FAR AS THE OTHER OUTLETS, THERE'S MORE EXPLICIT MAGAZINES LIKE *PLAYERS* AND . . .

[*grumbles*] Nah. Nah. I never shot that. Nah. You know if a girl ever talked about doing any nude pictures, I'd recommend she *only* do it for *Playboy*. That's the only thing that's got any class and she's gonna make some money. The other magazines are trying to show somebody's liver! [*laughs*]

HOW HAS THE ATTITUDE OF THE MODELS CHANGED OVER THE YEARS?
I think there's a little more awareness now 'cause *Jet* is the only magazine that really celebrates Black women all over the world—except *Essence*. 'Cause everybody picks up the centerfold. Even Bill Cosby has called me up and used a couple of girls he saw in *Jet* for his TV show. That's why we really keep doing it.

HAVE YOU SUBMITTED ANY PHOTOS THAT *JET* WOULDN'T PUBLISH?
Yeah, there's some they don't use. And then sometimes they start getting complaints: "Why are there so many light-skinned girls in there?" 'Cause that's the only ones that came in the studio! *Jet*'s not prejudiced—they'll jump over ten light-skinned girls to get to one really pretty dark-skinned girl. But the dark-skinned girls, the pretty ones—they gonna capitalize on [their situation] and go to *Playboy* instead where they gonna make a whole lot of money. That's why when people see some of the pictures in *Jet*, they say "Oooh . . . how did *she* make it?" Hey, that's all they had.

OUTSIDE OF *JET*, YOU ALSO PHOTOGRAPH WOMEN OF OTHER NATIONALITIES. ARE THERE ANY DIFFERENCES YOU'VE ENCOUNTERED AS FAR AS THEIR ATTITUDES ARE CONCERNED?
One time this Caucasian girl came in and I said, "Hey, we wanna blow your hair and then we want your hair wet." She said, "Aw, great!" And then a Black girl came up. I said, "We wanna blow your hair and then wet it." She said, "You crazy! As much money as I done spent for this?!" So it's a little different when it comes to hair.

Also with some of the Caucasians, we try to not shoot them from behind 'cause they don't have much back there. [*chuckles*] But nowadays everything is changing. I *seen* some Caucasians, boy!

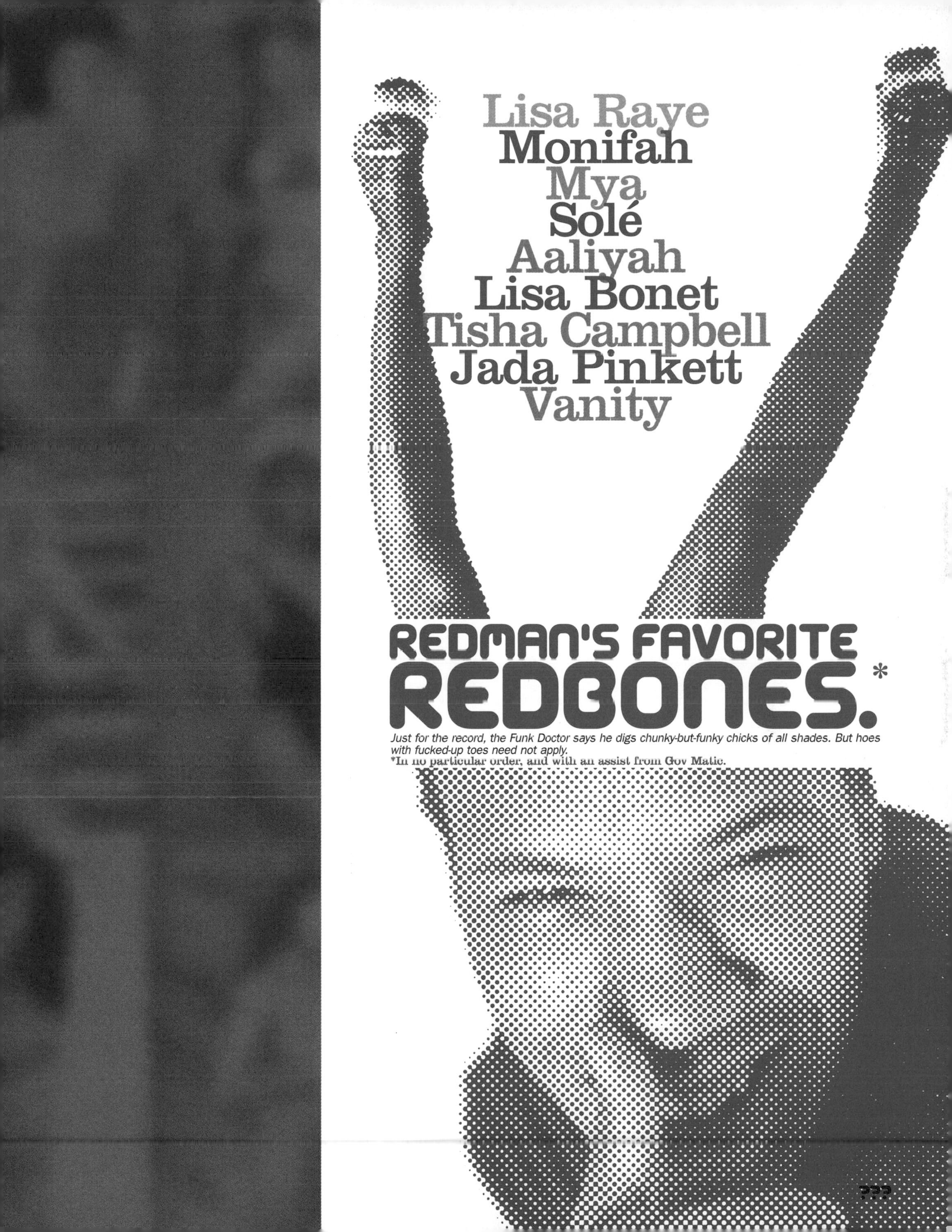

Lisa Raye
Monifah
Mya
Solé
Aaliyah
Lisa Bonet
Tisha Campbell
Jada Pinkett
Vanity

REDMAN'S FAVORITE
REDBONES.*

Just for the record, the Funk Doctor says he digs chunky-but-funky chicks of all shades. But hoes with fucked-up toes need not apply.
*In no particular order, and with an assist from Gov Matic.

LIBIDO LOCA:
WHY LATIN DUDES LOVE GOING "DOWNTOWN."

The Latin man's favorite pastime is not crossing the border line. It's crossing the panty line. Just what is the deal with José and the pussycats? Well, when it comes to going "downtown," males with Spanish backgrounds are the first to get their tongues a waggin'. Unlike their hesitant soul brothers, whose idea of eating out is strictly a table for two at Sizzler (except maybe for R. "You Experienced—and in Ninth Grade?" Kelly), Pepé and them can't wait to skip dinner and go straight to the poontang pie. *Que rico.*

Conquistador blood or native *sangre*—whether it be one or the other or the mix of the two—gets a lot of the blame for the Latin man's wild 'n' freaky streak. (It could be all that sangria as well.) But let's keep it real-o. Even that time of the month (no, not the first) won't always stop those few,

crazier Spanish *Papis* In Control from losing control and putting their mouths where their eyes can't see. (Hey, don't all Catholics drink blood?) To a lot of you that's just plain sick (and unsafe). And, frankly, that's what the power of the P can do to a small minority. Make you ill.

But then a lot of questionable behavior pops up in sex. Men like to get called "Daddy" no matter what the language. We often bring God's name, of all people, into it while doing it. In 2002, with no cure for AIDS, the old Eddie Murphy joke about sticking your Johnson in and having it explode (dammit, that was comedy, Gumby) seems more real than ever. Even so, some of us still don't even wear rubbers every time we bump uglies. (Maybe bringing God's name into it is a good idea.)

What the Latin man in the U.S.A. brings is a lot of tongue. After all, we are forced to speak two of the gringo's languages—Spanish and English. Well-exercised muscles the tongues turn out to be and everybody likes to put Latinos to work. So it's back to south of the border to dig for some clam chowder. And the Latin girls are grateful because after rocking them tight-as-hell pants all day, the coochie coochie could use some extra TLC.

In the porno flicks, the white cats lick pink panthers with the flicker of a stretched-out tongue. But the proud Latin man never goes back upstairs without a donut-glazed nose. That means the entire *lengua* was up in there, lapping away like a big friendly German shepherd, not a little scared Chihuahua. Like any other meal, Latinos must savor each and every one as if it were the last. It's embedded in our brains.

Blame it on the taco. Look at it. Think about it. The tasty yet fragile invention should be hot to enjoy and must be handled delicately or else it falls apart. There's an art to munching on tacos. Those who have done it their whole lives learn the best. Oh, and don't forget, fish tacos are real popular, too.

But what scrumptious dishes those Latina chicas are. They are all flavors under the sun. The fun part is guessing what color they are down there. Sure, it's all the same shade inside, but the hue of the entrance varies greatly. The Latin man likes to go to unknown lands and break a sweat.

Being horny all the time helps. Yes, a stereotype. But so true. How else do you explain that once a Latin man goes downtown and gets a taste, he's ready to keep going past the city limits? Fuck the red lights! Keep it gully.

ASSASSINATION DAY: GETTING TO THE BOTTOM OF J.LO'S DEARLY DEPARTED DERRIERE.

BY CRISTINA VERÁN

A few years ago, Jennifer Lopez, the pear-shaped *Puertorriqueña* superstar, single-handedly spearheaded a big-booty backlash against the supermodel types who for ages espoused *Schindler's List* chic. Long bound by the boney blond beauty barometer of America, women of color rejoiced in Lopez's triumphal tush-touting.

J.Lo joined the lengthy legacy of well-endowed ethnic icons like the nineteenth-century South African spectacle Venus Hottentot and her Herculean hindquarters to the risqué Rican TV-variety vixen Iris Chacón and her bombastic Boricua booty.

From living in the Bronx to *In Living Color,* La Luscious Lopez metamorphosed from flexible fly girl in 1990 to new-millennium foxy femme fatale as she took a ride on the *Money Train*, braved *Anaconda*s in the Amazon, and turned every head in *U-Turn*.

But there's no denying that the prominent posterior of this gluteus maxigoddess gained her as many die-hard devotees as her talents on screen. While hormone-raging *honquistadors* may treasure the chest, *los* brothas—on both sides of the border—make no qualms about playing like Teena Marie and going behind the groove. Her defining 1997 role as slain *Tejano* songstress Selena was one she amply and authentically filled, hip-shake, curves, and all. Finally, Hollywood began recognizing the real by recognizing the rear.

Sadly, however, a reassessment of J.Lo's gelatin reveals that her realness is less large these days than legend would have it.

Appropriately enough, it was in the posters for the film *Out of Sight* (1998), when things first appeared amiss. Posed with her back to the camera, Lopez's usually full fanny wasn't as full. As fast as the tech-stock bubble went flat, so had J.Lo's backside of dreams (as did her high-profiled Puff *Papi* Combs romance).

Soon it became apparent to paparazzi and fans alike that the queen of the hill, who had become annoyed at having to answer questions about her bountiful backyard (remember how homegirl whyled out on Triumph the Insult Dog at the 2001 MTV VMAs?), was abandoning her throne. (Interestingly, the successful all-sizes J.Lo clothing line shrewdly markets to "voluptuous" women, even though Mrs. Lo ain't so jumbo no mo'.)

Rumors flew that her handlers had pressured Lopez into working out with Radu, celebrity trainer to the derriere-deprived (beanpole Calista Flockhart is a pupil of his) who obsessively burn nonexistent baggage from their barren backsides. Could it be true? Had Jennifer been swayed by the dark side? Or, should we say, the white side?

If so, the repercussions could be far-reaching for the highest-paid Latina actress in history. Already J.Lo's street cred eroded a bit in the wake of the controversy over her use of the n-word in the song "I'm Real (Remix)." Would a more plump-rumped Jen-Jen have gotten a ghetto pass?

Her well-publicized divaish dressing-room demands and her desire to portray non-Hispanic roles would seemingly point to a whitewash. It now appears that Jennifer's vanishing heiny was the first warning sign.

Big booty owners and lovers of the planet unite! Dream of a brave new world when twenty-first century fashionistas in size fours will ask their favorite plastic surgeons for gel-filled *nalgas* as opposed to big honking hooters and the subway seats will be 30 percent wider to accommodate us all. Think big. The future is behind us.

Cristina Verán is a freelance writer, world traveler, and the proud owner of a big ol' imagination.

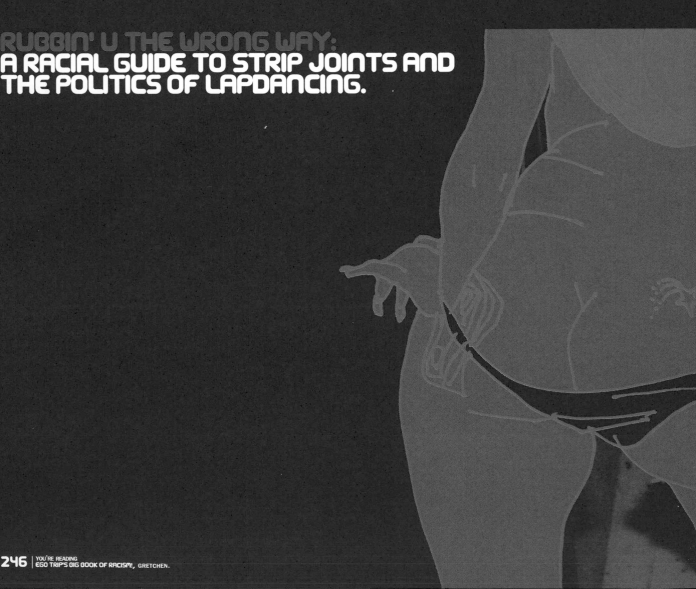

Let's be honest. Even the most devoted and proud Klansman stranded on a deserted island with a big bootied Boricua would have quite the dilemma. Give him a week and the horny burgundyneck (the sun people laugh at you, Phantom Menace) would be all up in that curvy temptress' gills like Johnny Gill. Word to Bill Clinton. Deep down inside in places you don't talk about, all horny heteros are colorblind punany-rushers like Usher.

That's why we love to make our jimmies holla with pleasure and pain (blue balls is an equal opportunity offender, you know) at the local tittie bar. It doesn't matter if you're stuck on a sticky private dancer who's carnation pink, burnt sienna, laser lemon yellow, or Indian red, greenbacks rule everything 'round this bitch. But before you horny lil' devils spend a little dough, ask yourself this: Is the Incredible Hulk hue the only color that matters in strip joints? Don't be afraid like Aaron Hall's baby mama. You can ask a few questions.

DO DARKER-SKINDED EXOTIC DANCERS GIVE MORE BANG FOR YOUR BUCKS?

Technically they do. Thanks to sexual taboos, Black boos (with tattoos) attract bonkers Archie Bunkers sick of their musty, decrepit Ediths at home. It's a two-way street, though. These girls love those old, lumpy, cigar-smellin' cottonballs because they know they want to release the dough to young Pam Griers with tight brassieres and ample rears. And the moolah flows quicker when chocolate bunnies thump and grind (and Peter meets cotton tail) while lazy Euro-beauty-sanctioned white chicks merely strike poses and throw up their noses.

Eureka! Emancipation proclamation with clothed stimulation leads to masturbation (but no master's dictation). Sistas are doin' it for themselves. Like in real life, Black women always have to work harder. If you can't pass, you shake that ass. Shake that ass, girl! Show dat work!

But for a real super-saver, you gotta hit that Dirty Dirty (Atlanta, stupid). Five bucks goes a long way with a Hershey Kiss (*Moui!*) focused on leavin' you weak in the knees. Just watch out for those Georgia Peaches (the light-skinded ones with Fendi bags and bad attitudes). Those Josephine Baker fakers will stiff you and put a dent in your bulletproof wallet.

RUBBIN' U THE WRONG WAY:
A RACIAL GUIDE TO STRIP JOINTS AND THE POLITICS OF LAPDANCING.

ETHNICALLY SPEAKING, WHICH POLE STRADDLERS REIGN SUPREME?

Good question. Damn good question. Are you ready, *ése*? No, we mean S.A.—South America. Brazil! It took a while for design-ing women (even the men are women) on Fifth Avenue to figure out what avid booty watchers have known for ages, Brazilian girls are *sin-tillating* when they're strutting their stuff on the catwalk. Put a couple of them together at a club, in let's say, Brooklyn, New York, and you have an instant party atmosphere. Thanks to their homeland experience of shakin' their rumps on floats for weeks on end during *carnav*al, they come equipped with the right experience to please your jeans.

And like a Brazilian wax, these ladies are smooth operators who come in all flavors (light, dark, you name it). Sometimes they look Spanish, but they actually speak Portuguese. How exotic! Plus, when it comes to actual body contact (fuck an air dance), like the D.O.C., no one can do it better. These broads are like machines—movin' and groovin' and puttin' in more work than Rosie, *The Jetsons'* mechanical maid.

ETHNICALLY SPEAKING, WHICH POLE STRADDLERS SUCK (AND WE DON'T MEAN IN THE GOOD WAY)?

Filipinas on our chinos is not our idea of a good time. These snooty booties are wanna-be white girls without privilege. Just 'cause college frat boys go ga-ga for that *moo shoo* doesn't mean you should drone on and on and on and on about your bullshit philoso-phies then front on an actual dance. Word to the wise with a rise in your pants: You can get more contact on a crowded subway.

You smoothed-skin parasites may be a sugar daddy's delight, but whatever happened to a little rub-a-dub? You know, the rea-son we paid to come into this den of flesh. Come to think of it, all A.G.'s (Asian girls) come up short like the paychecks Koreans dish out to Mexicans. No tips. There's no thrilla from a Manila wafer.

HOW DOES A WOMAN OF COLOR WITH REAL ATTRIBUTES FIND A JOB WITH HIGHER-CLASS CLUBS LIKE, FOR EXAMPLE, THE HOWARD STERN ENDORSED SCORES?

You don't. Face facts, whites love what you ain't got—a nice, big set of milk-colored knockers. In the '70s and '80s, every little

Mikey in the United States stroked his pee-pee to posters of Dolly Parton. And because Ms. Juggs never flashed her winners in that loser-of-an-'80s-flick, *The Best Little Whorehouse in Texas*, grown-up stockbroker Michael now demands hooters, hooters, and mo' HOOTERS—no matter how real or unreal they be.

All this, of course, makes sense since the lap-dancing W.G.'s whole aura is Plexiglas. Those pastie-rocking pasty faces prance around in their peroxide curls, utilize fake I.D.s like "Crystal," "Bambi," and "Maude," and show about as much genuine emotion as Yul Brenner busting caps in an amusement park.

Sorry, women with melanin, the only 'fro's you'll see in these white spots is when those post-op bimbos go to and fro the "champagne room."

But be pleased, beautiful, natural D-cupped ebonies. Those silicone drones' plastic bubbles are gonna pop. If not, they'll have severe back problems of Harry Bentley proportions.

WHY CAN'T A YOUNG THUG ROCKIN' HIS DU-RAG, HAT, AND SHORTS GET ANY LOVE AT THE CLUB?

The late, great Notorious B.I.G. once pleaded "If you got a gun up in your waist / Please don't shoot up the place" for a reason. Knuckleheadz be done doin' that shit, dun. But is it fair for a few bad apples to spoil the poontang pie? Hell, nah.

Racial profiling is real. You shouldn't be able to judge a crook—uh, book—by its cover, but America don't read and you thug-lifers need a makeover, anyway. It's time to hang up the trendy tracksuits on the top shelf and send a brother to Brooks Brothers. Go to a club dressed to kill (but don't kill), so you can cop a feel.

P.S., young guns: It costs to floss, so if you want the girls to bend, you gonna have to spend. Don't make the already-discriminatory dancers and owners discriminate even more and fuck it up further for your fellow perverts. Get your grind right!

ARE THERE ANY GENTLEMEN'S ESTABLISHMENTS WHERE BARBIES WITH PLASTIC BODIES AREN'T WELCOME?

Like Curtis Mayfield sang, "It's underground." Unfortunately for you, whitey, it's mostly a Black market thang—Black-owned, Black-operated, and Black-supported.

Dig, if you will, a picture, of you, a hundred brown sugars, and a couple hundred more brown drug dealers engaged in a transaction—shelling out ducats for economically priced, recession-friendly friction. It's like the Black Olympics—sexy mamas runnin' around from lap to lap like Tyra Banks on the track field in *Higher Learning*. Just don't blow the whistle to Five–0 or come packing with the wrong kind of trouble—the only bullet holes found here are not located on the walls, but on the posteriors of the women of the night.

Ex-mayor Giuliani and his sexually repressed oppressors couldn't stop all the good times. Tell the right wing to choke on a chicken wing. Even if you put all the mob-endorsed palaces of decadence out to pasture, there's still other places for young Lola Falonas to get their freak on. You can't knock the hustle of those monkey muscle relaxers for tryin' to make a dollar out of fifteen cents. Strip clubs forever!

10 NONWHITE PORNO ACTRESSES WHO SPEAK "GREEK" (IF YOU KNOW WHAT WE MEAN).

Dee (Puerto Rican)
India (Black)
Mariah Kane (Sicilian/Black)
Kira Kener (Scandinavian/Vietnamese)
Miko Lee (Chinese/Vietnamese)
Obsession (Black)
Tera Patrick (British / Thai)
Adriana Sage (Mexican)
Jasmin St. Clair (Indian)
Kobe Tai (Chinese/Japanese)

BEEN AROUND (THE WORLD) PORN GIRLS.

Veronica Brazil
Asia Carrera
Vanessa del Rio
Jewel De'Nyle
Deidre Holland
India
Kylie Ireland
Nyrobi Knight
Victoria Paris
Persia

AL GOLDSTEIN
ON WHY JEWS MAKE GOOD PORNOGRAPHERS.

The main reason Jews are good pornographers is because we heard nothing about sex when growing up. Christians have heard that there's a sin in pussy. But we've heard nothing [about that]. It's a clean blackboard for us, so we're drawn to it. We think sex is healthy. I wasn't a choir boy. I didn't have Catholic priests fucking me in the ass. Therefore, I could think about hetero-sexual sex [without guilt]. I didn't have to worry about the Pope and his dress and whether it was that time of the month for the Pope or not.

Jews have hook noses, so we're very money oriented. There's money in pornography because there's money in pussy—both for hookers and for people who purvey pussy. We know there's profit in pussy. High profit. Pornography's a profit field for us. We love it. The markup is good. "Usury" we call it. [As far as the porn I produce], the pictures you see in *Screw* today are so old and so badly done, you can't even tell it's a [photo of a] woman. I mean, I bought all my pictures in 1971 for 30¢ each. In street pornography the Jews are wonderful.

There're plenty of Jews in porn, but some of the most well-known pornographers are not Jewish. You have Baptists like Hugh Hefner, good Italians like Bob Guccione, and trailer camp trash like Larry Flynt, who shoots his porn like a gynecologist. It's too close up. I don't want to see everything like I'm some fucking proctologist. On the other hand, Hefner doesn't even show pussies because he doesn't even know that women have pussies. He's only into big tits. Personally, I like my porn smoky and soft-focus like [the way] Lucille Ball was shot in her last days. I like it romantic. That's why Bob is my favorite pornographer. I can only jerk off to his stuff.

Big Al Goldstein has published Screw, *a weekly tip sheet for beaver hunters, for many years. But we think he loves food more than eating the cat.*

CHAPTER 8

EMBRACISM.

RACE CARDS: POP CULTURE'S GREAT RACIAL THINKERS.

COLLECTOR'S CHOICE®

33

LOUIS ARMSTRONG
ENTERTAINER

FIGHTING WHITES
INTRAMURAL TEAM

····· SAM PHILLIPS ·····
··· MUSIC LEGEND ···

RADIO PERSONALITY
CASEY KASEM

egotrip

STEVE PARK
ACTOR

egotrip 1997 MOST VALUABLE ASIAN
OUTSPOKEN LEGENDS SERIES™

47

Lupe Ontiveros
Actress

#45

JAMES "J.J." JOHNSON

···SON DOOBIE···
RAPPER / PORN KING

CRAIG HODGES
SHOOTING GUARD

•••••••• 55 ••••••••
•••• SAM PHILLIPS ••••

A longtime champion of Black music, Phillips founded the Memphis Recording Service in 1950, providing musicians like Ike Turner, B.B. King and Howlin' Wolf the opportunity to record when most other outlets in the South prohibited them. He subsequently founded Sun Records and produced and released sides by Rufus Thomas, Little Junior Parker and other legendary Blacks before stumbling upon a great white whale in '54, Elvis Presley.

•••• GREAT RACE-RELATED QUOTE ••••

"If I could find a white man with the Negro sound and the Negro feel, I could make a billion dollars." *
(A remark to his secretary before meeting Elvis)

••••• MO' FACTS & VITAL STATS •••••

- Founded all-female radio station WHER in 1955.
- Sold Sun Records in 1969.
- Inducted into the Rock 'n' Roll Hall of Fame in 1986.

He actually only made $40,000 when he sold Elvis' contract to RCA in '55.

FIGHTING WHITES
2002 UNC
11

This 2002 intramural basketball squad at the University of Northern Colorado (composed of Native American, Hispanic and Anglo students) chose a white man as its mascot, turning the tables on the practice of bastardizing American Indian images as good luck symbols. After news of the "Fighting Whites" broke nationally, many Caucasians actually expressed their love for the name, showering the players with congratulatory emails and requests to purchase "Fighting Whites" jerseys.

THE TEAM'S SLOGAN:
"Every thang's gonna be all white!"

MO' FACTS & VITAL STATS:

Several news sources initially erroneously reported the team's name as the "Fighting Whities."

In an online poll, 50% of those asked agreed with the team that Indian mascots are offensive, 3% believed the term "whities" to be more offensive than "reds," 11% believed "reds" to be more offensive than "whities," and 36% weren't offended by either term.

2002 PRINTED IN THE U.S.A.

33
LOUIS ARMSTRONG
GREAT RACE-RELATED QUOTE:

"You take the majority of white people, two thirds of them don't like niggas, but they always got one nigga they're just crazy about, goddamnit. Every white man in the world has one nigga at least that they just love his dirty drawers. Ain't that a bitch?" (From his audio diary)

Jazz's originoo big poppa was often lambasted by younger Blacks for promoting a Tom-ish public image. But Satchmo got the last laugh on his critics 30 years after his death when his audio diary was made public in 2001. Among the highlights were his 650 reels of tapes: his profanity-strewn tirades on racism, and his blunt advocacy of getting weeded and self-medicating with daily laxatives.

MO' FACTS & VITAL STATS:

- Though unsure of his exact birthdate, Satchmo claimed that his born day was July 4, 1900 to symbolize his patriotism.

- Enjoyed first crossover hit in 1929 with the racial lament "(What Did I Do to be So) Black and Blue."

PRINTED IN THE U.S.A. BY LESBIANS

Lupe Ontiveros

- Born in El Paso, Texas.
- Began acting career as an extra in 1972.
- Spent 15 years as a social worker in L.A. and Compton, CA before going Hollywood on that ass.

Like a Chicana Hattie McDaniel, this veteran actress has picked up Tinseltown leftovers—mostly housekeeper roles, but also hard-working matron type parts—in numbers that have reached double digits, infusing them with dignity and gettin' crazy paid at the same time. And the years of hard work is paying off in other ways. Hollywood's finally offering her more "breakout" roles like the neophyte theater director "Beverly Franco" in Chuck & Buck (2000). Fuck all that brown n' serve shit. This is one Latina that truly has it maid.

GREAT RACE-RELATED QUOTE:
"I have been given the most stereotyped, demeaning roles that Hollywood has to give out. Each time, I have taken on the challenge—to make those characters human, with a heart and a soul. I've done it with humor."
-(From the Massachusetts newspaper the Standard-Times)

62

#47
STEVE PARK

- Born in Brooklyn, NY.
- In the '80s, began doing open-mic stand-up comedy due to the lack of opportunities in acting.

Korean-American actor Park portrayed the ghetto grocer in Do The Right Thing, and was a series regular on In Living Color. His finest performance was as the lonely dork "Mike Yanagita" in the Oscar-winning Fargo—a role Park was blasted for by Asian-Americans who felt it perpetuated the negative stereotype of the weak Asian male. Fed up with Hollywood after enduring racist incidents on the set of Friends in 1997, Park placed his yellow ass on the line and wrote a mission statement entitled "Struggling For Dignity" that challenged the film and TV industry to change its evil ways.*

GREAT RACE-RELATED QUOTE:

"[The cast and crew of Friends], by virtue of their status, money and power, are among the most privileged people walking the face of the earth, yet they behaved as if they were bankrupt in spirit and incapable of expressing simple human kindness." (From "SFD")

*Park hasn't been heard from since.

Bono vox Casey is much-loved across America, whether as the voice behind "Shaggy" from Scooby Doo, or as host of radio land's weekly countdown of national top tunes, America's Top 40. But where the Lebanese-n-proud Kasem really shone was when he wrote "Arab Americans: Making a Difference," an essay in which he bigged up (and outed) dozens of significant folks of Arab descent for the uncivilized to recognize and appreciate.

GREAT RACE-RELATED QUOTE:

"Arab-Americans are grocers and governors, physicians and farmers, Indy 500 champs and taxicab drivers, financiers and factory workers, bakers and bankers, salesmen and senators, TV stars and TV repairmen, teachers and preachers, Heisman Trophy-winning quarterbacks and neighborhood sandlot heroes. Name it, and an Arab-American has probably done it." (FROM "AA: MAD")

MO' FACTS & VITAL STATS:

BORN KEMAL AMEN KASEM. ● INDUCTED INTO RADIO HALL OF FAME IN 1985. ● ONCE ANGRILY SCREAMED AT HIS STAFF, "CAN SOMEONE AROUND HERE USE HIS FUCKING BRAIN?!" ON A STUDIO OUTTAKE MADE INFAMOUS BY HOWARD STERN.

94

The three-point sharpshooter for two Chicago Bulls championship squads was also an outspoken activist down with the likes of the Nation of Islam's Minister Louis Farrakhan. When the champs paid the traditional visit to the White House in '91, Hodges rocked a dashiki and handed George H.W. Bush a letter asking him to kindly get off his ass and help Black folks in America. Cut by the Bulls after helping them repeat in '92, Hodges alleged he was blacklisted by the NBA because no other team had the balls to sign him. But his lawsuit against the league was quietly dismissed.

★ MO' FACTS & VITAL STATS: ★ ★ ★ ★

★ Won the NBA All-Star Game Three-Point Shootout three years straight, 1990-1992.

★ Once lauded as "probably the most conscious cat from the NBA in the past thirty years" by Public Enemy's Chuck D.

★ GREAT RACE-RELATED QUOTE: ★ ★ ★ ★

"I can't go [to the White House] and just be in an Armani suit and not say shit."
(From the Village Voice)

••••SON DOOBIE••••
••106••

Son got wreck as the Puerto Rican leader of Funkdoobiest, a groundbreaking interracial rap trio rounded out by a Native American (Tomahawk Funk) and a Mexican (Ralph M Tha Funky Mexican). In '95, he kept it colorful by swinging sex episodes with a bevy of busted, multi-culti chickens in his X-rated video, Porn King.

• • GREAT RACE-RELATED QUOTE: • •

"I'm on that latino supremacy shit. We was there from the giddy up and nobody give us fuckin' no props. We perfected every fuckin' art of hip hop there was at the time. Whether it was breakdancing, the b-boy shit, Cazals, Lee jeans—all that stems from Latinos. Rap being a Black thang—we're gonna squash that bullshit to the max."
(From BeatDown)

••• MO' FACTS & VITAL STATS •••

Favorite old school porn picks: Caligula; the Dark Brothers' Let Me Tell Ya 'Bout White Chicks; Let Me Tell Ya 'Bout Black Chicks.

Enjoyed brief popularity in the late '90s as a radio personality on L.A. station Power 106.

HECHO EN PUERTO RICO

JAMES "J.J." JOHNSON
#45

Though the militia movement is typically associated with angry, white men packing heat, Johnson co-founded one of the first militias to gain serious notoriety, the Ohio Unorganized Militia. Characterizing militias as "the Civil Rights Movement of the '90s," he became a popular mouthpiece for the campaign for several years. However, Johnson abandoned the armed crusade in 1997, claiming it was not effective, and got down with another white-dominated crew, the neo-Confederates.

GREAT RACE-RELATED QUOTE:
"I Don't Want to be Black Anymore."
(The title of one of his post-militia essays)

MO' FACTS & VITAL STATS:

≫ Has addressed constitutional groups of various types in over 35 states. ≪

≫ According to www.jj-johnson.com, he lives by the motto, "If my ancestors would have been armed they would not have been slaves." ≪

PRINTED IN THE U.S.A. BY ANGRY SONUVAGUNS

I AM RODNEY KING:
STEP INTO THE WORLD OF A LEFT COAST TROUBLE MAN'S EAST COAST NAMESAKE.

Sharing a name with someone famous must be fun galore. After all, every single place you go it's like *Cheers* all up in that bitch—the banter's clever, the laughter's hardy, and everybody knows your goddamn name. But what happens when an innocent civilian suddenly finds himself sharing a tag with a figure of infamy? You think you know, but you have no idea. *ego trip* gets down with our man, Rodney (last name King), to find out.

HOW DID IT AFFECT YOU WHEN YOU HEARD ABOUT THE INCIDENT WITH RODNEY KING BEING BEATEN BY THE LAPD?
It was a horrible thing that happened. I wasn't in New York at the time, so all my boys I hung out with thought it was me at first. Then they was like, "Nah, Rod is in school, it can't be." It was a shocker.

WHAT'S THE STRANGEST THING YOU'VE EXPERIENCED AS SOMEONE NAMED RODNEY KING?
I used to work at Elektra Records in the L.A. office in Beverly Hills a few years ago. And the job required me to drive through Simi Valley [where the Rodney King trial took place]. I was like, ooh, this is ill—'cause that was his tracks. It was like *Blair Witch Project*. I told this woman I was working with, "I'm not gonna drive out there. You're gonna have to drive me out there and back."

HOW DO PEOPLE REACT WHEN THEY HEAR YOUR NAME?
Back when it happened I had to pick up some money from Western Union. I told the woman my name and she was like, "Sir, do not play like that. There's some serious things going on right now!" I showed her my college I.D. and she was like, "Oh, I'm sorry."

I get it to this very day, though. Like, for example, I went to the Garden to go see the Janet Jackson concert. I was like, "Yo, Rodney King here to pick up tickets." When you say the name you get like fifty people turning around, like, "Is that him?" If you're on the phone with someone you don't know and you say your name, they say, "Can you

hold on a minute?" I know they're probably crackin' up—especially when I call credit card people. But it doesn't bother me.

HAVE YOU EVER HAD TO DEAL WITH THE POLICE WHERE YOU HAD TO PRESENT AN I.D.?
Fortunately—knock on wood—I haven't been in trouble where I had to go through that. There was only one time when I was driving back from visiting one of my college buddies in Maryland and I was speeding coming off an exit, and a cop stopped me. I gave him my I.D. and he said, "You have a famous name." I didn't say anything. He just gave me my ticket and I went about my business.

THE L.A. RODNEY KING DOESN'T SEEM TO BE ABLE TO GET HIMSELF TOGETHER, EVEN AFTER ALL THESE YEARS. ANY THOUGHTS ON HIM?
I'm not knocking nobody, and I don't know what goes on in the mind of any [other] individual. But if you throw a few million at a person and they still don't know how to act, I don't know what to say. I have no comment.

DO YOU HAVE ANY ADVICE FOR ANY OTHER RODNEY KINGS IN THE WORLD?
Keep your track record clean. If your rap sheet is good, you have nothing to worry about.

HAVE YOU KNOWN ANYONE ELSE WHO SHARED A FAMOUS NAME?
Just my brother—Stephen.

AMERICA'S PIE:
HOW "FOREIGNERS" MAKE "CAKE" IN THE U.S.A. (BECAUSE, HEY, SOMEBODY'S GOTTA DO IT).

ITALIANS
WHERE THEY WORK: The Olive Garden, FIAT dealerships
FINE MAKERS OF: ices, track suits
FINE IMPORTERS OF: spaghetti straps

ETHIOPIANS
WHERE THEY WORK: parking lots
FINE MAKERS OF: *Rap Pages* magazine (last incarnation)
FINE IMPORTERS OF: famine chic

GREEKS
WHERE THEY WORK: twenty-four-hour diners
FINE MAKERS OF: coffee cups, souvlaki, gyros, and the like
FINE IMPORTERS OF: anal tongue darts

ARABS
WHERE THEY WORK: convenience stores
FINE MAKERS OF: thirsty bath towels and robes, hashish pipes
FINE IMPORTERS OF: crude oil

BRAZILIANS
WHERE THEY WORK: shoe shine stands
FINE MAKERS OF: bikinis
FINE IMPORTERS OF: dirty samba dancers

KOREANS
WHERE THEY WORK (SORTA): nail salons, delicatessens, liquor marts
FINE MAKERS OF: in-store ice grills
FINE IMPORTERS OF: Seoul Power

DOMINICANS
WHERE THEY WORK: livery cabs, Jheri Curl Juice Inc., overseers at Haitian slave camps
FINE MAKERS OF: fried banana dishes
FINE IMPORTERS OF: various fine goods produced by Haitian slaves (really)

EAST INDIANS
WHERE THEY WORK: taxicabs, hotels, newsstands, 7-Eleven, and Subway franchises
FINE MAKERS OF: curry dishes, spice girls
FINE IMPORTERS OF: spices

JAPANESE
WHERE THEY WORK: office buildings everywhere, sushi restaurants (even in landlocked states)
FINE MAKERS OF: Shoji screens, "cool," *Hello Kitty*, superior electronics
FINE IMPORTERS OF: Asahi beer, superiority complexes

FILIPINOS
WHERE THEY WORK: Jollibee, Ronald McDonald House, the Marcos House, Depeche Mode fan club
FINE MAKERS OF: Phillips screwdrivers
FINE IMPORTERS OF: Manila envelopes

YUGOSLAVIANS (OF THE "FORMER" REPUBLIC)
WHERE THEY WORK: auto shops that specialize in Yugo repair
FINE MAKERS OF: Puma footwear
FINE IMPORTERS OF: Yu-go-figure-it-out!

UKRAINIANS
WHERE THEY WORK: Veselka (on 2nd Ave. at 9th St.—open twenty-four hours!)
FINE MAKERS OF: lentil soup
FINE IMPORTERS OF: borschtshit

MALTESE
WHERE THEY WORK: malt shops
FINE MAKERS OF: chairs
FINE IMPORTERS OF: falcons

OTHER LATINOS
WHERE THEY WORK: Major League *Beisbol*, mailrooms
FINE MAKERS OF: babies
FINE IMPORTERS OF: themselves, beans, elbow grease

CHINESE
WHERE THEY WORK: computer software outlets, massage parlors, Chinatown
FINE MAKERS OF: Chinese fast food, Mexican fast food
FINE IMPORTERS OF: fire crackers, China white, Hefty bags of green plastic Army men

MMMmmm…

ISRAELI EXOTIC DANCERS
WHERE THEY WORK: Hooters, seedy strip clubs
FINE MAKERS OF: woodies
FINE IMPORTERS OF: a good time

So you're in Money Makin' Manhattan doing the tourist thing—buying yummy hot dogs off the street, checkin' out *The Producers* on Broadway, going up to the Black churches in Harlem where the African-Americans sing so angelically. "New York is sooo great!" you say to yourself as your plaque-yellow taxicab shuttles you from happenin' haunt to happenin' haunt. But as one washes down his or her last foot-long with a splash of pineapple cola, one starts to wonder about the passionate conversation that Habib the cabbie is holding down on his (driver legal, nonhandheld) cell phone while swerving through about a ton of muffler muck. You scream as the vehicle narrowly misses a head-on collision with Big Scott the UPS man's big brown beast.

"Ubdooolaaahhholarrrlll! It is okay, suuurrrd!" is Habib's response. Fuck it, this gentleman is getting a slim tip because of his careless tactics, you tell yourself. Still, you wonder as you slam that door and step into the dingy core of the Apple:

WHO ARE ALL THE MIDDLE EASTERN / EAST INDIAN NEW YORK CABBIES TALKING TO?

1. ALLAH
Because the way these gentlemen drive, He must be the only reason why most of us make it home alive. All praises due!

2. MOHAMMED
Ditto.

3. THE HAREM
With representatives here in the States and back at home, that's a whole lotta mouths to feed. Not to mention baby-mama drama for days.

4. FAISIL, RAJESH, RAVINDRA, MADHU, ETC.
The homeboys keep him up on what's poppin' 'round the way.

5. DISPATCHER LOUIE DE PALMA
Because there's always a Napoleon-sized white man in the background tryin' to tell a brova how to live, what to say, and how to say it.

FedMex

"When It Absolutely Positively Has To Get There After A Siesta."

Manu Al Labor

Arabic Manicure, Pedicure & Hand Jobs

✂ "WE CUT LADY FINGERS (OFF)." ✂

270

OPEN

BODY CARE
FACIAL
NAILS

ETHNIC BUSINESSES DOOMED TO FAIL.

DROPODOPOULOS'

GREEK CHINA SHOP

SPECIALIZING IN SECOND HAND PORCELAIN (SLIGHTLY CHIPPED)

IATA

Italian-American
Transit Author

Going Your Way... When We Feel Like
(or, for the Right Price).™

From Best To Warsaw.

Dimwicz Brothers (not related)
Exam Preparation...The Polish Way.™

3 Convenient Locations to Serve You:

KOREAN CHARM SCHOOL

"But You Pay First"

GET UR ROLL ON:
A SIDEWAYS LOOK AT EVERY BLACK WOMAN'S STRONGEST WEAPON.

It's damn near a hazard when dating a sista of African-American descent. A few months ago, you thought everything was lovely: You and your brown-skinded baby doll are gettin' to know each other and it's all love—especially when you get real fortunate and finally get to tap that ass one night to the sweet tones of Maxwell's ascending falsetto. You're thinkin' to yourself, Oh, shit, this bitch ain't like the rest: no door-knocker earrings, no gum-smacking. And, most important, no signs of the Black woman's silent assassin—the neck roll.

But then it happens. One Friday night you just ain't feelin' like goin' out to the movies. But she insists that y'all go out and do somethin'—anything. You suggest, in your most sincere voice, stayin' in the house and bonin' 'til the sun comes up, but she ain't havin' it. She mutters some slick shit that you barely catch, but you sure as hell comprehend what comes after. Girlfriend bites her bottom lip and, in what seems like slow motion, pulls her head back in one cir-cular motion in perfect synchronization with her shoulders. And—boom!—you've been hit. Just like that.

You see, to be truly able to handle the Earth one must be prepared to handle the neck roll, the trickiest combat tool in the Black woman's attitudinal arsenal. When it comes to intimidation, a brother can just stare at you face-to-face and threaten to tap that jaw. For females that's unladylike. So their version of bravado is the roll, which lets you know without a word that you just can't step on her and think it's okay. No burning beds here, muthafucka! It's an exaggerated exclama-tion point to the things she already said to you and a promise of even more harsh words to come if you don't lead this convo toward a positive direction.

Where'd it come from? They all get it from their mamas. Who did they get it from? Angela Davis. That bushy-haired ball-breaker must have started this shit. Big Mama D knew that half her strength came from the kink in her hair and the roll in her neck. Fuck a gun, Angie Stoneface bucked down pigs and disrespect-ful collard-green chewers with her body language.

Once the neck roll broke from its incendiary revolutionary stance, it inevitably seeped into popular culture, landing onto the big screen in films like the gal group fiasco, *Sparkle* (1976). Becoming a requisite diva gesture, it natu-rally reared its ugly head in the gay male community. Soon every Little Richard (and Liberace, for that matter) with attitude was accessorizin' his wiggle and snap with the "roll." The disco era was filled with this sort of illicit behavior. But these kings of queendom didn't claim the roll as their own. They soon reverted back to the snap as their true and preferred power source. (As one gay publicist puts it—quotin' the vignette "The Gospel According to Miss Roj" from his favorite off-Broadway show, *The Colored Museum*—"When I snap my fingers, I take a beat away from your heart." Ooh, child!)

Lately, the roll has suffered some backlash. Sistas are taught by their in-denial mothers not to use it for fear of being viewed as ignorant and unclassy. Well, you can deny the lie, ebony princesses, but you can't hide the truth. Just wait 'til conflict arises, then it's B.I. as usual: The roll will roll over all oncomers. Although the act is still troubling to many members of the male species, all true Alexander O'Neal–styled men maintain a progressive perspective: Cocoa B'z should never abandon their history. No one likes a phony macaroni. Besides, if men and women are truly destined one day to understand each other fully, we must embrace our pasts. Stay grounded, shorty. Roll that neck. Like Whodini and Millie Jackson once advised, let's be ourselves.

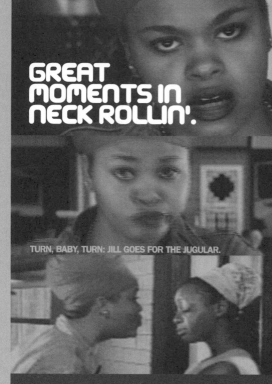

GREAT MOMENTS IN NECK ROLLIN'.

TURN, BABY, TURN: JILL GOES FOR THE JUGULAR.

ANY PAM GRIER BLAXPLOITATION FLICK (1970–1975)
Angela Davis didn't have twos like this.

DIAHANN CARROLL IN *CLAUDINE* (1974)
A classy lady has to lay the smack-down on a nosy whitey.

CHILDREN OF TELEVISION PRODUCTION: "THELMA" AND "PENNY" FROM *GOOD TIMES* (1974–1979) AND "DEE" FROM *WHAT'S HAPPENING!!* (1976–1979)
Three the hard way.

"CLAIR HUXTABLE" VERSUS "ELVIN THE DUDE" (*THE COSBY SHOW*, 1987)
Resortin' back to her nappy roots, the lovely lawyer lady puts her daughter Sondra's fiancé in his place.

MADONNA IN *TRUTH OR DARE* (1991)
Relishin' the clout she commands over fossil Warren Beatty, the material girl quips with a quick snap, "I always get what I want." (Must have been spendin' too much time with her cotton-candy dance troupe.)

JILL SCOTT'S "GETTIN' IN THE WAY" VIDEO (2000)
A modern-day minstrel show of estro-gen filled with essential wig-pullin' tips. Be careful or your seeds will grow up the same way.

HAIR-BRAINED.

It's something like a follicle phenomenon. Black folks are forever being asked lots of really stupid questions about Black hairstyles by non-nubians. Fuck Selsun Blue and White Rain. *BBOR!* asked dread-headed Philly native Ayana Byrd, coauthor of *Hair Story: Untangling the Roots of Black Hair in America* (St. Martin's Press, 2001), how she feels when a white person asks . . .

"HOW COULD I DO THAT TO *MY* HAIR?"

"That question makes me bristle because I always have the suspicion that—even if they sound sincere—they're looking at the style as the exotic flavor of the month. It's cultural appropriation in a lot of ways, often without any understanding of historical background. It's like when Justin Timberlake was wearing cornrows for a while. Young Black men with the style were being discriminated against—they couldn't hail cabs or get jobs—because of the messages that people *thought* they were trying to send with their hair . . . and then Britney's blond [ex]-boyfriend pops up and announces that he did it to increase his 'thug appeal.' What the fuck?! Stop acting like Bo Derek created cornrows!"

"HOW OFTEN DO YOU CLEAN YOUR HAIR?"

"That one makes me feel like whoever's asking it is not-so-secretly thinking that my hair's a little dirty, because, after all, doesn't *everyone* need to wash their hair at least a few times a week? Even if someone is consciously asking 'why' in order to increase their cross-cultural knowledge, in the back of their mind they're still probably thinking it's 'stinky.' The truth is that Black hair is a lot drier than white hair and you'll totally fuck it up if you wash it every single day. But, unfortunately, white hair's grooming habits are what nearly everyone in this country sees as the norm. We just need to recognize that there are different needs, not different levels of hygiene. Don't believe the hair hype.*"

"HOW DO YOU KEEP YOUR HAIR FROM BREAKING LOOSE?"

"At least that question sounds like it's coming from an 'Oh, please explain this to me' kind of place. It doesn't necessarily have a value judgment attached to it; it's just plain old curiosity. But we Black folk are always hyperaware of the facial gestures that white people make when they ask questions like that. So if you do get around to asking someone how they're maintaining some gravity-defying 'do, do make sure you don't look like you're stifling a giggle. Or you might be subject to a Black attack."

"OH, IS THAT ALL *YOUR* HAIR?"

"That makes me wanna be like, 'Is that all of *your* hair?' Don't ask me that shit. It's always an annoying question—one Black people aren't beneath asking either. But it's extra annoying when a white person asks this, because you're thinking that they're thinking, Black people's hair can't grow that long. But, come on, now, this ain't the '80s! Everybody knows what a weave looks like in this day and age. And if it isn't all my hair, leave it to me to make that announcement. It's comparable to asking someone if her breasts are God-given—you'll know if you're close enough to the person to be asking about their cup size. Same with suspected fake hair. Wisen up."

"CAN I TOUCH IT?"

"This one comes off like they think I'm an animal in a petting zoo. Don't EVER ask this question unless you are a close friend or family member of the person. And don't just *touch* someone's hair. It makes you just wanna punch a fool in the face. Whose hair do we touch without asking? Cute dogs. Small children, maybe. My thing is you don't touch a grown person's hair unless you're equating him/her with some sort of foreign, alien thing. Do blondy Heather-people sit around and touch each other's hair? Nooo!"

*Editor's note: But don't sleep on mane mag *Hype Hair.*

DON'T HATE THE PLAYER...

THE FORGOTTEN BOARD GAME THAT'S AN IMITATION OF LIFE.

BY OLIVER WANG

Buying property is tough enough. Now imagine you're a Black purchasing your forty acres in a white neighborhood: You might have pockets pudgier than Al Roker and still get locked out at the gate. That's the premise behind the mind power publication *Psychology Today*'s 1970 board game *Blacks & Whites*, its version of *Monopoly* with racism added as a thorny twist.

The layout is exactly like *Monopoly*, with each property square named after real locations—humbly beginning with Harlem and Watts, moving on up to Atlanta and Georgetown, and finally arriving at Palm Beach and Grosse Point. There's also familiar depots like the police station and "Go" (called "Treasury" here). The difference? In *Monopoly* any player automatically collects $200 for passing "Go." In *Blacks & Whites*, passing "Treasury" as a white player nets you $50,000. A brother? $10,000. If whitey gets knocked by po-po, he pays $10,000 to get bailed out. Blacks, on the other hand, are "held one turn for questioning." Hey, life ain't fair. But it gets better (or maybe worse). There are four zones of property: "Ghetto," "Integrated," "Suburban," and "Estate." Either race can buy into the "Ghetto" and "Integrated" zones. A few Blacks can make it to the "Suburban" zone; but the "Estate" zone is whites only, unless brothaman can cough up a cool million in assets.

The best part is the game's version of *Monopoly*'s "Chance" cards, called "Opportunity" cards here. Each one is different depending on which race you play. For example, one Black Opportunity card reads: "[Chicago's] Mayor Daly re-elected. You are picked up and taken directly to the police station for interrogation." Another says, "Congratulations! You are an All-American fullback and have been signed by the Rams. Collect $300,000 bonus. Collect $100,000 instead of $10,000 each time you pass the Treasury." (Sorry, white girls not included.) For whites, similar folly or fortune awaits depending on which "Opportunity" turns up. One white card states, "You have contracted a strange skin disease. For your next three turns, make your moves as a Black player." Another, "Stock dividend from company that makes tear gas. Collect $40,000."

While certainly innovative, the game play for *Blacks & Whites* gets complicated quickly with its endless rules and regulations—just like real life. For example, *Blacks & Whites* introduces mortgages and bankruptcy into the fold with different rules for each race. If a Black player goes bankrupt, "he goes on welfare and collects $5,000 from each white player." If a white player loses all his money, "he is out of the game, psychologically defeated."

And defeat is the agony everyone can understand. Originated by psychology professors at UC Davis, *Blacks & Whites*' packaging includes testimonials on its popularity: "The National Alliance of Businessmen reported that Black organizers were using the game to sensitize their white advisors and financiers." Racial sensitivity, property management skills, and competitive play all in one? Let's see *Scrabble* do that.

Journalist/DJ Oliver "O-Dub" Wang is only really discriminatory against subpar grooves. Check him out at www.o-dub.com.

DEED

LEVITTOWN

Value
$240,000

Rent
$24,000

Mortgage
$120,000

DEED

HARLEM

Value
$50,000

Rent
$10,000

Mortgage
$25,000

Mayor Daly reelected. You are picked up and taken directly to the police station for interrogation.

© 1970 Communications/Research/Machines/Inc.

Referees, cop cars, old television sets . . . At first glance, America would seem to possess a severe disdain for all things black and white. However, one city manages to confound the nation's predilection for color-conflict and display a healthy acceptance for interracial interaction. We're talking about the metropolis that reps caffeine, rainy dayz, Nirvana, the Space Needle, Supersonics, Seahawks, and *Singles*; the country's most polite city; the place where, the latest U.S. census reports, more biracial love children are birthed than anywhere else in our great land: Seattle.

Where else, but the birthplace of Starbucks, could this sweetest of taboos be so readily embraced? Appropriately enough, the latte is Seattle's favorite beverage—a coffee drink that is more milk than anything. (And what did Malcolm say about the strength of the brew?) Whether you live in Sea-Town or are just visiting, you and your other-colored loved one need not fret finding a place to step out. Visit one of the following establishments and find your forbidden love celebrated.

RED ROBIN / 17300 SOUTHCENTER PKWY.
While any Red Robin will do, the preferred RR for Black-white dating is this location. The draw here is the gourmet burgers—beef or chicken (for non-red-meat-swallowing chickens)—and the side of bottomless fries that comes with every burger order. Save room for dessert, and indulge in the mountain-high mud pie, which, like your relationship, beautifully blends chocolate and vanilla with other sweet, sweet flavors.

TGIFRIDAYS / 1001 FAIRVIEW AVE. N.
Overlooking Seattle's Lake Union, TGIF is an interracial dating hotbed. Perhaps subliminally drawn in by the high-contrast stripes of the TGIF logo and server uniforms, high-contrast couples feel right at home here. The drink menu is extensive, and foodwise the Jack Daniel's barbecue creations have proven popular with diners of all shades.

CHARLIE'S / 217 BROADWAY E.
In need of DL interracial dining? Check this prime late-night supper spot located in the heart of anything-goes Capitol Hill. Forget the main dining room and move your honey directly to the lounge in back. Better yet, feel like a goodfella as you enter Ray Liotta–style through the alley. (Mister) Charlie's sports a full bar and pub food, plus old-school tabletop *Ms. Pac-Man* for the true playas.

SUMMER NIGHTS ON THE PIER / PIERS 62/63 ON THE SEATTLE WATERFRONT
A can't-miss date. Picture the sun setting across the water over the Olympic Mountains, and music drifting over your

SLEEP LESS, MIX-A-LOT MORE IN SEATTLE:
A GUIDE TO INTERRACIAL DRINKING, DINING, AND MINGLIN', BABY.
BY AARON COUNTS / ILLUSTRATIONS BY TODD JAMES

head and up the hill into the city as you and your ivory lover sip a locally crafted microbrew (or for the bourgie-bourgie, a fine local Chardonnay). Man, you're in there! Skip the world music and folk-rock events in favor of the pure baby-making R&B events. Don't sit too close to the stage, though, or you may get called out by the performer, as Jill Scott did during her July 2000 show, when she observed, "There's a lot of brothers out there with white girls." Word.

MUSASHI'S / 1400 N. 45TH ST.

Want to prove to your Asian girlfriend that you're not just any white male graduate student? Do it with raw fish at unassuming Musashi's. Musashi's prepares some of the tastiest (and most affordable) sushi and sashimi in the city. The California Rolls are top-notch, as is the *maguro* (tuna). The *hamachi* is popular also, but suggesting its English name ("yellow tail") as a new pet name for your girl will end your date in a hurry. Cash only, fool.

FOLKLIFE FESTIVAL / SEATTLE CENTER

Any festival that claims to "celebrate the diversity of ethnic and folk communities" is bound to bring out the postmodern hippies, but none more so than Seattle's Memorial Day tradition, Folklife Festival. Folklife has the highest number of white guys with dreadlocks (a/k/a "dreadmocks") per capita of any organized Seattle event, and their love of things "ethnic" doesn't stop at music. Baldheaded or dreadlocked sistas, get UR freak on. A word to the scent-sensitive: Remember, Folklife is a patchouli-mandatory, bra-and-deodorant-optional event.

ANY LIVE HIP HOP SHOW

Interracial dating within the local hip hop scene can easily be undertaken in eleven easy steps: 1. Consult your local listings to find out if local authorities are allowing hip hop in the city. 2. Brag to your date about how your boy has a show this weekend. 3. Have your date pick you up on the night of the event. 4. Get to the spot and attempt to get in free. ("Come on, man, that's my boy on the mic.") 5. Try not to act mad when you have to pay. 6. Get inside and don't introduce your girl to any of your peeps. 7. Kick it with the brothers while your date chills at the table alone. 8. Keep an eye on the table just in case somebody else steps to your girl. 9. On the ride home get in a liquor-fueled argument about how bad you treat her. 10. Have sex and sleep over at her place. 11. Repeat next weekend.

BONUS / ANYWHERE IN VANCOUVER, B.C.

A mere two-hour drive to the north brings you to Seattle's Canadian sister city, Vancouver, British Columbia. Even brothers *not* looking for a white girl might not stand a chance against the chocolate-craving European women in the local night clubs. Sporting bolder moves than their sistas to the south and ubiquitous black stretch pants (a/k/a "Canada Pants") to show off their Canuck curves, these white women, to paraphrase the Godfather, know how to use what they got to get just what they want.

ego trip's Seattle correspondent Aaron Counts is a living, breathing testament to the power of interracial love.

DO THE WHITE THING: ENTER THE WACKY WORLD OF CAUCASIAN RECREATION.

BY DAVE BRY

White people are a truly confounding lot. Take a look around the next time you're at a yacht club or Neiman-Marcus. It's evident. Whites have a tendency to act in ways that just don't make a lick of sense. Being the complexion of driven snow myself, I occupy a privileged position from which to observe and assess America's dwindling majority on a day-to-day basis. (I can, in fact, and frequently do, walk among them virtually undetected.) Tapping into my years of experience as a white person, I've attempted to shed a little light on some of the more inscrutable aspects of white behavior.

BIRD WATCHING

The result of generations of slothful leisure and rampant inbreeding, the basic musculature structure of the white anatomy has begun to atrophy. For this reason, certain motionless nonactivities have been elevated in status. The hobby of "bird watching," for example, wherein a white person can spend hours sitting in the forest or by the side of a lake keeping track of the different avian species that fly into view, and then pretend that this affords a real sense of accomplishment.

COW TIPPING

When Klan rallies went out of vogue in the 1940s, America's rural young whites were left with very little to do on a swingin' Saturday night. Blacks had not yet invented rock 'n' roll, or premarital sex, so corn-fed country teenagers were forced to find their own fun. With the pastime of creeping up on a helpless bovine as it sleeps, pushing the gentle, 800-pound creature over into the mud, and high-tailing it out of the pasture before farmer John comes running out with a shotgun, generation after generation of heartland whites have taught themselves the value of teamwork, risk-taking, and cruelty to animals. (However, the practice strains Hindu-American relations to this day.)

50 WHITE BOYS IN A TELEPHONE BOOTH

During the 1950s, when the first signs of the civil rights movement began appearing, many of America's young, middle-class whites didn't know quite how to react. Borrowing from the African concept of *umoja*, or "unity," groups of collegiate whites began cramming themselves into the smallest, tightest places they could find. The more the merrier. The closer the better. Whatever turbulent societal upheavals were to come, those spunky kids wanted to demonstrate to the world one simple idea: We are

267

white and we are in this (telephone booth) together.

MEDIEVAL SOCIETIES

Some whites deal with their race's decline by focusing on a simpler time, when blue-eyed knights and fair-skinned maidens lived chivalrous lives in the cottages and castles of a Europe centuries past. Fledgling whites often experiment in this arena by playing *Dungeons & Dragons* or similar role-playing games. Older adherents, though, may forgo contemporary mores altogether and join the local medieval society. In a bold, almost courageous display of geekiness, these full-grown adult whites gather in public—wearing handmade costumes, tunics, and such—to joust with wooden lances, drink home-brewed mead, and converse with fellow weirdos in a hearty olde English brogue. Dragon breath included.

BUNGEE JUMPING

Having been rendered largely inconsequential after opening up legitimate sports to other races, white "athletes" were forced to come up with an exercise so terrifying, so seemingly painful, and so utterly pointless to modern life that no one else could possibly have any interest in competing. Hence, the bungee jump. Of course, whites didn't actually invent the ritual—ancient vine jumping existed thousands of years ago in the islands of the South Pacific. However, they did revive the activity in the late 1970s when Oxford University's Dangerous Sports Club began holding regular jump-offs. Similar to ice hockey (minus the ice, ice-skates, sticks, puck, goals, team-play aspect, and fighting, and with the addition of gravity and a long, stretchy cord), contemporary bungee jumping now resides securely in the white domain, where it shall forever remain.

POLAR BEAR CLUBS/WEARING SHORTS ALL YEAR ROUND

Each autumn, as the end of the mating season approaches, whites molt. Shedding the thin, outer layer of skin that has been exposed to the sun's harmful rays all summer, they grow a tough, leathery covering, naturally adapted to the harsh Arctic winds of northern Europe and Norwegia. This "winter skin" explains the oft-televised Polar Bear Club phenomenon—groups of elderly whites running around empty January beaches in their swimming trunks, taking a happy dip in the lethally frigid Atlantic Ocean. It also explains the common sight of a group of white adolescents smoking cigarettes out on their high school's patio, wearing nothing but blue jeans and Metallica T-shirts in subzero weather. Or the heavyset white hippie, strolling down a city street in the snow, wearing shorts (as well as earmuffs) and smiling.

HIGH FIVES

Due to a lack of motor skills and coordination, most whites have never been able to master the complexities of the common, congratulatory hand slap— the traditional response to "Gimme five," "Gimme some skin," etc. Thus, during the 1980s, the whites developed an easier-to-master alternative to perform with one another while watching sporting events. "High Five!" says the white excitedly, holding a flat, open hand up near eye-level—a target nearly impossible for his friends to miss. (Yet sometimes, somehow, they still do.)

BATTLE-BOTS

As nineteenth-century German philosopher Friedrich Nietzsche noted, the will to power is like a deep, unquenchable thirst for white people. Having watched their race's tenuous grip on the reigns of the world slip during the latter half of the twentieth century, many whites look to technology as a last hope. A subset of brainy white engineers is known to be hard at work creating an army of evil robots with which they hope to enslave the entire planet. The gladiator-style cable television show *Battle-bots* exists as a demonstration forum for these remote-controlled automatons, allowing its fervent white viewers to indulge their basest (albeit sexless) Roman emperor fantasies via a *T2*-like outlet. They're going (going) back (back) to Cali (Caligula).

Yes, Dave Bry may have a complexion resembling driven snow, but he's on fire, baby. That's right, he's a redhead! He's also an editor at blazing hip hop street bible XXL. *God bless!*

10 OBSERVATIONS ON WHITE PEOPLE
AS REVEALED BY THE TIBETAN FREEDOM CONCERT, RANDALL'S ISLAND, NEW YORK, 1997.

1. **WHITES WILL SLAMDANCE TO ANY FORM OF MUSIC**
   From "Bonita Applebum" to U2's "One," it just doesn't matter. From the people that brought you the NRA, the atomic bomb, and the Clapper, comes the knock-down, drag-out do-si-do two-step that's taking a rhythmless nation by storm. Express yourself!

2. **WHITES WILL DO ANYTHING TO RETRIEVE A FRISBEE**
   If only the Native American Indians had a Whammo when the Pilgrims landed at Plymouth Rock, the massacre of their people could have been entirely avoided with one long toss.

3. **WHITES LOOK ANYTHING BUT WHITE THESE DAYS**
   Dreadlocked, b-boyed-out, and with more piercings than half the tribes in the Brazilian rain forest, whites are on a mission to get ethnic on that ass. Whatever happened to the "grunge" look?

4. **WHITES ENJOY WALKING IN PUBLIC SHIRTLESS**
   Ever wonder why those "No shirtless patrons will be served" signs are in every Hardy's and Denny's in America?

5. **WHITES LOVE HACKEY SACK**
   So much so, that they'll pay $40 a head just to stand at the back of a concert and ignore the music being performed. Kicking a dirty piece of stuffed fabric around in a circle must have been a sacred rite of passage in the Caucasus Mountains. The gods must be (going) crazy.

6. **WHITES WILL WEAR ANYTHING**
   Outcooling the next man (a white man) is admirable. But trying too hard inevitably leads to rainbowed hair, ugly eyeglasses, and big jeans that drag through puddles. Take it off!

7. **WHITES LOVE TO YELL "WHOOO!"**
   It's the most common response to such staples of crowd participation as "You all having a good time?" "Make some noise!" and "Let me hear you say, 'yeah'!"

8. **WHITES LOVE MUD**
   Just ask Roger. Sliding and wrestling face-first through a foot-deep quagmire of the land seems to be even more refreshing than raping it.

9. **FOR WHITES, MONEY IS NO OBJECT**
   Why else would they willingly drop $5 on a polysorbate-80-infested cup of kangaroo sperm masquerading as a milkshake? As a side note, on the second day of the weekend-long soiree, the same roach lar-vae-flavored concoction was peddled to an unsuspecting Black *ego trip* staffer for six greenbacks. Shame on a white nigga for trying to run game on a nigga!

10. **WHITES ARE DESPERATELY AWAITING THE NEXT WOODSTOCK**
    Some would sit on a dirty blanket in the middle of a Staten Island landfill if they thought Jewel was gonna fart the national anthem. (And when Woodstock actually returned in 1999, you know what happened: raping and pillaging, "Attack of the Valkyries" style. Val-*holla*!)

FEAR OF A BLACK POOL PARTY. BY GRANT COLLINS

Black people have a peculiar relationship with water. I'm not talking about drinking or bathing. I'm talking about the uncomfortable pairing of African-Americans with any kind of water-related recreation. I'm a Black, and I can say with 99.8 percent accuracy that we don't surf, we don't go boating, we don't really swim. And we don't go to any water-slide theme parks either—that's for Mexicans. The Hamptons? Maybe for P. Diddy, Jigga, or some other brave soul a couple years ago. But with a few exceptions, Black people won't even live seaside. Generally, we like our fun, and lives, on the dry side.*

I know of what I write. See, I grew up in Los Angeles, the city that epitomizes the "California dream." I believe it's written somewhere in the state's charter that on the weekends you must go to the Venice Beach boardwalk. Not a bad idea if it was like that Kool and the Gang "Cherish" video—the one with all those beautiful sistas by the sea all wearing flowing white wispy-things and walking in the sand barefoot eating chicken. All right, I made up the chicken part, but it's a lovely image. It's the way things should be.

*Curiously enough, the AK-47 of squirt guns—the Super-Soaker—was the invention of diabolical African-American aerospace engineer Lonnie Johnson in 1988. It's really popular (and feared) in depressed Black communities. Go figure.

Instead, the video for the Gap Band's "Party Train" is more like how it really is—an unruly freak show scarier than Freaknik. The girls all wear too much make-up, their hair-sprayed 'dos looking like chocolate Magic Shell. The dudes look like the GB's Wilson brothers themselves, clad head-to-toe in black, or rocking unsightly Speedos. They don't actually get too close to the ocean—that's for Mexicans.

Why is this? I've tried to explain it to myself many times, many ways. Perhaps it was the culturally traumatic Middle Passage hundreds of years ago that instilled this aversion to large bodies of water within the psyche of the contemporary African-American. Like some sort of evolutionary programming whereby the salt water conjures up unconscious associations with slave vessels. That would explain a lot. Or I think of those old news clips from the early years of the civil rights struggle, where civil disobedience was met with the stinging thrust of fire-hose-expelled H_2O by the (white) man. Such tragic events must leave collective scars.

"So the Black man don't like water. Big deal." I tell myself such lies to keep my mind sane. But then I think some more. And then I weep. I weep because nothing can explain the twisted suburban social phenomenon known as the Black Pool Party.™ This is where my ebony race confronts its fears and lets it all hang out. This is where, free from the shaming eye of public scrutiny, the African-American indulges in bacchanalian splash-happy revelry. This is where I get the willies.

Since moving to the East Coast, it's been a long while since I've braved a BPP, but from what I remember, it ain't pretty. My friend Keith (who owned a pool, by the way) was a lot more social than I was and he'd convince me to troop it with him to wherever the action was. And in the summer the action usually took place at someone's house, next to a concrete hole in the ground, three feet deep on one end and twelve feet deep on the other, filled with water. It was at these functions where I would face the inevitable facts of BPPs: There's always a fat guy in the pool with his clothes on [1]. Right down to his sneakers. He stays in there God knows how long. (How does he do it? *Why* does he do it?) There's the requisite skinny guys with Jheri Curls running around [2], posing the imminent threat of leaving the water awash in an oil slick of *Exxon Valdez*ian proportions. As for the females, well . . . there's nothing wrong with big asses—unless you got some big-ass stretch marks. Cheek streaks ain't nuttin' nice.

And then there's mayhem. There's waaay too many people up in that pool/hot tub/Jacuzzi. Like a human stew. Like when my grandma used to cook oxtails every Friday. Except it's people. Rowdy people. Rowdy off of one too many Bacardi and Cokes, or Alizé, or Henny, or whatever. They start acting up. Splashing niggaz. Doing cannonballs [3] and getting the barbecue all wet and shit. Little children cry. (It makes little children *cry!*) And then, there's Big Greasy [4]. He just knocked down a couple (burp!), and he's ready to throw a couple of ladies into the chlorinated bowl—despite their wails of protest.

I can still hear their screams as Big Greasy commits this *numero uno* no-no. You see, damn near every Black woman in this country perms her hair straight [5], and damn near every one of 'em avoids a maritime frolic else they risk their coifs returning to a (gasp!) natural state. Ever seen a Black woman who just got all coifed and then tossed in the pool? She ain't smiling. Barring those with good hair, you'd think my sistas wouldn't even go to these things. It's too dangerous. But, still, they come. And Big Greasy is there waiting for them.

Don't believe me? Don't know a Black person? Try searching on-line for a copy of N.W.A's 1990 *Wet 'n' Wild* pool party, and see for yourself. This video is the *Star Wars*, the *Titanic*, the 800-pound gorilla in a bathing suit of BPPs. You will see horrible things. You will cringe. But most importantly, you will understand.

This has been a secret fear of mine for a while now, though my California days are long behind me. Still, every summer I loathe the phone ringing, fearing that it's my homeboy Keith about to suggest we trek to the latest suburban splash fest. "Hey, man, you down with BPP?"

Nah. You know me.

Grant Collins has actually been known to run through a sprinkler or two in his day.

STILL SCARED? BE SURE TO ALSO AVOID . . .

THE PARKS...
on Cinco de Mayo.

CENTRAL PARK..
on Puerto Rican Day

MAIN STREET..
on St. Patrick's Day

DETROIT...
on the day any of the city's professional sports franchises wins the championship. Or Halloween eve (a/k/a "Devil's Night")

TOP 10 PLACES YOU CAN FIND BLACKS AND LATINOS TOGETHER.

10. Lowrider car show
9. War reunion concert
8. Boxing ring
7. Swap meet
6. The N.W.A song "Dope Man"
5. The movie *Colors*
4. Ice-T's crib
3. Taco Bell/KFC
2. Compton
1. Prison

MARIACHI MADNESS: MY ROWDY MEXICAN NEIGHBORS.

BY DAVE ALVARADO /
ILLUSTRATION BY TODD JAMES

Next door to my new apartment live some Mexican dudes. I'm talking real Mexicanos, the kind of *vatos* who don't speak much of the *gabacho*'s language but still find work. The types that almost always walk the streets in teams and care deeply about who wins the next Necaxa, Cruz Azul, or América match-up. These cats all own something with the image of the Virgin Guadalupe on it, love flannel (and flan), and know every Tigres del Norte song by heart.

One of them (a light-skinded dude with sorta blue-greenish eyes) actually reminds me of Chomi, my cousin Benny's friend down in Ensenada. The others all look like lean, not-too-tall mod-ern-day Aztec warriors with brilliant slicked-back, jet-black hair decked out in the latest bootleg Sean John.

All my life I have been around Mexicans. Being a Chicano from Los Angeles has made it easy. But even when I moved to Nueva York in 1996, I was surprised to find a lot of my brown brothers stationed everywhere, holding down bodegas, restau-rants, and even blocks (*churros*, gotta love 'em). Still, I can't say I ever resided so close to any of *mi raza* till now (our apartments share a wall). I grew up in the spacious suburbs, and of all the apartments that I lived in after I moved out of my parents' house, none of them had Mexicans (sun people) or Chicanos (-U.S.-born sun people) living next door. (Amazing, but *verdad*.)

The first thing I noticed about my neighbors was that they're some Mexican LL Cool Js. Meaning they can't live without their radio. Or, in this case, stereo, which bumps mariachi, ranchera,

banda, them ill narco ballads with the drug-smuggling lyrics, cumbia, and anything else stamped "Hecho en Mexico" on it from dusk to dawn. On a daily basis.

In the beginning I admired the tunes that give me a taste of the *madre*land. A week later I began to dread that 10:00 A.M. musical kick-off when they prepared to go to work, especially since these homies often let the speakers thump past 3:00 in the *mañana*. (Last night, they broke out a microphone and karaoked to some sad Mexi-tunes. It was 2:15 on a Tuesday night/Wednesday morning. Friday or Saturday nights, they might throw a party that goes till 6:00 in the morning. So they're actually more like Mexican Ice-Ts.)

Then, one day things were surprisingly quiet. I finally heard the music coming from other apartments. Stuff like the theme from *Ghostbusters*, "Who Let the Dogs Out," and Lipps Inc.'s "Funkytown" (a song my cousin Chino loved back in the day). When, in a bizarre twist, one of my Mexican neighbors came home early and started blasting Backstreet Boyz (maybe he had a hot date with a *guera* that night), I began to realize that things would get worse for my ears.

It wasn't long before I discovered that my neighbors are also noisy in other ways. They crash into walls, knock over furniture, and basically love slapping the shit out of each other. (All in *bueno* fun, of course.) It seems like they got this thing going where they all take turns torturing the scrawniest guy who screams in pain then laughs about it.

I'm not sure how many dudes live in the tiny apartment,

but I do know they got friends who visit. All the time. I also know that they all love to cuss. The vulgar language doesn't bother me, though. Neither, I guess, do the yells some of them let loose at any given hour. (I don't know what it's called but everybody knows what yell I'm talking about—that wild, long-ass *"ay ya ya"* Mexican yell.)

The funny thing is that shortly after I moved into my new spot I went back to L.A. to visit. I was in my mom's kitchen, looking out the window, admiring this lowered, vintage Chevy truck parked in the driveway of the house across the street where my old *amigo* David Murphy used to live. I asked my ma about who was living there now.

"Ay, cállate. Ni me lo menciones," she said. ("Please, don't even mention it.")

It turns out that the new residents are (according to my dear ol' ma) these loud, obnoxious, womanizing, motorcycle-riding party animals. They had a huge crazy bash last Saturday night that went on till the sun came up.

With a souped-up ride like that in the driveway, I tell myself, they must be—

"Mexicanos," says my mom, completing my thought. *"Como joden."* ("They cause a lot of racket.")

Then she asked me what my new neighbors were like. I told her they were Mexican and left it at that.

Dave Alvarado is a freelance Mexican.

ego trip EBONICS: The New Racist Slang.

NOW THAT THE WORLD'S IN THE DEEPEST SHIT IT'S BEEN IN IN YEARS, RACISM'S MORE WIDELY ACCEPTABLE THAN EVER. WANNA BE DOWN? SURE YOU DO. WELL, LOOK OUT. YOU'RE ABOUT TO GET PLUGGED UP INTO *ET*'S LATEST GLOSSARY OF REVOLTING VOCAB. Y'ALL WILL BE FLAUNTING THAT NEW STYLE OF SPEAK IN NO TIME.

amigga\ah-mih-gah*noun*: 1. your Mexican homie (ex. "Julio is the hardest worker in the Korean deli. That's my amigga.") 2. a derogatory term to describe a Mexican trying to be Black (ex. "I don't see no watermelon in that burrito, amigga.")

anti-Kinte\an-tee-ken-tay*noun*: a Black person who doesn't believe he/she originates from Africa

Big O'Jasm, The\big-o-jazzim*proper noun*: the lingering climactic feeling of resentment whites get over the whole O.J. thing (Get over it.)

blacsimile\blax-si-mah-lee*noun*: a second-rate imitation created by or directed toward Black-Americans (ex. "BET offers great blacsimiles of shows originally shown on MTV last year.")

bootie tang\boo-tee tang, or boo-tay tang*noun*: an Asian girl with a big ass

bronounce\broh-nownss*verb*: the act of switching dialects appropriate toward Black slang—usually conducted by non-Blacks, or Caucasional African-Americans (ex. "Damn, I really blew it with Yuniqua from the projects. If I'd only bronounced her name correctly!") **(Synonym: afronunciation.)**

carte-negro\kart-eh-neh-groh*noun*: an unlimited-ride ghetto pass

Caucasional\kaw-kay-zhun-al*adjective*: of or relating to acting white from time to time

chonky

chip hop\ chip-hop\ *noun*: Chinese hip hop (And when the East is in the house, oh, my God!)

chonky\chawn-kee*adjective*: a term used to describe a full-figured ("thick") Caucasian hottie (ex. "My man Orenthal only goes out with them chonky bitches. I ain't mad at him, though.")

coco puff\ko-ko puff*noun*: a Black person who has never served time in jail or prison (derived from the slang "cream puff," as in a "softee")

craccolade\krak-o-layd*noun*: praise bestowed on an unworthy white (ex. "Man, that Fred Durst fucker sure gets a whole lotta craccolades. And that cracker sucks!")

crackavellian\krak-ah-vel-ee-an*adjective*: a term used to describe shifty, conniving behavior by a white person against non-whites (ex. "The Tuskegee experiments was some ol' moonshine bullshit of crackavellian proportions, yo!")

dreadmocks\dred-mox*noun*: anyone of European ancestry who prefers his/her hair (usually blond) styled in dreadlock fashion

eboneezer

eboneezer\eh-bon-eez-er*noun*: an elderly Black gentleman tight with his moolah (You can't take it witcha, bruh.)

ethniche\ehth-neesh*noun*: a special place or area of expertise for folks of a specific ethnicity (ex. "Mrs. Wong's small, dexterous hands enabled her to carve out her own ethniche toiling for Kathy Lee's Chinatown sweat shop.")

fauxesha\foe-eesh-ah*noun*: 1. any non-African-American female who assumes the mannerisms of a teeth-sucking, neck-whippin', "talk to the hand"-gesturing, "don't go there"-warning Black girl 2. a Black TV (transvestite) star

foolatto\foo-lah-toe*noun*: Someone who claims he/she is of mixed heritage, but is not (ex. "That pasty cake says she's one-eighth Cherokee on her mother's uncle's side. What a foolatto!")

German Munster\jer-man mun-ster*proper noun*: one cheesy-ass kraut

has-bean\hazz-been*noun*: a washed-up wetback (ex. "Maria Conchita Alonso is a has-bean. You hardly see her anymore. I miss her.")

Havana Trump\hah-vah-nah trump*proper noun*: a really rich Cuban bitch

heeb-bro\heeb-broe\ *noun*: a half-Jewish, half-Black male (ex. "Lenny Kravitz is one lucky heeb-bro, my amigga.")

hindecent\hin-dee-sent\ *adjective*: a word that describes a Hindu who leaves the house without her bindi (ex. "Get back in the house, girl. You look hindecent.")

hindigestion\hin-dee-jes-shun\ *noun*: the stomach pains that come from eating a flurry of curry in a hurry

hindigestion

hispandemonium\ hiss-pan-de-moe-nee-um\ *noun*: the chaos that results when more than two Latinos gather together in a public location (¡Viva la razor!)

hispandering\ hiss-pan-der-ing\ *verb*: the act of hiring Latino help by non-Latinos at reduced rates **(Synonym: el cheapo)**

honquistador\ hahn-kee-sta-door\ *noun*: a rude Caucasian that moves into your otherwise non-white neighborhood (ex. "Damn, dawg. Fort Greene has been claimed by honquistadors! Cancel Kwanza.")

hung-lo

hung-lo\hung-low\ *adjective*: a word describing a big-willied Asian gentleman (rare)

impostafarian\im-pos-tah-fair-ee-an\ *noun*: one who adopts false Caribbean island patois, mannerisms, and/or style in order to score some Black Starliner-powered weed, pick up chonkys in the East Village, and/or avoid employment; also **impostafairyan**\ im-pos-tah-fair-ee-an\ *noun*: a homosexual, white power extension of the above

indiosyncrasy\in-dee-oh-sin-cruh-see\ *noun*: a peculiar habit reflecting Native American tendencies, like alcoholism, or the urge to scalp paleface

inferierror\in-fear-ee-er-or\ *noun*: the act of mistaking a person of color for the help (ex. "I feel awful. I naturally assumed that young Black buck with the soiled messenger bag was a courier, not my boss' lover! What an inferierror I've made! I'm Irish pond scum!")

ishtarbaby\ ish-tar-bay-bee\ *noun*: an Arabian child who is born privileged, has all sorts of opportunities, and still fails

jeuphoria\ joo-for-ee-ah\ *noun*: a joyous sensation akin to that felt by an Israeli with a winning lottery ticket

jewbacca\ joo-bah-ka\ *noun*: an overly swarthy, follically enhanced Jew

latingle\ la-teen-gull\ *noun*: 1. the funny feeling you get in your pants when you see an attractive Latin person 2. post-*chica* house crabs (and they aren't edible)

jewbacca

latinot\ la-teen-not\ *noun*: a white bitch who pretends she's Spanish

melanincompoop\ mel-ah-nin-kum-poop\ *noun*: a person of color on some "I'm too pale" shit

Mexican't\ mekse-cant\ *verb*: the act of preventing a Mexican from doing anything (ex. "Jethro, see them beaners across the border? They Mexican't get over here. Nya ha ha!")

micadamia\ mick-ah-day-mee-ah\ *noun*: the phenomenon of an Irish person who seeks higher education, drops out (guess why, McBoozer?), and goes nuts

miscegeneric\miss-eh-jen-er-ik\ *adjective*: mixed to the point of blandness, like Tiger Woods, or your boo Shari *"Hotel"* Belafonte

orienterprise\or-ee-en-ter-prize\ *noun*: a highly profitable Asian-owned/operated business smack dab in the middle of an economically challenged community. The Yoo-hoo costs $3.50. (Boo-hoo.) Oreos, $5.00 (Misfortune cookies.)

slurveillance\sler-vay-lance\ *noun*: the offensive feeling a person of color gets upon walking into a store and knowing all eyes (the whites of 'em) are on him/her (ex. "I can't get my shop on at Bloomingdales no more. The fuckers that work there got me under strict slurveillance—following me all over the store and shit!")

suntanamadré\ sun-tan-ah-mah-dray\ *noun*: a Hispanic mom who tells her kids to stay out of the sun so they won't get too dark

vanillitant\ vah-nil-ah-tant\ *adjective*: staunchly "white" in attitude and demeanor (without the white sheets) (ex. "Kyle in accounting got all vanillitant when we asked him to dance at the company's '70s party.")

CONSPICUOUS: 16 WORDS 'N' CATCHPHRASES THAT SOUND RACIAL/ETHNIC BUT AREN'T (OR ARE THEY?).

1. brown out
2. caucus
3. chicanery
4. chigger
5. chink in the armor
6. jape
7. jewelry
8. jigger
9. jink
10. jubilee
11. judicial
12. niggardly
13. niggle
14. nigrosine
15. nip and tuck
16. spigot

P.S.: I H8 U: INTRODUCING RACIAL E-MAIL ACRONYMS AND ABBREVI-HATE-TIONS.

BOEICM:
bugging-out eyes in coonish manner

BRBGYAAIB:
be right back, gotta yell at an insubordinate Black

IMRO:
in my racist opinion

IN2H2S:
Indian name too hard to spell

LMYO:
laughing my yarmulke off

MEG(LS):
Middle Eastern guy (looks suspicious)

NBWG:
nothing but white girls

NHE:
no habla Español

NP:
nigga, please

NTSRB:
not to sound racist but

RE:
rolling eyes

ST:
sucking teeth

TABITR:
there's a Black in the room

TIE:
type in English

TP:
"those people"

WHA:
with heavy accent

WOW2PM:
waiting on whitey to pay me

MILLENNIUM RACIST PARTY: WHO'S ON THE GUEST LIST?
BECAUSE EVERYBODY PLAYS THE RACIST FOOL. WITH NO EXCEPTION TO THE RULE. LISTEN, BABY.

1. THE OPEN RACIST

M TO THE IZZO: Attended Duke University hoping to encounter a gentleman named David.

FUN FACT: His bumper sticker says it all: NIGRA FALLS IS FOR LOVERS. (AND THEY WILL FALL, EVERY LAST DAMN ONE OF 'EM! CHRIST WANTS IT THAT WAY.)

2. THE ACCIDENTAL RACIST

M TO THE IZZO: Though seemingly benign, you can light this fella's ire in the heat of the moment—when he's ordering fast food and can't understand the hamburger helper behind the counter.

FUN FACT: Whoops, he did it again!

3. THE PART-TIME RACIST

M TO THE IZZO: On the job he's all jokes. But after work he's all jerky—as in beef with other races: whites are blue-eyed devils, Blacks are savages, Asians are sneaky (and quick with the abacus), and Latinos are more hot-blooded than Foreigner (check it and *si*).

FUN FACT: Buy this guy a beer and he'll be your best friend.

4. THE CLUELESS RACIST

M TO THE IZZO: Doesn't realize she's being racist when she listens to rap and sings the n-word.

FUN FACT: She says she's very "JAP-y."

5. THE RAH-RAH RACIST

M TO THE IZZO: A get-up, stand-up cheerleader for his/her respective race/ethnicity.

FUN FACT: The perennial favorite quote: "I'm not anti-_____, I'm just pro-_____."

6. THE HE'S-MR.-KNOW-IT-ALL RACIST

M TO THE IZZO: This Izod-clad clod/stuffed shirt bases his biases on academic research, monkey development, and kangaroo court cases.

FUN FACT: The president of Guatemala couldn't get this guy laid.

7. THE SELF-HATING RACIST

M TO THE IZZO: Denies his cultural heritage, doesn't mix with his own kind, assimilates at all costs, and listens to the Smiths. (More Morrissey, Mom, please?)

FUN FACT: Lactose intolerance is the root of his pain.

8. THE RACIST IN DENIAL

M TO THE IZZO: Sends her kids to multi-culti schools, considers hitting a *piñata* a hate crime, and would love to go one-on-one with Denzel in *He Got Game* (or one of his Boys Club of America commercials).

FUN FACT: Tips her Chinese groundskeeper, Ugandan au pair, and Samoan personal trainer lovely during the holidays.

9. THE TRENDY RACIST (A/K/A THE CULTURE VULTURE)

M TO THE IZZO: This motherfucker thinks he walks to the beat of his own funky drummer. He fancies himself a man Blacker than Pepsi with more pep in his step than Cheryl "Pepsi" Riley, but he's paler than all three Pep Boys—Manny, Mo, and (cracker) Jack. But that's not all. He places his Taco Bell order in the Aztecan language of *Nahuatl*, swears in Mandarin while guzzling Mandarin orange Slice, claims to have added his own chapter to the *Kama Sutra*, and his style of dress is that of an Arizona shaman sprinkled with a lil' bit o' Shah (of Iran) flava.

FUN FACT: He knows how to do Black hair.

10. THE MILITANT RACIST

M TO THE IZZO: Is it possible to be *too* Black? She doesn't think so: She never puts milk in her coffee, only fucks with one-third of Neapolitan ice cream (guess which third?), and is highly offended when people call her a "chicken fajita." (She wears headwraps.)

FUN FACT: Her mother's boyfriend is white.

11. THE REFORMED RACIST

M TO THE IZZO: He once rocked a shaved dome, steel-toed Doc Martens, and possessed a Skrewdriver record collection that would make Chuck Bronson in *The Mechanic* whimper with envy. But age and maturity have made him see the error of his ways. (Just like *American History X*, when the main dude got raped in jail and he stopped being racist—that showed him.)

FUN FACT: He doesn't exist.

EPILOGUE.

It ain't over. The party's not over.

One hatemonger told two friends, who told two friends, and so on, and so on, and then . . .
After the Millennium Racist Party came the after-party, and . . .
After the after-party was the hotel lobby, and . . .
After the Belvy, they started swigging Cris . . .
And after a few hours it looked something like this . . .

Fin.

C'etait de la merde.

ABOUT E.T.H.N.I.C.*

SACHA JENKINS

Don't get it twisted: Sacha Sebastian Jenkins is a Black man who'll never be a veteran. And he really doesn't have to bust gats for the stars and white stripes because his original (and not-so-original . . .) kinfolk have fought in every stinking war this fine nation's been caught up in ("Jenkins" certainly ain't Mandingo for "Black family," potna). Revolutionary. 1812. Civil. Scranton. 'Nam. America, America—Jenkins Blacks have shed their grace for thee!

Philadelphian Horace Byrd Jenkins Jr. had to break tradition; he didn't want no parts of the 'Nam, so legend has it that he avoided the draft the old-fashioned way: he faked the sweet funk. Recruitment office peeps would be surprised to know that Horace Jr. and his Haitian wife, Monart, would go on to bring seeds Dominique and Sacha to life. Now that's a taste of chocolate!

Today Sacha Jenkins is proud to be all that he can be. He travels and writes, and enjoys music and animals. Jenkins is a Leo who spends his quieter moments up in Bearsville, New York, with his lovely Irish-Jew companion, Meegan. Call him "nature boy" and he won't get mad at 'cha. Just don't call him "boy."

ELLIOTT WILSON

Elliott Jesse Wilson Jr. was named after his father who just happens to be Black. That makes Elliott Jr. Black too. (Hey, we don't make the rules.) He's also Ecuadorian and Greek courtesy of his mama, Berta Victoria. A Nueva York dweller, Wilson looks like your average Puerto Rican, but please don't ask him for directions in Spanish—the only language he speaks other than English is hip hop. Shit, it pays the bills. It's not like he had much of an education to fall back on.

Actually, EJ used to love school. Ms. Introzzi, a buxom blond woman, was Wilson's third grade teacher. She was his favorite. But one day things went terribly wrong when the kids were instructed to fill out one of those census form thingamajigs. The innocent mixed boy with good hair questioned his trusted tutor about which box he should check for race—"Black" or "Spanish"? (Wilson didn't feel like acknowledging his Greekness that day.) Ms. I. informed the lad to check "other" and write in the word "mulatto." Wilson, who had never heard the word before, did as he was told. Later, he looked up the word in the dictionary. "'F' Ms. Introzzi and 'F' school" soon became his mantra. But make no mistake, Wilson hates to be mistaken for a tragic mulatto. He prefers the term "yellow nigga." EEOC, holla at your boy.

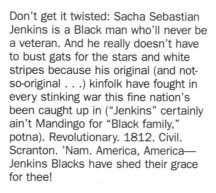

*ego trip's Head Niggaz in Charge